UNFINISHED BUSINESS

STEPHEN BONSAL

UNFINISHED BUSINESS

INTRODUCTION BY

HUGH GIBSON

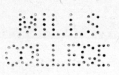

1944

Doubleday, Doran and Company, Inc.

GARDEN CITY, NEW YORK

THIS BOOK IS
STANDARD LENGTH,
COMPLETE AND UNABRIDGED,
MANUFACTURED UNDER WARTIME CONDITIONS
IN CONFORMITY WITH ALL GOVERNMENT
REGULATIONS CONTROLLING THE USE
OF PAPER AND OTHER MATERIALS

To

ARTHUR KROCK

*who intercepted this chronicle as it drifted toward the archives of some
historical society and who is not afraid to share with his
grateful, admiring friend the brickbats
its publication may provoke*

But no man who is correctly informed as to the past, will be disposed to take a morose or desponding view of the present.

MACAULAY: *History of England*, Vol. I, Chap. 1.

Contents

Introduction

Colonel Bonsal once told me the story of how this diary came to be written.

One winter's afternoon in Berlin, in 1915, he observed a distressed and bewildered American, a sheet of paper clutched in his hand, trying in vain to get help from passing Germans in finding his way. One after another they ignored him or brushed him aside, and seeing the way open for a good deed, Colonel Bonsal came to the rescue and took charge. He led his compatriot to the one shop in Berlin where English newspapers could still be found, interpreted for him, and left him at the door, never thinking he would see him again, and soon.

On the following day the two men met again, by chance, at the American Embassy. Bonsal was introduced to Colonel House, who hailed him as a good Samaritan. Like most good Samaritans, he was promptly called on for further service. To be exact, he was impressed to act as interpreter in a series of important meetings with German political figures in which Colonel House was engaged. In the course of this association the two men became firm friends, and when the time came to prepare for the Peace Conference Colonel House cabled General Pershing, asking for the services of his former associate, who was at that time an officer at General Headquarters.

Starting as adviser on Balkan affairs, Colonel Bonsal soon became the close associate of Colonel House in all matters bearing upon the peace. He was chosen to sit with President Wilson and Colonel House and interpret for them the proceedings of secret meetings where no stenographic notes were kept and no official translations made.

At the request of President Wilson and Colonel House, he made a daily practice of writing up his notes in the form of a journal, which was freely used for reference in checking the memories of our delegates. Colonel Bonsal jotted down not only the strictly official proceedings, but also a running commentary on the daily happenings in the meetings and the personal and human side of the interchanges.

I remember hearing Colonel House, during the Conference, speak with admiration of the author's special fitness for his service with President Wilson and for the inquiries he carried out not only in Paris but in Germany and Central Europe, of his knowledge of European and Balkan affairs, and especially of his genius for self-effacement —or what Colonel House called his "low visibility."

For a long time before and after the turn of the century Colonel Bonsal was probably our most distinguished foreign correspondent. He traveled extensively, following the armies in many wars, some of them with his lifelong friend Richard Harding Davis, with whom he shared various colorful experiences. As an illustration of the extent of territory covered by Bonsal it has been said that first for the *Herald* of James Gordon Bennett and later for the New York *Times* he had visited and "surveyed" all the countries of Europe, Africa, and Asia (with the exception of Persia), and all the republics of South America, before the Conference of the Nations assembled in Paris in 1919.

Writers on the subject of the Versailles peacemaking have usually made free with the names of the great, but to Colonel Bonsal most of them were more than mere names. Many were acquaintances or warm personal friends. There were such figures as Clemenceau, Lloyd George, Balfour, Smuts, and Masaryk. Besides being the trusted associate of President Wilson and Colonel House, he was on excellent terms with Senator Lodge and, as his diary shows, might well have bridged the gap between him and the President but for the unfortunate "blackout over Washington" caused by the President's illness.

This is no story of the peacemaking written in the light of later events; it consists of excerpts from a diary written at the time, without any attempt to cover up mistaken judgments or even to improve literary style. Of all the host of books written about the Versailles Treaty and the drafting of the Covenant of the League of Nations, I do not know of another based on notes taken in the actual meetings and written up day by day. The account constitutes an original source, rather than being compiled from original sources. For that reason it is of genuine historical importance. The author might have made some of his points more effectively by doctoring the original text, but has declined to do so on the ground that this would impair the integrity of his diary.

After World War I Colonel Bonsal was urged to publish his recollections, and on his objection that this might be indiscreet on the part of a professional writer who had been given access to confidential information, President Wilson told him, "You can't be too indiscreet for me. I give you full absolution in advance."

Recently his friends, among them Arthur Krock, a severe and discriminating critic, to whom this book is dedicated, sought to convince Colonel Bonsal that it was his duty to publish his notes. He held out against such pleas until it became clear to his informed mind that we were beginning to repeat the same mistakes that led to the tragedy of Versailles. It becomes daily more urgent that we learn to find a safer way amid the old pitfalls, and it is to be hoped that we may profit from Colonel Bonsal's objective, straightforward story.

HUGH GIBSON

New York

UNFINISHED BUSINESS

[*Some confusion may result from the fact that entries recorded, say on April 12th, follow those that were made on the fifteenth. It is true, as stated in the text, that the Diarist has, without changing a word or a comma, permitted himself to rearrange some of the entries according to the subject in debate and not chronologically. In this way everything that was said upon the problem before the Commission is given in a single entry even though several days may have elapsed between the statement of the contrasting views advanced and the rejoinder that followed. In this way the debate is concluded, or, as was more often the case, reached what engineers who are called upon to cope with natural phenomena, such as avalanches and landslides, term the "angle of repose." The Diarist admits that after an interval of twenty-five years he considers it more important to do full justice to the views expressed than to specify the day and the hour when they were spoken. S. B.*]

PART I

The Armistice

November 7, 1918.

I have been so busy during the past seven days, fetching and carrying, translating notes, condensing interminable conversations, and talking over the Paris telephone (alas, and getting nowhere), that I find I have not been able to make a daily record of the many happenings of this momentous week. How I wish I could resume my familiar role of a detached observer and be relieved of the subordinate but exacting tasks that now fall to my lot.

Today, however, there is a breathing spell, and I shall endeavor to recall what it seems to me has happened. After the preliminary skirmish on the morning of October 29th, in Colonel House's apartment on the Rue de l'Université, the great men came together once again at the Quai d'Orsay in the afternoon. It was evident that the plenipotentiaries, Clemenceau, Lloyd George, Balfour, and Sonnino, were one and all disinclined to accept the Wilson program as a whole. Lloyd George opened the ball by asking House a very pointed question.

"If we agree to this armistice," he asked, "do you think we are accepting Wilson's terms—all of them?"

"I certainly do," answered House.

Then the Fourteen Points were read and reread. Now Lloyd George would read one with a wry face, and then Clemenceau would take a hand in the discussion. After each point had been brought out, House would read the explanatory remarks, the "commentary," as it was called, that had been drawn up by Cobb and Lippmann under the guiding hand of the Colonel, and which, when cabled to Washington, had met with the President's approval. The discussions that followed clearly revealed the points of difference and the fact that the plenipotentiaries, far from getting together, were drifting farther apart. House finally intervened, making, as he afterwards admitted, the longest speech of his life. He said:

"If the Allies are unwilling to accept the Fourteen Points upon which Germany has based her request for an armistice, there can be, as far as I can see, only one course for the President to pursue. He would have to tell the Germans that the conditions which they had accepted are not acceptable to the powers with which America has been associated."

The words "has based" and "has been" fell upon the little group like a cold douche. And then House continued:

"America would then have to take up direct negotiations with Germany and Austria."

Lloyd George sprang to his feet, his eyes ablaze.

"Would that mean a separate peace between America and the Central Powers?"

"It might well," said House.

Now that the deep rift—indeed the yawning abyss—became apparent, everybody tried to back away from it. Everybody talked but said nothing; finally Lloyd George suggested that the meeting adjourn and that the delegates, each in his own way, should attempt to draw up changes and reservations to the Points that it was hoped might be found acceptable to all at the next meeting. An hour later House sent to Washington a full account of the delicate situation that was developing and in an almost incredibly short time received the following cable instruction from Mr. Wilson:

"I feel it my solemn duty to authorize you to say that I cannot consent to negotiations that do not include the Freedom of the Seas and the League of Nations. I hope I shall not be compelled to make this, our final decision, public."

That night House put on his thinking cap to excellent purpose, and on the morning of the thirtieth, as arranged, he conferred with the plenipotentiaries assembled at the War Ministry, Clemenceau presiding. Again everybody wanted to talk, but House expressed the opinion that the subject had been fully threshed out, that both standpoints had been fairly and fully developed, and, as a result, he said:

"I have decided to advise the President to lay before Congress the peace terms which he has approved, and also the terms that England and France and Italy apparently insist upon. In this way he would be giving the war-making powers all the facts, and ask for their decision. The question I think he would present is this: 'Should we make peace with Germany, now that she has accepted our terms, or should we go on fighting Germany until she is forced to accept the terms that France, England, and Italy apparently insist upon?' "

Appreciating the gravity of the situation and how disastrous an open debate on the question of war aims would prove, and in full knowledge of the prestige that Wilson enjoyed in the liberal and democratic groups of the allied countries involved, an adjournment was proposed and agreed to, and a few hours later the British reservations on the debated questions reached House. They differed greatly both in spirit and letter from the verbal objections which Lloyd George had made. Lloyd George now asked merely that the question of the Freedom of the Seas be not regarded as settled, but that he and others should be permitted to discuss it at the sessions of the Peace Conference "in the light of the new conditions which have arisen in the course of the present war," he explained in an informal note to House several hours later.

Lloyd George wrote: "There may be confusion here. Freedom of the Seas—what does it mean? The Tiger says it means that we shall have to abjure our inalienable right of waging war and he will have none of that. But we do know what a blockade is and what a blessing it has proved to be. It is the weapon to which we owe our lives and our victory. If I broke it or even blunted it Parliament would vote me out of office in twenty-four hours. And Parliament would be quite right."[1]

[1]As this account of what took place on this momentous occasion has been disputed by several prolific writers who were not present it seems only proper to print here the testimony of Count Luigi Aldrovandi-Marescotti, who in his capacity as secretary to the Italian Premier was also present. He acted as interpreter to Sonnino, the Italian Foreign Minister, as I did to Colonel House. Aldrovandi published his memoirs of the war years in Milan in 1937 under the title of *Guerra Diplomatica*. As to what happened he writes:

"There now followed (October 29, 1918) a lively exchange of views on the Freedom of the Seas. Lloyd George gave many reasons why he could not accept this clause. 'It would,' he said, 'inflict grave injury on British interests.' Clemenceau suggested that the question should not be discussed at this time but Lloyd George said, 'It is impossible for me to conclude an armistice if I must accept this clause.' Colonel House then took the floor and said, 'President Wilson has announced these conditions (the Fourteen Points) to the enemy and if they are not agreed to the President would have no alternative but to announce to the enemy that the conditions (his) had not been accepted by the Allies. The question would then arise,' he continued, 'would not the United States be compelled to negotiate with Germany directly and on its own account (*per conto proprio*)?'

" 'Would that signify that the United States might negotiate a separate peace?' inquired Clemenceau. House replied, 'It might lead to that.' "

Count Aldrovandi goes on to say: "Colonel House was perfectly calm as he made

Now that Germany is crumbling and the end of the war is evidently in sight, attacks on the President's policy which after all paved the way to peace are appearing in the Paris press. The first volley, at least the first that has caught my eye, was fired (October 26th) in the *Echo de Paris* and it is signed by the industrious Pertinax. He writes, "The Allies are bound by nothing that Mr. Wilson wrote or even typed on his famous typewriter." Many of the jackals have taken up the cry of this scurvy pack that Pertinax leads, but their campaign is serving a purpose which most certainly they did not foresee. Many important French groups are rallying to the President and expressions of good will are flooding the Colonel's mail. Included are letters from the Grand Confederation of Labor, from the League of the Rights of Man, and the Republican Coalition. They have sent in a joint resolution warning the Government not "to lend its ear to the excitations of the Chauvinist Press that is often more responsive to the spirit of conquest than to the desire for justice." It is clear that Pertinax has builded better, much better, than he knew. He is helping the President with very important sections of the French people.

November 8th.

It was on November the 4th that the Supreme War Council approved the memorandum of the Allies addressed to Wilson, which accepted the Fourteen Points, reserving, however, the right for further discussion on Point Two, and also a clearer definition of the reparation clause. It was in this way, you might say, the war ended. On November the 5th the memorandum reached the President and

---

this declaration. He seems to be a man without nerves. Neither his voice, which is rather low, nor the expression of his face, which is tranquil, changes. He remains serene and courteous and yet he does not appear cold (*freddo*).

"On the morning of October 31st," continues Aldrovandi, "we continued to work on the Armistice terms: in the morning at the home of Colonel House, in the afternoon at Versailles. Sonnino said he accepted the Fourteen Points as far as they refer to Germany but he wishes to make it quite plain he does not accept them with reference to Austria. Foch then commented on the military situation. He said, 'The German Army is disorganized and its morale is depressed. It is retiring continually and it staggers like a man who has lost his balance. In withdrawing, the German Army continues to devastate the country methodically but it only accepts battle where it has to.'"

On November 3d Aldrovandi writes, "Another reunion at the residence of Colonel House. Orlando introduces many details as to the interpretation of Point Nine with reference to Austria-Hungary and Roumania. Lloyd George says it is not necessary to mention these matters as we are discussing an armistice with Germany.'

"House said, 'I think it best not to refer these matters to President Wilson. It is unwise to increase the number of objections.'

" 'With that opinion,' said Clemenceau, 'I agree with all my heart.' "

was sent on by him to the Germans, with a statement to the effect that the actual terms could be obtained from Marshal Foch, if applied for.

"I am not at all sorry," commented House, "that these reservations providing for the future discussion of several of the Points have been made because they emphasize complete acceptance of all the other Points. The Allied governments, reluctantly, I admit, but also undeniably, have committed themselves to the American Peace Program. This is indeed a turning point in history, and a triumph for our great President. I was not always confident we would achieve it. There are, alas, so many key men in the Allied governments who, to put it mildly, are not sympathetic to this program. We shall hear from them later."

As a matter of fact these men had been heard from already, and later were heard from more frequently than even House anticipated. At the meeting on November 2d Clemenceau proposed that the words "reparation for damages" be added to the reparation clause. The British, Belgian, and Italian delegates objected on the ground that such a provision was out of place in an armistice convention, but after a somewhat languid discussion the addition was agreed to. Evidently encouraged by this success, the French Minister of Finance, M. Klotz, proposed a further addition in these words, "With the reservation of all ulterior claims on the part of the Allies and the United States," or as he put it in French, "*Sous réserve de toutes revendications et réclamations ulterieures de la part des Alliés et des États Unis.*" This was agreed to, and also a clarifying statement was inserted to the effect that "by restoration of invaded territory it was understood that compensation would be made by Germany for all damage done to civilian populations of the Allies, and their property, by the aggression of Germany by land, by sea, and by air."

On November 8th the delegations met at Rethondes in the forest of Compiègne. The Germans formally asked for the terms and duly received them. These terms were accepted by the German Government on November 10th. The Armistice convention was signed at 5 A.M. on November 11th and at 11 A.M. on that day it came into force. So much for the record.

November 19th.

The hot fit is over and the satisfaction that we all felt on Armistice night is fading fast. I recall with amazement many of the foolish things we said and did; like millions of others, we gave loose rein to our joy. How we cheered that noble woman who, holding aloft a fasces of Allied banners on the steps of the opera house, sang the "Marseillaise," "The Star-Spangled Banner," and "Britannia Rules the Waves." Our behavior was more decorous as we attended the Mass of Victory and sang the Te Deum in the Cathedral Church of Our Lady of Paris, where, as some, a very few, recall, that other victory of Franco-American arms, celebrating Yorktown, was sung by order of Louis XVI in 1781.

But now sun spots are appearing in the orb of glorious victory, and selfish instincts, long held in check by the urgency of war emergencies, are asserting themselves. Strange, but nevertheless true, all the confident words that I listened to with greedy ears on that historic night have now died away, and what I remember is a word of doubt and uncertainty, perhaps of apprehension; it was spoken by Emmanuele, the clever Italian journalist, whose articles in the *Corriere della Sera* I had so much admired throughout the crucial stages of the war. I remember meeting him in the milling throngs and recall his careworn face seen under the glare of one of the Boulevard arc lights.

"Yes," he said, "we have armistice; the *ora formidabile* has struck."

The "formidable hour" that only comprised sixty soul-searching minutes has lengthened into a week and more. The hopes we cherished seem now unsubstantial; indeed, many of them I cannot recall.

The Colonel's desk is piled high with reports of unpleasant incidents that presage bitter discussion and future conflicts. I console myself with reading the morning paper. Now no longer is it filled with the casualties in fine print and then the asterisk which explains, "All second lieutenants, unless otherwise stated."

My second lieutenant is safe, as safe as the commander of a Handley-Page night-bombing outfit can be, even in time of peace. *Ora formidabile!* And the Lord only knows how we shall meet it. I recall the words that Tolstoy spoke to me that day years ago during the first Russian revolution as I drove away from his retreat at Yasnaya Polyana:[2]

[2]A month later, when the pleasing peace mirage which had entranced us on Armistice night had receded still further, I tackled Emmanuele for an explanation of his *ora formidabile* prophecy. "From where did you draw it, O! Minor Prophet?" "I don't know," he answered modestly. "Perhaps it was the atmosphere in which I had lived for the last six months of the war but more likely, subconsciously, I was voicing the words of Mazzini, who declared, 'The morrow of the victory has more perils than its eve.'"

"Yours is the only beacon light in a darkening world," he said; "keep it brightly burning, or else——"

It is going to be difficult. Only ten days have passed and with the pressure of danger Wilson's omnipotence has passed also. New claims and new interests are being presented of which we know little, and of which the powers we have brought into the haven of victory think we know nothing at all. Some of our people are beginning to say that Wilson should have made hard-and-fast agreements with the powers while the eventual issue still hung in the balance. Perhaps! But what a lamentable ending that would have been to the glorious and inspiring crusade that brought so many hundred thousand of our boys from the homes and the farms that many of them will never see again!

November 20th.

An interesting if somewhat belated dispatch came today from the Colonel's mysterious spy; he gives a vivid description of the German collapse. Evidently he was an eyewitness of many of the amazing incidents in Kiel as well as in Berlin. Apparently on October 29th, the very day on which the members of the Supreme War Council were gathered together *chez* House, listening to the Armistice terms which the Germans might and in the judgment of Marshal Foch should have, in case they asked for them, a desperate move was planned in Berlin. The German High Sea Fleet, so long waterlogged in Kiel Harbor and in the Canal, was ordered to put to sea or rather ordered to prepare for this venture. It was announced that Prince Henry would be in command, but he never put in an appearance and, in view of what later happened, this was fortunate for him.

On the morning of the thirty-first the battleships *Markgraf* and the *Kaiser* were getting up steam and preparing to weigh anchor in obedience to these orders when suddenly the men mutinied, took possession of the ships, and placed their officers, not in the brig, but in locked cabins. Half a dozen of the officers who resisted were killed, but as our informant admits no precise figures as to the casualties are available. The mutiny spread to the naval base and to the town; the soldiers and the sailors fraternized and elected workers' councils after the Russians' model. He reports that the mutineers have appointed a commission to go to Russia for the purpose of entering into close relations with Lenin.

As soon as this news reached Berlin disturbances broke out all over the city and the workers from the Moabit quarter took over the police stations. At the War Ministry it was decided to send out two regiments, who were considered to be still reliable, to disperse the mob and arrest the ringleaders whoever they might be, but the soldiers threw their weapons into the Spree and joined in what was now evidently a revolutionary movement. He adds, "There is still desultory firing in some districts, but the workers are everywhere gaining control. Karl Liebknecht has unfurled the red flag from the tallest tower of the palace where only a few hours ago the last German Emperor, and King of Prussia, held court!" .

The Colonel is greatly impressed with this startling news although not all the details are as yet confirmed. But evidently he would prefer that the uprising should go no farther. "If all this is true," he remarked, "the Government with which we have entered upon an armistice would seem to have been overthrown and we can't tell with whom we can negotiate peace. It is to be hoped that now the revolution has accomplished its purpose the situation will be stabilized. What an inglorious end this is for the German Navy—incredible," was his comment.

November 22d.

Now that we have an armistice of sorts a tremendous discussion has arisen as to why Paris has been chosen as the scene of the Great Assizes and why, apparently, President Wilson has decided to take part personally in the discussions which will follow. Many, including Lloyd George, regret the decision that has been made and are quite voluble in expressing the opinion that it is the worst possible choice. Perhaps it is advisable to set down the circumstances that led to the decision, in so far as they are known to me, although I do not regard the matter as having the paramount importance that so many attach to it.

When House was leaving Washington to initiate the Armistice negotiations the President suggested Lausanne as the most suitable place for the Conference. He emphasized the fact that while undoubtedly the people of this Swiss town were pro-Ally in sentiment they were well behaved, unpleasant scenes would not take place, and besides the hotel accommodations were ample. By the time he reached Paris, House leaned personally toward Geneva and at his first meeting with Orlando he found that the Italian Premier was also in favor of the city of Calvin. In the midst of the Armistice discussions, on October 29th, Clemenceau announced that he hoped that Versailles would be chosen. House told him that Lloyd George, Orlando, and he himself were in favor of Geneva. It was agreed, however, that discussion was premature, it was, after all, not at all certain there would be a peace conference, and so the matter went over.

A few days later, when it appeared that Geneva had been definitely settled upon (when and if), a cable came from the President indicating that he had changed his mind and had reached a decision that later he was to regret most poignantly. In this cable, under date of November 8th, the President urged House to leave nothing undone to have Versailles chosen, and the reasons he advanced were as follows: "At Versailles friendly influences are in control, while Switzerland is saturated with every poisonous element, and open to every hostile influence."

While House confided to his diary that the President's second choice was a great mistake and that "he does not appreciate the influences we shall have to contend with in Versailles-Paris," he immediately set to work to carry out the President's wishes. Lloyd George for some days proved obstinate, but House overcame his opposition in a characteristically adroit manner. Knowing the dislike of the great press lord for the little Welshman, House induced Northcliffe to enter into the melee, and on November 11th the *Times* of London (his paper) announced, "The Conference must be held in Paris." The skirmishing continued for some days, but on November 20th House was able to cable the President that "his choice had prevailed."

The reasons why the President decided to take part personally in the Conference are more obscure. Undoubtedly, however, the President is mistaken in thinking that he came in response to the wishes of his friends. Many of them indeed ventured to dissuade the President from carrying out this purpose the moment they learned what was in his mind. As had been their custom during the last tense months of the war on every Wednesday afternoon the financial and economic advisors met with the President in the White House to confer with him on their current problems. On this particular Wednesday, three or four days after the Armistice, they were all on hand, and one after another they talked with Wilson. Vance McCormick had his talk, longer than usual, and Harry Garfield waited in a window embrasure with his memorandum in hand. "It was amazing, indeed magical it seemed to me, the way the President jumped from one problem to the next, always clearheaded and always with lucid thought and mind on the question presented," was the comment of the Fuel Dictator.[3] On this day Garfield noticed that when Mc-Cormick left, the President looked out the window for a moment and then called him in. After the current fuel problems had been discussed Garfield lingered on until the President said, "What is on your mind, Harry?" (They had been professors together at Princeton and were on terms of close intimacy.) "I want to ask you not to go to Europe," said Garfield. "Not to take an active part in the Peace Conference. I and many of your other friends for whom I am speaking fear that if you do go you will have to descend from your present position of world arbiter. You will necessarily become a combatant in the hurly-burly. You will become a contestant in the struggle, in the struggle of which you are the only possible referee."

The President grew very thoughtful. "There is much in what you say, Harry. I am indeed confronted with a difficult decision. But now listen to me and weigh my thought. Here in America I understand what is going on throughout the country. I know even before the public what is likely to happen at the Capitol. But Europe is far away, and the voices that come to me from there are so confusing. Half my time, and more, is occupied with decoding dispatches that come from Europe—and must come to me personally. So you see—at least I see—that by going abroad I would save time and would be helped by more direct contacts." Garfield bowed and was about to withdraw and then he blurted out, "May I say, Mr. President, how greatly I admire your ability to face alone all the problems we have to submit to you!" The President smiled and drawing Garfield to the window said, "I'll let you into a secret. Between each of the momentous interviews to which you refer I take, as you may have noticed, a peep out of the window. I watch the birds and the squirrels going about their daily tasks. I cannot tell you what refreshment there comes to me from watching them."

Downstairs Garfield found that McCormick was waiting for him. "What did you talk about so long with the President?" he asked.

"I begged him not to go to Europe—to remain here on top of the uneasy world," said Garfield.

"That is exactly what I talked to him about," answered McCormick, and there were many others who in these days expressed similar views and fears.

When the Colonel reached France (October 26th) he had not the remotest idea that the President had any thought of coming to Europe,

[3]Communicated to me by Dr. Garfield in 1932.

but soon from many sources he learned that the idea was uppermost in his mind and also that it was being hotly debated in Washington. Under his instructions to make contacts with European leaders and to keep the President advised as to their views, it was impossible for House to hold himself aloof from the controversy, much as he would have liked to. So on November 14th he cabled:

"Americans here whose opinions are of value are practically unanimous in the belief that it would be unwise for you to sit in the Peace Conference. They fear it would involve a loss of dignity and deprive you of your commanding position. Clemenceau has just told me that he hopes you will not sit in the conference because no head of state should sit there. Cobb wires from England that Reading and Wiseman voice the same view. Everyone wants you to come over to take part in the preliminary talks. It is at these meetings that peace terms will be shaped, just as the informal conferences of last month determined the German and Austrian armistices."

A few hours later House cabled: "It is of vital importance, I think, for you to come as soon as possible for everything is being held in abeyance. Clemenceau assumes that the preliminary discussions will not last more than three weeks while he believes that the Peace Conference may take as long as four months. In announcing your departure I think it important that you should not state that you will sit at the Conference. That can be determined after you get here. The French, English, and Italian Prime Ministers will head their delegations."

Even for such a trained diplomatist as House, here was presented a most difficult situation. Any suggestion that the President should not come to Paris, or if he did come should not take an active personal part in the negotiations, meant that the chief responsibility for American representation would devolve on the shoulders of House. And it must be admitted that at this juncture even House's diplomacy failed to conciliate the President, and his reply, though cloaked in cable code, discloses his irritation. It ran:

"Your telegram upsets every plan we had made. I am thrown into complete confusion by the change of program (this is far from an accurate statement. No program had been settled upon, consequently none had been changed). The suggestion that I should not sit as a delegate but that I should be received with the honors due to the chief of state seems to me a way of pocketing me." Then with evidently rising indignation the President continued: "I infer that the French and British leaders desire to exclude me from the Conference for fear that there I might lead the weaker nations against them. I play the same role in our Government as the Prime Ministers do in theirs. The fact that I am head of the state is of no practical importance. I object very strongly to the fact that dignity must prevent us from securing the results we have set our hearts upon. It is universally expected and generally desired here (?) that I should attend the Conference, but I believe that no one would wish me to sit by and try to steer from the outside. I hope you will be very shy of their advice and give me your own independent judgment after reconsideration."

This cable put House in an even more difficult situation than before. He had been sent across the water to sound out the leaders of opinion in the countries with which we had been associated in the war and in conjunction with whom it was our task to make an honorable and durable peace. Now the President urged House to turn a deaf ear to their opinions and their advice and to send only his own independent judgment after reconsideration, which of course was tantamount to saying that his advice on the subject, hitherto expressed, had not been independently arrived at. Never had I seen the Colonel so perplexed, but with less than an hour's delay he handled the situation so loaded with dynamite with his accustomed wisdom. He had now no doubt as to the coming of the President, so he cabled:

"My judgment is that you should determine upon your arrival here what share it is wise for you to take in the proceedings." And then House sought to change the cable conversation into a field which he hoped would prove more advantageous, but here again he was unsuccessful. The illusion under which the President labored that all the European powers were banded together against America was, as the sequel shows, to become with him an obsession. "I do not note any signs of a reactionary conspiracy among the European powers," House cabled. "As far as I can see all the powers are trying to work with us rather than with one another. Their disagreements (among themselves) are sharp and constant."

After a short cooling-off period there came the following answer from Washington which as I decoded it with Gordon Auchincloss I found reassuring: "The President," it read, "will sail for France, immediately after the opening of the regular session of Congress, for the purpose of taking part in the discussions and the settlement of the main features of the Treaty of Peace. It is not likely that it will be possible for him to remain throughout the formal Peace Conference, but his presence at the outset is necessary in order to obviate the manifest disadvantages of discussion by cable in determining the larger outlines of the final treaty about which he must necessarily be consulted. He will of course be accompanied by delegates who will sit as the representatives of the United States throughout the Conference. The names of the delegates and the date of the meeting will be presently announced."

I thought, of course, that the Colonel's wise counsels had prevailed, but the Colonel shook his head. "I hope you are right, but I fear that nothing is definitely settled."

No one had been more eager to learn what course the President had decided to pursue than Clemenceau, and so I was not surprised when he turned up with Tardieu an hour after this fairly definite cable, at least as I considered it, had arrived. He was gratified that our President would be pleased to propose him for the presidency of the Congress (which he had offered to do in a separate cable), but added it would not be necessary. As the Congress convened in France, automatically, the French Prime Minister would be called upon to preside. But Clemenceau was very persistent in trying to find out whether the President would sit in with the delegates. To his repeated inquiries the Colonel could only answer that after reaching Paris the President would decide. The persistence of the Tiger in making these inquiries revealed an angle of the situation which few had suspected. He knew that President Poincaré was most desirous of being called to the French peace delegation. And if this could be arranged, as the Chief Magistrate of France, he would have to be chairman. To his intimates Clemenceau stated that he would resign rather than submit to association with a man he so cordially disliked and distrusted. If the Chief of the American state sat in the Conference his presence would offer something like a precedent for the presence there also of the French President. As long as this cloud hung over the Conference, Clemenceau would have been delighted had Wilson remained in America, but once this danger was removed, and with Poincaré definitely out of the running, he greatly preferred, as he often stated, to have Wilson within reach rather than at the end of the cable. . . .

House, realizing that Wilson's mind was made up, did not argue the matter further. He did not even send on to the President the friendly, if strong, remonstrance of Masaryk against the President's coming to Paris (in the interview with House on December 7th, at which I was present). He merely said, "Evidently the President is convinced that his presence here is absolutely necessary if liberal forces are to win through, and he may be right." But on one position the Colonel stood by his guns. By cable he repeated his previous advice to Wilson not to reveal what action he proposed taking until his arrival in Paris. "I think it best that only on your arrival should you determine what share it is wise for you to take in the proceedings." Then once again he added, with the purpose of dispelling the President's suspicions, "As far as I can see all the powers are trying to work with us rather than with one another. Among themselves their disagreements are sharp and constant." To this the President merely answered he was coming to Paris, but on November 19th another cable from him came although this time it was couched, in part at least, in the third person. It read:

"It is not likely that it will be possible for the President to remain throughout the formal sessions of the Peace Conference. If the French Prime Minister is uneasy about the presidency of the Conference I will gladly propose that he preside."

This settled part of the problem but, in my judgment at least, not the part that most interested and indeed harassed Clemenceau. He feared that if Wilson had insisted upon presiding Poincaré would have been in some measure justified in saying that in this case France also must be represented by the Chief of State—and the diplomatic archives of the nations furnish, I believe, some support for this view. However, the Tiger made it quite clear that he would be the kingpin of the French delegation or he would not sit as a delegate at all. So Poincaré did not insist upon what may, after all, have been merely the plan of his too-zealous friends.

PART II

The First Draft
of the Covenant

THE SESSIONS OF THE COMMISSION IN THE HOTEL CRILLON
FEBRUARY 1—14, 1919
PARIS

January 2, 1919.

As I came into his study this morning I found Colonel House, always so calm and composed, visibly—but pleasantly—affected. Before him was the speech which the President delivered in Manchester (England) on the thirtieth—the words which they had so carefully, so prayerfully considered together last week. The substantial paragraph which should be long remembered both at home and abroad reads:

"There is a great voice of Humanity abroad in the world just now which he who cannot hear is deaf. There is a great compulsion of the Common Conscience now in existence which, if any statesman resists, will gain for him most unenviable eminence in history. We are not obeying the mandate of party or politics, we are obeying the mandate of humanity."

The Colonel was so exalted that I did not have the heart to tell him again that while there is a great voice of humanity appealing to the peoples of many lands there are millions who will not listen to it even when these convincing words of promise fall from the lips of the Crusader from across the seas they hailed only a few weeks ago as Salvator! As late as a month ago these words would have met with almost unanimous approval—but not today. Today there are many millions who will not see beyond their noses, who are grateful for what the Great American and his gallant soldiers have done but who are quite determined that he shall not spoil the peace with his "quaint" ideologies. I have told the Colonel so often of the pretensions and the

15

bickerings among the wild tribes with whom I must spend my long days that today, with an almost perfectly happy man before me, I did not have the heart to rub it in. Soon, very soon, he will realize into what disturbed waters our ship of state has sailed. Half to me and half to himself the Colonel continued: "That was indeed a trumpet note. In ringing out the Old Year the President not only heralds, he ushers in the brighter days to come. It was a clarion call to all men of good will to rally behind the flag of the New Freedom."

It was all that and more, but in view of my daily contacts with delegates arriving from Asia and Africa as well as from Europe I am not confident that they will fight for Wilson now as stoutly as he fought for them in war. I hope I'm mistaken, but certainly I expect squalls—and even storms.

January 18, 1919.

In accepting the presidency of the Peace Conference today M. Clemenceau gave the delegates assembled from all over the world a taste of his quality. No typescript was in his hand, there was no rustling of papers. He drew his inspiration from the world audience before him. No "releases" came to us or to the representatives of the world press; and I am glad I took down his noble words just as they were spoken, as they came, not from his secretariat, but from his great heart. He said:

"I cannot avoid trying to express my deep gratitude to the illustrious President of the United States, to the British Premier, and to Baron Sonnino, for the words they have spoken. I am profoundly touched by their attitude and I recognize in it a new force which will aid all three of us, with the co-operation of all the delegates, to push to a successful conclusion the difficult task that awaits us. In a word from these expressions of friendship I draw a renewed confidence in the success of our joint efforts. . . . It is indeed a noble and a lofty ambition which animates us, and I pray that success may attend our labors —but this success cannot be attained unless we are determined to realize our high ideals. This I said in the Chamber of Deputies a few days ago, but I want to insist upon it here. The achievement of our purpose is not possible unless we remain firmly united. Here we have met as friends, from here we must go as brothers. That is the thought that is uppermost in my heart today, and I would add that all else must be subordinated to the necessity of a union growing ever closer between the peoples who have taken part in the Great War. The League of Nations is here. It is in you, but you must inspire it with the breath of life, and this we cannot do unless that purpose and determination is in our hearts.

"If, as I have already said to President Wilson, we are to accomplish our great purpose, there must be no sacrifice which we are not ready and willing to make. I do not doubt that you enter upon our joint labors in this spirit, and I am confident we shall achieve our high purpose, but this can only be done if, in a spirit of impartiality, we reconcile our interests which are only apparently conflicting. We must be inspired by our clear vision of the world that is to come, the vision of a greater and a nobler civilization.

"The program of this Conference was drawn up by President Wilson; as you see it is not merely a territorial peace having regard to expanses of territory, however vast, that will occupy our attention. It is not merely to establish a peace, speaking in the terms of continents, that we have come together. We meet to establish for all time peace among the peoples of the earth.

"This, our program, speaks for itself. I shall not add a superfluous word. Let us work speedily and well. Gentlemen, to our task!"

February 1st.

I have made it a rule, of course with an exception now and then, not to confide to my diary any of the spectacular events that have followed upon the *ora formidabile* of the Armistice. I have omitted all reference to the pageantry with which the cavalcades of kings have been greeted as they came to the City of Light, and I ignore the visits of the President to the capitals of Europe now breathing freely after the tortured agony of war. These events are in the hands of competent remembrancers and assuredly they will not escape history. My task has been the humble one of jotting down things seen and words heard of less spectacular character which may, taken together, shape the future and perhaps control it and which, engrossed as he is with major tasks, may have escaped the Colonel's attention. From this rule, however, I deviate today in recording the words with which on the day when the delegates to the Peace Conference met in the first solemn conclave (January 25th), the President asked for the appointment of a commission to draft the League of Nations Covenant which is to be the statute of the Parliament of Man and, as many hope, will bring peace to the war-racked world.

His words were: "The United States in entering the war never for a moment thought it was intervening in the politics of Europe, Asia, or of any part of the world. Its thought was that all the world had now become conscious that there was a single cause which turned upon the issues of this war. That was the cause of justice and of liberty for men of every kind and place. Therefore the United States would feel that its part had been played in vain if there ensued upon it merely a body of European settlements. It would feel it could not take part in guaranteeing this European settlement unless that guarantee involved the continuous superintendence of the peace of the world by the Associated Nations of the World."

A trumpet note it was; the Colonel was affected as were all present. Tears streamed down the rugged face of M. Léon Bourgeois as he recalled the gallant but unsuccessful battles he had fought for peace and to safeguard civilization at The Hague, and at all the other conferences. Clemenceau listened to the President with his eyes closed, and certainly his features, which can be so expressive, did not reveal his inmost thoughts, but he was courteous and immediately set in motion the machinery of reconstruction which the President asked for. Bourgeois came up to us as we of the American group were leaving the scene of the great pronouncement. "Light and leading has come to us at last," he said, "and it has come from the West."

I accompanied House back to the Crillon, and in a very few minutes he was his practical self again, examining the situation the details of which were soon to be placed in his skilled, competent hands. At last he said, "The President has given them an unfailing compass for their guidance. If the Covenant goes into all the treaties we shall be bound to the European settlements. If not—not. They, both at home and abroad, have fair warning. The issue is joined."

As the difficult task of drafting the Covenant between the peace-loving nations begins in a few hours it is probably wise to recall and review some of the antecedents of the great plan. Of course it must be admitted, although a most depressing admission, that the idea goes back to the dawn of history and that none of the cherished hopes based upon it have been realized. William Penn, with his brotherly scheme of founding a paradise in Pennsylvania, brought the plan across the stormy Western Ocean into the new world from which Mr. Wilson now brings it back to wartorn and bleeding Europe. There may be many details of the incubation or rather the revival of the idea in its present form that are still obscure, but while doubtless not a complete narrative I shall here set down the record in so far as it is known to me.

Early in 1915, in one of the darkest periods of the war, Colonel House began to work on a plan to prevent what had happened, to the disgrace of our civilization, from ever happening again. By July 1918 he had, with the assistance of Hunter Miller, who is as able as he is unobtrusive (and who is with us now), hammered out what he called "A World Constitution."

Many months before the Armistice House was bombarded with suggestions and proposals from leading French statesmen (but not from Clemenceau) as to what the League of Nations, on which so many hopes of peace were based, should be. But as early as July 1918 he was forced to the conclusion that what the French, or many of them, had in mind was a continuation of the war alliance, with complete control of the peace conditions and absolute exclusion of the Central Empires from the comity of nations. When Sir Edward Grey (in this month), by publishing his plea for the admission of Germany into the ultimate League, provoked a storm of unfavorable criticism in the French press, House from Magnolia wrote the President frankly admitting his misgivings, indeed his fears (July 1918).

House and Miller had before them the Phillimore plan, so called from the eminent English jurist who drew it up, and several provisions of it were incorporated in the Constitution. It was about the middle of July (1918) that House in his summer home at Magnolia sent on his sketch plan to the President. From his covering letter it would appear that House had in mind to restrict full membership in the League to the Greater Powers. He expressed the hope, and also the belief, that the plan would be so fair and so just that, assured of its protection, all the lesser powers would concur and later "join up." This preliminary sketch was written hurriedly in thirty-six hours upon the receipt of an urgent call from the President, and, as House told me later, "It should not be regarded as representing my mature thought on the problem." It was, however, as he explained, "a venture in practical idealism," and it provided for a council, dominated, it is true, by the Great Powers, but with, as he thought, adequate representation assured the lesser states.

With this draft before him, and perhaps with others, the President set to work on his own plan. In the House sketch the word "Covenant" was used, in this connection perhaps for the first time, but as President Wilson in his addresses to the Congress had often spoken of his objective as a "covenanted peace" House may have simply clothed his idea in the President's language. He certainly never showed any pride of authorship in bringing into world-wide use the Old Testament term. House's sketch was fully utilized by the President in drawing up his plan which later became known as the First Official American Draft. Out of the twenty-three articles in the House sketch all but five were incorporated in the President's plan. There was also by this time before the President a French draft drawn up by M. Léon Bourgeois. It was sent to House from Paris and submitted by him to the President. Its salient feature was a provision for an international military force under a permanent staff, later to be so frequently referred to as the "Sheriff's posse of the league of law-abiding nations."

During the period of incubation which followed, as requested by House, Elihu Root and ex-President Taft made suggestions and some of these helped to shape the President's plan. About the middle of August (1918) Wilson paid House a long visit at Magnolia (in Massachusetts), and the sketch and the plan were compared and some changes in language as well as in structure were made. It was agreed to hold the plan in confidence until a more opportune moment for launching it arrived. Both the President and House were agreed that its publication at this time would start bitter controversy rather than fruitful discussion.

The draft that resulted from this conference at Magnolia is the one that Wilson took with him when, months later, he sailed for Paris. My clear understanding is that there were no further changes in this document until on the eve of the Conference the President and House got down to work at the Crillon. A suggestion of General Smuts as to mandates was now taken over, although his idea is to be found in the Fourteen Points, and the President incorporated his own idea of an International Labor Bureau with the main purpose, in Wilson's words, of "having an eight-hour workday throughout the world." Another article, an original idea of the President's according to House, was inserted. It "required newly created states to accord equality of treatment to all racial and religious minorities." Still another suggestion of the President's was inserted, and that assured to all member states the right to intervene with proposals of conciliation when war threatened. In a conversation at this time with Professor Seymour of Yale, the President explained the motive behind this proposal. He said: "When troubles threaten I want any nation to have the right to butt in. There must be no more private wars."

With some slight changes in language, and with these important additions, the resulting document became known as the Second Paris Draft. Some confusion resulted from the fact that at this moment a new British draft was sent to House and by him was submitted to the President. Orlando also submitted an Italian draft and some minor points of his were accepted. The President did not like the new British draft and the British did not like the American draft. Wiseman told House that "his people thought that the Americans were grabbing the whole shooting match and there was trouble ahead." House put both drafts into the hands of Miller for America, and Hurst for Britain, with orders to iron things out, that is, "to smooth the ruffled feathers."

These unfortunate gentlemen worked on their difficult task day and night, but the result of their collaboration only reached the President yesterday (February 2d) and he did not like it at all. He told House "it has neither warmth nor color." After much discussion, however, this draft was accepted tentatively, and it became the basis of the discussions which now ensued. This is as briefly as I can tell it the *historique*, the antecedents, of the document upon which the delegates are to work from now on in conformity with the resolution adopted, at the President's insistence, in the Plenary Session of the Conference, held on January 25th, which reads:

"It is essential to the maintenance of the world settlement which the Associated Nations are now met to establish, that a League of Nations be created to promote international co-operation, to insure the fulfillment of accepted international obligations, and to provide safeguards against war.

"This League should be created as an integral part of the general Treaty of Peace, and should be open to every civilized nation which can be relied on to promote its objects. . . .

"The Conference, therefore, appoints a committee representative of the Associated Governments to work out the Constitution and the functions of the League."

February 2d.

I had been told by the Colonel (who, being a man of one language himself, with generous exaggeration regarded me as a master of many tongues) that I was to act as interpreter for the President and himself in the sessions of the League of Nations Commission; that is, that I was to interpret from French into English for their edification. While by no means eager for the task, I was not greatly afraid; of course I had never done any long-winded verbal interpreting before, but then, in wartime, you have to do many things you could avoid in the piping days of peace. However, as the great men of some seventeen nations assembled in the charming salon of the Hotel Crillon, for the first meeting of the Parliament of Man, I was advised by the Colonel of a shift in plan and a new responsibility from which, but for the respect I knew was due my uniform, I would have fled incontinently. The non-English-speaking members of the Commission had approached him with a request that, as it was reasonable, he concluded must be complied with. They did not speak or understand English, they admitted, and yet they did not want to lose the meaning of a single word that fell from the President's lips. They requested that an interpreter be placed in their midst to pass on to them the winged words and the message of the one whom they (or at least many of them) regarded as their Messiah. And so in a moment I was drafted away from the head of the Council table, Frazier was given my place, between and a little behind (within whispering distance) the President and House, and I was catapulted to the other end of the table where I was beset on all sides by inquiries from Venizelos, in Cretan French, from Diamandy in Roumanian French, from Dmowski in Polish French, and from Vesnitch in the French of Belgrade. They were patient and kind and I, indeed, survived the first session, but could I continue?

That was, indeed, a question! Kind Fate now intervened and I was relieved from a painful situation. Sorry I am that the change brought discomfort to the immensely capable Frazier; he caught a terrible cold, and his voice trailed off into a treble, and I was reinstated in my original position, while Frazier was sent out upon important business which required brains and not merely a stentorian voice.

But what was to be done now for our non-English-speaking foreign Ministers? Means certainly had to be contrived to let them know what it was all about. In my quandary I looked into the "linguistic pool," as we called it, and drew out a young professor of high attainments and also excellent French, and placed him in the uneasy chair I was so glad to vacate. But, unfortunately, this scholarly professor was awe-stricken by his august surroundings; instead of passing on the golden words of the President, he would hem and haw; indeed in diplomatic reticence he excelled the trained plenipotentiaries by whom he was surrounded! After one completely blank evening, at the unanimous request of those who had with increasing indignation listened to his eloquent silences, the professor was withdrawn and duties more in harmony with his undoubted talents were assigned to him. Again I dived deep down into the linguistic pool and fished out a young lieutenant from Louisiana, who spoke excellent French and also the musical English of the Deep South. He was drafted to the job in which he acquitted himself admirably. He, an American "sovereign," was not at all awe-stricken by his close association with the representatives of the shattered monarchies of Europe, or with the outstanding new men of the budding democracies. As a matter of fact, he ruled them with an iron hand, but it was gloved, and they liked him, in fact they ate out of his hand! The youngster was born to command, and someday I expect to see him representing his state under the dome of the Capitol in Washington.[1]

The job of whispered interpretation to the President on one side and House on the other that again devolved on me was the most arduous task that I shouldered during the Conference. And even when the speeches ran on for three or four hours, as they often did, my taskmasters would not let me condense, which I thought, and always shall think, was a mistake. But my vocal cords survived the test. However, as I saw Frazier rushing about upon his important duties, always lowering his words to a gentle whisper as I appeared, I often wondered whether his voicelessness had not been merely diplomatic! After all, Frazier was a trained diplomat, the most successful exponent of the art that we produced at the Conference.

At the first meeting of the Commission to draft the Covenant of the League, with Woodrow Wilson presiding, the following were present:

President Wilson	
Colonel House	*United States of America*
Lord Robert Cecil	
Lieutenant General J. C. Smuts	*British Empire*
M. Léon Bourgeois	
M. Larnaude	*France*
M. Orlando	
Senator Scialoja	*Italy*
Baron Makino	
Viscount Chinda	*Japan*

[1] I regret that I did not record his name in my diary and that now I cannot recall it. I still am confident that someday he will come into his own, that both for the things he will say and those he will leave unsaid he will "command the applause of the listening Senate"—in Washington, of course.

M. Hymans	*Belgium*
M. Epitacio Pessoa	*Brazil*
Mr. Wellington Koo	*China*
M. Jaime Batalha Reis	*Portugal*
M. Vesnitch	*Serbia*

At the fifth meeting, held on the evening of February 7, the following were admitted to the Commission and from then on took part in the deliberations:

M. Venizelos	*Greece*
M. Dmowski	*Poland*
M. Diamandy	*Roumania*[2]
M. Krámář	*Czechoslovakia*

Thus bringing the membership of the Commission to nineteen.

The first meeting, as I have noted, took place on Monday afternoon, February 3d. Fifteen delegates should have been present, two for each of the Great Powers, and one each for the five lesser powers, with special interests—in distinction to those with general interests. However, the delegate from Portugal was late. After the proceedings were under way he came bustling in with the announcement that his instructions had been delayed. Nobody seemed to attach the same importance to his instructions that he did. The President, presiding, opened the proceedings without fanfare of any kind. He told the delegates they were about to undertake a most difficult task. He told them that never again should civilization be confronted with a situation such as they all met with in 1914. It was their task to see that what happened then could never happen again. Then, he continued, the civilized powers, inspired by their common interests, had combined against the Central Empires and so the basis was laid for a League which today world conditions make imperative. Then,

"For some days we have discussed methods of procedure and they have been put together in a skeleton plan which I now hold in my hand. This I will now submit to you and, if you approve, we shall use it as a basis for discussion."

[2]Jan Bratianu, the Roumanian Prime Minister, sat once or twice with the League of Nations Commission, a mute and forbidding figure. Then he turned over the representation of his country to M. Diamandy. Some months later even more difficult duties were assigned to M. Diamandy. He was sent to Budapest to sit on the High Commission which tried rather unsuccessfully to compel the commanders of the invading Roumanian forces to show some respect for the orders of the Supreme War Council, sitting in Paris. On this commission General Bandholtz, United States Army, was our able representative.

Bourgeois (France) protested. Delegates should be given an opportunity to study the draft before being called upon to discuss it.

Orlando (Italy) agreed, however, to discuss the draft, which he understood had been arrived at in informal conversations between the President, Cecil, House, and Smuts.

Bourgeois yielded, but stated that in his judgment, if the meetings were to be more than a formality, a secretariat should be chosen and should assist at all the sessions.

WILSON: "The important thing is to make progress. We must get under way. The record will take care of itself."

CECIL: "We should get down to work; we must push ahead. There has already been a great deal of discussion. We must get down to the details. The whole world is watching, anxiously awaiting the result of these deliberations."

WILSON: "I call this an informal meeting because we have not had the time to organize. It also seems to me that if our sessions are formal, with secretaries making copious reports, each day's proceedings would be subjected to prolonged discussions."

At the second session (evening of February 4th) the Preamble and Articles I and II were adopted without too much difficulty. But with Article III a snag was struck; it deals with the composition of the Council and the representation on it of the lesser powers. In deference to the wishes of Cecil, it had been omitted from the Hurst-Miller draft. It very soon developed that the majority of the delegates were strongly in favor of admitting representatives of the lesser powers to the Council, as a minority of one, however, as had been provided for in all the Wilson drafts.

Wilson now opposed enlarging the Council. The larger the membership, the slower would be the progress.

"It is of course our purpose to call in the lesser powers and also the neutral powers as progress is made. It should be remembered the Commission is not settling the fate of any particular nation. It is settling the fate of all."

Wilson then pled for informal exchange of views until the instrument had taken shape; then formal conversations would be in order. Orlando concurred; he stated that the function of the Commission was to study, to explore the field.

In face of the general opposition, Cecil now withdrew his plan. Nine delegates voted in favor of the admission of the lesser powers, and none in the negative. It was agreed, then, to place the situation before the Conference at a later date. Apparently Greece, Poland, Roumania, and Czechoslovakia for the present are to represent the lesser powers on the Council.

Still the discussion did not die down. Hymans (Belgium) was very vehement in his opposition to what he called the control of the Council of the League by the Great Powers, and he was supported by Vesnitch (Serbia), in a more moderate tone, however. Hymans declared that the lesser powers would not accept any plan by which they were excluded. Wilson stated that he believed there was no objection to a plan providing for the membership of the five Greater Powers and a minority representation of the smaller powers to be selected by themselves. Hymans apparently accepted this proposal, but with no enthusiasm. We shall hear from Belgium again.

There now followed heated discussions over the language of the Preamble and the first two Articles. It was quieted by a statement from Wilson to the effect that the delegates should bear in mind that the language of the document was provisional and of course subject to review. At the third session, on the following day, this dispute came to the fore again, and I think it wise to give what was said then in this place.

CECIL: "I strongly advise going slow on the proposal to give the smaller powers four representatives on the Council. Our purpose is, of course, to make the League a success, and that demands the support of the Great Powers. Two representatives of the lesser powers should suffice."

"What you propose," shouted Hymans, "is a revival of the Holy Alliance of unhallowed memory!"

Wilson sought to placate the little man by saying:

"We should remember that the political independence and the territorial integrity of each State, member of the League, is to be guaranteed by all powers, great and small alike. Bearing this in mind, I do not think injustice would be done the lesser powers by limiting to two their representation."

Later.

At the third session (February 4th) the President read Article IV of the draft which deals with the executive officer of the League and its seat. The executive is spoken of as Chancellor (later changed to Secretary General), and the seat of the League was left in blank. Hymans (Belgium) took the floor. "I see that the future seat of the

League is not designated, and while my action may be premature I avail myself of this opportunity to express the hope of my government and my people that Brussels may be designated. We are all of the opinion that this choice would be symbolic of all that we have fought for and may have to fight for again in future battles."

Wilson said all present had the greatest admiration for the gallant Belgian people and also full appreciation of the facilities that would be available in Brussels, but it was deemed advisable to defer the choice to a later meeting. The President's statement was greeted by all present with energetic nods of approval. I am confident that the matter will be turned over to a subcommittee and I am equally certain that Brussels will not be chosen and that Geneva will be.

III Session.

At the first meeting (turning back for a moment) of the Commission nothing was said about recording the deliberations and no arrangements were made for so doing. At the second session, however, M. Bourgeois again urged the appointment of a secretariat with a staff of stenographers working under the secretaries. Larnaude supported the request of his colleague. "Unless a record is kept we shall be working in the dark." The President tried to defeat the French demand, with a light touch, however. Laughingly he said, "I am opposed to a record being kept because I want to keep an open mind; I want to be able to say on Wednesday quite the opposite of what I may have said on Monday." Then, growing serious, he added, "The task of this Commission is like that of the body of men who drew up the Constitution of the United States. On that great occasion the proceedings were withheld from the public until their work was concluded. I hope this Commission will see fit to follow this illustrious example. We should proceed in an informal manner for the purpose of safeguarding our discussions from misrepresentation. I want to keep an open mind, and I think we all do. Informal procedure would, I have no doubt, assist us to this desirable end. Nothing should be given out until our work is completed and we can present it to our governments and to our peoples as a rounded whole. I am afraid if a detailed record is kept there may occur leaks, and this would increase our difficulties—already considerable."

The French delegates returned to the charge after the meeting. They were supported by all the delegates except the President, and at the third session the President gave way and secretaries were appointed. At the fourth session they were placed at a side table some distance from the conference table at which the delegates sat and must have had difficulty in following the proceedings. They were most discreet and their reports, I am told, were meager, although I admit I have never seen any of them. Bourgeois carried his point, but it was a triumph of form rather than of substance.

We then adjourned to meet tomorrow evening at the same place and at eight-thirty. There had been much desultory talk and even suggestions of revolt against the method of procedure which the President and House have worked over. But with a little grumbling our plan has been approved. During the first reading the rough draft is to be taken up and debated article by article. There are to be secretaries but no stenographers present. At this announcement moans from the French, and the President graciously consented to "putting out communiqués to the press when we agree that it is advisable—when we all agree."

I have gloomy forebodings. Not a few of the delegates will "leak" to their favorite newspaper when leakage promises to be helpful, and of course the burden of newspaper unpopularity under which the President suffers will be increased by what many have already called "the revival of Star Chamber proceedings by one who promised Open Covenants, openly arrived at."

While they may prove helpful, my records made in this haphazard manner[3] are certainly not so reliable as would have been a report of the proceedings drawn up by a competent shorthand man who, keeping out of the verbal melee, would have had nothing to do but to retain the words as they were spoken. While generally written up within a few hours of the conclusion of the sessions, on at least two occasions other duties delayed the write-up of these notes for several days. Under these circumstances it would be absurd to insist that my report is *verbatim et literatim* correct; but, on the other hand, I am confident that in the main I have set down accurately what was said and that the manner and the bearing of the speakers is faithfully recorded. Perhaps still another word of explanation may not be amiss. These post-sessions records of the deliberations have grown so voluminous that I find they are crowding out more important papers from the Colonel's safe where, as an extra precaution, they were stowed away every evening. Yesterday I went over these records, and this morning I have, as our instructions demand, taken down to the

[3]They were made after the sessions—at times only on the following day.

incinerator in the cellar those memoranda whose period of usefulness is at an end.

Further, I shall not retain in my diary my running accounts of some of the major battles that were fought over the Covenant. The results will be found in the draft that is now or soon will be open to world inspection and, after all, it is the results that count. I am hopeful that I shall be serving a more useful purpose by giving the details of some of the unsuccessful skirmishes and also by preserving the language of many of the amendments and additions which were not adopted, but may well be heard from later on. I shall also retain anything that may be helpful in drawing a picture of the men who for the moment are masters of the world. Each and every one of them wants to redeem this war-racked world and make it a better place to live in; unfortunately each wants to achieve this desirable end in his own way and has a very poor opinion of the other fellow's way!

February 4th.

Surrounded by a cortege of the Republican Guard and a squadron of cuirassiers, the President drove yesterday to the Chamber through streets and boulevards thronged with happy, cheering people. It was indeed a wonderful sight. Wilson was pleased and touched, and he showed it. All Paris was at his feet. In his address to the deputies he departed quite a little from the text of the discourse he had proposed to make. He said:

"America is paying her debt of gratitude to France in sending her sons to defend your country, but she does more: she is helping to re-unite world forces so that never again shall France be isolated; never again will France have to ask the question who will come to her assistance in her battle for right and justice."

At these words the Chamber broke out into tumultuous applause. The very largest interpretation is being placed upon these words, one more far-reaching, I should say, than was intended by the speaker.

February 6th.

Miller's darling project is to insert in the Covenant a provision for compulsory arbitration; all the minor powers who have heard of it support the idea enthusiastically. However, Lord Robert Cecil came in this afternoon and he made it exceedingly clear to House that England, at least, would have none of it.

"I hate to be a stumbling block to the realization of a dream, a

world without war, which I confess exerts a strong appeal upon me.
But in this present situation it would be far from wise if we allowed
our hands to be tied; they must be free to fight for the right as we see
it. We are ready for very drastic restrictions, we will go a long way
in accepting what Mr. Bryan called so wisely 'Cooling-Off Periods.'
And we are willing to accept delays, during which frayed tempers
might be restored to normal, but, in the end, if other more civilized
methods fail, we must have the right to seek the arbitrament of arms.
I trust, as you do, that we may never be compelled to call upon it.
Indeed, in hopeful moments I think we never shall, but I cannot assume, at least not just at present, responsibility for discarding war as
an instrument for the maintenance of the peace of the world."

Lord Robert's nerves are getting frayed, and I sympathize with him.
M. Léon Bourgeois is his *bête noir*, as he is mine, and with, as I think,
more substantial reason, for I have to translate his interminable
speeches, while Cecil and the rest of the great men can let their
thoughts wander off to more agreeable pastures. And they can also
go to sleep, which has happened several times with two of them. Yesterday Cecil's nerves got the better of his manners, and in the subcommittee, according to Miller (I was not present), as Bourgeois began his familiar and oft-repeated plea for an international army, Cecil
raised his arm on high and seemed to be overcome by an utter weariness which he could find no words sufficiently eloquent to express.
At last, catching breath, he said,

"Oh, M. Bourgeois! Do not begin that all over again. We have
heard you so often and so patiently. Your plan will lead nowhere, but,
stay—I am wrong; I shall tell you what it will lead to. It will lead to
the complete abandonment of our present work for some sort of a
league of nations. And when that is apparent, for my part I shall certainly recommend to His Majesty's Government an alliance between
America and Great Britain to regulate the world, with France left
out, because—because—of incompatibility of temper."

February 7th.

Should they ever fall into critical hands, I owe an explanation of
how and why these diaries and these much-too-copious memoranda
were scribbled by one who, before the great catastrophe overtook us,
was completely immune to the diary contagion. For my deplorable
activity I offer this word of explanation. It was enforced—not voluntary. From the first days of our collaboration, which began with the

Armistice negotiations, at his request I made full reports on the situation as I saw it to Colonel House, and also reports on the attitude of the press, and at times condensations of the views of the Colonel's fellow negotiators obtained by personal contacts with them or with their advisers. At times, I may add, special investigations on contentious points were entrusted to me.

The Colonel approved of this method of work, but as the situation became more complicated, and memoranda and reports from many sources were showered upon him as fell the leaves of Vallambrosa, he asked me, except in special cases, to make my reports verbally. This, he thought, would save me from the labor of much writing, would spare his eyes from the task of constant reading, and also would afford him an opportunity to question me on angles of the questions in regard to which he might want fuller details than those I gave him. This change of method was most agreeable to me, but, as is not seldom the case when you think everything has been comfortably arranged, difficulties and objections began to develop. The field I had to survey was very extensive; it did not merely run from Dan to Beersheba! Continents were involved and scores of nations were demanding their day in court. Not seldom when I was ready to place before my chief in writing, or, if he preferred, verbally, the mass of information that I had so painfully acquired, the spotlight of the Conference would be shifted to another quarter of the globe and to another national or perhaps international problem. What was I to do with all this encyclopedic knowledge and technical information? Of course I had to conserve it against the day when, surely, this postponed question would pop up on the agenda again. It did not seem wise, and it was probably impossible to carry all this information in my small head, and so I fell into the habit of jotting down memos in a shorthand which no one but myself could read, and out of these entries grew the many-volumed diary, written with soft pencil and with a want of clearness which was designed to baffle the spies with whom so many thought the Hotel Crillon was infested. However distressing the aftermath may be to those who, like myself, are compelled to read this diary, it was a wise move. When the negotiators returned from excursions far afield to the problem they had dropped weeks before, I could confront my chief with fairly authentic notes and was not compelled to rely exclusively upon my fallible memory.

This reservoir of information helped me in many difficult moments, and I sometimes hope that it will prove of value and of interest at a later day, when many of the dark shadows which we thought had been exorcised from the face of the world return, as return they may. And it may be wise for me to extend my confession a little farther and to let in a little more light on my *modus operandi.* A careful reading will reveal that there are gaps in my diary, and I hope to disarm criticism by frankly admitting that I do not pretend to present to possible readers a complete narrative. Many things happened at the Conference in which I was not personally involved, even in my subordinate capacity, and as to which I cannot claim to have firsthand knowledge. To fill out these gaps, it has been frequently suggested to me that I should consult the House Papers, now available to students in the Sterling Library at Yale, and perhaps also the memoirs of other participants, and indeed all other source material. I have not followed these suggestions, for a reason which seems good and sufficient to me. The only value that I can claim for my testimony as to what happened at the Great Assizes is that it is a personal record of things seen and of words heard. It is not a rounded historical narrative, but the personal testimony of one who viewed the scene as he believes without bias and without favor and certainly from a point of vantage. The complete history of the crucial events that took place in Paris in 1919 is a task that awaits some future historian. To him, perhaps, these fragmentary notes may prove of value. Checked by the reports and testimony of others, they may prove helpful in placing before a future generation a true picture of a most critical moment in world history, which certainly tried men's souls. There is consolation in the thought that possibly future generations may profit by our mistakes.

Baron Makino (Japan) told the Colonel yesterday that he had been instructed by Tokyo to bring before the Commission a proposal to recognize race equality in the Covenant, preferably in the Preamble, and that he had been instructed to press for its adoption. House has done what he could to convince the baron that this course will prove anything but helpful to the purpose of his government, of which he personally approves. Having failed in this, the Colonel has drawn up several drafts which he hopes will satisfy the Japanese without making little Hughes of Australia put on his war paint. One of these, in a personal and off-the-record visit from Balfour, he submitted to him. The draft was rather reminiscent of our Declaration of Independence. "All men are born free and equal. . . ." Balfour listened but said, "I think this idea is outmoded. All men of one particular nation are born free and equal, but I am far from convinced that a man from Central Africa could be regarded as the equal of a European or an American." House insisted that the time had come when the policy of excluding Japanese from almost all the world's surface must be stopped or at the least curtailed; "Japan is a great and growing nation. Their people are confined to small, crowded islands and, shut out by all, they have no place to go." Balfour said he sympathized with the Japanese and would do all he could to advance a practicable solution of the problem, "but Hughes will not admit them to Australia and if I am not mistaken your people in California are opposed to even limited immigration. We shall have to look elsewhere—some place farther afield."

House suggested Brazil, and they both agreed to speak to President Pessoa on the subject. And they did, but he gave them no encouragement: "We have all the race questions that we can manage now," he stated. "The bars are not up against the Japanese as yet, but they would be put up if they came in any numbers. It would be better for all concerned if they did not come."[4]

On the day following the Portuguese delegate served on me a brief memorandum of the remarks he would have made at the Plenary Session (on January 28th) had not, he asserted, the opportunity of speaking been withheld. It pointed out that the great Treaty of Versailles in 1783, in which the United States had been so vitally concerned, was introduced with the announcement, "*Au nom de la Très Sainte et Indivisible Trinité, Père, Fils et Saint Esprit* [There shall be a Christian Peace, universal and perpetual, on land and sea]. *Ainsi soit-il.*" Even as late as the assemblage of the powers at Berlin in 1878 the delegates pledged themselves "*Au nom de Dieu Tout-Puissant.*" The Portuguese delegate has gloomy forebodings as to the consequences of the omission of all mention of the Deity in our World Charter which he deplores. I think I rehabilitated President Wilson in his

[4]The Makino-Chinda proposal as now submitted reads:

"The equality of nations being a basic principle of the League of Nations, the High Contracting Parties agree to accord as soon as possible, to all alien nationals of States, members of the League, equal and just treatment in every respect, making no distinction, either in law or fact, on account of their race or nationality."

When the religious clause was withdrawn (Article XXI of the original draft of the Covenant), Makino agreed not to further press the race-equality clause. In a sense it was a Religious-Racial deal. Everyone was glad to have the matter settled in some sort of way, except the Portuguese delegate, who again said his country had never signed a treaty unless the Deity had been specifically called upon to preside over its fulfillment. Perhaps his government would not authorize him to sign. Cecil, strict churchman that he is, for once flippant, said the Conference would have to take a chance on this.

estimation by showing to him our President's original draft of the Covenant which included a religious clause.

This was a field day or rather night at the Peace table, and for once General Smuts, as chairman of the committee charged with the difficult task of drawing up the mandate provisions of the Covenant, held the center of the stage, and the general opinion is, including the President's, that he performed his job superbly. Hitherto Smuts has spoken almost as rarely as House. His best work was done in the committees and in missionary work with recalcitrant delegates when he could play what our Texas Colonel called a "lone hand," an activity in which he, too, excelled.

I do not think the Peace table and those who sat around it has ever been quite so excited. Smuts had been working on the project for more than a month, and the rumor was widespread, and generally credited, that the committee was split wide open and that Smuts had gotten nowhere with his darling project. Nobody knew what the draft would contain; but based on rumor and gossip all the delegates had before them on the table amendments which they thought were vital and which they intended to propose. All the capitals of the world were keenly alive to the importance of the moment, and the foreign offices were sending interminable cables of instructions to their bewildered agents. The mandate provision is not only important in itself but as I thought a signpost and a warning as to what will be the reception of other and even more important articles, if that is possible. I had prepared myself to take notes, no stenographers being present, and I think mine is almost a verbatim report of what was said and what was done.

After reading the proposed article, dealing with mandates (it was listened to in what seemed to me to be an ominous silence), the President called upon Smuts to take the floor. Blushing profusely, the South African opened his speech of explanation and apology in a very modest strain. And if this was tactics it was very wise.

"It is true," he began, "that I present this article to your careful and, I hope, prayerful consideration, with some misgiving, because I would be less than frank if I did not tell you that I am ashamed of it; and, as I have abundant reason to know, all the gentlemen who worked with me upon it, each and every one of them, are also disappointed at the result of our labors. But do not misunderstand me; distressing to our pride as is this confession and falling far short, as does our plan, of the objective which we hoped to attain, the article that we place before you is the best we can do now. In this belief we are all united.

"For the last month we have worked over the provisions of the article, the mandate problem, day and night; we have weighed every sentence, every word, indeed I may say every letter because we were of the opinion that, if we succeeded, it would be the cornerstone of a new and a better world procedure. The result, as you will readily see, is far from admirable, it is not grammatical, and it is anything but coherent, and yet let me warn you, it is the best that we can do, that any of us can do at this moment. We admit that we have lopped off an improving provision here and struck out or stuck in, in the most confusing manner, a safeguard here or there. We admit that the original purpose with which we set out upon our task is not easily recognizable, but upon patient scrutiny you will find that it is there and that while it may not be an ideal solution, it is, I can assure you, the best that your delegates will agree to at this juncture in world history.

"If you give your sanction to our work you will demonstrate that world public opinion is in favor of the ultimate self-government of all peoples, without distinction as to race, religion, or color, or previous condition of servitude. It also provides for a careful supervision and scrutiny as to the way in which the mandates are exercised and how the officers who shall be responsible for this great task are to be appointed by the Council (of the League). The power and also the responsibility remains with you. . . .

"I shall conclude as I began: the article we now submit to you is a poor production. Upon that point the members of the Committee are unanimous. But we submit it does stand for the two great cardinal principles which I have outlined. We are ashamed that we have done no better, but one virtue at least we have. We know our limitations and we frankly admit them. What we offer is not the cornerstone of a new era but we hope it is the opening wedge that if pushed will open wide a door to better things. A year hence, when the world has enjoyed a breathing spell and men less war-crazed have taken our places, I believe, and so do all my colleagues, that it will be possible to improve our plan, to convert it into something of which we can all be proud. These are my hopes, and they are shared by all my colleagues. If you approve we think that the system we have devised will help to maintain and to extend our civilization in those regions where today it is weakest.

"Now I shall close on a word of warning, based on the knowledge which has come to me as the result of many a long, weary, and at times bitter discussion in the committee. You will see many things you would like to change—just as I do, but I beg of you if our plan is pointed in the right direction, let it stand. It is not as responsive to your ideals, or to mine, as we had all hoped to make it, but hold your hand, restrain your natural disappointment, for if our edifice, poor as it is, is touched, I firmly believe it will fall to the ground, not to be raised again I fear in your day and mine."

Smuts's manly confession and frank warning against permitting the Committee battles to be fought over again in the Commission won out, and the mandate provisions on both the first and second readings were accepted, rather than approved without any substantial changes. "If you pull out a single plank," said Smuts in a quite audible aside to Makino, "the whole edifice, miserable as it is, will come crashing down."

It was a great triumph for Smuts, and the President quite visibly was pleased. He is not so insistent now upon details as he was a few weeks ago. He is pinning his faith to the cooling-off influences of time and the interpretive work of the League, as the war scenes and the animosities born of them recede and fade from memory.

February 8th.

However, in the afternoon session the long-gathering storm broke with great intensity. Despite the warning of General Smuts when he submitted the mandate clause that any changes would bring tumbling to the ground the agreement that has been so painfully reached, there are rumblings in many quarters. The French are dissatisfied with it because they say it lacks "clarity." In reality, they fear it will prevent them from raising black troops in Africa which have been so useful in the war. The representatives of the Dominions do not like it because our President insists that the mandatory powers should be regarded as trustees, and not as bona-fide owners of the new territories they are to take under their wings. The paragraph most discussed is the last sentence of Article XVII which reads:

"No military or naval forces shall be formed among the inhabitants of the territories (formerly belonging to the German or the Turkish Empires) in excess of those required for purposes of defense and of internal police."

Here again it is advisable to hark back to the initial discussions in the Council of Ten. On January 30th all the delegates from countries with colonial possessions or aspirations assembled in M. Pichon's spacious room at the Quai d'Orsay, but M. Clemenceau, scenting battle from afar, was on hand to preside. The Australians and the New Zealanders joined with the French in their request for "more light," particularly on Article VIII. Mr. Massey (Australia) said he was in favor of the direct annexation of the so-called mandated states. He thought that, owing to geographical contiguity to the mandatory state, they could be best administered as integral portions thereof, with, of course, such safeguards as prohibitions of the slave trade, arms traffic, and the prevention of the military training of the natives for other than police purposes. He and his colleagues strongly favored the principle of direct annexation, believing it would enable them to proceed more quickly with the development of the territories concerned. They were united in wishing a clear statement from the President on the subject.

President Wilson asked:

"Are Australia and New Zealand presenting an ultimatum to the Conference? Evidently you want the outright annexation of New Guinea and Samoa. Unless you secure these concessions, will you oppose the agreement, and if they are not granted, will you withdraw from the discussion?"

Here ensued a long delay because again the electrical apparatus which Mr. Hughes, the Australian Prime Minister, needed to follow the proceedings got out of order. Finally, after the President had repeated his views several times, Mr. Hughes said:

"Like my colleagues from New Zealand and South Africa I am in favor of the direct control of the mandated territories. Apparently the President is not in accord with our views. What are we to do? I at least shall follow the instructions of my government."

General Botha (South Africa) now spoke at great length, but, fortunately, in a more conciliatory spirit. He admitted that it was through the eloquence of Mr. Lloyd George that he had been induced to accept the disputed resolution. He trusted most sincerely that President Wilson would also agree. He believed that they should not be stopped by small things; if they could gain the higher ideal, small things should not be allowed to block the way. He appreciated the noble ideas of President Wilson and they would succeed if they were accepted by all. Our common objective is to attain a better world understanding. Then he added:

"Personally, I feel very strongly over the question of German

Southwest Africa. I think it differs entirely from any other question the Conference is called upon to decide. I hope, in a spirit of co-operation and by giving way on the little things, we shall overcome the obvious difficulties and realize the high ideals which we all share."

Mr. Massey (New Zealand) now answered the President's opening inquiry.

"As a public man I never make threats," he said; "those imputed to me in the press or elsewhere are without foundation. If I cannot get what my government wants, I am ready to accept the next best proposal, which is that set forth by Mr. Lloyd George."

Lloyd George now intervened with the statement that as everyone had now made his position perfectly clear, he hoped the Conference would accept his resolution as a provisional decision, subject to revision hereafter.

The French now entered the arena, M. Pichon speaking.

"France cannot renounce the right to raise volunteers in the countries under her administration," he said. "Before powerful American troops had come to her aid, France had resisted for a long time, aided by the British Army, but it was quite certain that but for the help she had previously received from her colonial possessions, her situation would have been most critical. We hold it absolutely necessary that France be empowered to recruit, not conscript, volunteers from all colonial territories under her control. This is absolutely necessary for her security."

President Wilson inquired if this decision referred to territory to be controlled as mandated states as well as her present colonies. M. Clemenceau now intervened, expressing acute dissatisfaction with the course of the proceedings.

"You must remember," he said, "and certainly we cannot forget, that France is the nearest neighbor to Germany. As so often in the past, at any moment in the future we can be suddenly attacked. We do not know if it is possible to disarm Germany, but we know we should attempt it. We appreciate that Great Britain has responsibilities in all parts of the world, that she cannot concentrate all her strength upon one point; we appreciate that America is far away and cannot come at once in the hour of danger to the assistance of France. Our situation is quite different from that of other powers more happily situated. America is protected by the breadth of the ocean, Great Britain by her fleet. The League of Nations, yet untried, must not begin by placing France in a position of peril, and that would happen if we were not permitted to raise volunteers in the territories under our administration. The people of France would resent such an arrangement and have a just grievance against any government that accepted it."

Lloyd George said that Great Britain has native forces in Uganda and Nigeria, just as France has troops in Senegal and elsewhere, but they are not equipped to carry on offensive operations outside of their home territory. He then contended that the clause under discussion would not prevent the raising of volunteer forces: "It will not prevent France from doing in the future what she has done so successfully in the recent past, but it would prevent Germany from organizing great black armies in Africa for the purpose of clearing everybody else out of the country. I for one can see nothing in this agreement that prevents France raising an army for the defense of her territory."

"If we have that right," said Clemenceau, "I ask for nothing more."

Lloyd George explained:

"The resolution is only intended to prevent a mandatory from drilling natives and raising great armies."

Clemenceau: "We have not the remotest intention of doing that. If this clause does not prevent France from raising troops in African territory under her control, I am satisfied."

President Wilson said that Mr. Lloyd George's interpretation was consistent with the phraseology of the Resolution and Clemenceau again said that he was satisfied and the Resolution was accepted.

The meeting now took up the question of Turkey, in which Mr. Wilson said that for the present the United States could not participate —she not having declared war on Turkey. Lloyd George thought this was a little matter and "could be easily arranged with the Turks," and then he spoke at some length of the great expense that Britain was now being put to in occupying these territories for the common security. He believed that in this part of the world they were maintaining a force of at least a million men and that it was causing an enormous expenditure, one that Britain could not face for long, especially as she had not the remotest idea of becoming the mandatory power over many of the territories she now occupied and protected. On this subject, he was quite certain, very awkward questions would soon be asked in Parliament.

In view of this burdensome situation, Lloyd George stated that he must *insist* with his colleagues (but not in the harsh military sense of the word) upon the definite appointment of the mandatories at an early day. As soon as this was done, the British troops could be withdrawn and the mandatory power could enter upon its responsible duties.

Mr. Wilson now stated, and for the first time publicly, his position as to the mandates and the reason why he opposed the immediate designation of the mandatory powers. He said he was disinclined to see his country shirk any burden that duty imposed, but at the moment he could think of nothing the people of the United States would be less inclined to accept than military responsibility in Asia. He would, if now asked to assume a mandate, be compelled to ask for a postponement, for time in which he would try to bring the American people to the point of view which he wished them to assume. He therefore asked that the whole question of the military occupation and control of these various regions be referred to the Supreme War Council. Lloyd George agreed—thought this would help to clarify the situation —but Clemenceau was not so certain. He said everything would depend on the development of the situation in Russia. He added:

"We as well as the British and the Italians have troops in Odessa. What are we going to do with them?"

Nobody answered.

The following draft resolution, apparently the joint work of Lloyd George and the President, was then approved. In part it reads:

"The military representatives of the Allies and the associated powers at Versailles are directed to report as to the most equitable and economical distribution among the powers of the burden of maintaining order in the Turkish Empire and Transcaucasia pending the decisions of the Peace Conference."

It would appear that the buck has now been passed to those idle gentlemen in Versailles (Supreme War Council), but, as a matter of fact, at least this is my judgment, now that the possibility of a black army has been secured for France and the Dominions have been assured possession of coveted territories more or less contiguous, everything is arranged, although the names of the powers that are to assume the mandates will not be published until later.[5] One clash, however, still remains unsettled on the agenda; that is the competition between France and England for the Syrian mandate. Emir Feisal says no mandate is necessary or desirable and that if the principle of self-determination were to be honored, the Syrians would ask for his rule.

[5]The definite allotment of spheres of influence and responsibility was only settled in London—months later.

But if a mandate is insisted upon, they would vote to have it exercised from Washington.[6]

Here I think it wise to interpolate a few details as to the preliminary discussion on this thorny problem. When the question of mandates was first formally taken up in the Council of Ten (on January 24th) the sea was serene and apparently there was every prospect of smooth sailing. This unanimity led to the immediate adoption of the first paragraph of the resolution presented by the British which reads:

"Having regard to the record of the German administration in the colonies, formerly a part of the German Empire, and to·the menace which the possession by Germany of submarine bases in many parts of the world would necessarily constitute to the freedom and security of all nations, the Allied and Associated Powers are agreed that in no circumstances should any of the colonies be restored to Germany."

After it had been read, for further emphasis, Lloyd George added:

"In behalf of the British Empire I would like to say that we are opposed to a return to Germany of any of these territories under any circumstances."

Wilson said:

"We are all agreed upon this point."

Then Orlando (Italy) and Makino (Japan) assented, but a few minutes later the Council came into heavy weather. The form of the mandate had to be considered, also the designation of the mandatory powers. Both promised difficulties, and they were not slow in materializing.

The French Colonial Office wants to annex parts of the Cameroons and Togo Land and the three British Dominions want to annex, respectively, German South-West Africa, New Guinea, and German Samoa, and they want outright possession, they do not wish to act as trustees. Mr. Wilson, apparently with the purpose of chilling the enthusiasm of the land-grabbers, said:

"Many of these mandates would constitute a burden, and a very serious burden at that."

Discontent became apparent as the clause was read providing for "The prevention of military training of the native for other than police purposes or the establishment of fortifications or military or naval bases, and the training of the natives except for the defense of their territory."

[6] An arrangement later described in some detail.

Then Clause VIII of the resolution was read, modifying Article XXII of the Covenant (first draft). It says:

"Finally, the Powers consider that there are territories, such as South-West Africa and certain islands in the South Pacific, which, owing to the sparseness of their population, or their small size, or their remoteness from the centers of civilization, or their geographical contiguity to the Mandatory State and other circumstances, can be best administered under the laws of the Mandatory State as integral portions thereof, subject to the safeguards above mentioned in the interests of the indigenous population."

The at first *sotto-voce* mutterings now became distinctly audible, and the clash of interests came out into the open. The quarrel as to the disposition of the German colonies filled the morning session and ran on into the afternoon meeting with increasing intensity of feeling. Hughes of Australia, indeed, made several outrageous attacks on the President, which, however, Wilson did not take up at once or even later because, as one of the Australian secretaries explained to all present, Hughes did not understand the President's point of view owing to the fact that, as so often before, his electrical hearing apparatus had failed to function.

February 9th.

One might assume that with all his tremendous responsibilities the President would not find the time for the petty attitudes and gestures which disfigure his character as they do, I fear, so many great men. But, unfortunately, he finds the time. He takes every opportunity of sowing ill feeling between House and Lansing, and they deserve great credit in refusing to participate in a personal feud, which the President apparently seeks to provoke.

Why the President brought Mr. Lansing to Paris is an enigma, unless it was with the malicious purpose of heaping indignities upon him and seeing him squirm. But Lansing does not squirm. He overlooks the slights, he ignores them, or, more probably, he pretends to. During his frequent absences in England, Lloyd George is always succeeded by his Minister of Foreign Affairs, Balfour, who takes his place. But Wilson always demotes Lansing and chooses House to represent him—a course which is not according to protocol and a mortification for Lansing. Again, when Orlando is away, Sonnino takes his place, and when Clemenceau was invalided, Pichon rattled around in his shoes. From the moment of his arrival in Paris, the President ignored his fellow delegates, and this must have been especially galling to Lansing who, as Secretary of State, was next in the line of succession to the presidency, after the Vice-President. From the earliest day after his arrival the President always came to the Colonel's rooms on the third floor of the Crillon. When, as rarely happened, their signatures were wanted, the President would summon the delegates to House's office and then dismiss them. The commissioners, being human, did not like this. Of course their personal reaction was not very important, but this treatment was damaging to their prestige as delegates who were called upon at times to sit on important committees. House thought that the commissioners should not be treated as office boys, and as the results of these snubbings became apparent, he spoke to the President on the subject. He suggested that what had happened was through inadvertence, and he asked the President to hold the meetings of the commissioners, if not as was usual, in the office of the Secretary of State, at least alternatively in the rooms of the delegates, Lansing, White, and Bliss. The President agreed to the suggestion, although he said public comment had but little weight with him. Finally, he did agree to hold all the commission meetings in Lansing's office; however, he spaced them so that they only took place once or twice a month!

This evening M. Bourgeois came to the meeting in an unusually jovial mood, but as he brought with him a fat sheaf of manuscript I braced my bronchial cords for a long speech. He showed several pages to Larnaude, and as they chuckled and said "Vilson-Vilson" a number of times it was evident they had something on the President and expected important, even devastating, results from the discovery. Some days ago I had heard that Tardieu had received from New York a consignment of ten cases filled with copies of Mr. Wilson's prewar and later speeches, and putting two and two together it did not require clairvoyance to divine what was coming. . . . When he was given the word Bourgeois began in as near a mellifluous tone as his raucous voice permits of:

"As it has a very direct bearing on the subject which we have so frequently discussed here, unhappily without reaching any satisfactory result down to the present, I wish to remind our distinguished, our most distinguished guest, and our presiding officer, of the noble words he spoke, which all Frenchmen treasure in their hearts, when our horizon was perhaps darker but I fear not more filled with dangers, yet to be conjured, than it is today. In May 1916, when the war was still far from America, you said, M. le Président, 'We are participants, whether we would or not, in the life of the world. The interests of all nations are also our own. We are partners with the rest of the world.' "

Then, raising a menacing finger, M. Bourgeois continued: "In September of that year you said 'we can no longer indulge our traditional provincialism. We are to play a leading part in the world drama whether we like it or not.' A few weeks later, M. le Président, you went still further in your encouragement to those of us who were in the toils of ruthless barbarian invaders. In November (1916) you said, and how we hung on your words, 'It does not suffice, as some would have us, as some suggest that we do again what we did when we were provincial and isolated . . . for now we are in the drift of humanity which is to determine the politics of every country in the world.' Then, M. le Président, allow me to recall the noble words with which you entered the war, words which gave hope and courage to every French man or woman, however sorely tried they were. These words were, 'The new world order must make provision for common action against aggressors.' And you added, 'If the moral force will not suffice, the *physical* force of the world shall.' "

Pausing for several moments of silence which he evidently regarded as most dramatic, M. Bourgeois concluded with, "And now today you are asking my countrymen and all the devastated lands of our Allies to be content with the shield of a Covenant without striking arms but merely illuminated with the noble words and the notes which you hurled against the invaders—but to stop them you needed force, and it was, at last, forthcoming. I beseech you to look at the situation once again. Without military backing in some force, and always ready to act, our League and our Covenant will be filed away, not as a solemn treaty but simply as a rather ornate piece of literature."

It was not easy to put back into English, for the President and House, Mr. Wilson's speeches, but as most of them I knew by heart my retranslation, from the Gallic version, was received with an indulgent smile and with only one minor correction from the author of these noble words. Evidently the President at first was not inclined to make any reply, but after a short whispered conversation with House he said, "I am grateful to the French delegate for his gracious comment on words which came from my heart, were ever on my lips when the world was in the stress of desperate war. Need I assure him that my attitude has not changed, but the situation has, and to meet it

I think it wise to now proceed to examine a number of questions on the agenda which have long awaited our close attention."

I thought the President extricated himself very adroitly from a situation which was not an enviable one. Evidently M. Bourgeois thought so too. He, with a despairing gesture, slumped back in his chair, and at least an hour elapsed before he and M. Larnaude went into a huddle to prepare another pitfall for their distinguished but wary guest.

February—undated.

After the religious clause was today again postponed, M. Batalha Reis (Portugal), Professor at the University of Coimbra, who loved to bring to light forgotten pages of history, approached the President and said:

"If you permit, I would like to make an inquiry of you, in your personal capacity as a world-renowned teacher of, as well as a maker of, history. What interpretation should be placed on this undoubted fact to which I venture to call your attention? The Treaties of Westphalia (1648), which were under discussion for two years, deal at about equal length with matters temporal and spiritual. Ecclesiastical settlements engrossed as much time as did the territorial adjustments, yet here today, when we are engaged on problems of even greater importance, the delegates seem averse to any reference to the Church or mention of the Supreme Being. What conclusion do you deduce from this striking contrast?"

"I think," said the President, after a short pause, "that the world has progressed since the sad era of the Thirty Years' War. By the instrument to which you refer the independence of Switzerland, where all Christian religions flourished, was recognized; and it was further agreed that all signatories to the Treaty were in the future to permit freedom of worship and liberty of conscience. I cannot say that all of them lived up to these stipulations, but it was a step, a great step, forward."

Then the usually silent Makino chimed in. He had evidently been reading his Martens:

"The right of immigration was also assured by this treaty to all nations. I fear that provision has also not been honored in our draft with a strict observance."

It seemed to me that for once our historian-President was stumped, and wisely, I think, it was agreed that this exchange of views should be omitted from the record of the proceedings. It was, after all, but an informal conversation!

In the short exchange of views between the President and the Portuguese delegate, who was continually urging the invocation of the favor of the Almighty in the Preamble to the Covenant, that now ensued, I saw that House thought to enter the parley and then changed his mind, and, as so often, held his peace. When we were alone I asked him what he had had in mind to say and he replied: "You see that was exactly the course that the Founding Fathers of the Confederacy pursued at Montgomery in drafting their Constitution in 1860. Then I decided to say nothing because my information might have further complicated matters and certainly it could not be regarded as a favorable omen! And by the way, who was that great statesman who said 'the things I have left unsaid have not hurt me half as much as the things I have said'? I can't recall his name—but he was a great man."

February 9th.

For the second time the admission of India to the League, which had been on several occasions sidetracked, was brought up again, and, of course, by Cecil.

"Does the President propose to admit India, or does he oppose her admission? It seems to me it should not be forgotten that during the war India mobilized a million men. The British Government has treated India according to her Colonial program, long tested in the school of experience. It is true that part of India is autocratically governed, yet it is willing to be so governed. And it cannot be denied that the greater part of India is democratically administered."

Again many views were expressed as to what constituted a self-governing state, but no definite conclusion was reached. Finally, the President stated that he was in favor of the admission of India and the discussion died down. But the calm was of short duration: M. Bourgeois started another fray by stating that there should be a very definite separation in the Covenant of the sheep from the goats.

"There should be a classification," he said, "of those who have reparations to make. Those who, like Germany, have violated laws human and divine, these should not be admitted on a basis of equality."

Mr. Wilson now talked at some length in favor of delay and the postponement of a decision on this point. Among other things he said was this:

"Not all the States here present are regarded by all the other States as having a good character."

As far as I can make out, then, the Article was provisionally adopted, but the way was left open for future consideration.

February 10th.

The President showed today unmistakable signs of irritation with his co-workers on the Peace Treaty. Attempts are being made, and they are many and subtle, to separate the Treaty from the Covenant, but they are not as many or quite as Machiavellian as the President chooses to assume. Much can be said in favor of rushing ahead with a settlement of territorial and reparation matters. Foch reports, no doubt correctly, that the Germans are "welshing" on all the disarmament clauses of the Armistice protocol; on the other hand, our information is that the Spartacist uprising in Germany is by no means quelled and that should Moscow send the promised munitions and above all the money that has also been promised, the Weimar people would have their work cut out for them.

Since the President has come to grips with Balfour and Lloyd George, not to speak of Clemenceau and Orlando, plus the cynical Sonnino, he is more and more convinced, as he unwisely announced before he arrived in Paris, that only he and some, not even all, of his delegates are on the side of the angels! If he gets a treaty, and now he must be convinced that no treaty would be worse than the treaty that is within his grasp even if it falls far short of the ideal he dreamed in faraway America, it will contain provisions of which he does not approve, but if the treaty is intertwined with his Covenant, now practically finished, then a step forward will have been taken and the wicked predatory powers will be at least pledged to assist in its improvement.

Of course those in favor of a quick preliminary treaty can and do advance many plausible reasons in favor of at least two solemn but separate compacts to start the world upon its new course, but the President is adamant and will not yield an inch, and in the circumstances I think he is right. The two compacts must be "intertwined"; that is his favorite word, and it is a descriptive one. He will sign the Treaty even if, as he fears, it will contain things of which he cannot approve but only if it is "intertwined." Those who say that the two documents will have equal force even when signed and ratified separately the President denounces as sophists and sometimes I hear he uses an uglier word. Even a blind man could see the disadvantages of further delay, which the President's plan entails, and truly the danger of the present state of uncertainty is very great, but still I am convinced that the President is right. He is dealing with men who are not entirely trustworthy, and from what he has learned by bitter experience in the last six weeks he knows that any treaty they sign will be in great need of copious libations of holy water such as will flow, it is hoped, from the font of the Covenant.

February 10th—later.

Irritated by a statement in an English paper today to the effect that the disapproval of many Senators already formally, if not officially, expressed boded no good to the Covenant and made its acceptance by Congress uncertain, the President expressed his dissent—indeed his indignation. "Those Senators do not know what the people are thinking," he insisted. "They are as far from the people, the great mass of our people, as I am from Mars. Indeed they are out of touch with the thinking, forward-looking masses of people throughout the world. Naturally they cannot understand them."

House shares the President's optimism, that is up to a certain degree. He regrets Wilson did not bring with him to Paris Mr. Root or someone of standing and authority in the Republican party. Then the responsibility and later the glory would be bi-partisan. He hears from political observers that many at home think the President is seeking a personal or at all events a party success, and further that very few of them have a very clear idea of the President's purpose and his high objective. Mr. Kohlsaat, the editor, whom the Colonel regards as a keen observer, writes from Chicago, "I think the great majority of our people are still behind the President—but I fear they are very far behind him." House did not like that. He is sending to some of his friends, including Kohlsaat, memoranda and reports on the actual situation which he hopes will dispell the darkness in which he thinks they are groping.

Later.

Larnaude said this evening he was anxious to know who or what body would pass upon the question, sure to arise frequently, "Is a treaty inconsistent with the Covenant?" Would it be the Council or a special tribunal? The President answered promptly: "The decision will lie with the court of public opinion." Larnaude trembled with pent-up emotion. He is reported to have said *sotto voce* to Bourgeois, "Tell me, *mon ami*, am I at the Peace Conference or in a madhouse?" It was an aside, so we did not have to take it up, but of course we gathered that the dean of the Paris law school has a very poor opinion of the Court of Public Opinion. Orlando now delivered himself of a lengthy dissertation as to the difficulties that lowered in the path the President was determined to pursue. Orlando dragged in a mention of Metternich which irritated the President. "We should not allow ourselves to be impressed by what may or may not have happened in the past, nor should we dwell on former failures. Our task is to build for the future," said the President.

A few minutes later a sigh of relief passed around the table. The President announced that now all the articles of the draft had been gone over once. Everyone was pleased, and all chose to forget that an imposing mass of amendments and additions were piling up on the desk of the drafting committee. Battles royal would be fought before all these were "ironed out," to use the Colonel's favorite phrase for this work in which he is most certainly the outstanding champion.

February 13th.

Today, on the eve of his departure, the President gave House, and in my presence, very definite instructions for his guidance while he was away. He said: "During my unavoidable absence I do not wish the questions of territorial adjustments or those of reparations to be held up." I would have concluded from these words that the President left House in control, but House did not so interpret them. "The President does not mean that I am authorized to definitely settle anything," he explained, "but he does hope that I will get the problems, one and all, in such shape that on his return they can be submitted to him for final judgment. I am glad of these limitations on my powers," said House. "The President has been so absorbed in his struggle for the Covenant that he does not fully appreciate the obstacles that still beset his path. Let me give you but one illustration. The President is unalterably opposed to the creation of the Rhenish republic, and justly so, because if we acquiesced it would torpedo our doctrine of self-determination upon which the future of our better world order depends. And yet if we close an eye but for a moment there it is—rearing its ugly head."

I think the Colonel is taking quite a risk in accepting merely verbal instructions from his chief. Both President Cleveland and Dean West, involved in the interminable Princeton controversy, are on record as saying that the President's memory has blind spots, and I also venture to call his attention to the fact that while on October 14th he was instructed by Wilson "to leave the details of the probable armistice to the judgment and advice of the military and naval advisers of the United States and of the Allied governments," a very few days later he ignored them and accepted the mere internment of the German fleet, against the wishes of our Admiral Benson. And as to the Army, Pershing was ignored or at least thinks he was. As to the treatment of Pershing, it is only proper to say that his attitude was not crystal clear. On one day he was in favor of sending his army into Germany and on the next he apparently agreed with Foch that the extra campaign—the march to Berlin—was not necessary and might well prove costly. "Men always fight better on their homeland, defending it against invaders, than they do on foreign soil," was his final word.

"Of course, of course," commented House. "I would like to have specific instructions in writing, but as the 'Governor' never gives them we can dismiss that idea."

February 14th.

Absit omen! Some do think it ominous, but the Colonel and I are determined to laugh it off. Yet, it cannot be denied that yesterday, within a very few hours after signing the pact of peace and the Covenant, the members of the League of Nations Commission fell openly into inharmonious groups. The question that divided them was how and where their "counterfeit presentment" should be achieved. Of course this is an important matter. The faces of those who have fought for peace in this the first Parliament of Man must be preserved through the world press to enjoy the respect and perhaps the veneration of generations to come who, profiting by their labors, will assuredly rise up and call them blessed. For at least ten days the photographic division of the Signal Corps had been badgering the Colonel on this subject. Its ranking photographer maintained—and not without reason—that the League for the most part was made in America, that its acceptance was made possible by the presence of our President, further that the discussions which have now come to a happy conclusion took place on American territory. (In view of the price which Uncle Sam is paying for the Hotel Crillon this temporary lease should carry with it extraterritorial rights, and perhaps it does.) Insisting on these facts, the Lieutenant of the Lens claims that it is an American show and consequently that the Signal Corps is entitled to the first picture. He also fears—and I happen to know that his fears are not entirely without foundation—that some enterprising newspaper photographer may steal a march on the corps and get the first picture. "It will go over big at home," he claims; "it will be published from coast to coast, from Pole to Pole. It is a document that will live in history like the Magna Charta and the Declaration. We are entitled to the first show—anyhow we must get it."

The Colonel agreed, and yesterday the photographers came in with all their formidable paraphernalia. When strange smells emerged from cans and filled the great council chamber, no one looked his best; and when it was reluctantly admitted that the picture would have to be taken by flashlight, the President put his foot down, and he put it down quite energetically. "I hate flashlight or calcium pictures," he protested. "Everybody looks as though they were laid out in a morgue and besides the flashes hurt my eyes." The Colonel hit upon a compromise scheme to meet the emergency, but he was not very enthusiastic about it. He, too, thought that the picture of the Peacemakers should be taken in the historic chamber where they had concluded their preliminary labors, but as this was impossible, except with the artificial agency which the President vetoed, the Colonel thought the best thing that could be done, perhaps in the circumstances the only thing that could be done, was to shoo all the delegates out of the Council room and have a picture taken by flash of the historic table where they had labored. Then move the delegates into another apartment where heaven-given light alone would suffice to preserve their features for all time.

This movement of the mighty men was not easy; it had to be explained in many tongues, and some thought it foolish, and then the picture of the empty table without the documents piled mountains high and with no one sitting around it they thought a travesty on their labors. "I call it misrepresentative," said the Portuguese Minister, and he without more ado slipped away. The rest I herded into the new apartment which they had never seen before, and in a few moments with his magician touch the Colonel had placed them in clusters about the President and all seemed satisfied. I thought I had nothing further to do in the matter and was making an unobtrusive getaway when the President, who for some minutes had shown signs of irritation, called me back with, "You mustn't leave me in this

Tower of Babel." So I stood by him, but as far as possible·in the background, as became my subordinate position. Also behind the great
men lowered a Belgian and a Polish secretary, but I cannot recall their
names probably because I never knew them. Today a proof of the
picture has come, and the Signal Corps promises to supply it to the
press of the world. The Colonel says that I look as if I was trying to
run away. That feature is certainly a true picture of the scene. I was.

But House found consolation in the counterfeit presentment of the
empty table. "It is an historic scene," he contended. "It presents a picture of a greater Independence Hall in which the representatives of
the enlightened powers will draft the Covenant that should, we hope,
safeguard the world from war and all the misfortunes that follow in its
train. And you should faithfully record how the Greater Charter of
the emancipation of a war-stricken world was hammered out." Among
the reasons why I suggested I was incapable of filling this role was the
fact that even the phonographic duties of interpreting the speeches of
the delegates were far beyond my powers and certainly most fatiguing.

February 15th.

The tenth and last meeting of the Drafting Commission, Lord
Robert Cecil presiding in the absence of Mr. Wilson, was held on
the afternoon of February 13th. It was marked by protracted debates
on the French amendments. In the strongest form they called for an
international force, a sheriff's posse to enforce the decisions of the
League Council. In the mildest form they provide an international
staff to prepare for and to cope with military emergencies as they
arise. They were all voted down, but the French were successful in
having an addition made to Article IX which reads:

"A permanent commission shall be constituted to advise the League
on the execution of Article VIII and on military and naval questions
generally."

Kramář (Czechoslovakia) sought to amend Article VII by an
amendment to the effect that the military and naval restrictions imposed on Germany should not be affected by her subsequent admission
to the League. This was voted down.

There followed a long debate as to the manner in which the exchange of military information between the States, members of the
League, should be carried out. M. Diamandy (Roumania) thought the
exchange should be obligatory, not merely voluntary. Kramář then
said:

"On this subject I have deep anxiety. I share the apprehension of the French delegates. From the day Germany is admitted into the League we shall be obliged to depend on her good faith. I am not alone in not having confidence in her good faith. As between the Allies, supervision of military changes is not necessary, but as far as Germany is concerned, we should be vigilant. I know the Germans well and I have no confidence in them."

"I am satisfied," said Larnaude (France), "with the control we have established over the rearmament of Germany in her present situation, but once Germany is admitted—what then?"

Venizelos (Greece) said:

"We should, of course, impose on Germany, as a condition to her admission, our right to control her military activities."

Kramář then proposed this addition to the Article:

"Special control conditions affecting military and naval forces, imposed on any State by the Treaty of Peace, shall not be weakened or in any way affected by its subsequent admission into the League."

Cecil, presiding, now advanced the suggestion that the military authorities of each nation would keep the League correctly informed as to possible military preparations. To this Larnaude disagreed vehemently.

"We know only too well that the experts are frequently caught napping and not seldom are misinformed. Let me give one illustration. At Charleroi, at the beginning of the war, we were confronted by thirty more German divisions than our experts told us it was possible for them to bring into action."

M. BOURGEOIS: "Public opinion in France is unanimous in demanding an effective form of supervision and I must ask for a vote."

The French plan was now disapproved by a vote of twelve to three, only Bourgeois, Larnaude, and Kramář voting for it.

Kramář's amendment, an addition to the Article, was now taken up and voted down. Speaking for it, Kramář said:

"The Germans are even now asking for admission into the League; very soon, in the name of justice and equal treatment, you will not have the strength to refuse them. It is not necessary to supervise the military activities of the Allies, but there must be an absolute control of the German armed forces."

M. Jacquemyns, substituting for M. Hymans (Belgium):

"I, and the whole Belgian nation, share M. Kramář's distrust of the German Government and people, but in our judgment no precautions will be of any avail until the German mentality has undergone a change. In our view the only effective precaution is to refuse her admission into the League. Once admitted, she would say: 'This is my house quite as much as yours. I insist upon equal treatment and footing.' "

Kramář's proposal was voted down. I do not recall the vote, but it was overwhelming.

Bourgeois now returned to the attack and spoke at great length in favor of his original proposal. In brief, his argument was about as follows:

"The lessons of the recent past demonstrate the fact that the risk of sudden aggression is very great and that it can only be met by an international army composed of contingents of the associated nations always prepared for joint, concerted action. Unless we make these preparations well in advance, it is certain that much time will elapse before the associated contingents can become really effective. As in 1914, in Belgium, regions important to our military defense would be invaded and devastated. Is this wise? Should we not prepare for eventualities which are really probabilities? In view of the opposition which it has provoked, we of the French delegation have abandoned our plan for an international army and even for an international staff always in being, but I do ask now for your approval of this amendment." It read:

"A permanent organism for study and preparation which shall have the special mandate of insuring effective defense in case of aggression."

Cecil (Britain) said that this would mean that plans would have to be drawn up to meet the possible invasion of all countries. Larnaude replied that this was a caricature of the idea that was in the mind of his colleague, and indeed of the French people. Undoubtedly it had been the practice in the past for the German General Staff to work out plans for the invasion of every country in the world, and similar plans might well be prepared by them in the near future. "We must be prudent and plan against the danger of such invasions. It is absurd to think that the League of Nations will be able to impose peace unless the world knows that she has at hand the means to do it, and to do it promptly."

BOURGEOIS: "If no preparations are made, we shall be surprised as we were in the past. Through want of preparation and foresight, we suffered losses which I fear are irreparable. But when we created a united front, we secured the victory."

CECIL: "I understand the view of my French colleagues, but my thought is, if we try to do too much, we shall accomplish nothing. I have gone as far in this matter as the public opinion of my country will support me."

LARNAUDE: "We pay homage to Sir Robert in full appreciation of the spirit of conciliation which he has always shown. We have now brought before you the considered judgment of the French delegation. If we are defeated, we shall remain good friends, but we shall also remain of our former opinion and—with our fears."

Bourgeois' original amendment, which he called "A practical application of Article IX," read:

"In case of aggression, menace or danger of aggression, the Council of the League will see to the measures suitable for insuring the execution of the obligations."

The amendment was defeated. I have no record of the vote, but it was decisive.

Bourgeois now tried the patience of the Commission which had been worn somewhat thin by many of his long and rambling speeches at previous sessions in favor of some recognition of the pioneer work of The Hague Conference. He insisted that his nosegay of approval and grateful recognition be inserted in the Preamble or at some other appropriate place in the Covenant. When this plan was first proposed, President Wilson had asked Colonel House to assure M. Bourgeois that he fully appreciated the work he and his colleagues had done at The Hague, but that he did not think it wise to remind the world of the complete failure of the first assault that had been made upon the entrenched positions of the predatory powers. However, today Bourgeois resumed his attack and developed at great length all his previous arguments.

"It is a serious matter," he said, "to ignore completely what we did at The Hague in 1899 and in 1907. Many, inspired by motives that I shall not characterize, have sought to discredit the first great attempt of the civilized nations to organize a regime of peace and justice in the world. If we pass over in silence what was then attempted, we should appear to condone, even to approve, their words of criticism, and indeed of ridicule. It would be a great mistake if we do not uphold the work that was attempted at The Hague. In fact we should be its most ardent champions. I am proud to have been there, and I do not think that our work was ineffective or should be passed over in silence. I am proud that I was intimately associated with the representatives of the United States, of Great Britain, and with the spokesmen of thirty-two forward-looking and law-abiding countries, who on that historic occasion declared their adherence to the rule of law and to a regime of international justice. That was noble pioneer work, and it should not be forgotten. I think, indeed, it should be emphasized, and proclaimed, that there are real achievements to the credit of our organization. Through arbitration we prevented war between Russia and England over the Dogger Bank incident; between Germany and France when the deserters were arrested at Casablanca; between France and Italy at the time of the Carthage dispute. I therefore formally ask that mention of these notable achievements be inserted in the Preamble."

Cecil, speaking from the chair, said:

"Nobody thinks of forgetting the notable work of The Hague Conference. The question is one of form. Is its insertion suitable?"

BOURGEOIS: "It is not a question of form, it is a question of vital importance."

Here Venizelos, by an innocent question, most certainly did not pour oil on the troubled waters:

"Is there really a permanent Court of Justice at The Hague?" he inquired.

Flushing deeply, Bourgeois answered:

"I have the honor to be one of its members."

Hymans (Belgium) now endeavored to have added to the mandate Article words which he said would safeguard and clarify its meaning, but he was urged both by House and by Smuts to take this up in the Plenary Session. The Commission was moving swiftly now, and Articles from XVII to XXVII were adopted. All inquiries and suggestions of changes were put over to be ventilated in the Plenary. However, Article XXI was not presented. It provided for religious freedom and, paired with the Japanese proposal for racial equality, was omitted. Brazil, China, and Roumania expressed deep regret at the omission, and again the delegate of Portugal said that he feared his people would be reluctant to subscribe to a treaty on which the blessing of Deity had not been invoked. He could not recall a treaty to which his country had given its signature without mention of the name of Almighty God and the Blessed Trinity. . . .

No opportunity was given to refer to these omissions in the Plenary Session on the next afternoon at which President Wilson read his first draft of the Covenant. Those who wished to make suggestions and even changes were assured that ample opportunity would be given them later on. As a matter of fact, the world press gave an erroneous idea as to what happened on this occasion. It was announced that the draft had been adopted; such was not the case. Clemenceau announced from the chair after the report of President Wilson had been concluded:

"This report has been deposited with the Bureau of the Conference for examination and study by all the interested powers. The Bureau will lose no time in summoning the Conference as soon as it is in a position to bring up the report for discussion."

Despite the charges that were made by many Senators in Washington, at this time no one was committed to acceptance of the Covenant, not even President Wilson, who inspired it. His work was now simply submitted to the world for study and prayerful examination.

In my judgment, at least, the determining factor in dropping the religious Article was the suggestion of Baron Makino that the Japanese proposal for a formal recognition of racial equality should be dovetailed into it. Makino maintained that questions of religion and of race could well go together. Makino accepted his defeat with characteristic dignity, merely reserving his right to bring up the matter at a later date.[7]

February 15th.

In his speech at the Plenary Session yesterday, moving the adoption of the League of Nations resolution, the President said things that were far from welcome to the ears of many listeners here as well as in Washington. He made it quite plain that he was not inclined to "pull his punches." He repeated what he had said at the first Conclave but with increased emphasis. "The United States in entering the war never for a moment thought it was intervening in the politics of Europe, Asia, or of any part of the world. Therefore the United States would feel that its part in the war had been played in vain if there ensued upon it merely a body of European settlements. It would feel that it could not take part in guaranteeing those European settlements unless that guarantee involved the continuous superintendence of the peace of the world by the associated nations of the world." And

[7]The reason why he did not do so, at least not very energetically, is not far to seek. With the Monroe Doctrine "and other regional agreements" later excluded from the sphere and action of the League, the Japanese delegation was inclined to rest on its oars. It had every right to do so.

he concluded by saying: "If we return to the United States without having made every effort in our power to realize this program, we should return to meet the merited scorn of our fellow citizens. . . . We should not dare to abate a single item of the program which constitutes our instructions. . . . We are here to see, in short, that the very foundations of this war are swept away. . . . The representatives of the United States are never put to the embarrassment of choosing a way of expediency because they have laid down for themselves the unalterable lines of principle."

Once again the President proclaimed himself a crusader. Once again he pointed to the Holy Land of Peace still far ahead. There was great applause, but there were some blank faces too. Our Richard the Lionhearted will be confronted, is confronted, with a paynim host. The Colonel was moved to tears, and he was not the only one who showed deep emotion as they shook the President by the hand. "You have raised a standard to which all men of good will should repair," said Lord Robert Cecil. "Should?" That word was well chosen, but to me it had an ominous sound.

February 15th.

Last evening we all went to the Hotel Murat and from there escorted the President to the station which was beflagged in his honor. The red carpet was spread and the waiting rooms with palms and evergreen plants and flowers had been converted into a tropical garden; a cheering sight after the drizzling rain that had been falling all day. President Poincaré and his lady were there and Clemenceau and his cabinet. All the American delegates were on hand and most of the foreign ambassadors and delegates. As the Colonel had had a long talk with the President in the afternoon and received his instructions, he kept in the background, but the President's attitude was most cordial. Just before he mounted the railway carriage he came over to House and placing his hand on his shoulder almost affectionately he said, "Heavy work before you, House." I rode back with the Colonel from the station and found him extremely thoughtful and rather depressed.

"He goes to meet the Senate——" began House, and then stopped.

"You do not seem hopeful of the encounter," I suggested.

"Hopeful, yes, but not confident. In the Washington battle the President will need diplomacy, patience——"

Here I pitched in with, "You are always urging me to speak right out in meeting and I'm going to do it now! I think you are unfair to the President. What patience has he not shown in dealing with that pestiferous mosquito Hymans of Belgium; and with what diplomacy has he avoided a complete break with the subtle Scialoja from Italy." Instead of the rebuke which I had expected and perhaps deserved the Colonel said, as his face brightened:

"How glad I am to hear you say that and how true it is. How true it is that if the President could bring himself to behave with the Senators as he has with the mixed and motley crew of world delegates here, if he could bring himself to unbend and be friendly with them, if but for a day, his troubles and ours would be over. But you see in Washington and particularly in the Senate the President is confronted, or at least he thinks he is, with ancient quarrels and feuds of long standing. So I can only hope and pray. Much, very much, is at stake; indeed all we have fought for and won at such cost."

Seeing that I was still skeptical and thought his criticism a little unfair, the Colonel took me further into his confidence but with the understanding, of course, that what he said was to remain "graveyard," that is, buried in my diary.

"Perhaps it is premature, but in my judgment you can never look over the probable field of battle too soon, and a man in my confidence has been making a tally of the probable vote on ratification of the unfinished treaty in the Senate. It is clear to me that not nearly as many Senators, as the President thinks, are 'sold' on the Treaty and the Covenant, but if he plays his cards well he will win. So today in our talk I told him I was already counting noses, and as that made him laugh I went into details. I urged the President to extend some courtesies, to even extend an olive branch to Hoke Smith, the Senator from Georgia, with whom, as I knew, he had been 'feuding' for some years, why I never knew but I was now to learn. 'If you whistle Hoke will not come to heel,' I suggested, 'but if you ask him to come to the White House and assist you he will come and stay with you.'

" 'I shall do nothing of the sort!' answered the President, and for a moment his eyes blazed with anger. 'That man is an ambulance-chaser. I scorn to have any relations with him whatsoever.'

"Aghast, I inquired for details, and the strange story of the feud came out. It seems that, unhappy coincidence, Hoke Smith and Wilson hung out their law-office shingles in Atlanta in the same month and the same year." House continued, "As I see it Smith was a hustler and Wilson a Southern gentleman inclined to stand on his dignity. Smith got a few clients, perhaps he did chase ambulances, but Wilson got none except a few family lawsuits that brought in no fees, so Wilson soon returned to academic life and Smith went on his way to the Senate.

" 'But, "Governor," ' I insisted, 'this man's vote is important, it may be vital. If he did chase ambulances thirty years ago, do not ostracize him. Let him, too, help to save civilization.'

"The President laughed now, and that was a good sign. 'I don't think his vote will be important and I'm sure it will not be decisive. I shall receive him, of course, as the Senator from Georgia, if he calls, but, House, no nosegays, no olive branches in that direction.'

"Wilson wanted to change the subject, but I was insistent, and we talked for an hour about the conflicts that awaited me in Paris and were also awaiting him in Washington. He seemed now in a reasonable mood, and so I ventured to say, 'Governor, I hope you haven't lost your admiration for Burke. Your essay on that great man was the first product of your pen that enthralled me.' 'Of course not, of course not,' was his rejoinder. 'When in doubt I always consult Burke or Bagehot or both. But why your question?' 'Because I recall your Burke said "to govern is to compromise." ' He laughed and shook his finger at me and then he grew serious. 'I know the situation you have in mind, but for once I do not agree with you or with Burke, if you have quoted him correctly. I have found that you get nothing in this world that is worth while without fighting for it.' And so you see why I am hopeful, but not confident, of the outcome of the battle that awaits the President in Washington," concluded House.

Certainly the President has achieved a number of notable successes during his stay in Paris. It is equally certain, however, that many major problems remain unsolved. First, Reparations; second, French Security and the Left Bank of the Rhine; third, the Adriatic and the Shantung problems. House fears the return of the President which was announced for four weeks later. In his judgment, the President could best direct future negotiations from Washington. There he would be in a calmer atmosphere and have the advantage of enjoying close contact with developing American opinion. However, House has been designated to take charge of the negotiations while the President is away. Could he make a suggestion that would result in prolonging the period of his authority and greater responsibility? Confident that an expression of opinion would be misunderstood by some and would have no effect on Wilson, the Colonel did not repeat the views he had expressed so frankly in October 1918, when he urged the President not to personally enter the melee:

"We must leave the decision to the President, where it belongs," were his words on the only occasion, at least in my presence, when the question was again raised.

February 16th.

With the President on the high seas, with the first draft of his Covenant in his pocket, now no longer a secret document but, by the miracle of almost instant communications, already informally at least before the Congress and the world, the time has come to make what record I can of how what many regard as a miracle was wrought. The delegates, those who assembled from all over the world to take part in the Great Assizes, have had ten sessions in a large and spacious room on the third floor of the Hotel Crillon adjacent to Colonel House's private quarters. In the center was a great table around which at first the delegates of the Great Powers sat, later to be enlarged by the addition of five representatives of the lesser tribes. To one side was a smaller table at which sat generally Hunter Miller and his colleagues of the drafting committee. Later, when the President's objections were overruled, another little table was introduced at which the secretaries of some of the delegations sat when, after the third session, they were finally admitted to the hearings.

This is how we worked: At the great table the President presided; to his left sat Colonel House. I sat between them but a little to the rear as became my humble functions. The President held in his hand the Hurst-Miller draft, reading aloud one by one the articles as they were submitted for discussion. The President did not like this draft but he accepted it as a basis of discussion, because Lord Robert Cecil was very insistent and the President appreciated that without the support of the British the project would get nowhere. At first the procedure followed was to await the conclusion of the remarks of the delegates and then for me to translate them. However, this took up so much time that the plan was modified and I was told to translate sentence by sentence in a low voice, while the speaker held the floor—a procedure which while timesaving was much more difficult for me. The suggestion I made, that I be allowed to try my hand at condensing the speeches, often repetitious and discursive, was frowned down upon. And here I must say a word about myself and the manner in which the records I am incorporating in my diary were made. My duties as instant translator of all the speeches, sentence by sentence, were very exacting and, I may add, exhausting. The delegates only spoke from time to time as the spirit moved them but from me there flowed incessantly a Niagara of words (their words; not always well chosen). After the sessions I generally made as soon as possible a résumé of what had been said. This was helpful to me, and as my chief maintained it was of assistance to the President on several occasions when memories were at fault and impressions clashed—as they did frequently.

"We're engaged in drawing up a world Constitution," said House; "under it, I trust that civilization will be safeguarded and a new and more humane era shall be opened to all of us. It is your duty to play the part of James Madison of Montpelier in recording the drafting of this great document. I hope you will."

"Madison had many qualifications which I lack," I protested. "He, too, had to cajole balky horses, but Madison only had to listen to plain English and set down what he thought was worthy to be recorded; while I, alas! have to put into plain English speeches that are often made in the barbaric French of Warsaw, of Zagreb, of Belgrade, and, worst of all, the French of Crete. You really ought to have a man like Professor Montoux, who has spent his life in straightening out mixed metaphors and simplifying the remarks of incoherent statesmen."

"You are doing quite well," said House.

"But I would be a better Madison," I insisted, "if I sat idly on the side lines and took notes."

I then asked, not for the first time, what is our objective? And the Colonel answered, as he often did, with a Texas story:

"One day Bill MacDonald, the chief of the Rangers, came riding up to Big Foot Wallace's ranch and said, 'Come on, Big Foot,' and in a moment Big Foot was in the saddle, and they rode and they rode, stirrup to stirrup, toward the setting of the sun. And the second day they continued riding toward the West and Big Foot never opened his mouth. And so it went on until the morning of the sixth day, when at last Big Foot opened his mouth and said, 'Gosh, Big Boy, where we're gwine?' 'I don't know, Big Foot, but maybe we'll have to keep after them varmints until the end of time.'

"I told the President that story last week," continued House, "and he liked it, but he added that 'although the sixth day has not dawned, I know where "I'm gwine" and I also know where the "varmints" are lurking.'

"I think the President is right," commented House. "There are spots in Europe where the good grass is rising from the parched earth; at least I think so."

"The news from Washington is none too encouraging," I ventured to say.

"True, true," admitted the Colonel. "But all those doubts will be brushed aside once the President takes to the stump and presents to the people the true picture of the world situation."

PART III

Clemenceau –
The Wounded Tiger in His Lair

February 20th.

Balfour was in the Colonel's office when the startling news came that Cottin had shot Clemenceau (February 19th) and his remark was: "Dear, dear, I wonder what that portends?" just as though someone had spilled a cup of tea.

"I don't know," said the Colonel, "but we must find out." He grabbed his hat and the lanky Balfour by the arm and hurried him into his car and sped away to the Rue Franklin. The Colonel did not know what it portended, but *he* meant to find out.

How quickly men change and how radically these changes upset calculations based on past performance! Who can recognize in the lackadaisical Arthur Balfour of the Peace Conference (although he is Foreign Minister of the British Empire in one of the most critical moments of its history) the man who held the Parnellites at bay in Commons for so many years, who smiled when Tim Healy dubbed him "Bloody Balfour," or when John Dillon roared, "we'll remember Mitchellstown"? Can this be the same man who energized the British Army in 1900 and sent that startling cable to the sluggish General Buller: "If you feel incapable of relieving Ladysmith, turn your command over to someone who can"?

But here at this tragic juncture in world affairs he seems again possessed by the spirit of philosophic doubt which afflicted him in his callow youth. Even the Balliol boys who seek to keep him awake, and also informed, are inclined to throw up the sponge. He is always surrounded by a coterie of female cousins, aunts, and nieces, and to these he monologues but really says nothing. If the Balliol boys say, "It is raining," his answer is, "Are you quite sure?" If they say, "For a wonder the sun is shining," his answer is, "Is that so—beyond the peradventure of a doubt?"

February 22d (Saturday).

Georges Mandel, regarded by some as Clemenceau's *fidus Achates* (by those who like him not as the "Tiger's jackal"), came in after lunch with an urgent message from the wounded Premier, and at two-thirty I accompanied Colonel House to his lair in the Rue Franklin, named after our Benjamin, who guided American diplomacy with such skill throughout the Revolution. It is in the Passy quarter where Franklin lived during his fruitful sojourn in Paris and is still redolent of memories of the truly great man who said "there never was a good war or a bad peace." I have these words frequently on my lips when, as is so often the case, pessimistic critics of the current negotiations call. As on my previous visit, the Tiger was seated in an armchair because his wound does not permit him to lie down. He was wrapped up in an old army blanket and the same unchanged foulard was twisted around his neck. He had on his characteristic skullcap and the gray gloves. He was as gay as a cricket and announced that he would attend the meeting of the Council on Monday although no one, least of all the worried doctors, thinks he will be able to do so. When House mentioned the opinion of the medicos the Tiger roared with laughter: "They are a gang of jackasses!" he shouted, "and who knows this better than I? Was I not a member of their gang for twenty years? Listen, *mes amis*, to a frank confession: I am responsible for many crimes, indeed for downright murders. Not in war, as many suppose, but in the piping days of peace, during the years I practiced what they call the healing art, in Montmartre."

He drew the Colonel to him and went on in English: "The slogan now is full speed ahead. As I cannot lie down since that madman shot me (the *attentat* took place three days before), I just naturally will not let anybody else lie down. I shall insist upon a little speed being turned on. I am confident that if we 'Americans' and the British and the French would only get together we could push through the Peace Treaty with Germany in a very few days and then we would be at liberty to take up the arrangements with Austria, Turkey, and the Bulgars—and those fellows should not detain us for long."

Unfortunately at this moment Signor Sonnino burst into the room and began to talk about Italy's claims, which he feared could not be properly formulated until we could see the situation more clearly.

Here the Tiger groaned and for the first time admitted he was in pain. To me he whispered, "It feels like an Italian stiletto," and then he turned and began to tease his patient and adoring nurse, Sister Theoneste, with his bizarre views on heaven and hell.

On our return to the Crillon, Frank Hitchcock was there, a former Postmaster General and a power in the inner circles of the Republican party. The Colonel greeted him cordially and offered him every facility to visit the army at Coblenz and to inspect the peace proceedings in Paris. When Hitchcock had gone, the Colonel reflected aloud: "Frank is here looking for weak spots. I trust his eyesight is not good."

February 23d.

It is not news that misfortunes never come singly, but that saying does not make the budget of today any easier to bear. A few hours after the shooting of Clemenceau we heard of the murder of Kurt Eisner in Munich. Then came the beetle-browed Bratiano with his Job's post, and hardly had he gone when Premier Voldemar Priene, the envoy of Lithuania, appeared, and he, too, was draped in the garments of woe. While of course it was not so intended, the clause in the Armistice prolongation of February 17th, by which the Germans are ordered to clear out of Lithuanian territory, practically turns the country over to the by-no-means-tender mercies of the Bolsheviki. He insists that the resulting deplorable situation can only be remedied by an exceptional ruling, in fact a new interpretation of this clause; it should be limited to the German-Polish frontier and should not apply to the German-Lithuanian situation. To avert otherwise inevitable conflicts he asks that the Supreme War Council announce that Section XII of the Armistice convention is in force, and will be enforced, except where the German-Lithuanian frontier is involved.

Two Poles came in then, recent arrivals from Warsaw, and said things looked dark along the Silesian border where the Germans were massing large bodies of troops, and also along the Vistula where several factions of the Poles were fighting among themselves. They said: "Paddy wants help." Then Butter[1] came in with a long memo from Beneš. Apparently even he, as a rule the most cheerful man of the Conference, is perturbed by the outlook. After reading the somber memo which I submitted to him, the Colonel grew thoughtful and said: "Unlike the good farm horse our panaceas do not seem to work

[1]Economic adviser to the Czechoslovak Delegation.

well in 'every spot and place.' There is a certain individuality in the troubled zones and that we shall have to take into consideration."

February 26th.

Two days after the "half-wit" fired his shots at M. Clemenceau (February 19th) as he was leaving his house in the Rue Franklin for a conference with Balfour and House at the Crillon, I was detailed to remain in constant attendance on the French Premier. Everybody took a serious view of the incident and the resulting wound except Clemenceau himself. Seven shots had been fired deliberately and at close quarters; fortunately, only one took effect. (The bullet, never extracted, had lodged very close to vital organs and caused him great pain throughout the ten years he was yet to live.) Clemenceau refused to allow the incident to be dignified as an attempt at assassination, and when he did speak of it he called it an "accident."

After the preliminary hearings of the would-be assassin were over, the prosecutor called upon the Tiger, bringing with him several legal luminaries who were engaged upon the investigation. They assured him that all the facts had been brought to light: that the man had no accomplices, that he was unbalanced in mind, and a menace to the community; then they asked the victim of the "accident" what he thought the sentence should be.

"How complicated are your duties!" exclaimed the Tiger. "Of course I'll help you all I can, but I'm glad I'm not a judge. When I think of the men who are continually sniping at me from ambush, I am tempted to say that this brave fellow who faced my walking stick with nothing in the way of a weapon save a machine-gun revolver should have conferred upon him some prize of valor, some Grand Cross or other. But I must not be impulsive, the women and the children and all the innocent bystanders who might have been hurt while the fellow was aiming at my miserable old carcass should be considered. Then his poor marksmanship must be taken into account. We have just won the most terrible war in history, yet here is a Frenchman who at point-blank range misses his target six times out of seven. Of course the fellow must be punished for the careless use of a dangerous weapon and for poor marksmanship. I suggest that he be locked up for about eight years, with intensive training in a shooting gallery."

The prosecutor and his assistants withdrew in some bewilderment and the "half-wit" was later given a ten-year sentence.

In the following ten days I was sent by Colonel House, during the absence of Mr. Wilson in America, the ranking member of our delegation, almost every evening to lay before M. Clemenceau the developments of the day and to receive any communications he might care to make to his fellow negotiators. The Tiger had turned the sickroom topsy-turvy with his eccentricities. To the complaining sisters who nursed him with such devotion, he had an answer that turned away their wrath:

"Before the 'accident' I was only a tired old patient and had to knuckle under; now I'm a martyr, and you've got to put up with me."

One of these eccentricities was to sleep from nine in the evening until midnight; then, bright as a button, he was ready for business, and, despite the protests of the doctors, his sickroom was thronged.

"I must make a peace," said M. Clemenceau to me in one of these midnight sessions, "based upon my belief and upon my own experience of the world in which we have to live. My responsibility is personal and non-transferable. When called to the bar of history, I cannot say, 'Well, I made these arrangements to conform to Mr. Wilson's viewpoint.' Mr. Wilson has lived in a world that has been fairly safe for Democracy; I have lived in a world where it was good form to shoot a Democrat. After a few weeks of sparring I became convinced that your President wanted the same things that I did, although we were very far apart as to the ways and the means by which we could reach the desired end.

"When he first developed his program, it seemed to me perfectly Utopian. I said to him, 'Mr. Wilson, if I accepted what you propose as ample for the security of France, after the millions who have died and the millions who have suffered, I believe, and indeed I hope, that my successor in office would take me by the nape of the neck and have me shot at daylight before the donjon of Vincennes.' After that we began to get together.

"Once I said to him, 'Mr. Wilson, have you ever seen an elephant cross a swinging bamboo bridge?' Mr. Wilson said he had not. 'Well, I'll tell you how he goes about it. First, he trots down into the stream to see if the foundations are all right; then he comes back and puts one foot on the bridge. If the result is reassuring, he ventures its mate. Then he gives the bridge a sharp jolt. If it stands that, he gives it his trust and advances. Now that's my idea about your bridge leading to the New Jerusalem. I may be, as they say I am, a springing tiger where my personal fortunes are concerned, but where the safety of France is at stake—— Well, there never was an elephant more careful or more cautious than I am going to be.' "

Last evening, four days after the "accident," I came to the Tiger's lair with several memoranda from the Big Three, about Dalmatia and the Saar, and their best wishes for an early and complete recovery. Sister Theoneste was in charge of the sickroom. She had been brought hurriedly from another case, it being well known from experience in a previous illness that she was the only person who could "handle" the Tiger. Even she could not tame him, but handle him she could. She was a middle-aged woman with a grave, intelligent face.

"So intelligent," said the Tiger in a quite audible aside to me, "and yet she believes in prayer, *c'est insensé!*"

"And you, M. le Président, you are a good man, but you would be a better one if only you would say your prayers."

"Copycat!" shouted the Tiger. "Renan said that years ago."

"I can't make you say your prayers," continued the Sister. "If I even tried to, your government would probably expel me from France, but I can and will make you take your medicine." And now she advanced toward his wheel chair with a glass filled with a very unpleasant-looking syrup. The Tiger tried to roll away, but she followed him full of menace.

"My Sister," he bleated, "how can you be so cruel?"

"Georges!" whimpered the Sister, in mock despair, "if you don't take it, the doctor will make a bad mark on my certificate."

"Give it to me; give me still another dose. Never shall it be said . . ."

Ah yes. It was not to be doubted Sister Theoneste knew how to handle the Tiger.

After he had been given a glass of sugared water to take the horrid taste out of his mouth, the Sister inquired:

"And what kind of night did you have?"

"A terrible night it was," he answered plaintively.

"But your temperature is almost normal."

"Perhaps, but I have had mentally and morally a great shock. Should I tell you about it?"

"*Pour sur;* to whom else should you tell it if not to your nurse?"

"Well, last night in my dream I walked to the gate of Heaven and there was St. Peter on guard as usual. He was chatting with an old woman outside the gate and she was in great distress. I could not but overhear their conversation, and soon I had a chance to take part in it. You know how I love to chatter.

" 'I fear you cannot come in,' said St. Peter. 'As you frankly admit, you do not come with a clean bill of health. Good woman, we have to be very careful as to whom we admit; *in extremis*, you failed to confess.'

" 'Death came so suddenly, my good St. Peter; when I sent for the curé, they could not find him, and soon I was on my way here.'

" 'Of course I'm sorry to refuse you, but there are the regulations. Clearly you are not in shape to be admitted.'

"Then I intervened, as anyone would have done in the circumstances.

" 'Good St. Peter,' I pled, 'this is but a little irregularity. Her curé was absent, *sans doute*, engaged upon some pious work . . .'

" 'But the law says even the faithful must confess before they can enter the Kingdom of Heaven,' said St. Peter.

" 'All you have to do,' I persisted—the poor woman was in such distress—'is to call to the gate one of the curés who here must abound, and then in a jiffy the letter as well as the spirit of the law can be complied with.'

"St. Peter was vexed and he gave me an ugly look, but I was so eloquent that he could not ignore my plea. He summoned an angel messenger—I think it was Seraphim—but I am not quite sure, and in a surly voice he said:

" 'Go fetch me a curé.'

"This one, whoever he was, came back in a few minutes and whispered something to St. Peter which did not please him, and he closed the door with a slam right in our faces. He peeped at us rather contemptuously now through the little *Judas*, and I heard him give another order to the angel messenger and heard him prance off with a hop, skip, and a jump. He was gone a long, long time, and when he came back, what he said made St. Peter still more angry.

" 'Well, well,' I said, for standing at the gate of the Promised Land so long had made me nervous.

" 'Well, I find there are no curés in Heaven,' snarled St. Peter; and then he snapped to the peephole and was gone.

"I turned to the distressed woman. But, really, what could I do, invite her to go with me to the other place? I was indeed in a baffling quandary. And then I woke up. Now, dear Sister, what do you augur from that dream?"

Sister Theoneste kept a straight face, but not without effort.

"If M. le Président would only say his prayers, good St. Peter would not keep him outside the blessed gate." Then in an aside to me, "Georges (no longer M. le Président) is *impayable*. He is such good company and such a good man that perhaps they will let him in anyhow. At least I hope so; and that hope I never fail to include in my prayers."

February 28th.

"I never said, as widely reported (the Paris papers were filled with suggestions to this effect at the time)," insisted Clemenceau in my talk with him this evening, "that Wilson was pro-German, but I did think and I probably said, as I generally say what I think, that many of his plans and proposals were unduly and most unwisely helpful to the Germans in their present unregenerate state. I confess that from my first cable contact with it Wilsonism alarmed me, and that is why on the eve of the Conference I announced in the Chamber, 'It will be more difficult to make peace than it was to make war.' Now who can deny that in peacemaking France is meeting with great opposition from all her Allies who were so noble and considerate while the battle was on? During the long war years we sustained the heaviest losses, we suffered the most, and now what is our fate at the Conference?

"We are blocked in our plea for security; only our undoubted claim to Alsace goes uncontested. For the little else we may obtain we shall have to fight and fight hard. I mean to do that very thing and Wilson knows it. There is one bright spot in the dark prospect. Wilson is as frank with me as I am with him. We have both placed our cards on the Peace table."

There is, it is true, one criticism of Mr. Wilson to which M. Clemenceau often returns, as indeed he did today, which seems to me not without foundation. "I told your President that, in my judgment, the grave fault of his attitude is that he eliminated sentiment and endeavored to efface all memory of the past. A grave, a very grave fault it seems to me. It was then I would say, 'I am the last, the only survivor of the Protest of Bordeaux—against the infamy of the Treaty that the Prussians imposed at the point of the bayonet. M. le Président, I speak for our glorious dead who fell in the two wars. For myself I can hold my tongue, but not for them.'"

In one of the many rude discussions that took place between the Tiger and Lloyd George, Mr. Wilson, the Presbyterian elder, was by many accounts compelled to intervene to prevent the fisticuffs which seemed imminent. As he retired to his corner, the little Welshman said: "Well! I shall expect an apology for these outrageous words!"

"You shall wait for it as long as you wait for the pacification of Ireland," was the hot reply.

Clemenceau's comment on this incident, without wholly admitting its truth, however, was amusing. "I can well understand why the youth of the world hates war, more power to them! But for us oldsters it is not so bad; as a matter of fact, war life rejuvenated me. It gave me back the health I had lost, and think of it, there was old George doubling up his fists and squaring off. If Wilson had not intervened, I would have given him a clip on the chin with a *savatte* stroke."

Only one thing at this moment can be vouched for as certain, and that is that the relations between the Entente Powers and their chiefs, consecrated by the death of millions of youths, are strained; indeed, they are near the breaking point.

March 1st.

At this time, as he said for my personal guidance and for the benefit of the generations to come, the Tiger made a remark which I trust I shall bear in mind when, as I hope, my writing days—for the public, not for sealed archives—begin again. He indeed repeated it so often that it took on the shape of an injunction.

"Someday," he said, "you will put down in writing what you saw at the war and during the course of the Conference and what you think you know about it all. Just as I will, without doubt, though many a time I have taken an oath not to do so, and then may the Powers that be (wherever they may be located, whether up aloft or down below) have mercy on our souls! Now out of pure friendship I am going to give you a tip which I fondly think is worth all the 'C' bonds the Germans are trying to fob off on us in lieu of real reparations payment. It is this, *mon cher ami!* Beware of documents! They are the pitfalls and ambuscades which the crafty jugglers of the day plant in the path of the unwary historian, to waylay, in fact, to mislead him. When you come to write, set down what you have seen with your own eyes and what you have heard with your own ears, and even if you pursue this discreet policy you may wander from the straight and narrow path." Then with a sly wink he added: "All we old newspapermen know that this does happen. An unavoidable professional risk, I suppose."

Here by innuendo M. Clemenceau was referring to what might be regarded as our first meeting and what came of it. Many years ago, in 1889 to be exact, with but a fringe of bushes intervening, in Count Dillon's Neuilly garden I, and at least twenty other newspaper correspondents, had witnessed a sensational and, in its results, the most surprising duel of that day. The principals were Boulanger, the general of the Revolution and of the Revanche, and M. Floquet, the Premier of France, whose nearsightedness almost reached the point of total blindness. Clemenceau, acting as his friend's second, advised the Prime Minister to assume a somewhat unusual posture of defense, but, as the sequel proved, it was justified by the event.

"You can't fence," insisted the Tiger, "and the general can, or at least he ought to. Extend your arm with your *épée* straight before you and the general, in a rage at having to cross swords with a decrepit *pekin*, may rush upon it."

And that is what happened, and after the brave general had been carried away from the field of honor by the waiting stretchermen, M. Clemenceau had shocked us all with an outburst of gay and certainly most unrestrained laughter. Now he thought, as did so many, that the Boulanger bubble was pricked and that the people of France would never follow such an ineffective swordsman in the campaign across the Rhine which seemed imminent. But for once the Tiger was mistaken, and the popular faith in the Paladin of the Black Horse survived for at least another six months. In answer to his remonstrance at my account[2] of his unseemly behavior on this historic occasion, I said: "If you wish it, I will omit that episode from the definitive edition of my memoirs."

After a moment's reflection M. Clemenceau said: "I will not ask you to go as far as that. While, of course, I displayed all proper respect to the wounded warrior, as became a veteran duelist and a 'correct' one, still it is a gay story, and there are not many of them floating about in this dismal world today. You can tell it your own way. I'll never contradict you. We old newspapermen must stand by one another if for no other reason than that no one else will."

March 2d

Albert, the Tiger's shadow and valet, is a handsome fellow and a lucky one. He went through the war on the Western Front without receiving a scratch.

[2]*Heyday in a Vanished World.*

"He's lucky, and that is one of the reasons why I like to have him around," said Clemenceau. "I seem to remember that whenever a ranking officer was suggested for an important post, Napoleon would always ask—is he lucky? Well, Albert is lucky. While he has done many foolish things he always comes out smiling and as plump as a partridge. *Ce garçon* loves contrasts and seeks out remarkable experiences. One I will tell you about. For years he valeted the richest man in the world and now he valets me, the poorest, and yet he is always smiling. Of course, when he brings me my soup at midnight, I try to induce Albert to tell me how Sir Basil Zaharoff coined his millions, but he will only tell me how he spent them, and in the spending line I am not in need of instruction. He says that throughout the war, day and night, Sir Basil's agents were on guard at all the railway stations of Paris and when the *permissionaires* arrived on leave they were each given forty francs.

"And why? Albert explains that 'Sir Basil could not sleep at the thought that our poilus on short leave in Paris would have to go without their beloved *pinard*.' What a strange animal he must have been. He could not sleep at the thought that some of our *braves enfants* went thirsty, and yet the thought that hundreds of thousands of men are blown to bits by the bombs he manufactures never worried him in the least! A strange animal, indeed one of the strangest that the war has brought out of their caves," soliloquizes the Tiger.

PART IV

With General Smuts to Southeastern Europe

VIENNA—PRAGUE—BELGRADE—BUDAPEST

NOTE: General Smuts left on his tour of southeastern Europe on April 1st and the following excerpts are from the diary of Colonel Bonsal, who joined him in Vienna. Generally, but not invariably, they are headed by the day of the week and not by the day of the month. While, as will appear, Colonel Bonsal on this tour covered a good deal of ground, he was back in Paris on the afternoon of April 11th to resume his duties with the Commission engaged in drafting the League and the Covenant.

March 30th.

The Colonel came in this morning, quite excited. "Smuts," he announced, "is leaving tomorrow night for a tour of investigation and, as we hope, of pacification in southeastern Europe. With him on the mission will be a Frenchman and an Italian, and he has asked me to let you accompany him as the American representative. He intimates that the Frenchman and the Italian will merely serve as camouflage or window dressing but that he wants you, whom he regards as a 'common-sense' American, to assist him because you are perfectly familiar with conditions down there before propaganda got to work and covered up the facts. Here," explained the Colonel, "as regards the Covenant, things are at a standstill and will remain so for two or three weeks, and by that time you will be back. Perhaps Smuts will not accomplish much but he will learn a lot about the actual situation at first hand and that cannot fail to be helpful. Here we have put all the pressure we can upon the stubborn factions, and, while it is sinking in, for the present it is best for us merely to tread water and hope for the best. I told Smuts I would like to have you go and Hankey[1] is arranging the diplo-

---

[1] Hankey, a marine officer, acted as secretary and co-ordinator to the British Commonwealth Commission. Some years later he was raised to the peerage as Lord Hankey and played an important role in the after-the-war conferences.

matic passports and the reservations on the international train to Vienna where the real tour begins."

I welcomed the change and, awaiting further developments, set to work to clear my desk.

At the appointed hour on the following morning (April 1st) I was at the station. On hand also was Major Hankey, the bear leader of the British Empire delegation, and a General Thomson. Hankey was in a rage, or pretended to be. I never knew which. "There has been a mix-up," he explained. "Of course the telephone is to blame. Smuts left in great haste last night but you can overtake him in Vienna. There he will wait for you, and no harm done." To this the tall, red-tabbed general agreed, but he was put out and seemed to think that the telephone was not entirely to blame, and this first impression was confirmed later on.

Thomson and I were not at all pleased with our stuffy and far-from-clean compartment on the French train and we drew up a formal complaint which we proposed serving on M. le Conducteur in the morning. But the cold, searching light of the dawn revealed how extremely lucky we had been—and were. Out in the corridor, taking what ease they could on uneasy *strapontin* seats, unshaven and unwashed, were a number of princes of the blood and half-a-dozen great ones of the earth whose lofty lineage and diplomatic passports had gotten them on the train but had not secured for them the accommodations they were accustomed to. So our displeasure vanished, and having concluded that as a transport officer Hankey was a wizard, we tore into scraps our complaint and moved into the dining car for morning coffee.

At Buchs, Paderewski boarded the train, very friendly but most mysterious as to whence he came and where he was going. Suddenly a real baby blush overspread his face, and, with the characteristic gesture of pushing up his back hair which later on during the sessions in Paris we found so amusing, he said:

"Sometimes I wake up at night and cannot be comforted. Why? I'll tell you. It is the memory of that morning in November when I arrived in Paris and burst into your colonel's bedroom at seven-fifteen. How I must have harassed him! That is one of the things I could only have done for Poland. Do you think he will ever forgive me?"

He was pleased when I assured him that all his visits were welcome and all were timely whether he came at midnight or early morning. "You cannot come at an untimely hour," I insisted, and indeed mine were true words. "Paddy is the Colonel's pet," as I once heard the yeoman of the guard explain. "We boys think he likes 'Paddy' better even than the Tiger."

We found General Smuts at the British Embassy in Vienna. There all the cabinets and archive cases were still covered with the Spanish seals of His Catholic Majesty, which had protected them through the long war years. The South African soldier-diplomat greeted me in the most friendly manner, but he was noticeably curt with Thomson. Of this frigid reception the explanation only came some days later, when I learned on excellent authority that Smuts was displeased with this last addition to his party and would have stopped Thomson if he had learned of his assignment in time. It all goes back, apparently, to the bad feeling that has long existed between Smuts and General Henry Wilson, a wordy and pompous ass, who presides over the British imperial delegation to the War Council in Versailles, because it is said "he can outtalk Lloyd George." Wilson, I learned, was furious that so important a mission should have been entrusted to the interloper from South Africa and without asking leave of anyone had sent Thomson to keep an eye on the proceedings which Wilson regarded as most irregular because he had not been consulted.

This was not the first time I noticed that the red tape which enmeshes the brass hats is even more disastrous in its effects than it is among the civilian delegates and that it afflicts all nations pretty much alike. Be this as it may, Smuts evidently concluded that Thomson had been sent to spy on his movements and decided to exclude him as much as possible from the proceedings. I think Thomson personally was wholly innocent, and when Colonel Cunningham, whom we found in temporary charge of the Embassy, asked him rather stiffly why he had come, he answered: "Oh! for a lark." And that was, I think, the truth.

Smuts offered no explanation of why we had been left behind in Paris, but the cordiality with which he greeted me and his coldness to Thomson gave color to the explanation I have already given. "Well, here you are, Thomson," was all that the lieutenant general said as he caught sight of the man he regarded as an unwelcome recruit. It seems that the ill feeling between Smuts and Sir Henry Wilson dates back to the Boer War, when they fought under opposing flags. Now Wilson as chief of the Imperial General Staff opposed the choice of Smuts for the mission, and when Lloyd George insisted he sent Thomson, one of his men, and a devoted adherent, to keep tab on the South African. Smuts had evidently thought to escape this surveillance by anticipating his departure by twenty-four hours. Left at the post, Smuts hoped that Thomson would remain there, and of course it was not a matter of great importance that I also should be left behind. I did not mind, but Smuts evidently thought I might take umbrage and laid it on with a shovel in the presence of Colonel Cunningham, the British agent in Vienna, and of poor Thomson, who was hurt by his treatment and had reason to be.

"I am so glad you have come," the Afrikander repeated over and over again. "I shall lean heavily on your assistance because you are perfectly familiar with the politics and the other conditions in the countries we are about to visit, of which so many of us are woefully ignorant. You, indeed, can be helpful."

The general's thanks sounded a little more sincere when I interrupted to tell him that I had brought along with me his batman or soldier "striker," who had also been left behind in the hurried departure.

"Splendid, splendid!" he said. "I'm an old soldier, but I'm lost without that man." The inside story was that the batman could shave the general without awakening him—a rare accomplishment in Europe, but not unknown among Chinese "boys." Indeed I enjoyed the ministrations of one such artist myself in Peking years ago, but only for a month. He was, alas! in my service only on loan.

Domestic matters having been settled, Smuts drew me aside and talked politics. "You have missed nothing by not being with me the few hours we spent in Budapest. Nothing came of our gesture, but I am glad we made it. It is clear that Bela Kun will not last long and I am advising Paris to assume a waiting attitude. Kun will soon be displaced by the Majority Socialists, and while they are by no means men after my own heart with them I think we could discuss matters— seriously."

Late in the afternoon we boarded our special train and reached Prague shortly before midnight. There was at the station a huge gathing of military men and civilian officials of the new state to greet the general and do him honor. Some palace or other of the vanishing territorial lords, now deserted by its owner, had been arranged for our occupancy, but in view of the shortness of his stay Smuts decided that we should all remain on board the train where we had now shaken down and were fairly comfortable.

Thomson, with the temporary rank of brigadier general, with whom I now shared a compartment for several days, was an English officer of an unusual type. During the war he had served in military intelligence and also with a combat unit in Palestine under Allenby.

He talked incessantly about the tangled affairs of Europe and was outspoken in his prophecies of the dark, dire things that were to come. Generally I thought they were based on false premises and misinformation, but he had a slant on the collapse of Russia which was new and I thought interesting.

"If the government of the Tsar had made a separate peace in 1917 little Nicholas would be alive now and probably still on the throne. Those who advised him to take this course were denounced as pro-Germans, and in a sense some of them were, but they were for the most part simply Imperialists who wished to safeguard the Empire against the rising tide of democracy—if you wish to call it that. It was stupid of us to cajole Kerensky and drive him back into the war, and it was stupid of him to allow himself to be driven."

Out from his tunic now and again, indeed quite often, Thomson[2] would draw a small photograph of Lenin. He would look at it for a long time and then slip it back into his pocket again. "A remarkable man! a most remarkable man!" he would mutter, and I certainly was not in a mood to gainsay him.

. . . Certainly in his talk with Masaryk on the morning following our arrival in Prague, General Smuts had no assistance from me or from any other member of the mission. It was strictly a tête-à-tête. He was closeted with the President for half an hour, and when he rejoined us he kept his own counsel. In the meantime we passed the time in wandering through the interminable corridors of the Hradčany Palace and wondering as to the why and the wherefore of the many paintings of sea battles that were hung along them. Perhaps they tell of the days when, on the authority of Shakespeare at least (no great shakes as a geographer, it must be admitted), there was "a seacoast of Bohemia." I was then summoned into the presence of the new chief magistrate of the brand-new republic, and had I been miffed, which most certainly I was not, by my exclusion from the first meeting, I would have been consoled by the fact that he talked to me twice as long as he had talked with the great Afrikander.

At first, for the moment at least, Masaryk turned away from the world in turmoil and indulged his reminiscent mood. Again he referred to our first, our, at the time, little-noted meeting and the small gathering of friends that welcomed him a short year ago on his arrival

[2]Thomson, on leaving the army after the war, became the closest adviser of Ramsay MacDonald on European affairs. He entered Parliament as a Laborite and was raised to the peerage when MacDonald came into power. He died with all his fellow travelers in the airship disaster at Beauvais in France on his way to India.

at the Union Station in Washington from the far-flung battle line in Siberia.

"That was an important moment in history," he reflected aloud, "not because of my insignificant person but because of the great cause I had the good fortune to represent. At last I had come to the city where the noble Wilson was continuing the battle which the great Lincoln had only half won. In a few days, thanks to the President's sympathy and assistance, the crusade for the liberation of all peoples was under way."

I mentioned with what interest I had noticed the great ships putting out to sea, at least from the palace walls and galleries. The President smiled but evidently was not inclined to elucidate this historical mystery. "Yes," he said, "Prague has had many changes and transformations, and in the wars of long ago she suffered many vicissitudes. Prague was once an imperial city and, seated here, the Hapsburgs ruled the world in their unhappy way. Our purpose is to make of Prague the Mecca of Democracy. We have the task to liberate Central Europe. From here must radiate the only gospel acceptable to free men. It is a great and noble task but I am confident my people will prove equal to it—with God's help!"

Only then the President came back to the actual, indeed the urgent, situation. Fortunately, for I had no instructions and would have been unable to answer them, he put to me no questions as to the American view of the political situation, but he admitted that things were not moving so smoothly in his reconstructed country as he had hoped. "And as they will," he added confidently, "when the war fever subsides and our people see clearly the important peacetime tasks with which we are all confronted." On one point the President was evidently a little anxious. Undoubtedly the rumor had reached him, as it had come to us, that a certain Czech general, dissatisfied with the proposed territorial adjustments, was preparing to "pronounce" against the new government in true Latin-American fashion. Masaryk was evidently aware that his sober, intelligent policy was not universally popular and that some of the hotheads were decidedly restive.

"When I saw Colonel House in Paris," he said, "I told him that the German fringe and the scattered German settlements along the northern and western border of historic Bohemia present a difficult problem. What is to be done with them? We cannot expel them as did the Berlin Government the unwelcome Poles in the provinces which at various times, but always by ruthless force of arms, they had annexed. If we tell them to go with their Germanic brethren and take with them their poor farms, we abandon our only defensible frontier, and it is exceedingly doubtful that such a solution would be acceptable even to them. Most of these people fled to the Sudeten hills to escape German control and they have long and unhappy memories of why they sought refuge with us.

"And, unhappily, there is another aspect of the problem that should not be overlooked. Surely it will have to be met. These German settlers, although they came as refugees, for nearly three hundred years now have lorded it over their Czech neighbors. They have for political and racial reasons always been favored and indeed at times pampered by the Hapsburgs. Some of our people think—and unfortunately how very human is the thought—that with the change in the fortunes of war their day has come and they may wish to profit by it. It has been suggested (the motive is obvious) that by joining up with Austria the best solution is found or at least an escape is presented to the German communities, to avoid their more pressing problems. Those who think so take, I fear, a superficial view of the situation. The war that was not of their choosing has left the Sudeten people greatly impoverished and their economic condition would be worsened by being annexed to the Austrian poorhouse. To cite but one reason which is ignored by those favoring annexation to the Reich. Within the borders of the Austrian Empire, at least before war came, these people have prospered through their little cottage industries. Now they fear, and not without reason, that once they become a part of the great German industrial machine their means of livelihood would be wiped out. Please tell Colonel House about my hopes and also my fears. They will not be surprising to him. He knew better than I did when we talked last fall that the peace would develop problems but little less difficult than those that beset us during the war."

Acting on a sudden impulse, Masaryk began to fumble among the papers which littered his desk.

"I want to read to you," he said, "the draft of the message which I sent to your great President on New Year's Day (January 1919). With characteristic modesty, the President did not publish it."

Then he went on and read it.

"On this great day, when the darkness that has for so long hung over us yields to the light of liberty, I salute you, Mr. President, in my name and in the name of our redeemed Czechoslovak State."

Apparently he was translating it from his native tongue and it came rather slowly.

"Our nation, Mr. President, will never forget that you by your support of the cause of liberty and justice brought about the downfall of that immoral combination of states formerly known as Austria-Hungary. Much less can we forget that you by your firm decision in favor of our rights, at a most critical moment, made possible the revolution that has brought about our national independence. We salute in you the great exponent of the political ideals of the noble American Republic. Those ideals represent the creed, the hope, and the aspirations of my people. The Czechoslovak Republic stands today ready to defend them against a world in arms."

Then the President darted off on another tangent and began to talk politics, indeed, world politics:

"The era of imperialism has closed," he said. "The self-seeking, ruthless plans of the Germans, of the Russians, and of their imitators, the Austro-Hungarians, have failed, as did those of Napoleon. The little states are free. The war task is accomplished, but a still greater task lies before us: it is to reorganize not only eastern Europe, but the world as a whole. As I see it, we are on the threshold of a new era in which the human race feels its unity. My people are determined to contribute all that is in their power to the realization of this sublime task."

I told President Masaryk that Colonel House, and also the president of the Conference, M. Clemenceau, had received a memorandum from the German minorities in Bohemia setting forth their hopes, their fears, and their claims. Apparently Masaryk was not entirely satisfied with what he had already said upon this, so he returned to the subject:

"The territory which the Sudeten Germans occupy belongs to us and with us it shall remain. We created this state and it is we who have restored it, with the help of world democracy, to its present independent status. I should be glad indeed if the German minorities would collaborate with us; that would be, I think, a wiser policy than the one they are called upon to follow by a few of their leaders whom I consider unworthy of their confidence. Unhappily, these men have adopted a Pan-German program and seek to array their misguided followers against us. Let them remember that it is we who built this state. They came to us as emigrants and as colonists; their juridical status should be as clear to them as it is to us. They should also remember the occasion when we stood together and together how we were deceived; they should remember that with us in 1861 they demanded of the Emperor in Vienna that he come to Prague to be crowned King of a united Bohemia. I trust they will stand with us now when a nobler future beckons us both.

"I hope and pray that an accord will be reached; but I do not close my eyes to the difficulties that have to be surmounted. It will not be easy to forget that out German minorities, as well as the Germans of Austria, approved the atrocities of the Hapsburg soldiery; that they did not protest at our treatment; indeed that in many, many instances they participated in the crimes of the war years. I recall these unhappy memories not in a vindictive spirit; we shall accept their participation in building our new independent state, but they must not be surprised if in the light of our bitter experiences we act prudently and without haste. I can assure them that their fate is in their own hands and that as a law-abiding minority they shall enjoy equality of citizenship and full national rights.

"As to the Germans of the new Reich on the north, that is a different matter. Our relations with them must be determined by the attitude they assume—ours will be correct. Of course we cherish the hope that the total defeat of Prussian militarism will result in the redemption of an emancipated German people. We trust that they will abandon their dreams of expansion to the east and of political supremacy over their neighbors. If their activities concentrate on the development of their resources, our relations with them might become cordial. I trust so."

☆   ☆   ☆

The situation that caused Masaryk to leave Paris so hurriedly last December evidently still exists and causes anxiety to neutral observers as well as to the new government so recently and so suddenly installed. It cannot be said that today the Czechs are one happy family. The Bolshevik propaganda is said to be spreading and certainly in the Kladno districts it is going very strong. At least three orators, who may or may not be emissaries of Moscow, are touring the country; namely, Slivine, Vorel, and Zapotecsky, and where necessary their meetings are protected by the police. Their talking points, as reported to me, are, first, that the peasants and the industrial workers are even worse off than they were under the Austrian regime. Second, that the Entente is sending beribboned generals to organize an army but does not send much food to feed the starving people. Third, that the millionaire exploiters are still in control and that consequently the famous Revolution of October 28th stands revealed as a swindle. They exhort the people to gather their strength for a second revolution, one that will bring the warmth of the Bolshevik sun to the shivering, starving people of Bohemia. Those near the President say that he does not attach any importance to these radical orators. "I shall continue to handle the situation in the American way," is his reported comment. I hope the sequel will justify this attitude, but there are many here who disapprove of it.

Later I had a long talk with little Caesar,[3] a glorified office boy in the *sub rosa* Czech Legation in Washington during the war, before recognition came, and now one of Masaryk's secretaries. Escorted by a mounted guard, Caesar took me for a drive through the beautiful capital. How different it is from the mourning city I last saw in the dreary days of March 1915, when the hard-fisted Magyar troops were in control and the jails were crowded with political prisoners, men and women. The town was bathed in a white mist through which now and again the golden spires of the many churches emerged in radiant glory. As we passed through the Square of Good King Wenceslaus and over the Charles Bridge, many groups drew to the curb and cheered us. "I have let it be known," explained Caesar, "that you were a friend in the dark days." Pledging me to secrecy (but of course I have no secrets from my diary), Caesar told me it had been the wish of Masaryk to rechristen the town of Pressburg, redeemed from the Hungarians, as Wilson City, and he had only desisted upon receiving an intimation from the President that he preferred the old Slovak name of Bratislava should be restored.

Little Caesar was amused at the only request I made of him on our sight-seeing tour, but upon this I was insistent. As in all my previous visits to Prague, I now wanted to see again the strange little cell-like dwellings in which the medieval kings of Bohemia lodged the alchemists and the other magicians of their dark but hopeful days. These little hovels lean against and indeed form an humble part of the Hradčany Palace. Here these wise men were fed and clothed and passed their time in exploring the earth and searching the heavens alike for the alkahest, the universal solvent, that would enable them

[3]My charming young friend was really M. Císar, but we gave him the more familiar name in memory of our bouts with the Commentaries.

and their royal patron to treat refractory ores, even to convert common clay and shining pebbles into refined gold. It seemed to me that this was a job almost topical, and that it should appeal to the rulers and the statesmen of this disastrous day who are called upon to invigorate depreciated currencies and restore to life the industries which have been shattered in the whirlwind of war. Some of these latter-day magicians are gathered together even now in Paris and are loudly proclaiming their panaceas. Temporarily, at least, they are better housed and better fed than their predecessors of medieval Prague, but I fear the long-sought alkahest still eludes their eager grasp!

In one of our halts Caesar produced his memorandum also. He wanted me to know that Masaryk in his inaugural address had used the words that Lincoln had spoken on the tragic battlefield.

"This nation," he said, "under God, shall have a new birth of freedom—and that government of the people, by the people, for the people shall not perish from the earth."

Two hours later we were on our way back to Vienna. The warm, almost hot sun had now burnt away the concealing mists and we had an excellent view of the scenes of farm activity through which we were passing. The people were at work, at hard work, men, women, and children; horses, cows, and dogs, harnessed and coupled together, were plowing and harrowing the long-neglected fields.

Before we reached Vienna, Smuts sent for me. He wished to set me straight as to the various versions of his talk with Kun which have appeared in the papers. "Unfortunately," he explained, "his first answer to my inquiries as to the course he meant to pursue was so offensive to our allies, the Roumanians, that I declined to receive it. My information is that the little man is at the end of his tether and my purpose was to facilitate his departure which cannot be long delayed. I came here with the impression that we have neglected the many and grave problems resulting from the collapse of the Dual Monarchy. As a result of my personal survey this impression has deepened into a strong conviction. In my talk with him it was clear that Masaryk also was of this opinion; he insisted that there should be no further delay in tackling problems too long neglected."

"Hearing nothing from Paris," Masaryk admitted, "I have been forced into entering into tentative negotiations as to our boundaries with the Reich through a German agent who is now in Prague."

After a moment's reflection, Smuts went on to say that further delay was unwise and would prove costly. "It is absolutely necessary for the

Supreme War Council to call a subconference to deal with the problems which we have inherited upon the demise of Austria. Where should it be convened? That also is quite a problem. If it is summoned to meet in any of the capitals of the Succession States that would not fail to provoke bickerings among the statesmen of the brand-new political creations. When I return to Paris I shall insist upon such a conference being called, and in my judgment it should sit in Paris."

We pulled into Vienna late in the afternoon. I separated from the mission and went to the hotel to enjoy a rest, of which I was in great need. In the morning I learned that Smuts had been called back to Paris; the tour to Belgrade and Bucharest had been abandoned. Now he was to delve into the baffling Irish problem. Perhaps Dublin was to be his next port of call and of course I immediately advised Paris of this sudden and radical change of plan.

When, on the following day, my instructions came, detaching me from the mission and instructing me to continue certain researches as a "lone wolf," I sought out General Smuts, but as I did not find him I saw no reasons why I should not tell the other members of the mission I met with that I was not returning to Paris with the general that evening. According to Thomson, this step provoked severe criticism from at least one of my colleagues, little Captain L'Hopital, one of Foch's socially ornamental aides, in distinction to his fighting aides, who represented France on the mission, and who burst out with, "I have heard of shirt-sleeve diplomacy as practiced across the Atlantic and now I see it. This is very discourteous to our general. The American commandant should return to Paris with General Smuts and then when released act according to his instructions."

To keep the record clear, I went after Smuts again, found him this time at the English Mission, and explained the point of etiquette that had been raised. He roared with laughter. "I approve of your course. I suppose I'm something of a shirt-sleeve diplomat myself. I think it would be absurd for you to go to Paris with me and then return." Then he said something about L'Hopital which I shall not repeat; it would not further cement the *entente cordiale*. "I give you my blessing and my thanks but on one condition. I, too, wish I could remain down here longer. We are just beginning to find things out, but the P.M. has wired me he wants me to meddle in the Irish business and after all that is nearer home. The condition I make on releasing you is that when you return to Paris you call on me and tell me what you have found out."

Vienna, April 4th.

There came for me today a telegram which put me back in diplomacy, even in secret diplomacy. And yet it was not in code, but open and aboveboard for anybody to read, and it ran:

If a complete set of Grillparzer's works, the 1872 edition, is available, secure an option and wire me the price.
Signed: HAROLD JOHNSON

I understood now why I had been detained in Vienna and detached from the Smuts mission. My instructions had nothing to do with the sale of the Viennese dramatic poet's works, and if, through a leak in the telegraph office, the Graben booksellers had run up their prices, they would have suffered a costly disappointment.

Before I left Paris, I had had a long talk with House and out of it had been arranged the enigmatic telegram which I had drawn up and now received. For some weeks the papers had been filled with rumors to the effect that the brand-new Austrian Republic had decided to throw in its lot with the Reich. These telegrams came from Berne or Basle, the starting points of so much misinformation. But, on the other hand, they might be trial balloons and probably were. As early as mid-January Clemenceau had spoken to the Colonel as to his anxiety on the subject, and he discussed the question again at some length with House on the day that I left Paris to join Smuts.

"I have instructed Allizé, our man in the Austrian capital, to urge upon Chancellor Renner not to tie up with Berlin—or, rather, Weimar. Certainly not before we take up with him the Austrian Treaty. He must remember that by the Armistice terms he is under political duress. And in view of the leisurely way we are proceeding with the German Treaty, the Austrian Treaty is hardly in sight. Allizé is not at all certain that his words have sunk in and he complains that he is getting no support from his Italian colleagues, who are so busy robbing the picture galleries that they have no time for matters of less import. "I think it would be helpful," concluded Clemenceau, "if you advise Renner to stand pat until he or his delegates come to Paris to discuss permanent arrangements."

House agreed. He, too, thought it more considerate to give a friendly word of caution in advance rather than an order later on to the Austrians to withdraw from a position which it was feared they might be induced by the many Berlin agents in Vienna to take up.

"If the President approves, I will do as you suggest," said House.

And the Grillparzer telegram showed that approval had come from Washington and I was to make an essay in shirt-sleeve diplomacy. I sent a request to the Presidency (Presidium) asking for an audience at eleven o'clock that morning. The answer came back promptly, and an hour later I presented myself at the Ballplatz. Karl Renner was a plain man, undistinguished in appearance. He had risen to his unenviable eminence in the hard way. He had been a printer, then a subeditor, and finally, by sheer merit and persistence, had become the editor in chief of the *Arbeiter Zeitung*. Unlike Bauer and several of his more brilliant colleagues, Renner wrote but little; he contented himself with executive supervision of the paper and in keeping his eyes on the Kassa.

I gave my message as briefly as I could. For a moment he was silent, and then he began to speak, slowly.

"It is unfortunate," he said, "this message has reached me so late, but I hope not too late. Botho Wedel, the German Minister, has just left me and what I told him he is even now wiring to his government. It was that we would join with the Reich. I was quite frank with him and I told him that we were doing it without any enthusiasm; I made it quite plain that the lessons derived from our relations during the war were too fresh in our memories for that. What else was I to do?" Renner inquired of me. I could see no *ausweg*, no other way out. He left me an hour ago, and I told him that I would submit his proposal to the Council in the morning and that I hoped that our alliance would be more successful in organizing the Peace than it had been in winning the war.

"Of course this expression of opinion, this word of advice from the American delegation will carry great weight with us; it will certainly reawaken the doubts that were expressed in our last council, but—what can you offer in the way of assistance? We know that we cannot stand alone. Austria-Hungary has been dismembered, not by the Allies, but by the action of the little nations who formed the Empire. Now, what can you offer us?"

I told Renner frankly that I could offer him nothing, that I had complied with my instructions and that it would be unwise for me, and anything but helpful to him, if I exceeded them. I did suggest that it might be proper for him to recall that America had shown great reluctance in declaring war on the Austrian Empire.

"We refrained from doing so until we were forced by the course of events. There is a reservoir of great good will for your people in America. Practical evidence of this is the relief program now under way, of which you spoke with so much appreciation when I first came to Vienna. It will be continued; we will do all we can for the people who, as we believe, without being consulted, were trapped into the war and who are now its most-to-be-pitied victims."

Poor Renner paced up and down the apartment and then with a sigh returned to the ornate desk at which had sat Metternich and so many of his princely predecessors. Then he straightened himself up and said resolutely:

"I do not know how we can manage it. I shall, of course, have to confer with my colleagues, but you can tell Colonel House that somehow and in some way as yet unexplored we shall follow his advice."

An hour later I sent my telegram: the desired edition of Grillparzer was available at a fair price, and it meant that at least for the time being the *Anschluss* was postponed. There would be no immediate action, and that indeed was all we asked for.

This was the only occasion on which I saw Renner seated at the desk where Metternich spun his alliances or where in my own day I had so often fenced with Graf Kalnoky about the Balkan situation or, and this was more to his liking, gossiped about the coming horse races in the Freudenau. For reasons that I could understand, and approved of, Renner preferred to confer with me at my hotel. The beautiful desk of Metternich I thought rather turned up its nose at its new occupant. There were, moreover, other notable changes in the furniture of the historic salon. The busts of Kaunitz and the other famous chancellors of the Austro-Hungarian monarchy which had looked down upon the inquiring correspondent from America, as recently as 1915 when I here interviewed de Burian on the prospects of war or of peace, had been removed. And that was wise; they certainly had no place in this new *galère!*

Vienna, April—undated.

"Would you like to talk to Paris?" said young Captain Clapp to me the other day.

"I should say I would," was my answer, "but, of course, it is impossible." (Telegrams were greatly delayed and letters rarely reached me and always many days old. Lacking definite instructions, I was in something of a quandary.) Clapp is a telephone expert attached to the Hoover organization and, as it turned out, something of a miracle worker.

"Nothing is easier," explained young Clapp. "We have a perfect connection with Paris via Cologne. I established it some ten days ago, but we have to be very secretive about it because if it were known the authorities 'here or there' might take it into their heads to interrupt it. We are working entirely through subordinates, telephone men like myself, and we are in agreement to send no military information."

That was not a handicap for me. I had no military information to send. Within twenty minutes I was talking to House at the Crillon and our conversation was as clear as if I had been talking from Versailles. This system of clandestine grapevine communication was a great resource to me in the following days and I hope it did not prove too great a nuisance to the Colonel.

Vienna, April 9th.

Evidently the wires are crossed between Archibald Coolidge, of the Enquiry, and the delegation in Paris, and doubtless this is one of the reasons why I am detained here. Coolidge says, in his indignation, that a letter to Santa Claus has a better chance of being answered than an inquiry sent to the delegation! The Peace Commissioners come back with the statement that if you ask Coolidge for facts to aid in an appreciation of the actual situation, he replies with a learned disquisition on the Pragmatic Sanction. He is a learned man, but *muy pesado*, as the Spaniards have it. And he is living in the eighteenth century.

On the other hand, Professor Brown, in Budapest, is regarded as a "pink," by some even as a Bolshevik, because he pays some attention to the Bela Kun movement in Hungary. I have had an opportunity to read some of Brown's dispatches, and they are excellent. The highhanded proceedings of the territorial lords and magnates share with Moscow responsibility for the anarchy that prevails on the Hungarian plain. Most of the agents down there, diplomatic and otherwise, are greatly handicapped by the fact that all wire communications are interrupted. Thanks, however, to the Hoover organization and the diplomatic as well as mechanical ability of their telephone expert, Captain Clapp, I now talk to my colonel in the Crillon whenever I want to. It is difficult to maintain, but I am sworn to secrecy, for if this surreptitious means of communication were even suspected, a way undoubtedly would be found to interrupt it.

Vienna, Tuesday.

To escape the hospital smell that pervaded the Bristol, I went to the opera last evening. I was in uniform, and when I presented myself at the ticket window they were opposed to taking my money. "Soldiers, officials, do not pay," quavered a voice through the little window, but I insisted. I was hardly settled in my stall and was gazing up at the fourth or fifth gallery which was where I sat in my student days, when I was suddenly surrounded by what seemed the whole management. There they were crowding my neighbors, bowing and scraping.

"It was *unerhört*," they asserted. "I must occupy a box—otherwise they would die of shame." To be sure, as they admitted, the imperial box was crowded; there, where Franz Josef had so often snoozed throughout the performances, was a badly dressed flock of civil servants of the new government and their ladies. But we have an arch-ducal box we would most gladly place at your disposal. "*Euer Gnaden*, come! Do us this favor. No, no! *Euer Gnaden!* here you must not sit." Say it they did not, but in gestures they pointed with contempt to the fairly common herd by whom I was surrounded. But I wouldn't move. In Berlin, of course, I could be arrogant and assertive, but not in my dear Vienna. Just because I was in uniform, a temporary officer and a make-believe conqueror, I would not even seem to crack the whip. I would sit with my friends, the good, the *gemütliches Volk* of the Kaiser-stadt. At last the management withdrew and my neighbors beamed on me. I sat with them because in other years I had shared their joys and some of their sorrows, too. I had lived with them as a corps student with *Bummler aufgesetzt*. In 1915 I had driven many great nails in the Wehrmann in Eisen out on the Schwarzenberg Platz in the hope that by its forbidding mien and some mystic quality it would defend these *liebe Leute* from their war allies of the north, and if I was only a Wiener *Kind* by adoption I was the father of a real authentic child of the Kaiser-stadt because my second son had come to us one happy day in the Pelikangasse.

So I sat with the dear plain people who in former years had perched up in the highest gallery just as I did. As my thoughts were far away, in time at least, if not in space, it is perhaps not strange that I do not remember the opera and now only twenty-four hours later I cannot recall its name. It was, to be sure, a sad spectacle, and as the *tenore robusto* tottered across the stage I noticed how shrunken were his shanks, how feeble his voice. But truth to tell, I peopled the stage and the boxes with figures that have for the most part vanished from the scene. There I used to see Princess Pauline graciously giving to Count Hübner her hand to be kissed, the favorite of Metternich and perhaps the first of the old-school diplomats who had circumnavigated the world on his grand tour. There swaggered Count Kalnoky and here passed Taaffe with his soft, gliding step. And on the stage I saw Cerale and Fräulein Abel pulsating with life, resplendent in beauty, and yet now they are as dead as Maria Theresa, and Josef and Kaunitz and the King of Rome!

Wednesday.

Vienna, always a cave of the winds, with every breeze bearing upon it a fantastic rumor (such certainly was my experience here in my days as a correspondent), is even surpassing itself in this respect now. I shall make a brief record of the news that reaches me from many quarters, but I begin with one that is certainly not fantastic. Here it is in black and white in all the official newspapers. This one explains perhaps why the authorities are so desirous for me to live in one of the palaces and so protect it with our flag. The decree reads:

"All palaces, castles, and country houses with the adjacent buildings are to be taken possession of by the State to house the invalids, the sick, and all others who are without shelter. The up-to-now owners must turn their property over to the State without indemnity; the farm lands attached to these properties will be taken possession of when they are needed. In such cases (that of the farm lands) an appropriate indemnity will be paid. For the period of twelve months the previous occupants of these residences may continue to live in them, but they may only occupy the space absolutely necessary to shelter their families. From this date, none of these properties can be offered for sale or have existing mortgages increased."

Even the *Neue Freie Presse*, which since the revolution has piped down and can hardly be recognized as the organ of the bankers, is outraged by this plan, which it says infringes upon all law and equity. "The seizure of property without indemnity," it writes, "destroys the fundamentals of our civilization."

A few hours after this bombshell was exploded, I came across my old friend Fuchs, long the most active editor of the paper; he was seated on a bench out on the Ring just opposite the Stadt-Park.

"I am writing my editorial out here," he explained, "because the office is in turmoil and our printers have taken possession of the editorial rooms and are about to proclaim a soviet."

The publication of these decrees, expropriating private property, seemed to indicate that the radical wing of the Social Democrats is getting the upper hand and calls attention to a possible development of the Austrian situation which not a few have regarded for some weeks now as a probability. The Reds are now in control in Budapest and in much of Russia, and they also seem to be sweeping all resistance before them in the Ukraine—that vast reservoir of men and of greatly needed food. Should the Bolsheviks join up with the troops of Bela Kun and threaten Vienna, that would entail a campaign in eastern Europe for which hundreds of thousands of troops would be required. Many people are asking me what the Allies would do in these circumstances, and indeed Renner put the question to me this afternoon, and my answer was I did not know, but hoped that they would act intelligently. Naturally, he finds my answer unsatisfactory and unsatisfactory it is. It is true, of course, that a few days after the Armistice Foch proposed that we send a hundred thousand men to Moscow to "clean up," but his proposal fell on deaf ears. No one was in favor of another campaign, everybody wanted to be demobilized and go home.

Vienna, Thursday.

The papers here are filled, you might even say ablaze, today, with contradictory reports from western Europe in regard to the proposed war indemnities. Lloyd George is reported as saying that Germany must pay the full amount of war damage, even if it takes fifty years to do so. Wilson is reported as not backing him up very strongly. He thinks the Allies should be content with getting the money to replace what has been actually destroyed, and no more—reparation payments but no indemnities. Also, under unusually striking headlines the papers publish a report which they ascribe to Havas. This runs:

"Yesterday the budget committee of the French Chamber reached a unanimous report on the actual financial situation and the immediate prospects, and sent it on to Clemenceau. It reads: 'It is now clear that the financial burden of the French people will reach twenty-two milliards of francs annually, in which sum pensions for widows, the invalids of war, and also for civilians who have been crippled, are included. In the light of these figures, it is an elementary and a just demand that the enemy should be made to pay war burdens as well as damages, with priority being given to the bill for replacing what human values have been destroyed or impaired. The sums that will be required for this purpose should not be estimated on present capacity to pay; the future ability to pay, after financial recuperation, should be carefully weighed.' "

These reports have created consternation and some rather unusual expressions of sympathy for those whom the Viennese persistently call "the Germans of the north." "From our carcase they will get nothing," said Renner to me today; "perhaps a few feathers; and if they ask too much of Germany, they will kill the goose that might, with coddling, be induced to lay a few, a very few, golden eggs. But the end of Austria is in sight; the time has come to write *Finis Austriae*. No wrong or insult is being spared us. The Italians are taking from our public galleries and private collections pictures and works of art which belong to us as much as does the tower of St. Stephen's Cathedral. The Czechs are on the march and they have reached the Danube; some of their advanced posts are in Lower Austria; the Roumanians are devastating Hungary; the South Slavs are not lagging behind, they are within a few miles of Graz. I try to keep an open mind on the veto of the *Anschluss* which you brought me, but in my heart I feel that the Allies are acting in a very shortsighted manner. I am not blind to the consideration that weighs heavily with them. They feel, and feel very keenly, that the defeated Germans should not emerge from the war with an increase of territory and a greater population. I suppose they would not deign to read German history, but if they did, they could learn that, not so long ago, Louis Napoleon sent an ambassador to Nikolsburg to prevent the union of the northern and southern Germans; and that this ill-advised step led to Sedan. That they would see if they were not blind. I seem to remember that in one of the classics it is written that those whom the gods mean to destroy are first made mad." For the first time Renner was bitter.

These press rumors brought Botho Wedel, the German Minister, into action. He was now back from Berlin. He sent for an editor of the *Neue Freie Presse* and, expressing great indignation, asked that the following statement be printed: (This is on the authority of Fuchs.)

"Our delegation has been invited to appear in Paris on April the 25th to receive the Allied terms. I hope then we shall get some light on the future, but even now our position is clear. I cannot see how anyone should be uncertain about it. In accordance with the offer of the Allies, we accepted a preliminary peace on the basis of the Fourteen Points. This agreement we shall carry out, although in view of our losses and the distress prevailing among our people before and since the Armistice it will be difficult for us to live up to a peace settlement, even on the Wilson terms. Certainly we cannot do more, and I am confident we shall refuse to attempt it. No honest man would sign a promise to pay which he knows it is quite impossible for him to fulfill. We are all of one mind on this point, the Government, the National Assembly, and Das Volk. We have a proverb which runs: 'Where nothing remains, not even the Kaiser can collect,' and that, of course, applies to the presidents of a republic in a similar unhappy plight. Undoubtedly my people would even prefer a continuance of the anarchic conditions with which we are confronted, than to sign a treaty which would surely destroy Germany and make of us and our descendants slaves. No sane man would sign his own death warrant, and anyone who thinks we shall, has lost his sense of reality."

Friday, April.

M. Allizé (the French agent), who is always urging, at least unofficially, the union of Austria with Bavaria, handed in a note to Dr. Bauer, secretary of the Government for Foreign Affairs, yesterday, in which he broached a new topic, and also revealed the anxiety, which so many feel, that the present government here is turning very rapidly to the Left. He said:

"France, like the other Allies, is seeking to send food here for the distressed population; hitherto this has been scanty because with us at home very little food is available, and the difficulties of transport are great. Now, however, as the outlook is more promising, we have entered into negotiations with the proper authorities and are hopeful of being able to route food trains over Switzerland."

Then he concludes with a word of warning:

"All these efforts, however, will be arrested unless we receive assurances that law and order throughout Austria can be maintained; there must be no political interference with the distribution of food."

Saturday, April.

A man who knows history and recalls it, as so few of us do, wrote interestingly yesterday in the *Frankfurter Zeitung* about the flight of Emperor Karl:

"This is indeed poetic justice," he writes. "For hundreds of years the House of Austria sought to destroy the independence of the Swiss Confederation and the rights of free men. Had it succeeded, the Swiss would have become lieges of Austria and today they could not have offered a refuge to the last of the Hapsburgs, now landless and forlorn. Had the Swiss not driven out this family five hundred years ago, and by so doing preserved their independence, they could not be offering, as they are doing today, safe refuge and asylum to the last of this unhappy line. Today the Hapsburgs are flocking for safety to their home country they sought to enslave. They come as aliens to their old home, but, like all refugees from oppression, they are eligible to citizenship if they demonstrate that they have the proper qualifications for this honor and are alive to the responsibilities that go with it."

☆   ☆   ☆

This afternoon Dr. Lodgmann, Landes-Hauptman of German Bohemia, as rightly or wrongly he styles himself, came in with four or five of his indignant followers. He accused Masaryk of double-dealing, of disseminating misleading information, and indeed of many other and even more terrible things. He is especially outraged by a report in the Viennese papers that the new President (in Prague) proposes to give the Germans (of Bohemia) complete autonomy. "This news comes from Berne and we do not think much of news from Berne. Masaryk will never let us vote on the question as to whether we would like to join up with German Austria or remain with the Czechs as a self-governing state. He is simply trying to mislead the conference in Paris. If the powers really want peace, and I try to think that they do, they must take into consideration our situation, and they should remember that neither the people in Prague nor the delegates in Paris can determine our future; that is in our hands; there is no possibility of *Gemeinschaft* or even federation with the Czechs, and they are entirely responsible for this strong and universal lack of sympathy. If they should wish to put it to the test, we do not shun an election, but of course such an election would have to be held under non-partisan, international control."

An hour later came a delegation of the German citizens of Reichenberg. They are greatly excited as to the purpose of the Smuts visit to Prague. They think he wanted to urge Masaryk to send Czech troops into Hungary, and they sought to find out what I knew on the subject; this was easy. Officially I knew absolutely nothing; personally, I knew next to nothing.

They then placed before me a manifesto or a petition signed by five or six members of what they call the Provisional Government of

German Bohemia; among them was the name of the famous Dr. Herold. The petition was addressed to President Wilson and read:

"Hearing through the European press that the German populations of Bohemia, Moravia, and German Silesia are to be denied the right of self-determination, we, members of the Peoples' and of the Socialist parties, called upon to rule provisionally our communities, draw your attention to the injustice of this decision and request that our representatives may be admitted to the Peace Conference. If it is decided to hold a plebiscite, and that is what the ends of justice demand, we hope that you will insist that the vote be taken under the control of the Allied and Associated Powers. In no other way could a fair election be held. We do not hesitate to say that in case this step is not taken, there is grave danger to the peace of Europe. Three and a half million Germans will never submit to the alien rule that the Czechoslovaks are seeking to impose."

I accepted both of these statements[4] and promised to send them on to Paris by a courier who was passing through Vienna on the following day, but I urged them to also send formal copies to the secretary general of the Peace Conference, M. Dutasta. Many here are of the opinion, and among these are the members of our Food Administration, that Botho Wedel, the German Minister, is very active in stirring up these complaints. It is evident, however, that there is rough going ahead for Masaryk. How these people hate one another—talk of the Kilkenny cats!

[4](1932) So far as I know, this was the only public reference to the Sudeten problem at this time and for months later. The Germans of this hill country did not formally approach the Conference, and I am not aware that they attempted to do so. As a matter of fact, a fact that is so often lost sight of, they never had belonged to Germany and most of them settled in the Bohemian hills in the hope of escaping German rule. Renner was not the only man in touch with the Sudeten people who thought that the present was a most inopportune moment for them to join with the Reich Germans suffering deserved hardships, and perhaps some undeserved. It was not until the year 1930, when the world economic depression bore down upon them more heavily than upon the agricultural Czechs, that the Sudeten people gave ear to the propaganda that came to them from Munich and Berlin—with what effect all the world knows. While the Sudeten might have been more wisely treated, as some maintain, it is certain that no minority in Europe during these troubled years enjoyed such considerate and kindly treatment as they did. It is frequently asserted that President Masaryk was opposed to taking over the Sudeten and also averse to bringing into his republic the Carpathian Ruthenians of Russinia, as I think we called this mountain land at the time. These statements, however, are without any foundation in fact, at least as regards the Sudeten, as my talk with the President in Prague fully demonstrated. While he never broached the subject, at least not to me, I do think he was far from eager to annex Russinia. But nobody wanted this poverty-stricken province at the time, except Hungary, and no one wanted to enlarge the territory of what had been the misruled kingdom of St. Stephen.

Chancellor Renner, who, owing to the illness of Dr. Bauer, is also acting as Minister of Foreign Affairs, took me yesterday to visit the Burg, and though I suspected from the first that behind the courteous gesture there was a plan, perhaps a deep-laid plan, I was glad to go. I visited Francis Joseph's apartment. I saw that, as the tradition had it, there was no water laid on. I scrutinized his *Gummi* portable bathtub and saw that now it was full of holes. The starving mice that had formerly lived on the fat tidbits that fell from the imperial table, reduced to starving rations like all living things in the Danube capital, were gnawing on it. I sat in the window from which in 1904 I had seen the old Emperor presenting his grandson, little Karl, to the loyal populace. The old Emperor had smiled his empty, vacant smile and the people had shouted: "What a magnificent *Buberl* he is." Now the Emperor is moldering in the vaults of the Capuchin church and little Karl is a refugee in Switzerland. Wild-eyed people were pushing their way through the dark and dismal corridors and the few guards in evidence did but little to control their curiosity. And then Renner developed his plan.

"You would be more comfortable here than at the Bristol," he suggested, "and you would be better protected. Wild people from all over the monarchy are streaming into the starving city, and a man who is well dressed and well fed, who looks as though he had foreign *valuta* in his pocket, is far from safe. But if you moved here and raised your flag over the Burg you would be perfectly safe and you would protect the palace from the roving bands of hoodlums who may at any moment get out of hand."

I expressed my appreciation of the invitation but declined it. It would never do for a democrat with no heraldic quarterings to take up his abode where once the Caesars of the Holy Roman Empire had lodged. Besides, I had no flag except the little pennant which I flew from my car when I was fortunate enough to have one. That would look ridiculous flying from this great edifice with its hundreds of deserted, unswept, and smelly rooms. . . . Renner then very good-naturedly dropped the subject.

As to the contacts which General Smuts may or may not have had with Herr Renner before he returned to Paris, I have little or no information. In one of our talks Herr Renner said: "*Ich bin mit ihm nur flüchtig in beruhrung gekommen* [My contact with him was only of a superficial character]." Evidently nothing very satisfactory had resulted from the conversations that may have taken place—which are reported at great length in all the sensational papers.

I made a pilgrimage this morning to the imperial vaults under the Capuchin church where all, or nearly all, the Hapsburgs, with their secrets, their sorrows, their benefactions, and alas, as I also fear, their crimes, have been laid away. The aged monk who opened the postern gate to my knock seemed not a little nervous at the sight of my uniform, but after I dropped a silver coin in the little leather bag for contributions which he carried, he lit a great beeswax candle and led me through the purple twilight of the great cellar. I stood by the leaden coffin of Francis Joseph, whom I had seen as an act of penitence washing the feet of the selected beggars on Maundy Thursday, years ago. I tarried for a moment by the smaller leaden sarcophagus that contains all that was mortal of the beautiful Empress Elizabeth—she whom I had first seen in my boyhood as alone and unattended she walked through the garden of the Hofburg. What a noble bearing she had and what a carriage! To me she appeared as a goddess descended from on high, and in the words of Aeneas I hailed the beautiful vision as that of a *Dea certe!* What a strange life was hers and what a strange ending! Her troubled, tumultuous heart was pierced by a stiletto in the hand of a crazy anarchist, and those who saw the weapon say that it looked no more formidable than a hatpin— and yet it sufficed. At her side rests her unfortunate son, Rudolph, the hero, or the victim, of the mystery of Mayerling where he died. Ten weeks after the tragic event I came from Turkey to investigate the mystery that so intrigued the world. How Rudolph met his end I do not know, and I do not think the world will ever know. The official stories, as well as those put out by the Empress Eugénie, who had also lost an only son in the heyday of life, as well as the doubtless sincere gossip of Käthi Schradt, the Emperor's dearest friend, were invented with the natural purpose of misleading a morbid world. Someday, perhaps, I shall set forth the reasons why I do not think the Archduke shot himself after killing his mistress. They are, I admit, not entirely convincing. Of all the royal mysteries, that of Mayerling remains unsolved, and is likely to remain so.

With some show of emotion the monk now led me to the little vacant space, all that now remains unoccupied in this centuries-old charnel house. He lifted his eyes to the roof of the dark vault and said:

"Who will occupy?"

I had no answer; no one knows, and perhaps the leaden coffins will all disappear in the next whirlwind of war. Even in 1917, I am told, the suggestion was made by the editor of a fugitive Communist sheet that they be melted down into bullets to kill the oppressors who ride roughshod over the proletarian world.

As I turned to leave, I caught sight of my old friend of the Balkan days, René Pinon, now for many years the lynx-eyed observer of the European scene for the *Revue des Deux Mondes*. He had been kneeling in prayer, and as we walked out together he brushed the dust of the ages from his trouser knees. I think I understood his thought which, however, he did not voice. He was a loyal and patriotic Frenchman and he was happy that France had survived the world catastrophe that for four long years had menaced her; but he was also a true son of the Church, and a Rightist. There was moisture in his eye as he greeted me and surveyed the uniform I now wore as a pawn in the crusade to make the world safe for democracy. I do not think he mourned the fall of the Hapsburg emperors, but he did regret the disappearance of the great Catholic power which as recently as 1903 had exercised its traditional veto and prevented Cardinal Rampolla, suspected of being tainted by a touch of modernity, from becoming the successor to St. Peter.

Vienna, Tuesday.

I dined tonight with Admiral Höhnel; General Margutti was also his guest, but how different were the circumstances and the temper of the party from that evening in March 1915 when they dined with me at the Bristol. Then the Russians were being driven back over the Carpathians, according to War Office reports, and the war would be over in a few weeks! Now the war was over, and the government that had displaced the Empire had told them that as they had both been appointed to their respective services from Trieste, now annexed to Italy, they had better apply to Rome for their pensions. Höhnel was living on the sale of his stamp collection and the general, I understood, was living very much from hand to mouth.

For seventeen years Margutti had been the personal aide and adjutant to the Emperor Francis Joseph, and certainly no one was closer to him and deeper in his confidence than he. Naturally in these circumstances I gave a wide berth to war topics, but Margutti was not to be denied; with him the responsibility for the war was an obsession. Every few minutes he insisted: "I live over and over again every day those tragic hours when the ultimatum to Belgrade was

being fashioned. Even then all might have been well. The Emperor
knew that Francis Ferdinand could not have been brought to life
again. That was not a practical demand on the Serbians and he was
asking himself why thousands should die to avenge him? That was
the thought of my imperial master, and I was hopeful that with a
little good will in Belgrade peace could be preserved. Then, however,
almost daily the telephone would ring and Budapest was on the wire,
the Chancellery of the Minister President, and I was told that Count
Tisza had started for Vienna on a special train, that he had matters of
vital importance to lay before the Emperor-King and that I should
arrange an audience. I did arrange it in the great study, and I was
present at it, as I was expected to be, but of course, as was proper, I
kept my distance. While Count Tisza spoke in a loud voice, in a voice
that was unseemly and with an emphasis that shocked me, I could not
understand, I could not gather the meaning of his words, but the
import of his coming was clear. He wanted war! In all the years I had
served His Majesty no one had ever addressed him in such outrageous
tones. At times he bellowed, and the condescension of my imperial
master in trying to calm him was of but little avail. The Emperor was
visibly affected and was very upset after the Count left, but he said
nothing, keeping his own counsel and bearing his own heavy burdens
—as was his custom. It was Tisza who drove us into war," concluded
Margutti. "May God forgive him—I cannot!"

Truly a wonderful inside story of undoubted authenticity, and had
I been in my usual and normal role of a news correspondent a very
few minutes would have elapsed before I had placed it on the wire—
and what a world sensation would have resulted and from what an
unimpeachable source! But now I was dealing with the aftermath of
the great catastrophe and this, the true story though it was of its
initiation and origin, could wait.

I waited, meaning perhaps only to make a verbal report upon my
return to Paris, and how fortunate it was that I did. Within a few
days, under orders from Bauer and Renner, competent historians
explored the secret archives, and among the many illuminating dis-
closures was one in regard to these interviews in which Count Tisza
had presumed to raise his voice. His tempestuous words had been a
plea *not* to enter a war which was unnecessary and one in which, in
his judgment, whoever won Austria-Hungary would be the loser.
Further, a memorandum was brought to light in which Tisza had
marshaled all his very cogent arguments against the Serbian adventure.

Tisza was murdered in the presence of his wife by a group of cowardly soldiers who made him responsible for all their sufferings. And yet in killing him they wreaked their vengeance on the man of all others who was least responsible for the hostilities, although when the battle was engaged he, too, fought stubbornly. The incident has given me a realizing sense of the dangers of special cabled correspondence even when the most authentic sources are tapped. Those (Ambassadors and Ministers and such) whose dispatches are filed away in the secret archives have much the best of it. They do not come to light for years, and by that time no one cares—truth or fiction? "*Es ist alles eins,*" as they say in Viennese.

April.

Today, alone, I again visited the Burg Palace. All the great figures who in their little day had strutted across this scene, the aged Francis Joseph, the beautiful Elizabeth, the luckless Rudolph of the Mayerling mystery, have vanished now, and the millennial empire of the Hapsburgs lies in squalid ruins. But there was one in the hungry crowd who recalled the well-fed days. He was tattered and torn, but from his manner it was evident that in the happier days he had been a palace lackey and his thoughts ran to food.

"The Kaiser sat him down to lunch," he said, "and what they brought did not appeal to his appetite. 'I crave,' he said, 'a slice of salmon.' There was a hurried conference and then, greatly embarrassed and chagrined, the major-domo said, '*Majestät,* there is no salmon today!'

" 'Let us see your diet books,' remonstrated the Kaiser. They were brought, and then, 'I see you bought sixty kilos of salmon yesterday,' said the Kaiser. 'Is it all gone?' 'All gone,' bleated the major-domo. 'Well, for tomorrow order seventy kilos so that the Kaiser may have a *stückl*—a little piece.' "

"Seventy kilos of salmon," the famished mob that had invaded the Burg kept repeating as they wandered through the damp and dreary salons where in other days these great feasts had been spread and now were spread no more.

Vienna, April.

In the following days Herr Renner called upon me several times at the Bristol. It was evident he wished to discuss further the *Anschluss,* but as I had delivered my message and had no further instructions I kept off the subject. Our purpose had been achieved, at least for the present, and Allizé, the French agent, told me that, in high dudgeon, the German Minister, Botho Wedel, had gone back to Berlin. The secondary purpose of his visits was to renew his plea and to induce me to take up my residence in the Hofburg, but I was not tempted. He evidently feared that some of the mobs and the riotous demonstrations that emerge almost every day from the working quarters of the city would brush aside the few police who were guarding it and set the old palace, from which the Hapsburgs now have fled, on fire. My presence and the American flag would safeguard the edifice, but I declined the opportunity to dwell in the abode of emperors and kings and remained in my democratic quarters at the hotel.

But on other matters I liked to talk with Renner. He was, in my judgment, the most intelligent of the Austrian postwar leaders. I found him surprisingly fair to his political opponents. Like all the other actors in the tragic days, he was inclined to talk about the lost opportunities for peace and to point out who was responsible for losing them. Of Count Czernin's activities he took a very lenient view. It is so different from the popular, the almost universal judgment of the "sporting" Minister of Foreign Affairs that it seems to me worthy of record.

"Czernin went halfway toward a separate peace and then stopped midstream and all unite in blaming him, but the blame should be placed squarely on the shoulders of his predecessors—where it belongs," said Renner.

"Ballplatz had excellent information about the Balkan situation but did not act upon it. There was the report of the Markgraf Pallavicini, our Ambassador in Constantinople in 1913.[5] This able man had spent his whole life in the Balkans and he was as familiar with its currents and its crosscurrents as he was with the lines in the palm of his hand. Well, months before the war came he wrote officially to his chief that the monarchy was headed for war and if it was the desire in Vienna to avoid it there was only one way and that was to give Russia a free hand and to abandon the *drang nach Osten*. This report has since vanished from the archives but I have talked with many, and very responsible people they are, who read it. Curiously enough, it is also a matter of record that the report was turned over to the Archduke

[5]I was particularly interested in this statement. I had known Pallavicini in the days of King Milan in Belgrade when the "Pig war" broke, that harbinger of the great disaster.

Francis Ferdinand for his examination only a few days before he went to Sarajevo and met with his tragic end. . . .

"Now about Czernin being blamed for stopping midstream—for not driving on with his plan of a separate peace with the Western Powers, I do not think this is quite fair. Obviously his idea was to intimidate Berlin, to make Ludendorff and those madmen see that Austria was finished, and also that without Austria, Germany was lost. It didn't work, and we stayed on to the end. Now let us see what would have happened had Czernin pulled out of the war. Well, right off the Germans would have overpowered Austria before any assistance could have reached us from the Entente. Long before the Allied armies could have put in an appearance in Bavaria or Bohemia, as was planned, or rather hoped, we would have been snug in the Prussian military straitjacket. As a matter of fact, throughout the war the Germans had a large force in and around Vienna, and when they began to suspect that Czernin wanted to quit, they moved many divisions of second-line troops into the Tyrol to prepare for all possible contingencies. In the end Germany would have been defeated and she would have been compelled to hoist the white flag, as she did in October 1918. The war might have been ended perhaps a month or two sooner if Czernin had had his way, but the price? Austria and Bohemia would have been devastated, as Belgium and northern France and Serbia had been. Not even the Czechs would have liked that. As a matter of fact, I think Czernin was wise to desist from his project when he did. The evil wind was sown when his predecessors ignored the storm signals. Infelix, not Felix Austria, was to meet the whirlwind these old men had sown, and her complete destruction was inevitable."

When he came to speak of the greatest of the lost opportunities for peace, Renner's thoughts centered around the International Socialist Congress in July 1917, in Stockholm, and he admitted that responsibility for failure rested squarely on the shoulders of some of the Social Democrats.

"Czernin was not hopeful, but he helped us as much as he could and he also persuaded Tisza to give the Hungarian delegates passports that permitted them to reach Sweden but, alas! we came there empty-handed. We were forced to admit that the monarchy could not give up Trieste. Tisza said he would deserve to be shot if he gave up Transylvania and not merely the people in power in Berlin, but the very German Socialist delegates announced that they regarded Alsace-Lorraine as a German province and that German it must remain.

Would they consent to a plebiscite? Most definitely they would not. How wise Vandervelde was in speaking for his devastated Fatherland, when he said: 'What chance can there be for international action to further the peace movement when the German Socialist party remains silent in the face of the crimes of the German Army and excuses the barbarities of submarine warfare?'

"I and my colleagues went to the Congress in good faith but very soon we saw that it was a plan to trap us all into a Hohenzollern peace. Soon I doubted even the good faith of the Dutch Socialists who had called the Congress. They went to Berlin and conferred there with Zimmerman too often. How Branting, an honest man and a convinced Socialist, could ever have been induced to preside, I have no idea. Doubtless he was hoodwinked like the rest of us."

"I gather then," I said, "that you are of the opinion that the Socialist delegates to the International Congress for Peace were as far apart and no more open to reason than were the militants of the predatory powers?"

"I am afraid that is so," admitted Renner sadly. An admission which I think should be recorded for the guidance of generations to come who may in their time be involved in the horrors of a world war.

"What do you think of Mr. Wilson's leadership in Paris?" I inquired. Renner shook his head sadly. "I am not so sure of his leadership," he answered. "Your President might have imposed his program on the predatory powers in 1917, but today I doubt it."

"I see some of your papers suggest that our President wash his hands of Europe and go home to happy America. What do you think of that suggestion?"

"I think nothing of it," replied Renner. "Wilson will not get what he wants, the wild animals of many countries are on the rampage now, but he must stick to his guns and make the best peace he can. If not, the law of the jungle will reign in Europe."

Vienna, April.

A report of German plotting in Belgrade forwarded by our delegation in Paris reached me yesterday. It came without an expression of belief or skepticism, merely registering a rumor to the effect that German agents in Yugoslavia, particularly in Croatia, are planning to supplant the pro-ally, Regent Alexander, by his elder brother, Prince George. For some months now, as was well known, George had been under restraint, practically under arrest, in a country house near Nish.

Apparently the young man[6] is quite mad and after he had, in an outburst of passion, murdered one of his aides, he was placed in the safe seclusion out of which it is feared that the Germans are trying to entice him for some dark purpose.

I did not have much confidence in the yarn and yet as the Germans were very active in making trouble in Vienna, they might well be doing their stuff in the White City on the Save also. While I was deliberating what to do, "Jimmy" Logan, formerly of the Army and now in charge of the Food Administration in southeastern Europe, came in. He was leaving for Serbia in the morning with a train laden with supplies and medical stores for the typhus-stricken Serbs. Would I go with him? And I accepted even before he told me that he would have a private car and the right of way. I concluded it would be interesting, though depressing, to see Belgrade again, although now in ruins, and I would have an opportunity to smoke out the Prince George story. In any event, I would escape the importunities of the new government and the great lords who, almost on bended knees, were beseeching me to take up residence in their palaces and hoist over them our protective flag.

Certainly we traveled in luxury and comfort that far surpassed anything that had been provided for the mission of the Right Honorable Lieutenant General Jan Christiaan Smuts, and now there were only two of us to loll about in the private car. It was decorated with the Hapsburg arms and other reminders of the great tribe that had ruled for so many centuries over what had been until quite recently Felix Austria. And on the panels there were several reproductions of the famous Ville d'Este near Rome.

"I forgot to tell you," explained Logan, "this is, or rather was, the private car of the Archduke Francis Ferdinand, who in some way was descended from Beatrice d'Este, or Isabella, her also famous sister. In that historic villa near Rome he spent his honeymoon, and it was in this car that with his lady he traveled to the shambles at Sarajevo. In our little sitting room their coffins were placed side by side on trestles on the journey that brought them back to Vienna. The Austrian railway people think the car is haunted, or at least unlucky, and

---

[6]The rumor that came from Berne to our delegation in Paris was to the effect that an attempt was about to be made to place the elder and probably insane brother of Prince Regent Alexander on the throne and that discontented Croatian as well as foreign groups were behind it. If successful, it was hoped that the conspiracy would give the Belgrade Government an entirely new orientation. There was, as it turned out, no foundation to the story beyond the fact that Prince George was insane and was being held under proper and most necessary restraint.

they were very glad to turn it over to the Food Administration. We find it most useful in transporting medical supplies and the less bulky foods to where they are needed. Odd, isn't it? The car that carried that unlucky pair to their death, to where the avalanche of war and all its attending horrors started, helps us to alleviate some of the suffering and the epidemics that have followed in its train. Poetic justice, don't you think so?"

We traveled all day through a beautiful country, very different from the monotonous, if fertile, plains of Hungary over which I had traveled so often before on my journeys to Serbia and to Turkey beyond. With Bela Kun and his Communist cohorts controlling Budapest, the Magyar capital is boycotted by all the railways and there is some justification for this attitude. Logan tells me that the Smuts train is the only one that put into Budapest during the last two months and escaped confiscation at the hands of the Soviet!

The country we traveled through was not only new to me, it was most attractive. It looked like western Maryland and the upper reaches of the Potomac. For a moment we stopped at Zagreb, better known to me as Agram, and then we ran along the beautiful Save River, dotted with its crenellated castles, now for the most part deserted, and many of them in ruins

☆   ☆   ☆

I confess I did not greatly enjoy the unusual luxury of the Imperial-Royal train. Inured as I am to scenes of massacre and mass murder, the present atmosphere redolent of this personal tragedy depressed me. Often during the night I heard the last words of the dying arch-duke, who did not know the fate that had also befallen his wife, "Sophie! Sophie! Watch over the *Kinder*." Unmoved I had walked over the battlefields of Verdun with its half million dead, many un-buried with still protruding, beseeching arms, and with but a passing shudder I had seen the bodies of hundreds of the "hot-country men" who had, at the field of La Victoria in Venezuela, been cut to pieces by the cutlasses of Castro's Andinos. These things were horrible and, as I think, disgraceful to our civilization, but they were too horrible to grasp. On the other hand, it will be long before I shall forget the face of the little quartermaster captain who was mashed flat as a pancake on the Boulevard de Bonne Nouvelle in Paris twenty feet from where I stood, by the overturning of a lumber truck. And there is another dead soldier who travels with me, whose face I shall long

see, although years have passed and millions have died, many of whom
I have known and not a few of whom I knew intimately. It was on
the East Front in March 1915. We were halted by a patrol outside
of Memel where the street fighting between the Russians and the advancing Germans continued. Orders came from the High Command
we were not to go down into the city where fighting continued, and
in below-zero weather we stood until midnight on the brow of a hill
where a few hours before a Russian battery had been stormed with
heavy losses by a Landwehr battalion. We left our cars and ran up
and down to keep from freezing, but gradually fatigue and the cold
were bearing us down. The wind from the Baltic increased in intensity,
and it seemed as if we would be frozen to death, and indeed some of
us rather welcomed this escape from suffering. Then someone had a
bright, if ghoulish, idea. All around the battery lay the frozen, stiff
corpses of the men who, pulsating with life and vigor, had stormed it
but a few hours before. Our chauffeurs picked up the dead and piled
them together into a stockade and physically, at least, for the rest of
the night we were protected from the icy blast, but one, a middle-aged
sergeant with a great black beard, faced the corner into which I
crawled. He greatly resembled the crude picture of Stonewall Jackson
that presided over my nursery in the days when I first began to listen
to war tales. The dead sergeant and I, alive perhaps because of the
protection which his sturdy body afforded, lay side by side throughout
that long night, and so a personal contact was established which still
persists and so it will be, I fear, with my trip in the car which carried
the archducal pair to the romantic honeymoon in Italy and to their
death in Sarajevo. Of course I can do nothing about it and I should
try to forget them, but still I know that for a long time I shall hear
those piteous words of entreaty: "Sophie! Sophie! Watch over the
Kinder."

☆　　　☆　　　☆

Belgrade, in early April.

I wandered up the hillside through the ruins of the White City
with whose broad avenues and byways I had been familiar not so
long ago. All man's work has been destroyed by man's diabolical inventions. Only the Danube and the Save majestically flow on to their
union under the old Turkish citadel, and so I know I am in Belgrade,
or what is left of it.

At times there was such an uproar I thought that once again the capital of the Serbs was under fire, but that was not the case. Gangs of soldiers and civilians, urged on by the loud cries of officers and foremen, were clearing away the ruins that tell the sad story of the Austrian bombardment with which the holocaust of disaster began. Rapid-fire explosions rent the air, and now and again the wreckers brought to view the body of a man or a woman who had not lived to see this day of liberation. Generally the corpses were exceedingly life-like and some had homely utensils in their hands, showing that they were going about their daily round of duties when death came down out of the clouds, or from the ironclad monitors on the river. Entombed as they have been for four years in piles of brick and timber, these first victims of the war have been protected from the scavengers of the air who now, however, circle menacingly over the scene of desolation. As I climbed in and out of the ruins I heard scraps of every language known to man, and many of the speakers have come from faraway lands and over distant seas. I spotted two Filipinos and tackled them in scraps of Tagalog, but they shook their heads.

"Me Visayan," said one, and then they explained in scrappy Spanish that early in the war they had enlisted on an English ship as stewards and now were serving with the Danube patrol. At last I escaped the labyrinth of wreckage and before me waved invitingly the Stars and Stripes over a building still intact that was once the Turkish Legation. I hastened on to greet one of our most competent representatives, H. Percival Dodge, a career man upon whom I had dropped in at many faraway posts, in China, in Morocco, in Panama, and in Paris.

On the steps of the Legation I was delayed by an arresting figure, and soon I was in conversation with perhaps the only happy and contented man I have come up with in all the acrimonious days which have followed upon the Armistice. He was talking with the French-speaking butler, and not making much headway, but at sight of my uniform he turned to me with evident relief.

"I am Mikel Tusla," he said, "an American citizen," and he glowed with pride. His nakedness was covered with a scanty assortment of rags. He wore a fur cap from which the fur was gone and only the skin remained. His face was grimy and his feet were wrapped in rags. As we talked, a gentle rain began to fall and washed little canyons down his mud-caked face.

"I'm Mikel Tusla, an American citizen," he repeated, "but when I heard Mother Serbia was invaded, I came back home; and could I do otherwise? My brother had been killed and the little house on the hillside where I was born had gone up in flames! God! even in the days of the Turks our home had been spared. For four years I have fought with the Smedalia brigade and now that we have victory and peace, I want to go back to my Iowa farm—but there is difficulty."

I sat down on the doorstep and talked for some minutes with this happy man, without a shirt and without shoes, but who had an expression of contentment in his eyes to which I had long been a stranger. Then the Minister[7] appeared and proudly I introduced our fellow citizen.

"You should—and you shall—have a decoration," said the Minister. "Only last week the Prince Regent told me that all the boys who came back across the sea to fight for the homeland would be remembered."

This talk about a decoration failed to interest Mikel.

"I only want a little writing on my passport, to say it is good; you see, it was only good for two years, but it was not my fault that it took us four years to lick the 'Swabs.' Now that all is well in Serbia, I want to go home to my farm in Iowa and to my American children."

The Minister, after examining his army papers, wrote on that passport a citation that would make the heart of any soldier swell with pride.

Then Mikel turned to me.

"Would you mind if I touched your uniform? Someday my son will wear it."

"I shall be proud," I answered. And he laid his grimy hand on my insignia with something that was very like a caress.

"You must come to see me tomorrow, or any day, any hour, if there is any further difficulty," said the Minister.

"With that writing on my pass, there will be no difficulty," said Mikel Tusla. And he turned and went down the hill through the smoking ruins, the only happy, contented man I had met in months, and he was without a shirt or shoes.

"The melting pot," said the Minister, "and glory be to it."

I confess the atmosphere of the at once honeymoon chariot and funeral car on which I came to the smoking ruins of the Serbian capital had depressed me, and I planned to make the return journey by ordinary conveyance, but when after two days in the mourning city Logan

[7]H. Percival Dodge.

agreed to hold his car for me at least twelve hours I succumbed to the comforts, the creature comforts, which it afforded. If there are ghosts in this world they certainly must have infested that tragic Pullman. But of course there are none, simply devils and demons of flesh and blood, extremely like ourselves. We made a quick journey back to what had been the Kaiserstadt without any noteworthy experience except one just as we were running into the station. Hearing Logan and myself discussing once again the ill-fated couple, the porter said: "I want to show you something." We followed him, and in my sleeping compartment he pointed out, scratched on one of the panels, "Sophie and Franzl," but he was not a sensationalist. He admitted that he did not know whether the names dated from the honeymoon journey, when the honeymooners might have written them, as so many democratic trippers do on similar occasions, or whether it had been scratched there by some railway servant with a romantic leaning toward the vanished regime.

April, Vienna, Monday.

I am back from a brief dip in the troubled waters of the Balkans, for so many years my familiar swimming hole, where, surprisingly enough, I did not hear a hostile shot. In this respect it was a record-breaking journey. Down there, with stoical determination, all the peoples are digging themselves out of the wreckage that four years of war have wrought, and now back in peace-loving and traditionally frivolous Vienna I find myself involved in riots and in mass killings so surprising that at times I am inclined to disbelieve the evidence of my own eyes. I came back on the morning of what they call in Germany, and here, *Gründonnerstag,* our Maundy Thursday, a day of penitence and sorrow, on which it is traditional throughout Christendom for those who can to share at least a crust with the disinherited and the needy.

Leaving my bags at the hotel and feeling stuffy from the long railway journey, I immediately started out for a walk on the Ringstrasse. I noticed a greater number of police than was usual, and that most of them were mounted. Here and there I also caught sight of small detachments of troops half hidden away in the courtyards of the great apartment houses on the Ring between the Opera and the Parliament building. The fact is, however, that I paid little attention to the actual scene; I was living over again in memory what had happened on Maundy Thursday more than twenty years ago. On that day, through the courtesy of Count Taaffe, the Prime Minister, I had been invited to the Burg and had witnessed the medieval ceremony which then survived in the Holy Roman Empire as perhaps nowhere else. There in the great hall of the Hapsburg Burg, surrounded by the gorgeously attired dignitaries of the realm, the Emperor Francis Joseph, with a silver ewer in his hand, knelt down before a row of some twenty carefully selected beggars, and with perfumed water washed their poor, misshapen feet. Before the curious and the interlopers from distant lands arrived, the great Salle was already crowded with the mighty ones of the earth and the high dignitaries of the realm who had assembled to see the Emperor "with the pride that apes humility" perform this penitential act.

In appearance and garb, at least, the most striking were the Knights of St. John, the traditional defenders of the Holy Sepulcher, at this time, alas! still in the unholy keeping of the Turks. Two of them very graciously led us to a raised gallery from which we could in comfort survey the scene. They were gorgeously appareled in white satin robes with the Maltese cross of the Crusaders embroidered on their breasts and armlets. They had escort and other duties to perform and were constantly hurrying hither and thither, but the great dignitaries stood stock-still, waited and yawned. Among them were the men of the high army and navy command, the members of the General Staff with their haughty plumed hats, and not a few of the great magnates from Hungary, their tunics encrusted with medals and their shoulders covered with leopard skins. Among them also were the great territorial lords of the Empire, the Schwarzenbergs, the Liechtensteins, the Kinskys, the Trautsmansdorffs and scores more whose possessions are now scattered to the four winds, as are the dust and ashes of those of their caste who perhaps had the good fortune to fall in the battles on the Carpathian Mountains.

Suddenly the beggars, politely called pensioners, appeared—twelve men and twelve women; some were so feeble that they had to be supported by halberdiers and court servants. They were hardly in their places before the Emperor came in, and he was flanked by the cardinal archbishop of the apostolic city and the papal nuncio, the famous Monsignor Galimberti.

From now on the Church was in control of the ceremonial proceedings and it was the cardinal archbishop who gave the Emperor his cue. Reading from the Gospel of St. John, he announced: *"Posuit vestimenta sua* [He laid aside His garments]," and the Emperor obediently entrusted his sword and his hat to an adjutant. Then the Cardinal read "*et coepit lavare pedes Discipulorum* [and He began to wash the feet of the Disciples]." A servant now appeared with a silver ewer and preceded by a court chaplain who sprinkled the protruding feet of the pensioners with what was evidently perfumed or aromatic water, the Emperor began his task. Half kneeling before each of his humble guests, the lord of many lands wiped the moisture away from the now obviously shrinking feet. Then he gave them new socks and stout shoes. He led them to a great table, groaning under a weight of meat and drink, and, for the first course of this banquet, the Emperor-King served them with his own hands. The Emperor did not seem to enjoy the unusual experience, but he went through with it doggedly, with the determination with which he complied with all the requirements of his profession. The Emperor even tasted the soup and told one of the lackeys to put in several more pinches of salt, which he did. I do not think the pensioners enjoyed the repast. They ate sparingly and looked about with curious eyes. Then they were told that receptacles would be given them to carry away the rich food to humbler surroundings where they could eat more at their ease—and this pleased them. So their eyes wandered over the scene which was, I have no doubt, as strange to them as it was to me. So, following their roving eyes, I also looked about me.

. . . But evidently I am a poor substitute for Froissart. I cannot recall whether the beautiful Empress was there. Had she been there, the memory of her grace would doubtless have remained with me throughout the drab years that have followed. But I am almost certain she was not present; doubtless she was breaking in the wild horses of the Hungarian Pusztas down at Gödölo, and probably the carefully selected old ladies in their prim hats and gray smocks, now brought in, had their feet washed and were otherwise comforted by her ladies in waiting in a side apartment, to which we, the curious spectators, were not admitted. But, certainly, few other members of the Hapsburg family were absent. There was the sturdy Karl Ludwig, fat and rosy, although he is surviving his fourth marriage. By his side stood his eldest son, Francis Ferdinand, whose death at Sarajevo set the world ablaze and started the holocaust of disaster. Also, there were two little boys in sailor suits, the sons of the Archduke Otto, who was not present. He never attended Church festivities if he could help it, and on this day he could not have been present even had he wanted to; it was an open secret that because of a certain indiscretion the handsome Otto was being detained under arrest in a Tyrolean castle—at least for the duration of his uncle's displeasure.

The elder of the little boys was Karl, who succeeded to his great uncle's tottering throne in 1916. He could not cope with the difficulties that confronted him, and he is now in Switzerland in none-too-affluent exile. And there was little Elizabeth, a scrawny elf with a wizened but shrewd, uncanny face. She is the only child of the luckless Crown Prince Rudolph, who died so mysteriously at Mayerling, and the Princess Stephanie, who, plump and plain, survives her unhappy marriage, but, no favorite at Court, she is not present today. The Viennese of both high and low degree blame her for not holding her "man," or if she could not do that, for not having overlooked his gallantries. She is particularly criticized for the gala Court carriage she on a memorable occasion maliciously stationed outside the apartment of the soubrette Rudolph was visiting; that was a thing that had never been done in Court circles before—at least not since the days of Maria Theresa, who, after all, was a warm-blooded woman as well as a fighting empress, and who tried to rule her flighty Franz with an iron hand.

. . . Now came the last of the scriptural scenes. Preceded by a noble boy carrying heavy purses in a great basket, the old Emperor, with somewhat unsteady step, climbed upon the estrade where the Court pensioners sat, exalted. Around the neck of each of them he placed the corded noose of a purse, which doubtless contained the traditional forty pieces of silver. The eyes of the pensioners were wide open now.

Then, in the twinkling of an eye, the pageant came to an end. Preceded by the noble boys, the nuncio and the archbishop, the Emperor vanished behind an arras, and the assemblage disbanded. We went down the corridor and the gala steps out into the Schweizerhof. It was crowded with Court carriages and lackeys in gorgeous liveries. I recall helping a charming French lady into her carriage and also what she said, with a touch of cynicism, which, had it been overheard, in those days would have been regarded as treason.

"C'est jouer la comédie—mais au moins, la pièce est fort belle." To me it certainly seemed a strange pageant, a relic from the medieval world, which probably nowhere else survived. . . .

What a contrast is the scene with which I find myself confronted today. There are no gala carriages and no bemedaled courtiers to be seen. The Ring smells of the accumulation of garbage. Here and there a shabby taxi rattles by. Here and there along the broken railings of the Volksgarten there slinks an invalid soldier of the Hoch und

Deutschmeister, once the darling regiment of the Viennese, the pride of the Imperial City. How gaily they sang as I saw them sally out to war in 1915:

"*Ach du mein Östereich!*
Du bist ein schones Land."

Today they sang no more. Many had empty sleeves, all were pale of face, many seemed to be starving; some were asking for alms from those who had nothing to give, or pleading to be taken to the reconstruction hospitals, which were already overcrowded. And yet perhaps these were the lucky ones in contrast to their comrades I had seen in 1916, dying like flies in the prison camp at Khabarovsk on the Amoor in faraway Siberia. Lucky they doubtless were, but certainly they did not seem to know it.

. . . Deep in this reminiscent mood it was natural that my thought should travel back to the last time I saw the mighty ruler of this long-lived, millennial empire, whose ruins lay strewn before me. It was in February 1915, but what I saw then is as plainly etched in my mind's eye as though it had happened but yesterday. Francis Joseph was coming down the Mariahilferstrasse on one of his last visits to his post of duty in the Burg. Perhaps it was his very last as a few months later an attack of gentle pneumonia, that blessing to octogenarians, eased his departure from a world where he certainly could not have had any desire to linger. As I saw him for the last time he did not ride in a gilded Court carriage nor was he surrounded by the pomp and panoply of the Imperial Guard. Indeed he sat in his private *zwei-spanner* only to be distinguished from the public vehicles of that category by the fire and the beauty of the blooded horses that drew it.

The mighty Emperor whose empire was crashing about him was on his way to the Burg, to hold a war council, to hear the dark news that was coming in from so many fronts. By his side sat Count Paar or General Margutti, which of his personal adjutants it was I could not tell, so swiftly they passed me. On the box sat a "Jaeger." The great man was late, and the horses were being pushed. Persuaded, perhaps, that this was an historic moment, I stood still on the curb, almost spellbound, and my coat was flecked with the foam from the snorting onrushing horses. The strange old man was greatly changed. He seemed to me quite ripe for the end that awaits monarch as well as serf. His expressionless eyes were glazed and from one corner of his mouth there hung unlit the inevitable *Virginier* cigar, a libel on the noble state where really sweet tobacco is grown (only second to our Maryland crop), that the Austrian tobacco monopoly had proclaimed to the world, unashamed, for so many generations. Had the Emperor not said: "It would seem no misfortune is spared me"? But he was wrong. He, at least, was to die in his bed and still an emperor, while Kaiser Bill skulks, a refugee in Holland, and little Nicholas, but yesterday the autocrat of all the Russias, trapped in an Ekaterinburg cellar with all his nearest and dearest, has been butchered to make a Communist holiday.

Perhaps beyond the Styx, but never again in this world—this vale of tears, at least in part of their making—will the mighty men meet to reshape their dominions. Never again will the cloth of gold be spread for their Imperial Majesties on the dreary Polish plain of Skerniwicze. Never again in "shining armor" will they strut about on that lonely island in the fogbound Baltic, remaking maps of their world and redressing balances of powers. Indeed they will not ever again hobnob, and drink the waters at Tyrolean Ischl, which they were told, at least by the Court physicians, could not fail to have a rejuvenating effect on their senile bodies.

Now the old empires are being partitioned, and the new boundaries are about to be drawn by those who were for so long the underdogs. A herculean task it will prove to be, but one consoling thought suggests itself—they cannot possibly make a worse mess of it than did those who claimed to rule by Divine right. And at least Crown Prince Rudolph presents no problem except to the writers of mystery stories who have such unrestrained license in dealing with historic facts. About the mystery of Mayerling, as it is called, best sellers have been written in many tongues, but little light emerges. Unlike most of these brilliant fictionists, I did investigate the mystery. I did bring to light at least two long-veiled facts, but unfortunately they proved contradictory, and so while the unfortunate young man who was the heir to the apostolic throne has long crumbled into dust, the mystery, the deepest of the many in his line, survives and will doubtless always remain unsolved.

If I had a reputation to lose, say, as a transatlantic Sherlock Holmes, I could advance the plea that when my services were called in it was a cold trail, indeed it was three months old. I was in Constantinople when the news of the sudden death of Rudolph shocked Europe, and in a few hours the many versions of how it had happened set many tongues wagging. A few hours later I received a wire from the Commodore[8] ordering me to Vienna and urging me to elucidate the mystery. Nothing could have been more unwelcome to me. Owing to one or two minor achievements during my first sojourn in the waltz capital, my chief had a wholly exaggerated notion as to the sources of information I enjoyed there, and now I was sure that this myth would be exploded. A few hours later, however, another wire came, which was most welcome. "Have made other arrangements in Vienna. Stay with the Armenians."

Three months later the myth came to dangerous life again. I was called to Paris to confer on the tangled Macedonian situation but also instructed by the Commodore to stop off for a week in Vienna and "clear up" what was still known throughout the world as the Mayerling mystery. Neither the unfortunate man who had substituted for me nor any of his competitors had accomplished this and so I was put on the cold trail and told to go to it.

The discoveries I made, particularly the unmarked grave in the Heiligenkreuz, "peace Acre," cast doubt upon many of the popularly accepted solutions. It certainly was dug within a few hours of the tragedy—but unhappily it did leave my own theory in the "not-proven" class. I was, as so often before, mulling over the inconclusive end of my researches when suddenly I was recalled from my Rip Van Winkle dreams of court splendors and unsolved mysteries to the ugly present by musketry fire. I heard the rattle of sabers being drawn from scabbards and the cobbles in the driveway of the Ring rang with the approach of mounted men and the sharp orders that brought the slouching troops out of the courtyards and to attention fell on my ear. Fully aroused now and looking about me, I saw a disorderly mob of men, women, and barefooted children marching down the Mariahilferstrasse and I also saw that the police were drawing a cordon across the street which leads from the industrial quarters, with the evident purpose of preventing them from reaching the Parliament building a few hundred yards farther along. As they drew nearer I could see how miserably clad they were and I could hear their cries:

"We are starving! Give us bread and jackets! *Es Friert uns! Wir verhungern!* We are famished and we freeze."

In all the uproar and the confusion that followed, in which so unexpectedly I was involved, I cannot say that I have a very clear idea of how the battle began. Suddenly, however, shots rang out, followed

---

[8]The title generally given to the seagoing owner of the New York *Herald* both at home and abroad.

by volleys, and these were certainly not warning shots. Some of the police fell and many of the horses. There ensued a regular fusillade and peering from behind the newspaper kiosk where I had sought refuge, I could see that many of the starving workers had fallen and riderless horses were prancing over their bodies. Some of the workers were running away but other more resolute groups were pushing on. The troops now entered the melee, in support of the police, and soon the Ring was cleared of the living. Here and there lay groups of dead and tangled masses of the writhing wounded which showed how deadly the firing had been while it lasted.

When the shots became desultory and finally died away, or almost, I saw a sight which gave me full realization of the dangers starving people will face under the compelling urge of hunger. Men, and women, too, now crept out from their refuges in the adjacent buildings and though frequently fired upon could not be kept from hacking with their dull knives at the bodies of the horses that had fallen and then making off with hunks of bloody booty!

When the last of the rioters had disappeared and ambulances for the police, at least, arrived on the scene, I emerged from my makeshift bombproof which had served its unusual purpose and did what I could for the wounded. Many indeed were past helping. Among these was a handsome Englishwoman who had been shot through the heart and had died instantly. It developed from her papers that she was a Mrs. Thompson, a casual passer-by, as was I, the wife of a distinguished engineer who had come to Vienna on the invitation of the new government to advise them on the water-power projects that are being planned to give employment and bread to the thousands who are literally starving. After what I had seen of the reckless courage of the rioters who were risking their lives for a chunk of horse meat, there could be no doubt that the need is appalling and that our Food Administration is getting to work none too soon.

Vienna, Saturday.

Contrary to the expectations of many friends, I am back safe and sound from my sojourn of three days in Budapest under the Red Star, the hammer and sickle—the advance post of Bolshevism in Europe. None of the difficulties that had been expected materialized. Everything passed off so smoothly that I have an uneasy feeling that perhaps my journey was not clandestine after all and that the new authorities not only acquiesced in my venture but connived at it! The only unpleasant incident took place on the return journey at the new Austrian frontier about an hour out from Vienna, measured by the slow-moving and lice-infested train; here I was held up and accused of being an emissary of the Reds, who had come to corrupt the Austrians and turn them from their apostolic faith. I should say in explanation that the frontier guards I here encountered were drunk and later a very plausible explanation of their condition was forthcoming. It seems that the regular supplies of beer had given out and the customs men had fallen back on the local *Branntwein*, which is, I should say, corn liquor in its most deadly form. However, I was permitted to telephone to Renner's office in Vienna and the liberating word came almost immediately. The offending inspector collapsed, whether from the corn liquor or the rebuke he received I cannot say, and I resumed my journey in a roomy but by-no-means-clean cattle car.

Colonel House had insisted on my running down to the Hungarian capital for a "look-see," however brief. He was inclined to class the reports that he had received from the representative of the Enquiry there with those that came from the scholarly observer[9] of this organization in Vienna whose interminable dispatches dealt almost exclusively with the history of the pragmatic sanction; however, in this, for once, the Colonel was mistaken. The reports of Philip Marshall Brown,[10] were very clear, extremely fair, and always illuminating. I was sorry that he was away during my short stay in his bailiwick.

"But I want another point of view," insisted the Colonel over the telephone. "You need only stay down there a couple of days. You know Budapest from former visits and perhaps you will meet with people who, having confidence in your discretion, will tell the truth."

Well, the only difficulties I met with were in starting. In what guise or, rather, in what disguise, should I go? If I went in uniform, that would be some sort of recognition of the Red regime, and I was not authorized to take that step; if I went in civilian garb, and was apprehended, I might be regarded as a spy and dealt with as such. I finally decided on this risk, and even left behind me the diplomatic passport with which I had been provided when starting on the Smuts mission. I decided to go in the familiar role of a newspaper correspondent and in the civilian clothes which G——[11] of the Food Administration kindly

[9]Archibald Cary Coolidge, of Harvard.
[10]Later professor of international law at Princeton.
[11]Gregory.

furnished. I had no identification papers with me, and fortunately no one asked me for any. Once in Pest, in my best Hungarian, I told the shabby cabdriver at the station to take me to the Hotel Hungaria, my favorite refuge during the days of my Balkan adventures. He seemed surprised, but took me there, and on my arrival I found that the famous hostelry had been converted into government offices and there where the gypsy orchestra had played "To the Ear"—wild, fantastic music— the air was filled with the click of typewriters. He then took me to the Carlton-Astoria, I think it was called, and there I received a cordial welcome and registered as a journalist with residence in New York. This resulted in an unexpected complication. The clerk told me that all journalists received a reduction of 25 per cent on their bills. What should I do in all honesty about that? Fortunately, in the lobby there was a box in which all were invited to place contributions for invalided soldiers, and in this box I later deposited the amount of the professional reduction to which, for the moment, I was not entitled.

It was a greatly changed Budapest in which I now wandered about. The people were quiet but obviously extremely nervous as to the things that were about to happen. As I walked along Andrassy Street, a window fell and all within hearing ran like mad—they evidently apprehended bombs. While the situation was outwardly calm, most people seemed to think that they were merely experiencing the lull that precedes the storm. Three weeks before all the banks had been looted and all the stores sacked. At the moment of my arrival there was nothing left to steal. Kun ordered the "Lenin boys," for the most part released convicts, to the citizen army, urging them to face the invading Czechs on the north and the Roumanians advancing from the south. It was then they showed their true colors—and their teeth. Not a few of the officers who brought them these unwelcome orders were killed, and in and out of uniform the "boys" continued their depredations.

Since March 21st, when the Károlyi government fell (or rather evaporated), all the factories were taken over by the "State" and then perforce closed down because the only people who knew how to run them had, not unwisely, taken to their heels. In the first three weeks of the Soviet rule the Lenin boys probably murdered a thousand people—thrifty citizens who foolishly sought to retain the little money they had and the stores of food they had hidden away. Of course in a situation like this it is very difficult to control the figures of what were euphemistically called "casualties," but I believe the above figure is a very liberal underestimate. Kun tried to get these bandits to march against the invaders but with few exceptions, and indeed none among the cityfolk; they had no stomach for fighting. Loot! loot! and ever more loot was their dream—now about to be realized, they hoped.

While I do not claim to have enjoyed anything more than a superficial view of the situation, I do think that but for what is termed his "agricultural policy" Kun might have lasted a little longer.[12] It is quite true that, first off, the peasants of the Pusztas, or at least a goodly number of them, were enthusiastic at the thought of becoming small landowners, but when the commissars arrived they learned that the redistribution of the large estates did not work out as they had thought it would. It is true that the old territorial lords were displaced and that some of them who lingered around, most unwisely, were murdered by the Lenin boys who accompanied the commissars. But when it turned out that the old estates were to be converted simply into collective farms and that the profits resulting from their labors were to be pocketed by the State, following the bad example that had been given them a few days before, the peasants killed quite a number of the newly arrived commissars, and those who could were glad to return to Budapest and to the protection of the large force of Red soldiers that the little dictator had now assembled there.

Tuesday.

As far as I can make out this is the immediate background of the present very insistent Magyar problem. Nearly a month ago the Károlyi government collapsed under the weight of its stupidity. Apparently it was neither Tory nor Red, neither fish nor fowl nor even good red herring. Anarchy was spreading through the land, and at this juncture Bela Kun, the shrewd little Polish Jew who for some time, as an agent of Lenin, had been engaged in subterranean work in Hungary, entered the government and in a very few days took control of it. It is only fair to state that Kun was perfectly frank as to his intentions: he almost immediately proclaimed the right of the industrial workers to rule the factories in which they had slaved for so long; also the right of the peasants to the lands on which they and their forebears had been held as serfs for generations. His foreign policy was equally clear. In alliance with Moscow, and as its spearhead, he would overrun all the bourgeois countries who did not frankly accept the New Gospel and bring them to heel. In the first flush it cannot be denied that his program was warmly received in many quarters, particu-

[12]He sneaked out of Budapest three months later.

larly by the peasants who shouted innumerable *"Eljens,"* for Moscow
and for Kun. I am told, however, by some, that many of the peasants
thought that these alien catchwords were the names of fast-running
horses!

. . . Before leaving Vienna on the Hungarian venture I had talked
with my old friend, Rittmeister Pronay, and he had offered to be helpful and also discreet. In happier days I had known him as the commander of a squadron of that crack regiment, the Radetzky Hussars,
that witched the Prater and all Vienna with its horsemanship. Now
poor Pronay was a war invalid and his outlook dark indeed. Even before the coming of the catastrophe he had lost his estates at cards, I
think. Invalids were not wanted in Hungary any more than anywhere
else, and Renner, out of charity, was keeping him employed on a
mere pittance in drawing up a record of the casualties of the Great
War, the *listen* of those who had died, and those who had disappeared,
and those who were still marooned in the Siberian prison camps.

"We have reached March 1918," said Pronay. "We move slowly, I
and my comrades, but slow as we move someday we will reach Armistice Day, and then we, too, shall be on the bread line."

Pronay had wanted to give me letters to some of his loyalist friends
in Pest, but I had declined, believing that they would prove as em-
barrassing to them as to me. However, in some way that I did not seek
to discover he had advised many of them of my coming, and as a result clandestine communications reached me from time to time in my
room, and also were often discreetly slipped to me at the cafés and
restaurants which I frequented. They were generally typed on a
machine of ancient make and were always marked "P" to authenticate
their source. I must say that the information that reached me in this
way was not always convincing. It should be frankly admitted, however, that the situation was terribly confused. The Esterházys, the
Zichys, the Festetics, and the rest of Pronay's horsy friends to whose
statements I might have given some credence had fled the country or,
wisely, I think, remained in hiding. Count Károlyi, the pseudo-demo-
crat, in control for a few weeks, when the Red storm broke, had also
sought safety in flight. His hide-out was a closely held secret.

There was an amusing story told me of an incident in these last
troubled days in which the telephone played an unusual role. From
the last of the Hapsburgs, Károlyi, upon taking office, asked and received release from his oath of allegiance and publicly announced his

loyal adherence to the People's Republic, but he, too, not unwisely, I think, ran away before it was inaugurated. Perhaps I should throw a charitable veil over the conduct of the Archduke Joseph at this critical and, it must be admitted, most perplexing moment for a Hapsburg and a man of great wealth. He saved his estates and probably his life by throwing in his fortunes with the Reds. At least the Soviet-controlled papers announced that he also, again by telephone, had secured his release from his allegiance to the head of the Hapsburg house, now a fugitive, and had taken an oath to support the People's Republic. The papers were also printing in lurid letters extracts from a speech which must have sounded strange indeed as they fell from Hapsburg lips, if they ever did. As reported, his concluding statement was:

"With a little Bolshevism we shall pull ourselves out of the hole where the war has landed us." Evidently this archduke was a teachable fellow. He knew the times were changing—and that it was the part of wisdom to change with them.

On my arrival I was permitted, even urged, to attend a session of the Workers' and Soldiers' Council of the Revolution. Kun spoke very frankly and well, I thought, and by the aid of a volunteer interpreter I think I got at least the general drift of his remarks. My interpreter spoke very bad German and he explained that Kun spoke very bad Magyar, so he had a difficult role. Kun began by saying:

"Comrades, I will not beautify the situation which is one of danger to us all. We have lost the fight at Szatmár-Némety and the Roumanians are at the gates of Grosswardein; some of our men fought well; others, I regret to say, deserted their positions. But in Debreczen we have scored some successes; there the Workers have risen in their might and expelled the counterrevolutionaries. Everywhere the invading Roumanians outnumber us and are better armed. The great need of the young army of the new proletarian State is better weapons and more of them.

"We do not know whether the Entente means to hold the Roumanians to the line of demarcation which was fixed by Colonel Vix (acting for the Supreme War Council) or whether they would condemn us to the fate of the Paris Commune. At the present moment the Czechs are not advancing, but that may happen tomorrow and we must prepare for an invasion on this front also. There is no reason to despair, but I must admit that as far as munitions and arms are concerned, we are in bad shape. At present we can most certainly not undertake an offensive. Every proletarian in Pest must hasten to the front; and remember, even if we fail, we shall have sounded the tocsin that will awaken the proletarians of the world. We shall have notified them of the inevitable struggle that is coming and our fate, if adverse, will serve to warn them in time of the necessity to arm."

People's Commissar Bakany then took the floor with a stern warning to the bourgeoisie factions who, he said, the moment the Roumanians appeared, "threw off all concealment, put out the old flag, and shouted 'Long live the King!' "

He then moved that at least half the members of the Council and all the Workers who were not engaged on pivotal jobs should proceed to the front. It was carried, but the motion was weakened, I thought, by the proviso attached to the effect that the Workers' Council should decide which of its members should be sent to the firing line.

In my role of an inquiring journalist I had later on the same day a talk with Bela Kun. He was most accessible and outspoken. More clearly than what he said, a mere repetition of his speech at the Workers' Council, I recall his surroundings and his appearance. With a guide that was furnished by the hotel, and with the prestige of a tourist, a rare bird indeed in these revolutionary days, I was ushered into a cabinet council in the very same room where in former years I had interviewed in succession the former Prime Ministers of a vanished Hungary, the Tiszas, father and son. The portraits of Deak and of Kossuth which had formerly adorned the council chamber were gone, and their successors were sitting around a large table with heads close together. The heating apparatus in the palace, as everywhere else in the city, was out of order, and it was probably wise for the new counselors to sit in their overcoats—all wore imitation fur coats; and so good was the imitation that even the moths were deceived and had evidently been at work gnawing on the now-upturned collars!

I shall never forget Bela Kun as I now saw him at close quarters and cheek by jowl with his coterie of conspirators. He made upon me an indelible impression, but it is one that is difficult to convey. He had a round bulbous head and his hair was so closely shaven that he seemed to be bald; he had a short, squat nose, ugly thick lips, but undoubtedly his outstanding physical feature was his great pointed ears. Some people suggested, but under their breath, that with his great abnormal head and his small but very active body he looked like a lizard, and certainly there was a touch of green in his coloring. In a word, his figure was one that I have never seen duplicated in any of my wanderings.

Rumor has it that when the war came (1914) Kun was under arrest charged with the embezzlement of funds, but the charge was dropped when he was drafted into the commissary branch of the Hungarian Army. When the Russians made their great drive over the Carpathians in 1916 he became, it is said, a very willing captive. Sent to the celebrated prison camp at Tomsk in Siberia, he learned Russian so well that when the Revolution broke he was able to distinguish himself by his eloquent appeals to his fellow prisoners in favor of the new gospel. I was given copies of his awakening speech, his call to arms in seven or eight languages. It opens, and for that matter concludes, with the familiar words: "Proletarians of the World, unite. The hour of liberation has struck!" This speech and many others attracted the attention of Radek, the famous Russian propagandist, and through him Kun came in contact with Lenin and soon he was enrolled as a missionary of the Red gospel.

A few days after the Károlyi government was established, in the fall of 1918, Kun appeared in Budapest, officially at least as the representative of the Russian Red Cross. He brought with him many millions of rubles, ostensibly to succor the thousands of Russian prisoners and wounded, who were still marooned in Hungary. In the executive council, the so-called Commissioners of the People, by whom the renegade Count Károlyi was surrounded, out of the twenty-six who composed it at this time, eighteen were Jews, at least so I am informed. Be the religious and racial divisions what they may, it is quite certain that very shortly a majority of the counselors welcomed the latest recruit and fell under the spell of his eloquence, or, as some insist, of the Moscow gold which he distributed so lavishly.

I did not enjoy even a glimpse of Károlyi. He had disappeared two weeks before my arrival—and left no address behind him. Many and strange are the stories I heard about him, and probably some of them are worthy of credence. He was born to great wealth and broad possessions, in the renowned Magnat family whose name he bears, as most of them think, most unworthily. A great many fairies were not present at his birth and in their absence they certainly failed to shower rich gifts upon him. He came into the world with his mouth awry and he had to be provided with an artificial palate. Even with a mechanical device, when he raised his voice, it is said something more resembling a dog's bark than a human cry emerged.

At the age of ten, so the story runs, he startled his affluent parents by announcing that at the earliest possible moment he proposed starting a revolution! That was certainly a bombshell hurled in the midst of a family group that had much reason to believe that they were living in the best of all possible worlds. Cut off from a career in the army, and indeed from all official life, by his physical handicaps, Michael Károlyi found an outlet for his restless spirit in gambling. At the baccarat table in the Nemzet Club, for a hundred years the rendezvous of the great, the daring, above all the affluent, of Hungary, he played for high stakes and won or lost millions on the turn of a card. When in the last year of the war things began to look dark for Hungary, Károlyi was nearly dead broke and also interned in France as a dangerous alien.[13] Many think, especially those who have not a word to say in favor of a man who, whatever his motives may have been, was a renegade to his caste and a humiliation to his clan, that it was the need to rehabilitate his finances that induced him to enter upon the strange associations by which he will always be remembered.

In his earlier years Károlyi had been a frequent and generally an unsuccessful duelist, and some of the circumstances of the duel that he fought with Stephen Tisza, the last Prime Minister of Hungary (murdered by mutinous soldiers returning from the front at the time of the Armistice), is legendary, because of its great length and one-sidedness. The weapons used were sabers, and as Tisza was a skilled swordsman, he is said to have struck Károlyi thirty-five times, but merely with the flat of his sword! In later life he lamented his generosity. "I should have killed Michael that day," he said; "had I done so, I would have spared our country its deepest humiliation."

Catherine Károlyi, the devoted wife of Michael, one of the strangest figures in this lurid "incident," was a granddaughter of the great Andrassy, who, while he fought against the Hapsburgs under Kossuth, in later life became Minister of Foreign Affairs for the Dual Monarchy, and represented Francis Joseph at the Congress of Berlin and on many other important occasions. Catherine's own father was the Jules Andrassy who was sent by Czernin on a mission to Switzerland in 1917, probably to negotiate a separate peace. An attempt was made to cloak these clandestine negotiations, but it was unsuccessful, for one reason because Andrassy broke all the discreet rules of the diplomatic game by making at the time a frank speech in Parliament, calling upon the Government "to abandon Germany, bring back our troops from all the fronts, and save our homeland."

[13]He had been making a rabble-rousing trip to America and on his return journey he was picked up by the Allied authorities and interned in France for the duration.

Sensible words, indeed, but they were spoken too late. Apparently the only path still open to Austria led to the abyss into which she fell twelve months later.

In the early days of his startling political activities Károlyi was frequently insulted and indeed not seldom assaulted in public places. Whatever else he may have been, Károlyi was no coward, and he always reacted by challenging those who so despitefully used him; however, finally a court of honor held at the Nemzet Club handed down the crushing decision that "Michael Károlyi by his own actions was incapable of affording satisfaction to a gentleman on the field of honor."

Undoubtedly this sentence of ostracism, this denial of the privilege which above all others he and his peers cherished and so frequently exercised, the right of being *satisfaktions-fähig*, had great influence in pushing Michael into the Socialist and, as some charge, into the Bolsheviki fold.

Károlyi, to sum up, gave up the seals of office on March 21st (1919), several weeks before I reached Budapest. I make this statement, although I admit there is another story to the effect that he never had them in his possession, and this story may be true. The feudal lords were very jealous of the emblems of the historic rule of King Stephen, and the seals may have been buried, as were so many other historic symbols, to save them from contamination. But whatever insignia Károlyi may have had, authenticating his ministry, he turned them over at the hour of crisis to a certain Garbai, who had been in his cabinet. Garbai served for a few hectic hours as president of the Council, but within the week he was eased out by his own cabinet, of which Bela Kun was the most energetic figure. Kun inaugurated the new era by issuing an ukase that smacked of Moscow and which declared that all trade was a State monopoly and that all money, however held, in the banks or privately, belonged to the Government. In the lurid days which Budapest now lived through, while all the records available certainly come from untrustworthy sources, there is much reason to believe that more than six hundred people of some prominence were murdered, not for open opposition to the revolutionary regime, but because they were suspected of not being sympathetic "fellow travelers."

Certainly I was glad to get away from the city that in my hectic Balkan days had always been my favorite retreat. And I was lucky too. As Admiral Höhnel said in welcoming me back to the city of the

Waltz King: "You, as an American officer, in civilian clothes were *vogel frei*, anyone had the right to shoot you down!" But, as a matter of fact, no one bothered to do it.

Vienna, Tuesday.

Yesterday a *petit mot*, brought by a shabby *Dienstmann* came from Princess Metternich, asking me to call; evidently the great lady is no longer served by the gorgeous palace lackeys who in former days ran her errands and did her bidding. I felt I had been remiss in not calling without awaiting an invitation, but the new people with whom I had my contacts were not at all likely to know her whereabouts and so I had assumed, and indeed hoped, that the Princess had been able to escape from the mourning, starving city and taken refuge at one of her many country estates. I knew, of course, that they were all heavily mortgaged, but I also knew that for the time being, at least, a moratorium had been declared on all these ugly legal processes. This afternoon I was setting out to pay the call which I knew was a duty (she had been most kind to the wandering correspondent in former days), and was sure would be a pleasure, when I was advised that the great lady was downstairs and that with the consideration that was her due the manager had shown her into a salon more suitable for her reception than the dark entresol which was my abode. I did not want to talk of the present distressing days we were living, that would not have been tactful, but looking back I am not at all sure that the turn I gave the conversation indicated much *savoir faire*. I had last seen the great lady in her box at the opera, with the magnificent Count Hübner at her beck and call, so I talked of those gala nights which in the words, the true words, of the half-Viennese poet Metastasio, *"non si ritrovano piu."* Then, the broken, almost decrepit woman now before me was a charming, gracious princess and he the very ideal of a grand seigneur. So yielding to a sudden, perhaps an indiscreet, impulse, I asked:

"And how has it fared with your friend, Count Hübner, in these dark days?"

"Josef has been lucky; he has escaped the catastrophe. He withdrew from the scene in which he played such a great role before the lights went out. Yes, Josef was lucky."

"A remarkable man, a notable figure," I commented. "He gave me his book describing his tour of the world—quite an adventure in those days. In it he made an excellent prophecy, which I now recall. He said: 'When England is in danger, the lion's whelps will come together from the ends of the earth and save the mother country—even if the whole world is arrayed against her.' "

"Yes," said the Princess, "he was a wise man. But, oh, I am glad he did not live to see the fulfillment of his prophecy. And now, my dear Redman, I shall tell you a secret: In America, and indeed in many other democratic countries, the belief was held that in our Austria no one could rise to power unless he was *hoffähig* and had the sixteen quarterings of noble birth. (Today we are ruled by buttermen and saddlers, alas!) As a general thing that charge was true, but there were a few exceptions, and of these Josef was the most notable."

Here the Princess lowered her voice as though in fear of being overheard: "Though he became the leader of our nobility and a favorite of our Emperor-King, he sprang from very common clay. He was ennobled for his achievements and died as the leader of the House of Peers, but he was born a Hasenbredl, or something very plebeian like that, and his father kept a little grocery shop out in Mariahilf.

"How with these handicaps he was able to enter the Foreign Office no one, except himself, ever knew, for at that time I must admit it was a closed preserve to all but the curled and corseted darlings of the Court. He achieved many things in his remarkable career, but the way he surmounted this caste barrier was of all the most remarkable. Within a few months he attracted the attention and the favor of his exacting chief, Metternich. Then his ability won him rapid advancement. He was placed in charge of the negotiations which in 1848 brought about the abdication of the incompetent Emperor Ferdinand. By the skillful way in which he handled this delicate situation he won the confidence of young Francis Joseph. It was a fruitful contact and young Hübner profited by it—as did the young Emperor. When I saw him last in 1914, when the war clouds were gathering, the Emperor said to me:

" 'Pauline, how I wish our Hübner stood at my side; he would find a way, an honorable way, out of our dilemma.' "

For a moment now the unfortunate Princess turned away from the past with all its pomp and pageantry and ease and appraised the dark present and the still more somber future which opened before her and her class.

"How stupidly we managed it," she exclaimed. "Our good Emperor was living in the last century, he had no understanding of the actual world, and Hübner was not there to advise him, to guide him. How stupidly we played our cards! We were sorry for what had happened to Franz and to Sophie. But could we recall them to life? And was it worth the lives of millions of brave young men to revenge them and to maintain ourselves in those pig-infested provinces which after all belonged to the Serbs? Franz was dead, past recall, and we sacrificed our best and bravest, for what I ask you? Well, they tell me it was to re-establish our prestige. A stupid *Dummheit*, say I, and those sly fellows in Berlin pushed us into it. Well, they have fallen into the pit they dug for others but Austria, our dear Austria, is lost. To have escaped that I would have given that contemptible Peter Karageorgevitch a *Busel*, all the Vienna *Mädel* would have given him a hug, yes, *recht gerne*." When she wandered away from her courtly French the Princess spoke a Viennese that was the envy of the flower girls at Mme. Fossatti's and the songbirds of the Prater cafés.

"Josef was always a friend of the English," explained the Princess; "he understood their worth, he appreciated their immense reserves of strength. He kept Austria on friendly terms with England and her allies during the Crimean War, and he represented us at the Congress of Paris which ended this episode in 1856. But I must tell you that Josef, wide-awake and keen-sighted though he was generally, on one occasion was caught napping. But how unpredictable was Napoleon Third. Of that my husband and I myself had bitter experiences during our Paris mission in later years. Josef did not believe—to me he admitted it—that Napoleon was planning his Italian adventure that brought us into the first of our unfortunate wars. He told me that for a moment he could not believe his ears when at the famous historic diplomatic reception on New Year's Day 1859 the Emperor of the French stood before him and said: 'I regret that our relations with your government are not so good as they have hitherto been.' Of course that meant war, and we were caught napping, as usual, and in 1914 we were simply playing our traditional role," added the Princess, with some bitterness.[14]

The dear old lady's flow of reminiscences was here interrupted by a spell of coughing and this was followed by a severe chill. A leaky water bottle, a relic of the tourist days, was found by the hotel man-

[14]Hübner survived this misadventure and became Ambassador at Rome, and in 1867 he undertook the world journey which he described in his *Promenade autour du Monde*. Follower of Metternich and Schwarzenberg though he was, and leader of the Church and aristocratic party in the Upper House, Hübner was loud in his praise of the English colonial system and prophesied that the overseas Britons would save the mother country in any world conflict that might arise. He died in 1892.

ager and army blankets were also available. An hour later a Red Cross ambulance turned up and, placing the Princess in it, I escorted her back to the now-dark palace out on the Rennweg, once the meeting place of all who counted in the society of the Holy Roman Empire.

To escape the importunities of men who would lure me, and above all my flag, into their endangered palaces, I not seldom slipped out of the hotel and closing my eyes to the misery all about me, which I could not help, I would walk through the Graben and around the Ring conjuring up memories of the friends and companions of long ago who have disappeared in the whirlwind of war. One, and certainly not the least of those with whom in happier days I had sauntered through these historic streets, was the Cavaliere Constantino Nigra, the Italian Ambassador. What an opportunity I had, and how completely I muffed it! I still recall the weariness in his voice as he replied when in my role of an ardent news gatherer I subjected him to the modern *questio:*

"Well, if you must talk about the Yugoslavi, this is what we Italians think." Here was an *affascinatore* of the vanishing age which, as it recedes from view, exerts such a fascination upon all who are condemned to live in a prosaic world, and yet I talked to him about the Yugoslavi in an attempt to secure ephemeral copy about the ever-changing panorama of the Balkans!

After his retirement Nigra lived in Rome and Venice and was supposed to be writing his memoirs, which, however, so far as I know, have never been published. He certainly had a self-control which his great friend and chief, Cavour, lacked, and he was never misled by a feeling of gratitude. In the years in which I knew him, he was on the closest terms of intimacy with the Emperor Francis Joseph, although as a boy in the Bersagliere, before he was sent to Paris to win the friendship of the Empress Eugénie, he received at the battle of Rivoli a bullet in his right arm, and this wounded arm vexed him by always remaining a little stiff. Certainly it was not as supple as his tongue. He admitted to me on one occasion that he had made a few memoranda *pour servir*, but that he would never publish them. He confessed, however, that he was a secret poet and a diligent philologist.

"Someday," he said, "my *Canti Populari del Piedmonte* will appear; perhaps of all that I have heard and seen they alone are worthy to be preserved."[15]

---

[15]They were published some years after his death.

In Vienna as elsewhere there was much gossip in these days as to what was behind the extraordinary promotion which Nigra received that brought the romantic-looking lieutenant of Bersagliere from the tented field to head the Italian mission in Paris as Ambassador—certainly at the time the most important post in the foreign service of the rising state. Concerning this enigma, and a few others, the aged and weather-beaten Countess P——, after a hearty dinner, and with a long black cigar in her mouth, would delight the young people, who gathered about her table in the dining room of the Imperial Hotel, with her memories of the days that are gone. Her language was rather Elizabethan in its coarse frankness (I shall permit myself to bowdlerize it).

The old Countess would generally introduce her hair-raising yarns with this profession of faith, followed by the frank admission that sometimes, like many others, she strayed from the narrow path of verified truth.

"Believe me, *Kinder*," she would begin, "I try to keep separate *Geschicte*—which is history, from *Geschicten*—which is tittle-tattle. But I'm not sure I always succeed. Indeed, who can be? While Nigra had an insinuating way with the skirts, and his conquests were notorious, I would not venture to say that the wily Cavour sent him to Paris with the purpose of seducing the beautiful but neglected Empress Eugénie, but I do think that he reasoned this way. If Eugénie decides to punish her imperial husband for his notorious infidelities, it would be to the advantage of Piedmont to have the fascinating Nigra on hand to co-operate and assist her in her natural purpose, as any woman with hot blood in her veins will readily understand. But what actually happened, no one really knows except the good Lord, and what He knows is never communicated to us creeping terrestrial worms—and that is a good thing. If only He published memoirs!"

Vienna, Saturday.

Another request came today from Ballplatz, this time in official form, asking me to move to the Hofburg and occupy at least a wing of it. Again I declined, stating I would not do so unless instructions to that effect came from Paris. But a few hours later I was beset by a temptation that was much more difficult to resist than the previous invitations. The major-domo of Duke Philip of Coburg put in an appearance at my dismal quarters in the hotel. He came with letters from Admiral Höhnel and a card from Sternberg, who, like everyone else, I had known in Paris and Baden-Baden years ago when he was a prominent figure in the racing world—Sternberg has gone quite democratic and his visiting card simply reads, "Otto, a descendant of the former Counts of Sternberg." He did not deny his forebears but as to himself he has forsworn the title they had borne so proudly for many generations. Now he is seeking a job under the Socialist government. The major-domo was a sleek and comfortable-looking person, as was to be expected in a representative of the caste that had battened for years upon the largesse of princes. But for all that, his face was careworn and it was apparent that peering into the future he saw dark days ahead. However, he came straight to the point. "His Royal Highness," he explained, "is living on his estates in the country where he is safer. His little palace here is an architectural gem, as you will remember." (And indeed I did. It was altogether charming, and here Duke Philip lived with his wife, the rather plain sister of the beautiful Empress Elizabeth. Gossip in Vienna was that she had been selected as the consort of Francis Joseph, but that as he came to the Bavarian Court on *Brautschau* he had caught sight of her beautiful, dark-eyed sister, a little girl of thirteen, and had decided to postpone marriage until she reached marriageable age.)

"This architectural gem is in danger, we fear. Almost every day the street *Gesindel* gather in crowds before it, shouting foul words about his Royal Highness and throwing sharp stones. If you would only move in and hoist your honored flag, Your Excellency would be, as you should be, suitably lodged, and the palace would be preserved for the delectation of generations to come." With that the insinuating fellow threw a contemptuous glance about him at the sordid surroundings, which was all that the Bristol could afford its guests in these dark days.

Was I weakening or was I merely curious? Be this as it may, I must admit that through chattering teeth I inquired: "How about the heating?"

"Modern central heating," he said proudly. "True in the bins there is no coal, but a word from you and they will be replenished."

Shame on me, while I did not say yes, I did not say no. "My plans are so uncertain," I faltered. "My mail and important visitors come to the hotel almost every hour. To move would be inconvenient, any moment cable instructions may come transferring me to another equally vital post. Did you say that the central heating was in working order?"

"Perfect, only coal is lacking, and a word from you would procure it in any desired quantity."

I did not say yes and I did not say no, but the major-domo thought he had me. With a sweeping bow he withdrew, saying, "I shall wait on Your Excellency in the morning to learn your wishes." And true enough, he came in with my coffee.

"I neglected to tell you yesterday," he began, "that in the garage of his Imperial Royal Highness there are five cars. Three Italian Fiats and two admirable French cars." If he had mentioned those items the day before I do not know what might have happened. That was indeed a temptation to a man who was dependent on the whims of the transportation pool at the Crillon, with whom he stood none too well because of a smashing accident for which he was by no means responsible, but this added inducement had come too late.

"My instructions have reached me," I said. "I am leaving Vienna on Thursday." And then: "Thank His Royal and Imperial Highness for his hospitable offer and tell him that only the demands of my important duties prevent me from accepting it." The major-domo was crestfallen. He had thought he had me, and perhaps he had before those blessed instructions to return to Paris came. Would I have continued to resist the archducal palace—and the five cars in the garage? I fear that I, for one, will never know!

During the last days of my stay in Vienna I became greatly attached to a tall and lanky American soldier with an "affidavit" face who by some quirk of fortune had become attached to the Food Administration after the Armistice. As I suspected his origin, and his loneliness was only too evident, one day I said: "Virginia?" and he answered gladly, proudly, "Big Stone Gap."

"Then you must have known John Fox?"

"Know Mr. John? My father grew up with him. Many and many a time I sat on his lap." Detached from his organization, the boy was cruelly homesick and, poor reed that I was, he clutched at me as a drowning man does to a floating plank, and when I talked about John and how we had been together in the Santiago campaign, his features brightened wonderfully and he would say, "Do tell." He was depressed and oh, so homesick, and what really appalled him most, as he later admitted, were the strange words of the strange languages he heard on every side. Now that the war was over he wanted to go home and if that was impossible he wanted to be alone with the memories of his village and out of hearing of those outlandish words.

I gave him an extra key to my room and there he would sit when off duty, alone with his hopes and his dreams, because the American papers that I turned over to him did not detain him for long. "There was practically no news from Big Stone Gap in them," he commented. And sometimes we plotted together how he could rejoin his organization, and, above all, how he could get home where, as he asserted—I agreeing—he "belonged." One day he began to talk with me about a photographing "outfit" that had been abandoned in Vienna some weeks before. There was a lieutenant and three soldier photographers from Chicago. There had been some mix-up about their orders and their pay checks, and the lieutenant had taken what money there was and gone to Paris to straighten things out with the Signal Corps section that had been entrusted with the task of photographing "Europe—After the War." Soon he would return and continue their task, but down to the present the lieutenant had not done so.

"How do they live?" I asked.

"Hoover's men let them have rations but they don't need them. They are livin' mighty high, I should say, on what fat is left in this skinny land. They have gone into business and are making money hand over fist. They understand all these lingoes and are getting into every deal." Then in a tone of grudging admiration, "They are smart. I have to give 'em that. If you and I were left on our uppers as they wuz, I reckon we would jest naturally starve to death, but those boys are on the way to be millionaires."

The next day he pointed the "Chicago boys" out to me. They were in the back, or tradesmen's lobby, of the hotel and busy as bees. They belonged to a race that has often been persecuted, a people who have often seen their property expropriated, but have always risen superior to adverse fortune. They were now surrounded by groups of half-starved people to whom they were opening up business opportunities—for a consideration. "They say they are speculating, making business deals," said the Big Stone Gap man contemptuously, "but they are smuggling. Just now they have a corner in coffee."

I watched the Chicago boys for a day or two very closely, with feelings in which admiration and indignation were mixed about fifty-fifty. They had their fingers in every small business operation that was in progress in the Kaiserstadt-that-was. All the profiteers and *Schiebers* from the squalid quarters of the Leopoldstadt sat at their feet glowing with something that approached adoration. "If you let them go on they will have all the money that is left in this poor-folksy land," warned the Virginia boy, and he was right. The strain from which they sprang, the struggle for existence in Chicago which they had survived, had prepared them for the emergency that had now overtaken them.

I intervened. I put in a word at the proper quarter and orders and transportation came, and they departed for Paris with their pockets full of money. Once there I fear a rude awakening awaited them, the moment when they transferred their Austrian gains into a more substantial currency. But they would be able to cope with that and with any emergency that might arise, in civilian and commercial life, at least. And the Big Stone-Gaper paid them his tribute too. "Wonderful boys they were," and then he repeated: "Ef we had been left on our beam ends as they wuz we'd hev starved to death." And that was a true word.

Sunday.

Having heard that I was leaving, Herr Karl Renner came in this afternoon for a few last words. Obviously, and how natural it was, he wished to draw me out, but of course I stood by my instructions. "I came with a message and I have delivered it. Of course I shall be pleased to carry to Paris any suggestions you may care to make. I am sure they will be considered sympathetically by Colonel House and I believe by others who fully appreciate your unfortunate position." This pleased him and he said:

"We Austrian Germans are having a very difficult decision forced upon us. Our first thought, as we emerged from the ruins of the Empire, was to set about the building of a new country which should be a federation of free states. But if the other nationalities that were comprised in the old Austrian Monarchy do not co-operate economically and should threaten our undoubted right to self-determination, and it looks that way today, the conclusion is forced upon us that it might be wiser to join up with the German realm as an autonomous state, and that is what Botho Wedel promises us. Allizé, the French Minister, wants us to combine with a Bavaria emancipated from Prussian control. And that might be a way out, too, but of course the objective of Allizé is the security of France—naturally—and what we are striving for is freedom and social development along democratic lines for our own people. Would we find that in Bavaria? I doubt it. And what are we to say to the Sudeten Germans? Some of them want to join with us and are very greatly afraid of the Czechs. Having been on top in the Bohemian Hills for so long, it would be unpleasant for them to play the role of the underdog. But would it be right to invite several million poverty-stricken people into our own *Findel-Anstalt* (home for foundlings)?

"Whatever the decision as to our future may be, whether it is one of free choice or as a result of coercion, it bristles with difficulties, and this I hope you will endeavor to make plain. Few of our people are enthusiastic about union with North Germany. We have learned to know those people both in war and peace. Such a union would block our former channels of commerce and overwhelm our struggling industries. We would be confronted by new and untried commercial conditions. How would it work out? Of course no one knows.

"But, on the other hand, union would give us compensating political and social advantages. At least, so it seems; we would be safeguarded from national and racial conflicts and so be able to concentrate on the tasks that await all Germans, for as the war years have demonstrated, both here and in the north, our people are but little versed in the art of self-government. We want to live and we want to learn. Thank God, America is saving us from starvation but that may prove a poor boon indeed, unless we are given an opportunity to redeem our senseless past."

I begged poor Renner to be of good courage. I offered him my deepest sympathy! I could do no more, although I was well aware of how little was the value of sympathy in the actual situation. His unfortunate people are facing dark days!

Monday.

Yesterday I paid my farewell visit to Princess Metternich; her palace out on the Rennweg is dark and gloomy and oh, so cold. Once the meeting place of the noblesse, it is now dreary and deserted. No equipages block the driveway, and all the bedizened flunkeys have vanished. A crippled retainer took in my card. Like everyone else the Princess, once the toast in Paris and supreme in Vienna, has fallen upon evil days, and she has fallen farther than most, for her place was very high.

"*Die* Pauline," as the Viennese called her with affectionate familiarity, had always been gracious and helpful to me during my days as a correspondent in Vienna, and, unlike so many others, only once had she asked for her *quid pro quo*, and alas! on that occasion I had failed her. One of the papers had announced that Charles M. Schwab, the

American *Goldmensch*, was in Vienna for a few days. "I would so like to meet him," said the Princess. "I have grown up with men who were born with silver spoons in their greedy mouths. I have lived with *Rentiers*, with men, and women, too, who have wasted their substance and have wagered their estates on the turn of a card. Now I would like to meet a *Goldmensch*, one with the Midas touch, who has made his own money. And it is not mere idle curiosity," continued the Princess. "I'm thinking of starting a milk route (this was 1904). The people of Vienna need milk and I could supply it from my farms—if I only knew how to go about it. All my friends are wasters, they could not help me, but *Der* Schwab, he knows; he could."

For several days I ransacked the town for the *Goldmensch*, but in vain. He had gone back to the little poverty-stricken village in Galicia or in Slovakia, from which, a barefoot boy, he had started on the road to fortune.

On this sad day the Princess recalled my failure but with kindly words of appreciation. "I wish I could have seen him," she said. "That was a man from whom I might have learned much."

Then she voiced another regret, and this in poignant words: "When before the war my daughter married in Bavaria I felt the need of money. You see with us marriage is a costly business, and to meet the expense I thought of my noble forests in Styria.

"There was wealth lying idle—an undeveloped gold mine. I put myself in touch with a great lumber merchant and together we drove down there. How beautiful were my trees, tall and straight and full of sap and vigor. And the man could not conceal how he coveted them. '*Hoheit*,' he said, 'I will give you three million florins for your trees, and you will still have your land.' 'I must think about it,' I said. And indeed I did. That night I never closed an eye. I could hear the blows of the ax, the rasping, creaking noises of his sawmills, and I heard the fall of my stately trees—so full of sap and vigor. The lumberman came with the papers the next morning. 'Please sign here,' he insisted. 'I want to begin cutting next week, and I must bring my machines from the Bohemian forest.' 'You may go to the devil!' I shouted. 'May the *Henker* have you in his unholy keeping! Never, never will I sign the death warrant of my noble trees—so strong and stately—so full of sap and vigor!'

"Then the war came," and here the brave old lady sobbed but soon regained control of her emotions. "There was great need of timber on the Italian front and the army cut down all my trees to plank the roads, without which the big guns would never have reached the front. But the Government was very honest and the War Minister asked me what the trees were worth. I told him that I had been offered three millions but from Austria in her hour of need I would only take a million. He sent it to me in war bonds and with it came a bouquet of flowers. The war bonds are not worth the paper they are printed on now, but I shall always treasure the faded flowers. The bonds, yes, they are in that drawer. Do you think I could trade them in for a pound of sugar?"

This gave me my cue. I was leaving and I still had a box of sugar brought from Paris. I would send it to the Princess as a parting gift. For a week or two it would sweeten her dire distress. But as I went out of the hotel to carry out this mission myself, for in these days there is no one in Vienna who could be trusted with sugar, I came upon two pretty, ragged girls padding about barefoot in the snow and slush and sleet. *"Uns friert es Euer Gnaden* [We are freezing]." But they did not whimper; indeed as they sloshed about in the dirty snow they sang with their rich young voices:

> *"Es gibt nur 'er Kaiser-Stadt*
> *Es gibt nur 'er Wien,*
> *Es gibt nur 'er Rauber Nest*
> *Und es heisst Berlin!"*[16]

I liked these sentiments and the girls were pretty and brave, so I gave them half the sugar which I had intended to give wholly to the once-proud Princess who had fallen on such evil days. The girls kissed my hand in gratitude. They had a future and their present need was great.

Paris, April 12th.

In my first talk since my return with General Smuts today, he was not as reticent as to his bout with Kun as he had been in Vienna, but even so what he did say was not very enlightening. He evidently did not regard the incident as a diplomatic triumph and soon the conversation turned to other fields. He admitted, however, that he had told Kun that the scattered forces, more or less under his control, on the Czech frontier were violating the terms of the Armistice and that sooner or later this attitude would compel the Allies to take severe

[16]"There is only one Imperial City
And its name is Wien,
There is only one robbers' nest
And its name is Berlin."

measures. To this Kun answered that his government were not bound by the agreements which may have been accepted by Károlyi, and that as a matter of fact they were completely ignorant of their provisions. He then asked if the Roumanians were honoring the agreements they had made and Smuts admitted they were not, but he assured him that they, too, would very shortly be brought to book. I have a clear idea now that under his instructions from the Supreme War Council Smuts had tried to convince Kun that his regime was doomed—and had also offered to assist him (for the benefit of all concerned) to an easy "getaway."[17]

It must be admitted that the Roumanians also are not paying even lip service to the mighty men in Paris. Without a mandate and against positive and repeated orders, they are marching up through Transylvania and, further complications, thousands of old Magyar soldiers are flocking to the national standard of St. Stephen which Admiral Horthy has unfurled at Szegedin—and so another little war looms on the horizon!

True, the Czechs were on the Hungarian border, probably they had overstepped it, but no one really knew as the new boundaries had not been fixed. Smuts's first task was to prevent the clash that was so near and, by expelling Kun, to rob the advancing armies of all justification of invasion. Kun stayed in power much longer than Smuts believed he could. Smuts said in April the former Jewish insurance agent could not hang on for more than six weeks. As a matter of fact he retained power for many months, until August, and then made his escape to Moscow via Vienna. There is much reason to believe that before they left Kun and his crew had sent much loot and booty to Russia which would, they hoped, assure them of a comfortable, carefree existence in the years to come. However, these "old-age pensions" with which the White Hungarian papers taunted the provident Red refugees were confiscated by the Moscow Soviet and it is said that Kun has been forced to resume his former pursuit of writing life insurance. But now his methods and technique are quite different. It is said he does not write policies in the great international companies as formerly. You simply paid him premiums and as long as you kept them up you

[17]This plan was defeated through the obstinacy of Bratianu and by the weakness of the Allies in yielding to his demands. The talking point of the Roumanians, quite apart from their claim to Transylvania as the cradle of their race, was the fact, and it is a fact, that most of the loot by Mackensen's army had stuck in Hungary and that they wanted it back.

were safe from arrest at the hands of the Ogpu, in which he is all-powerful!

I should perhaps repeat here that in my parting talk with Smuts (before his return to Paris) he not only approved of my staying on in Vienna (as instructed by House), but urged me to try to realize his plan of a subconference to be held in Paris at which all the Succession States of the defunct Empire would be represented. He wished me to work on his plan, which had been interrupted by his call from Lloyd George to take up the Irish problem, and in his enthusiasm he announced that he was confident that within ten days I would be "herding the delegates" yet to be appointed to the peace fold in Paris. However, I received no instructions on the subject and naturally did nothing. Renner approved of the plan and told me that "in a hasty talk with him, Smuts had touched lightly upon the matter"—"*flüchtig beruht*" were the words he used, and that he was strongly in favor of the plan—but the invitation never came.

On my return to Paris, Frazier assured me that the plan never reached the Big Four, or even the Supreme War Council. He thought that in all probability Lloyd George had decided that Smuts should devote all his time and his great abilities to a solution of the situation in Erin which was, it is true, quite a man-sized job. Several days later, at a reception House gave to the delegates, Smuts came in and, pushing me into a corner, told me confidentially that his plan had not prospered and that he greatly regretted what he regarded as the unfortunate neglect of a golden opportunity.

He was pleased when I told him that Renner had authorized me to say that as far as Austria was concerned, the project was not dead. Hearing nothing further on the subject from Smuts and fearing that he had been diverted definitely from the only concrete plan he brought back from southeastern Europe, I (April 30th) accompanied the Colonel on one of his constitutional walks, and though I knew how beset he was with problems emerging from every point of the compass, I again explained, at considerable length I fear, the sad posture of affairs in the Succession States as I saw it. He, too, was impressed that something must and should be done, and right away. He took the matter up with the President and found that he, too, was favorable. He had no objection to the plan of a subconference but it soon developed the Italians had. At the moment the Fiume cauldron was at the boiling-over point—and so the vital and indeed most urgent matter was again postponed and later definitely dropped.

As an alternative, I suggested that a mission be sent to Hungary to take over when the Soviet regime collapsed, as collapse it would, although not as soon as Smuts had predicted.[18] This plan also won approval but was never carried out. It is true there were many, but certainly not more, important problems pressing for solution. Unfortunately, however, these problems were nearer at hand and those who pressed them carried more guns than I did.

Paris, April 14th.

Since my return I find much misinformation in circulation, and in circles which should be well informed, with regard to the wishes of the Austrian Germans toward the *Anschluss*, the union with the German Reich which, as I was instructed to tell Renner, is to be forbidden in formal terms by the Versailles Treaty. I am well aware that an opinion based upon but a few days' stay in Vienna is not very convincing and should not be accepted without further study, but, on the other hand, it should be taken into consideration that owing to many long sojourns in Austria in previous years I was able to make contacts with important people who would have been more reticent in their talks with a casual stranger. The result of all this preamble is that I have no hesitancy in affirming that the great majority of Austrians are opposed to the plan, at the present time, and that to the few who toy with the idea it is a counsel of despair. These people say "crippled Austria cannot stand alone, she must lean on someone, what crutch can you suggest other than North Germany?"

Even the people who favor the *Anschluss* see clearly what union would mean to Austria. As one of them said, "We shall become the granary, the very limited granary, of the Reich, and our infant industries will be put out of business by the greater productivity of the North German industrial plants." And whenever the subject was

---

[18]The Kun regime lasted longer by many months than Smuts predicted it would, and even longer than I thought, though I gave Kun a longer lease of power than did the Afrikander. Kun only skipped out in the following August (1919), and my information is that he did not get back to Russia via Vienna with the great treasure that the papers reported. My information is that the "Lenin boys" took charge of that. I have always thought that the devastation of Hungary by the Roumanians and the massacres of many so-called "Reds" at the hands of the Whites that followed on the fall of Kun could and should have been prevented by firm and timely action on the part of the Peace Conference.

broached I had ample opportunity to realize that the dislike,[19] even the antipathy, of the Austrian for the Prussian, has not been quenched by the common misfortunes endured during the Great War. On the contrary, I think it has been increased.

[19]The fact that practically from the outbreak of the war Berlin kept two divisions of second-line troops in and around Vienna, really an army of occupation, was not an idle gesture; indeed from 1916 on it was a wise precautionary move. They kept in check the partisans of a separate peace and also any danger of a revolt among the Slav factions of the Dual Monarchy. Had the plan to dismember Germany, urged at this time by many French leaders, prospered, I have no hesitation in saying that the Austrians would have welcomed a union with the Bavarians and the Catholic Rhinelands. And the Roman Catholic Church, so powerful in these regions, would have strongly favored this redistribution of the congregations, without the least doubt.

PART V

The Battle for the Final Draft of the World Compact

March 23d.

The first of the meetings of the Commission, since the return of the President from Washington, to review and indeed to revise the draft of February 14th, was held on March 22d in the afternoon and it lasted from three to seven. The Preamble and the first eight Articles were simply read, rather than discussed, yet it was quite apparent that the atmosphere of the future sessions was to be quite different from that which had prevailed in the past. While, as to the main points, the antagonists did not unmask their heavy guns or reveal their new objectives, it was clear that they all appreciated the awkward position in which Wilson had been placed by the hostile criticism of the first draft by so many of the Senators. The French were now encouraged to bargain more closely about the Rhine frontier, and Lloyd George was evidently seeking to secure a commitment for naval equality in return for his acquiescence in the Monroe Doctrine reservation. It was also clear that Sonnino would be more insistent with his Adriatic claims.

However, on the surface the session opened very quietly. At the suggestion of Wilson, presiding, Cecil explained that, under his chairmanship, there had been two meetings with thirteen representatives of neutral governments:

"I am happy to add that they all gave general approval to the Covenant."

The usually taciturn Makino (Japan) now went into action. He proposed an amendment to Article XII providing for a suspension of military preparations while a dispute was under examination. Textually it read:

"From the time a dispute is submitted to arbitration, or to inquiry, by the Executive Council, and until the aforesaid term of three months shall have elapsed, the parties to the dispute shall refrain from making any military preparations."

(It was sent on to the Drafting Committee.) We shall hear more about this proposal later.

Cecil proposed an amendment to Article II. It read:

"The proceedings of the Body of Delegates (afterwards known as the Assembly) shall be made public unless it is otherwise determined."

Larnaude opposed this—vehemently. Orlando suggested that the question be left to the experience of the future and Cecil withdrew his amendment. He then proposed that the number of representatives for each member state in the Assembly be raised from three to five. This provoked discussion and the amendment was withdrawn or postponed (ultimately it was adopted).

Hymans again proposed Brussels as the seat of the League. Wilson remained silent, probably because he has already made known his opposition to the Belgian proposal in personal talks with most of the delegates. He has stated that it would be advisable to have the seat of the League placed in a country that has not been engaged in the war. Not a single voice was raised in favor of Brussels; even the French did not support the proposal. The British are now all in favor of Geneva. While further consideration was postponed, it is evident to all that the question is settled. Geneva is to have a rebirth as the seat of the Parliament of Man.[1]

Senator Hitchcock, upon whom will devolve the duty of guiding the Treaty and the Covenant to the desired goal of ratification by the Senate, on March the fourth wrote the President a letter giving his views on the prospect. He also sent a copy to Colonel House. In brief, it reads:

"In my opinion, some of the Senators, even those who signed the Lodge manifesto on the Covenant and the League Constitution, will vote for it, I think, if it is a part of the Peace Treaty; and more will vote for it if certain amendments are made. Among these I would like to mention a reservation giving each of the High Contracting Parties exclusive control over domestic subjects. Also, a reservation on the Monroe Doctrine and a provision by which on proper notice a mem-

[1]This decision was reached later, and unanimously, by the Committee composed of Orlando, Smuts, Makino, and House.

ber state can withdraw from the union. It is important that definite assurance should be given that it is optional for any nation to accept or reject the burden of a mandate."

It is only too evident that the troubles with which they are faced in Washington blind at least some of the Senators to the witches' broth they are helping to brew here.

I here insert an account of our first contact with the neutrals.

This afternoon (March 20th) for the first time representatives of many of the smaller states which remained neutral during the war assembled in the Crillon and expressed formally their opinions as to the proposed League of Nations. The Swiss demanded that the permanent neutrality of their Confederation be recognized. The delegates of the Netherlands, of Norway and of Denmark, spoke at great length, and it is apparent that they share the same objections—which is fortunate and timesaving. M. Neergard, former Premier of Denmark, requested that the smaller states be given larger representation on what he called the "Executive Council of the League." For himself and his colleagues he said they were all in agreement in demanding a radical limitation of armaments and in forbidding the private manufacture of arms, munitions, etc. They also insisted that none of the smaller states should be called upon to enforce military or economic measures against an offending nation "unless they should have participated in the deliberations at which the decision was reached and should have formally approved of it." This was regarded by all as a reasonable request. Then the Danes advanced another request which is sure to meet with opposition. It was to the effect that any state which remained neutral in the last war, even though it had become a member of the League, could declare permanent neutrality and so be relieved from the obligation of taking part in any military action against an aggressor in the future. Also that its territory should be declared inviolable and that the passage of League troops across its territory be forbidden. The former Premier admitted that public opinion in his country had not crystallized as yet on this position but that in his judgment it was unanimous in favor of securing these reservations to be availed of when and if it seemed desirable. Wedel-Jarlsberg (Norway) wished inserted a reservation to the effect that the smaller states would not be called upon to participate in military measures against states not members of the League. Lord Robert Cecil, speaking at some length, poured oil on the waters which began to look distinctly troubled. His interpretation of these provisions of the

Covenant was that the smaller states would only be obligated to economic sanctions against offending nations. On the other hand, he insisted that they would have to permit the passage of troops that were proceeding against a nation rebellious to the decrees of the League.

Frankly, flatly, but not as violently as is his wont, Léon Bourgeois (France) opposed these suggested reservations. "All these reservations were nullifying," he declared. Adhesion to the League made all such conceptions of neutrality impossible. Then M. Loudon, former Minister of Foreign Affairs for the Netherlands, and long their popular representative in Washington, inquired: "Are all alliances defensive as well as offensive between the states forbidden by the Covenant?" M. Venizelos answered this rather vaguely. "In his judgment," he said, "in the new World Organization there would be found a place for purely defensive alliances."

House thanked all the delegates for their co-operation and dwelt on the fact, in his usual suave manner, that in a brief two hours of council all difficulties had been smoothed away. As we returned to our office I asked the Colonel to be more explicit, and then he said, "There has been no explosion or public indictment of the Great Powers, the 'big bad wolves,' for dragooning the little lambs, and that is what I apprehended—and not without reason."

Before the thirteenth meeting of the Commission, on March 26th, 8:30 P.M., the third since the return of the President, many negotiations "on the side" were in progress. Lloyd George and Clemenceau fully understood the President's plight in view of the situation in Washington, and they were, as stated more fully elsewhere, determined to profit by it. Clemenceau was now insisting on a better frontier, quite naturally, and Lloyd George professed increasing anxiety as to our naval expansion. These and other red-hot amendments are on the table or in the dispatch cases of the delegates, ready to be produced at any moment. To secure a cooling-off period, the President read a letter from the Swiss Government, asking formally that Geneva be selected as the seat of the League. Hymans made his third or fourth plea for Brussels, and a subcommittee was then appointed to study the subject and make recommendations. It was apparent that nearly all the delegates favored Geneva, although Larnaude maintained that the neutrality, which the Swiss wish to preserve, did not harmonize with this choice and would nullify it.

In consequence, as was natural, at this session there was considerable discussion of the peculiar position of the Swiss and a memorandum, drawn up I believe by M. Rappard, that had been filed with the Commission was turned over to a subcommittee for examination and report. In part it reads:

"Even if, as Switzerland desires, the League of Nations succeeds in legally and practically prohibiting war in the present meaning of the word, Switzerland must adhere to her traditional neutrality on account of the military executions ("sanctions" probably meant) which the League might be obliged to decree. In maintaining her neutrality Switzerland would then render greater service to the League than she could in taking active part in military measures even if these should be directed against some of her near neighbors.

"By reason of her neutrality Switzerland could keep up, as she had through the centuries, the tie that unites peoples of different races, different languages, and different religions. The League of Nations will have the greatest interest in admitting to the community of the League one, or several states, in the inviolable territory of which the international institutions could find a tranquil residence and therefore an atmosphere of impartiality."[2]

In a private meeting, preliminary to the formal session, Cecil proposed what he called a slight change in Article X by adding the words: "Subject to the provisions of Article XXIV" (now Article XIX).

Its purpose was to empower the Assembly (of the League) to advise on the reconsideration of existing treaties. Cecil thought that this addition would clarify, and yet by no means lessen, the responsibility that was implicit in the Article. Wilson did not agree. He said this was the Article on which the French relied for their security. He thought the change would weaken this important provision and he declined to accept it.

The question of withdrawal, which Washington, or at least many Senators, insist upon, now loomed on the horizon. However, before this problem was tackled an addition to the Mandate Article was agreed to. It provided that it was entirely optional with a state to decline or accept

[2]It was of course difficult to reconcile the Swiss point of view with the ideal of the League. The amendment to Article XVI seeking to do this was finally rejected at the meeting of April 11th. Both the French delegates and President Wilson, strangely paired, spoke against it.

In consequence Switzerland did not sign the Treaty of Versailles but she did secure a sort of left-handed security through Article 435 of that Treaty by which the parties to the Treaty "recognize the guarantees stipulated by the Treaties of 1815 . . . in favor of Switzerland, the said guarantees constituting international obligations for the maintenance of Peace."

a mandate. Cecil drafted and presented it at the request of House.

Then, suddenly, the withdrawal provision was by unanimous consent sidetracked and the proposal that the domestic affairs of the states, members of the League, should not be regarded as within the province of the League was taken up. This brought in the Japanese and the Irish problem and so while escaping from the frying pan, we most certainly fell into the fire! And on these subjects the President spoke at unusual length. As a constitutional lawyer, he thought the Federal Government had the right to override state land laws. If it did so in California, the question would be between the state and Washington and not between the United States and Japan. He said an Irish delegation had called on him, while he was at home, and sought to extract from him a pledge that he would ask the Peace Conference to make Ireland independent.

"I refused, of course. Since my return here I have taken up the problem with Mr. Lloyd George and I have asked him what he wanted done, if anything could be done. I told him," continued the President, "that the consequences of avoiding the issue might be that the Irish would start a campaign in the United States against the League and so raise racial and religious questions that we all wished to avoid. I am confident that such a campaign would be overwhelmingly defeated and that perhaps it might even contribute to the success of the League. My first impulse was to tell the Irish to go to hell, but, feeling that this would not be the act of a statesman, I denied myself this personal satisfaction."

Then, turning to Cecil, the President added:

"However, sooner or later, I fear a discussion of the Irish question in its relation to the League is inevitable."

With a melancholy nod of the head, Cecil acquiesced in this conclusion.

Continuing, the President said:

"It is apparent that many of the Irish organizations are convinced that by starting this discussion, and even provoking incidents here and there, they will compel international attention to their problem. All this leads up," explained the President, "to my fear that if we adopt an article excluding any interference in the domestic affairs of a state, member of the League, the Irish will regard it as a direct shot at them. Undoubtedly this would prove the tocsin for the outbreak of the Anti-League campaign in several countries which we all wish to escape—if possible."

The domestic-affairs article was now laid aside and there followed a great deal of rather desultory talk about the Monroe Doctrine reservation in which the President, House, and Cecil participated. Many of the drafts of the proposed reservation were gone over, including that of Senator Hitchcock, also Cecil's, and one that came from Senator Root by cable to Mr. Lamont. The only agreement arrived at before the discussion ended seemed to be that the Monroe Doctrine reservation should later on be bracketed with the somewhat similar Japanese doctrine in regard to continental Asia. Then the whole discussion went over for a subsequent meeting.

(In the main, the amendment to Article XV, ultimately arrived at, was in the language of former President Taft which came to House last week by cable.)

March 24th.

I am probably the only person in the Crillon who is not working on a draft of the reservation which the Senate demands on the Monroe Doctrine and which the President will see to it is inserted in the Covenant. Excellent draftsman that he is I'm surprised that the President does not take the matter in hand himself. But he doesn't, and my explanation is that the whole business disgusts him and he will have nothing to do with it except to see that it goes in—because it must. And scores of people outside the Crillon are also working on drafts. They come from all quarters. Lord Robert Cecil submitted one and the President did not like it. He turned down Hunter Miller's plan also. It seems that Miller did not even mention the Doctrine. "The Senate will not be satisfied by mere innuendo," said the President. Secretary of the Navy Daniels offered his plan, and then T. W. Gregory, the Attorney General of the United States here for a few days, on holiday, he thought—mistakenly—was put to work and he has produced the following:

"No coercive action shall be taken in the Western Hemisphere under Articles X, XVI, or XVII except at the request of the United States of America and the other states, members of the Council, if any, situated in that hemisphere." Nobody liked this, and when House broke this news to the Attorney General he said in perfect good nature, "That does not surprise me. I do not like it myself."

"That's splendid. You make it unanimous," said House. "Many changes and amendments to the Covenant have been rejected but none so unanimously as yours." Both Texans, Gregory is one of House's men and the Colonel is very fond of him. I think he has really been brought over to see if some way cannot be found to consider the war debts before our friends and Allies have forgotten all about them. But Gregory says "the money was lent by act of Congress and Congress will have to act, or delegate its authority, before the problem can be tackled by the President in any shape or form."

Later.

The suggestion and indeed the very language of President Taft have been accepted for the much-discussed reservation which is to be an amendment to Article XV. I wonder if there is any politics in this? Some undoubtedly will suspect the Colonel's fine Italian hand. In any event, the ex-President is now involved in the Covenant, indeed very closely.

House today endeavored to soften the President in his attitude toward The Hague Conference, but the President proved adamant and the Colonel's suggested "pat on the back" for poor M. Bourgeois went into the waste-paper basket. In fact, the suggestion seems to have irritated the President, and so he brought the matter up in open session.

"We have a great many difficulties ahead of us," he said. "I think it unwise to point out the failures of those who did not make the grade on the path upward and onward which we are now pursuing."

Nothing daunted, however, Larnaude proposed an amendment to the Preamble to the effect that,

"Our purpose is to take up and complete the work commenced at the Conference of The Hague."

It was meant, of course, merely as a consolation prize to Bourgeois, who had suffered so many defeats in the debates on the first draft. At the suggestion of Wilson, Cecil now spoke out in meeting; although his repugnance to all mention of The Hague incident was well known, he had certainly taken little or no pains to conceal it. He now said:

"The Commission has considered it advisable, especially from the point of view of the nations who will later enter the League, not to mention The Hague Conference. It has seemed wise that the instrument we are now drafting should be presented as a new plan and so avoid the criticisms and the strictures that have been directed toward the work of the earlier conferences. I have great respect for the work that was attempted at The Hague, but for the reasons stated I should regret any allusions to it."

Bourgeois now demanded a vote on the Larnaude amendment and he got it promptly. His amendment was rejected ten to five. Poor Bourgeois was brokenhearted. He came over to House and said:

"My life's work is wiped out."

House consoled him by saying that he would always be remembered as the precursor of the era of peace that now was dawning.

The rereading of Article III, especially the part dealing with the situation of the neutrals, led to a long and somewhat acrimonious debate. Smuts asked whether the neutrals who would adhere to the Covenant should be considered as original signers, or as later adherents. In this case, he maintained, they would have to be chosen by a two-thirds vote and, in his judgment, they would not like this. Wilson thought those who fulfilled the requirements of membership and who desired to loyally co-operate would not be frightened away by the test vote.

"They should welcome it," he asserted.

Later today (March 24th), in private conversation with Cecil and House, the President explained why he was far from patient when M. Bourgeois took the floor (and yet I the interpreter with the parched throat was the principal sufferer!) and came near to an explosion whenever The Hague was mentioned. "If I am correctly informed," he said, "M. Bourgeois was the leader of the talkfest at The Hague in 1899. He blazed the trail, or so his friends claim, but it ended in fog overhead and in bog underfoot. The whole business was wishy-washy—though well meant, of course. After talking for weeks, these loquacious delegates wound up with, not agreements—oh no, but with *voeux* or wishes. 'Pious' wishes they were, I grant you, but they were without binding force upon those who signed, or upon those who declined to sign. Now we are met here for hard-and-fast agreements, for binding stipulations, for commitments, and it is my task to see that no nation or group of men holds out on us—those silly pawns in the murderous game of power politics!" Then, after a pause, he added: "But of course I would not hurt M. Bourgeois' feelings. I respect them more than I do his plans for peace or the brains that hatch them."

More, much more than this happened in the session. But I shall have to postpone my account to a later, a more leisurely hour, I hope.

This morning a memorandum came to House in which the President states the changes in the Covenant he is willing to ask of the Commission for the purpose of placating the opposition that has developed at home, at least in Washington. They have been under discussion between the President and House for several days. "They go far, but I do not know whether they go far enough to ease the way to ratification by the Senators," said House. The President has little enthusiasm for them. He would greatly prefer to stand by the Draft Covenant (February 14th). He says: "I am yielding to men, to the judgment of men, who have little knowledge or appreciation of the world situation, but who, alas! control votes." And he added—and this is a belief in which I concur—"These changes we shall put through, but I fear we will find in the end that we have jumped out of the frying pan into the fire. Certainly the way will be opened for a flood of amendments which will surely delay us and may disfigure our solemn agreement—so patiently, so painfully arrived at."

The most important of the changes which the Senators demand and which the President will ask for and indeed insist upon is an addition to Article X. Roughly, in its present form, it reads: "Nothing in the Article denies to any American State the undoubted right to protect the integrity of American territory, when threatened, whether by a member of the League or by a non-member; or to prevent the further transfer of American territory to any power outside of the Western Hemisphere." Further, as an addition to the above or as a separate Article, the President proposes:

"If the difference between the parties in conflict shall be found by the Council or the Assembly to be a question which under international law is solely within the domestic jurisdiction of one of the parties, it shall so report and shall make no recommendation as to its settlement." This aims at continued control of the possible influx of yellow men.

The third amendment advanced at the suggestion, really the demand, of some in Washington is an addition to Article XXII which, if accepted as presented, will read:

"Ten years after ratification, a member State may withdraw from the League after having given one year's notice of its intention so to do, provided that all its international obligations under the Covenant shall have been fulfilled." Here is outlined the terrain over which the more arduous battles are to be fought. The President will win but he will have to make concessions—and even give hostages. Whatever may have been their purpose the recalcitrant Senators have handicapped the President in his fight to "make the world safe for Democracy."

March 25th.

House had sent to Mr. Root some weeks ago the draft of the racial-equality provision which Baron Makino wishes to have inserted in the Preamble, or attached to some appropriate Article of the Covenant. Here is Root's answer, at least in paraphrase:

"Don't let it in, it will breed trouble. In any event, you're going to have hard sledding, but with the racial provision, you will get nowhere in the Senate. And the people . . . ? On the Pacific coast, at least, they would think there lurked behind it a plan for unlimited yellow immigration."

Dmowski, the Polish delegate, came in today and made a statement in regard to Makino's proposal which pleased the Colonel. In his judgment, a Preamble should suggest, and perhaps even enumerate, what is pledged and agreed to in the Articles of the main instrument that follows, and certainly nothing else.

"As there is no reference to racial equality in any of the Articles," said Dmowski, "although implicit in all of them, a reference in the Preamble would be out of place and, indeed, misleading. It seems to me like giving a promise in a table of contents, and then omitting all reference to it in the text that followed. I think this would provoke criticism and perhaps excite suspicion. It had better be left out."

The outlook for the racial-equality proposal[3] of the Japanese is far from bright. Prince Saionji remains behind the curtain, but Makino and Chinda, harassed by cables from Tokyo, are evidently perturbed. They call on the Colonel almost every day, and he gives them all the consolation the situation affords. He maintains that racial equality is implicit in the fact that now for the first time the Rising Sun Empire sits with all the Great Powers in a world conference and he argues that with this recognition the Japanese should be content.

There was much talk today in regard to the German Colonial Empire, with particular reference to German East Africa. Fortunately, it was, for the most part, off the record. It covered again the ground which had been gone over by the Council of Ten in January. General Smuts led whatever discussion there was. There was very

[3]The clause which Makino and Viscount Chinda wish inserted in the Preamble or in Article XXI reads:

"The equality of nations being a basic principle of the League of Nations, the High Contracting Parties agree to accord, as soon as possible, to all alien nationals of States, members of the League, equal and just treatment in every respect, making no distinction, either in law or fact, on account of their race or nationality."

little, however, all being in agreement that German Africa had to be destroyed. I was particularly interested because I was in Berlin in 1890 when the Protectorate was established through agreements arrived at by the British, Portuguese, and the German governments, and when the Sultan of Zanzibar ceded his mainland possessions to Germany for a sum which was said to have been approximately one million dollars. It was about this time when the news came of the massacre of a large German force by the Wahabi tribe, that Bismarck, never an enthusiastic *Kolonialmensch*, is reported to have said that the disputed territory was not worth "the bones of a Pomeranian Grenadier." After the fall of the Iron Chancellor, the important element of prestige came into play, and very different ideas were advanced and accepted in Berlin.

While I never visited the Protectorate, I became at this time very well acquainted with the German pioneers in Africa, and in particular with Karl Peters, who distinguished himself by his cruel methods of dealing with the natives, particularly in the Kilimanjaro district; indeed, I listened to his recital of how he had executed men and women of many tribes who opposed German domination. It was a blood-curdling confession, and perhaps it is only fair to say that he was drunk at the time. However, it should be added that he was generally drunk throughout his disgraceful administration. After a long delay, Peters was brought before a military court, removed from office, and lost his commission in the German Army.

His successor, Major Herrmann von Wissmann, who went out as Imperial Commissioner, was a gentleman as well as an able officer. By his intelligent and conciliatory methods he effected something approaching a pacification of the disturbed regions. He was recalled, however, and shortly afterwards died. Then Count von Götzen was sent out; he is well known to many of us from having acted as Military Attaché of the German Embassy in Washington for many years, and he participated as an observer during our Santiago campaign (1898). He, however, was opposed by the *Kolonialmenschen* of Hamburg, who liked the Peters methods, and he was also unsuccessful in securing from the Reichstag the subsidies needed to build railways, or even roads, to the lake regions of the interior which might have developed the unfortunate country and given its inhabitants work. Later, in 1907, Herr von Dernburg was sent out; he now found all the tribes arrayed against German domination and is reported to have said (not in an official report, however) that he found the region to be "a hell on earth." "We must not allow such disgraceful conditions to be revived" was the comment of General Smuts, pounding the Peace table with his heavy fist.

The following discussion flared up in several of the ensuing sessions of the Commission. I am permitting myself to dovetail it as though what was said was a continuous performance.

A long and somewhat academic discussion followed upon the reading of the Article dealing with the question as to which states are eligible to membership in the League.

"I now propose," said Mr. Wilson, "a slight, but what I think is an important, change. In my original draft, I wrote 'Only States are eligible whose governments are based upon the principle of popular self-government.' While I think some such phrase highly desirable, I would like to insert now a more simple expression. I believe that the words 'self-government' more nearly approximate the idea we all want to express."

Larnaude, somewhat sadly:

"I once delivered fourteen lectures on *pays libres* and *non-libres*. Certainly Germany is not a *pays libre*, yet there are many here who advocate her admission into the comity of civilized nations." (A dig at the Colonel!)

Bourgeois made a long speech. His words were diffuse, but this is apparently what he had in mind to say:

"The definition which you seek is most difficult. What countries do not enjoy self-government? I suggest the phrase 'No State can be admitted unless its government is responsible to the nation'; in my judgment, whether the form is monarchical or republican is immaterial. We only have to ask is the government responsible to the people?"

LARNAUDE: "You are raising a thorny question of *droit publique*; for example, I believe I am correct in saying that Japan does not enjoy a responsible government, yet no one would suggest excluding her from the League."

"With us," countered Baron Makino dryly, "the Ministry is responsible to the Emperor," and then he added, "and, through His Imperial Majesty, also to the people."

"I'm afraid self-government is hard to define," admitted Cecil, and then President Wilson made a confession.

"For twenty years I have lectured on the subject, but I am reluctant to commit myself to a definition. To illustrate our dilemma, before the war no one regarded Germany as self-governing. The Reichstag was controlled by the Chancellor. On the other hand, there are many governments who live under legislation in some respects less liberal than that of Germany, and yet we regard them as self-governing and rightly so."

Then the President went far afield. He said:

"If we admit India, can we reject the Philippines? While we propose to grant the Filipinos their political freedom at the earliest practicable date, at present they are satisfied with their status, and I think it would be unwise to admit them to the League, although I am frank to say that I consider them farther advanced in the art of self-government than are some other peoples who are applying for recognition. We must admit that not all the States here present are regarded by all the other States as of good character. I therefore suggest that the Article with my amendment be provisionally adopted."

And so it was. It reads:

"Only self-governing States shall be admitted, also colonies enjoying self-government privileges."

The proposal to abolish compulsory military service, now taken up, was objected to from many quarters. This is Mr. Wilson's pet proposal and it was set forth in all his drafts. He succeeded in having it restored and provisionally approved. (It ultimately became Article VIII dealing with disarmament.) The President also succeeded in having restored the provision forbidding the private manufacture of munitions that had been omitted from the Hurst-Miller draft. This was evidently the President's good day, and when we adjourned he was bright and smiling.

It was at the twelfth session, on the evening of Monday, March 24th, that Wilson formally submitted the amendments which he had brought back with him none too cheerfully from Washington. As this fact was well known to them all, the President did not seek to disguise from his colleagues what an important bearing these changes would have on the American attitude. (They were all ultimately adopted, but none of them in the form in which they were first presented.)

The President proposed an addition to Article X, which ultimately became the Monroe Doctrine reservation. Also an addition to Article XV to the effect that, when a question submitted should be found by the Executive Council and the Body of Delegates (later the Assembly) to be one solely within the domestic legislative jurisdiction of one of the parties, it should so report and make no recommendation as to its settlement.

The President's third proposal was an amendment to Article XXIV permitting a member to withdraw from the League after a period of ten years and upon one year's notice. These amendments were phrased, it was hoped, to satisfy the criticisms contained in the Hitchcock letter, the cable of ex-President Taft (March 18th), and other criticisms of men who, while favoring the Covenant, were of the opinion that it could not be ratified in the form of the February 14th draft. The discussions on the Monroe Doctrine reservation continued off and on throughout the twelfth and the thirteenth sessions, and it was only adopted near the conclusion of the fourteenth session. But at this meeting there was a very heated discussion as to the withdrawal provision. Larnaude said bitterly:

"If the people of France thought that the League was to last for ten years only, they would regard it as bankrupt from the very beginning."

As usual, Bourgeois spoke at great length on the subject. He pointed out that the provision for withdrawal only after ten years of service, or membership, would be interpreted that the members expected a breakup, and, further, that an attempt was being made to hold them under duress in the meanwhile. He said he was willing to accept withdrawal after two years' notice, but he wanted the requirement of ten years' membership eliminated.

In the course of the discussion Orlando made several witty remarks. He said liberty of action was, of course, essential.

"*Mais l'important n'est pas tant d'être libre que de se croire libre* [The important thing is not so much to be free, but to think you are free]. If the States think they are bearing chains, they may decide to snap them in a brutal moment. I am in favor of membership, but the right of withdrawal must be reserved."

The President then formally introduced the Monroe Doctrine reservation with these words:

"The Covenant provides that the members of the League will mutually defend each other in respect to their political and their territorial integrity. The Covenant is therefore the highest tribute to the Monroe Doctrine, for it is an international extension of that great principle by which the United States said that it would protect the political independence and the territorial integrity of other American States.

"I have told my friends at home that the Covenant is but a confirmation and an extension of the Monroe Doctrine. This being so, they ask that a specific statement to this effect be placed in the text. So, as a concession to this reasonable request, I am asking the Commission to state definitely and explicitly what has already been taken care of."

This seemed to the French a favorable moment to renew the proposals that were nearest to their hearts; namely, some form of an international army on the Rhine frontier. This time they asked merely for an international general staff, but in a new and less pretentious form. They asked for:

"*Un organisme permanent,* to see that the obligations imposed by the Treaty are carried out and to assure their efficacy in moments of emergency."

And now, suddenly, doubtless with the best intention and yet it was confusing, Cecil harked back to the withdrawal proposal. This was probably by arrangement with the President, who now took the floor and spoke at considerable length. He said he was willing to abandon altogether the ten years' membership condition and to substitute a proposal to withdraw at any time upon two years' notice. Larnaude opposed this vehemently. He maintained that the fact of quitting by a great power would throw the League into confusion and perhaps result in a complete breakup. In answer, Wilson developed his views as follows:

"I have not the slightest fear that any State would take advantage of this permissive withdrawal clause. To me it is clear that any State so doing would become an outlaw; it would mean the cancellation of an arrangement on which most of us believe the world has set its heart.

"One of my difficulties," continued the President, "is that Americans demand complete assurance that they are not being called upon to give up the sovereignty of their States. I am confident, however, that the day is near when they will become as eager partisans of the sovereignty of mankind as they are now of their national or State sovereignty. But, for the moment, it is necessary to take into consideration current prejudices and make concessions to their sense of independence, of will and action. I confess I would find myself in a very awkward position if the amendment is not approved. Of course no State, once it has entered, would have a moral right to withdraw, but it would have a legal right, and that and that only is what the proposal concedes. I certainly assured my colleagues in America and other friends of the League that all here were convinced that the right to secede was implicit in the Covenant. They want it stated frankly and openly, however, and I am afraid the Senate will not come in if this is not done. I share with M. Larnaude his hopes and his noble aspirations as to what the League should be, but the most important thing of all is to make a start. If the Senate is not assured of a chance to withdraw, the difficulty of inducing it to ratify the League is very great. But once we have entered into the Covenant, I am convinced that the United States will stay in for all time."

Larnaude, the dean of the law school, evidently in a very bad humor tonight, followed with another violent attack on the President and the Monroe Doctrine reservation which we are insisting upon. "You come over here," he shouted, "and dictate what we should do and what we should not do, and yet you do not let us have our say as to what you propose doing over there!" The President, as always under these attacks, kept his poise admirably, but I fear that it was largely this perfect poise that infuriated Larnaude. Smilingly the President said: "I am convinced by what the French delegate has just said that at least for one of the delegates a more careful exposition of the purpose of the Monroe Doctrine is required and I shall endeavor to give it. At least one charge now advanced cannot be sustained. We most certainly did not come to Europe uninvited. We were urged to come, indeed we were besought to come, and our ideas as to how a settlement could be reached and a durable peace secured were formally accepted by France and by the other powers with whom in the world emergency we became associated. Indeed they became their war objectives and as such were proclaimed to the world—and to Germany."

March 26th (thirteenth meeting—anent the withdrawal amendment).

M. Larnaude, while admitting that his dear colleague, M. Bourgeois, had talked for two hours yet merely skimmed the surface of the vital subject, now whirled in with, "We shall astonish and depress an expectant world if we say, or merely imply, that we are making an experiment for a period of ten years. The world wants something definite and final."

WILSON: "I—none of us have the most remote idea of limiting the life or the duration of the League. Yet Sovereign States cannot be permanently bound. The ten years' period would safeguard their rights."

Orlando also wanted the right to retire, safeguarded, but he admitted that the provision of a definite time limit had its disadvantages.

"There is a possibility that all the withdrawals might come at the same moment."

Wilson then agreed to cancel the requirement of ten years' membership and also to substitute notice of only two years as a preliminary to withdrawal.

But Larnaude was far from satisfied.

"You are assuming that the League will prove tyrannical and that the States will be eager to withdraw. Such an impression might be disastrous. Non-member countries might combine against the League. The notice of withdrawal by a major power would throw the League into confusion," he contended.

As it neared midnight Bourgeois again brought up his amendment providing for an international staff. It provoked an uproar in which the protesting voices of Orlando, Cecil, Venizelos, and even Vesnitch could be distinguished. They would have none of it, and the troublesome question was again postponed. Wilson now appointed a committee to revise the work done or rather the amendments that have been submitted, and Cecil, House, Larnaude, and Venizelos were appointed to it. We were all so sleepy that it was only on the following day we realized that the humble drafting committee had been promoted and was now practically charged with the functions of a committee on revision. House told Miller that he was not good at phrase-making or word-splitting and that he, Miller, must sit for him on this committee.

It was at this meeting that a letter from Mr. Bryan was made available, at least to the American delegates. He stated that he was favorable to the League, but he thought that the Commission was neglecting "the waste places of the earth." He did not define them geographically. Mr. Bryan gave himself a pat on the back for his "cooling-off treaties"—the subject of so much newspaper ridicule during the stay of the Great Commoner in the Department of State. He certainly deserved the "pat" and more. Indeed the Bryan idea is implicit in the Covenant. Mr. Bryan also contended in this letter that the United States should have a larger representation in the League, one "proportioned to our voting strength, our wealth, and moral influence." He also opposed the two-thirds vote necessary for the admission of new members. "Many would be blackballed," he feared, and he concluded with the sonorous phrase: "The World League is for the World."

The French now propose a new article to establish an economic section of the League, with the objective of regulating freedom of transit and equitable handling of commerce. This drew fire from Mr. Wilson, and he spoke at considerable length. Obviously he had the Mexican situation in mind.

"This new clause," he said, "while doubtless not so intended, would introduce a dangerous principle. It is known, unfavorably known, in my country as the principle 'the Flag follows the Dollar.' My judgment is that no government should support its nationals in claims detrimental to the country in which their investments have been made. The League must be on its guard against accepting proposals of this nature. Since I have had anything to do with the Government of the United States, we have refused to support capitalists who have made unreasonable investments abroad and who seek unfair advantage over the people of the country where their investments are lodged."

Much desultory discussion followed, and then the Belgians proposed a clause dealing with international agriculture. The talk became discursive and Bourgeois, for the third or fourth time, brought up his plan for an international army or at the very least an international general staff. On the insistence of Orlando, Cecil, and Venizelos, the troublesome question was shelved again. It was now past midnight and everyone was sleepy. It should be admitted that the Commission now disintegrated rather than adjourned.

March 27th.

Yesterday's session of the Commission was stormy, and little was accomplished. Lord Robert Cecil was in a belligerent mood; his patience is often sorely tried by the little Belgian who is so frequently spoken of as the "pestiferous Hymans." Yesterday Hymans exasperated Cecil by voicing his old complaint. He said:

"The Great Powers are bullying the little States; they are not showing the proper respect for our national rights. With reason, the people of Belgium are suspicious, and we shall insist upon our rights."

"Good God, Monsieur Hymans!" Cecil broke out. "After all that has happened, do the people of Belgium suspect Britain of bad faith and of not respecting Belgian independence? Good God, Monsieur Hymans!" Cecil fell back in his chair, too full for utterance. And House very adroitly called the attention of the listening delegates to other matters on the agenda awaiting their prayerful attention.

A little later Hymans renewed his complaints. This time it was the mandate system that excited his suspicion. He suspected, evidently, that some predatory power was planning to steal the Congo; so Cecil whirled in with:

"It is clear to all but idiots that no state can be mandated unless it wants to be." But finally, however, "To quiet the fears of idiots," in the words of Cecil, the reservation was placed in the *procès verbal* of the discussion.

The thought long silent then found expression, that the clause covering the labor proposals was too narrow, and finally it was broadened to take in the white-slave traffic, opium smuggling, and a number of other international conventions. Speaking for Barnes (British Labor), Cecil said that perhaps the title Labor Bureau was neither appropriate nor sufficiently comprehensive. The President poured oil on the troubled waters and placated Cecil by adding the words: "Or such other appropriate organization," and this addition would seem to have been provisionally adopted, but I am not certain.

Teamwork between the French members of the Commission, Léon Bourgeois, former Premier, and Larnaude, dean of the law school, was noticeably lacking in this session. Larnaude coquetted with the Italian Prime Minister Orlando and expressed his disapproval of the darling project of his colleague Bourgeois, for an international staff to constantly and vigilantly survey the scene and to bring the Allied contingents to the danger points. He said he would vote against the proposal if it was pressed to a vote. Evidently the Colonel's frequent talks with Clemenceau are bearing fruit. Larnaude at least has been "instructed." However, it later developed he opposed an international staff only because he wanted an international army.

Then several of the delegates demanded to be heard. They wanted words inserted that would permit women to hold office under the League and to serve in the Secretariat. Someone complained that this might result in a woman becoming the Secretary General, but it was pretty generally agreed that this danger was not imminent. However, the woman question was on the carpet and the delegates proceeded to thresh it out at considerable length. It seems to have been provoked by the arrival of a delegation of American women who have been knocking at the President's door for the past few days. As a result of this suggested change in phraseology the legalistic Larnaude flew into a berserk rage. He does not suffer fools gladly—indeed, not at all—and he shouted:

"Everybody knows that in our Civil Code *l'homme embrasse la femme*—man embraces or includes woman."

Wilson agreed, but he shook his finger at the learned French lawyer who had at last introduced sex into the discussion.

"Naughty, naughty!" said our Presbyterian Elder, and Larnaude beamed and was as pleased as Punch.

"If no one objects," he said, "we will place in the record that *l'homme embrasse la femme.*"

No one objected, and it was adopted. And after a rather futile evening the Commission adjourned so that Larnaude might hasten to catch his suburban tramway.

"What a terrible waste of time the evening has been," commented the Colonel as we walked away, "but the President has at last agreed to receive the delegation of American women, and that is all to the good." House is delighted with this concession. He has talked to our women, finds them very intelligent, knowing exactly what they want to say and agreeing to say it all in twenty minutes.

"As a matter of fact," said the Colonel, "it would be a good idea to have all the delegates present. They might learn how to transact business."

(They were heard on April 10th.)

March 28th.

Bourgeois now offered an amendment to Article VIII dealing with disarmament. It called for what he said was a Commission of Contrôle and Vérification:

"Its members should keep us fully advised as to the actual condition of the armament, both military and naval, of the member States; also give us full information as to the status of such of their industries as could furnish, in emergency, war materials. In other words," he said, "I want a Commission to keep us informed as to military activities in the States that are members of the League, and in others as well."

The President opposed the proposal at some length.

"I fear," he said, "and indeed I anticipate that the visits of a Commission, such as our French colleague proposes, to ascertain whether the nations are living up to their engagements or not, would be far from pleasing to many. It might even be irritating. If we were proposing to form a Union of States and so constitute a Super-State, much might be said in favor of this method of supervision and control. But our purpose is well known. It is to avoid any suggestion of a Super-State, and under these circumstances, the supervision of the internal affairs of member States would be most difficult; I cannot approve the plan." Cecil joined with Wilson in his opposition. The proposal was dropped, but Bourgeois reserved the right to bring the matter up again, both in the Commission and at a Plenary Session.

The reservations to, and the changes in, the Covenant which evidently much against his will (only at the behest of Senators) the President is pressing upon the unwilling members of the League of Nations Commission may soften his enemies in the Senate, but they are playing hob with his popularity and even his power here. In a quiet, tactful way the Japanese are supporting him on the Monroe Doctrine reservation, for they hold that the term "and other regional agreements" readmits the Ishii agreement into the new code of public law which is being drawn up. The proposal that a member state should be permitted to withdraw from the League upon two years' notice is, however, the one that excites the most opposition in press and public. Lord Robert Cecil is doing missionary work among the delegates which it is hoped will prove helpful, but he has carefully abstained from committing himself either in the debates or in public upon the question. He asks only that the proposal be looked at "objectively."

Only Orlando supports the President's stand on this point and last night he spoke for twenty minutes on the subject. I have no doubt he expects a substantial return for his support, which is important at the moment. Boiled down, this was the sense of his rambling remarks: "He valued highly membership in the League. It seemed to him to be a precious privilege, but in case the League does not work out the way you expect it will, it is a comfort to know that you can throw off your membership with but a short delay."

With other and perhaps more important groups the President has lost prestige and I fear support because of these last-minute changes. There is always the dishonest opposition that will sulk until the President consents to pay the price which they demand for their support, and there is the honest opposition, that of the men who believe and say the President initiated the Covenant and that now he smashes it with a proposal which converts it into just another treaty that anyone can treat as "a scrap of paper." "Indeed now you can do it quite honorably, if you are not too precipitate, and give two years' notice. We were told and indeed we believed there was something sacramental in the word Covenant, that it was a holy compact that would in time redeem the world. Now it would seem it is not more important or lasting than a trade treaty you can throw over the moment it becomes unprofitable." So Larnaude—privately at least.

Important men of the Commission are not saying much but they are thinking a great deal. House hopes the changes will facilitate ratification in the Senate and stem the isolationist sentiment which he is advised is growing stronger in many quarters at home, but he admits that over here the President is paying a fearful price for these same changes. At public meetings and in their papers both Jean Longuet of the Populaire and Cachin of the Chamber are turning against the President and are doing all they possibly can to thwart what they consider is his purpose. Mme. Cachin who, having lived long in America, knows many of our phrases said to me yesterday, "Your President has sold the Liberals of Europe down the river." Longuet is even more bitter. Yesterday he wrote in his paper: "We must look our situation straight in the eye unpleasant as it is. We are confronted with the complete failure of the policy of the one man in whom we put our confidence." His bitterness is all the greater because in the beginning Longuet evidently regarded the President as a bashful "Red"; now he has concluded that the President is a hard-shelled, if cleverly veiled, Conservative, and is determined to "smoke him out."

I had quite an argument with the long-haired editor last night but accomplished little or nothing, I fear. He is not only disappointed; he believes that he has been deceived, and that, of course, leaves a sting. The only suggestion of a concession he made was the fact, which he admitted, that all the other delegates to the Peace Conference are more despicable than Wilson. "Of them, however, we expected nothing and indeed we did not allow them to enter into our calculations. One and all we knew them to be insignificant hypocrites. But Wilson—— These men accepted the Fourteen Points but with reservations; they would still pursue their Machiavellian path. Now we see, however, that a sinister comedy has been played before our eyes and Wilson is a party to it."

This evening session, in my judgment, was a total loss. It was marked by an outburst of bad temper from the English delegate who is variously described by the French delegates as Lord Robert, or "Sir Cecil." There were, I must admit, extenuating circumstances for this, from him at least, unusual departure. His nerves had been worn to a frazzle by verbal clashes with Hymans, who is so generally referred to as the "pestiferous Belgian." And more, indeed in overflowing measure, for the fourth or fifth time, M. Larnaude pinch hitting for M. Bourgeois—and reversing his attitude of three days ago—had brought up the French proposal for an international general staff to *contrôler* the military and naval establishments of the recent allies as well as those of the recent enemy states. And I had faithfully translated what he had to say. As a matter of fact, he had put in his plea so often that I could have reeled it off in my sleep. Being in an angry mood, Cecil took exception to my translation and taking the floor he said—and I had to translate his reproof—that I was putting an entirely wrong construction on the words of the French delegate. He asserted that the French proposal was not merely to *control* the armed forces of all nations but to *dominate* them, "to establish a super-sovereignty in the world we are planning. He asks that the role of an autocrat be assigned to the League and that it be invested with powers which only a vassal state would submit to."

We are told that even the crushed worm will turn, and so I saw no reason why an interpreter, however humble, should not defend his work. Be this as it may, I sailed right in. I should say that in his youth Cecil had evidently known a little French, of the Stratford-Atte-Bow variety, but it had grown rusty. I began with the remark that of course I had no idea what the French delegate had in mind, that my simple duty was to faithfully translate what he said. In doing this I find that the word *contrôler* which they use so frequently does not suggest domination or even control in the English sense of the word but simply to watch over, and to register the actual muster rolls of the various armed forces.

Dmowski (Poland) evidently enjoyed the verbal bout hugely and kept the French delegates informed as to how it was going. As a result warm smiles of approval came from Bourgeois and Larnaude while the atmosphere in the Anglo-Saxon corner grew *plutôt glaciale*.

For at least an hour the session degenerated into a talkfest. Words such as surveillance, supervision, inspection, audit, were trotted out and put through their paces in a way that would have amused, but certainly not have edified, the late Archbishop Trench and the very-much-alive H. W. Fowler. I kept out of it except to say, with Fowler, how often verbs derived doubtless from the same root in the passage of time acquire very different meanings. This for the instruction of Cecil, who was still trying to give the same interpretation to the French *contrôler* and the English control.

The incident depressed me, and not unduly I think. Here world leaders were assembled to form a federation of the world. It was indeed an opening session of the Parliament of Man. Almost everywhere

the "war drums" were still throbbing, there are battles along the
Baltic and everywhere in the Balkans, the Allied forces have been
driven out of southern Russia, misery and starvation prevail almost
everywhere, and in French garrison towns mutiny had raised its ugly
head and the men who were to prepare for the "peace of Jerusalem"
were engaged in kindergarten studies as to the value of words! What
diable had embarked me *dans cette galère?* I asked myself, and determined to abandon the crazy ship and return again to the study of my
Ethnic Factors, my colleagues of the Congress of Submerged Nationalities,[4] so many of whom were still hanging on in Paris and hoping
for hearings before the Great Assizes of the World Court. But the
Colonel refused to accept my resignation, and when on the following
day Cecil very handsomely apologized for his attack and said I was
entirely in the right I consented to hang on—but none too cheerfully.

March 29th.

By a coincidence, which I trust will prove a happy one, the seat
of the League of Nations, to impose peace and safeguard the pursuit
of happiness in this troubled world, was announced today, which is
also my birthday. The Committee on Location met this morning in
the Colonel's office and within five minutes the decision was reached
and the delegates dispersed to their various pursuits. It was a meeting
after the Colonel's heart, but truth to tell caucusing had been going
on for weeks and there have been brawls that promised ill for the
purpose that brought the nations together. And even this morning
there were what might be called *pourparlers* over the telephone and
also very unwelcome news was conveyed by the same instrument of
modernity. No! the delegates of Switzerland, Holland and Belgium
were not expected to appear but they were assured that if they desired
to be heard ample opportunity would be given them at a later meeting.

The League for peace, disarmament, and friendly council will take
up its residence very shortly in the ancient city of Calvin, and from
Geneva on the historic lake the new world polity will be formulated
and broadcast to a world that is weary of the old procedures. General
Smuts made the motion by arrangement with House and neither a
voice was raised nor a vote cast in opposition. The Colonel is pleased
with the result and above all with the speed at which it has been
reached. As he says, it is "these long talky-talky sessions of the Com-

---

[4]Colonel Bonsal was the United States representative at the Congress of the Submerged Nationalities which convened in Paris, September 1918.

mission that sap my vitality and bear me down." The President did not open his mouth, but it is evident he is pleased to have the matter settled as it was becoming a breeder of ill feeling. In the early discussion bouts the President opposed the choice of The Hague, which enjoyed support in many quarters because, as he said, it would revive memories none too happy of the Russian peace movement in the last century. He was more outspoken in his opposition to the choice of Brussels, and many of the things he said have, as usual, leaked out and given great offense.

Mme. van der Velde, the wife of the Radical Belgian delegate, said to me when I sat next to her at dinner last evening that while three weeks ago the people of Brussels hailed him as the saviour of the world, if he put in appearance there now he would be hooted. "But it will soon die away—and justice will be done to Wilson" were the reassuring words of the little lady. Knowing that I was talking to a left-winger if not to a "Red" I also leaked a little, but I trust for a good purpose. "The President's regard for the heroic Belgian people is unchanged," I insisted, "but he does think that the sufferings to which they were subjected during the war have upset their former noble balance and inclined them to imperialism." "And your President is right," interrupted Mme. van der Velde, "and no one knows it better than my husband and myself."

I have no doubt the decision was a wise one although of course either Paris or Brussels would have been a more pleasant place for the delegates to sojourn in. I had also suggested Vienna where now, no longer a Kaiserstadt, there are empty palaces and residences galore which would furnish splendid and immediate accommodations for the League. But the fact that Vienna and its future is in hot dispute, and with the *Anschluss* becoming with every day a more acute problem, Vienna was ruled out.

After the meeting Smuts and Makino came into my room and had a long talk about the racial-equality proposal which is hanging fire and is so filled with explosives. They asked me to remain and I was glad to do so, as it gave me an excellent idea of the style and technique of the South African when negotiating on delicate ground. He was exceedingly friendly to the formal Japanese delegate, but he made quite plain what course he would pursue if Makino insisted upon bringing the matter (the race question) before the whole Conference in a Plenary Session as it is rumored he proposes doing.

"Your position is incontestable and so is the status of Japan—so why raise the question? You know what my personal feelings are, but you see I am here officially, and so I must warn you that if you persist in your motion for which I have much sympathy, and if Hughes of Australia opposes it, as he undoubtedly will, I shall have to fall in line and vote with the Dominions, like a 'good Indian.'"

Kind words may butter no parsnips but they certainly softened Makino's attitude toward the white world, and when Smuts left him with a warm handshake I seized the opportunity to call his attention to the fact that the Japanese press, almost without exception, made America responsible for the stalemate on the race question and was attacking us most bitterly. When I pointed to the bundle of clippings on my desk which provided full justification for my complaint, Makino threw up his hands and said: "You are quite right and our press has been most unfair. I shall summon the correspondents in Paris to my office tomorrow and inform them of the facts," and I have not the slightest doubt but what he will.

When Makino went, Orlando came out of the Colonel's room where he had stayed on with a purpose not unconnected with Fiume after the short session closed. I noted that the charming old Sicilian was not in his usual amiable mood but rather had the air of a man who had been in a scuffle and was not at all certain that victory had perched on his banner. Rather unwisely Frazier, who from his long residence in Rome was on especially friendly terms with the Prime Minister, said: "I trust you and the Colonel have been making peace," but Orlando answered somewhat curtly: "*Je cherche la Paix*—my Peace! The only peace that will last." So he has given us ample notice. Orlando wants his own peace, just like all the boys—including the President.

March—undated.

Last night the Colonel was giving one of his grand dinners and Frazier and I naturally planned for ourselves a holiday, a carefree evening *en petit comité*. But as we put away our unfinished business in the safe our chief appeared. "I shall expect you to be present tonight. Two delegates down with the flu have dropped out. You must come to make up the quota of eighty." Smiling, he added: "You will have nothing to do but enjoy yourselves. I have unloaded the seatings and all the other troubles on the ceremonial officer." But this harassed gentleman, as it soon developed, like Jove, had nodded, and little Ali-Kuli Khan, the second Persian delegate snooping about the groaning board and surveying the place cards, saw that his first delegate, the

Prince from Tabriz, had not been assigned the place that was rightfully his. "His Highness sits far from where Mrs. House is enthroned," he complained. "He, the noble representative of a glorious monarchy that goes back six thousand years, indeed to the very dawn of history, is placed below M. Beneš, the representative of a republic that came into the world only six weeks ago. This would degrade my prince. I shall advise him to withdraw."

There was nothing of the silken Persian about Ali-Kuli Khan. He had, as consul, dwelt for years in America and had taken on much of our roughness, and now he was evidently mad all through. "I shall advise my prince to withdraw," he repeated, and Frazier, the coward, under pretext of looking for the ceremonial officer who was far away, rushed out of the room. "Let me explain to the Prince," I stuttered. Here at last was an opportunity to qualify as a diplomatist and lie for my country, and, as it seemed to me, no moral turpitude was involved! With blazing eyes Ali-Kuli Khan led me up to his chief, a tall and very picturesque personality. I began: "Your Highness, I should have advised you, but I trust even now it is not too late. The seatings tonight are not arranged according to protocol. This is a birthday party in honor of the new-born Republic of Czechoslovakia, its representative and his charming lady. His people, unlike the fortunate Persians, have long been in duress. Tonight it was the thought of Colonel House to welcome them right royally into the comity of nations from which they have been disbarred for so many generations. Consequently we have given precedence to M. Beneš and we hope that this gesture will meet with your sanction. Of course wherever he may be seated the place occupied by the delegate of a realm of such glorious history as Persia is always the head of the table." The Prince, who looked a trifle stern as I approached him, immediately relaxed and not only in excellent French but with a certain *élégance Latine* he said: "I think it is a graceful gesture, and I am most happy to yield the *pas* to the newcomer." Ali Khan was by no means pleased, but he bowed low to the Prince from Tabriz and the incident was closed.

But I cannot say that the Prince was the life of the party; in fact, there was no life or vivacity to the party at all. The Italians glared at the Yugoslavs, and even the neutrals were ill at ease, and the bright, enlivening talk of Mrs. House gradually died away into whispers. Frazier and I and some other young and unimportant folk, once the crisis was conjured, took refuge at the far end of the table. We were so far from the throne that we escaped the glacial atmosphere that enveloped it. We laughed a great deal but what it was about I have no idea. Near the throne sat Lady Asquith, Countess of Oxford, and she gradually succumbed to the surrounding gloom. Suddenly, with an energetic gesture, she rose, walked the whole length of the banqueting hall, and planked herself down between Frazier and me. As we made room for her she said: "Thank God I'm no longer in office. Why shouldn't I have a good time? Go on laughing, or I'll begin to cry."

We did our best, but it was not a great success. Lady Asquith was vivacious but so vitriolic in her judgments. She made a butt of poor Mrs. Lloyd George. "How wise is the little Welshman in keeping her at home." Then she began mauling the feminine entourage of Mr. Balfour. "Dear boys (of course we liked that!), have you ever seen such an unattractive bevy of women as those sisters and cousins and aunts that surround poor Arthur? For the honor of old England they ought to be put to death, painlessly of course but firmly, as Dean Inge said the world would treat another useless category of people when we become really civilized." Well, we were glad when the banquet was over, and so, judging from their precipitate flight, were the eighty participants in it. "I knew it would be terrible," commented the Colonel, "but it surpassed my most gloomy expectations."

"What were you laughing at at your happy end of the table?" inquired Mrs. House, but frozen to the marrow by Lady Asquith's bitter tongue we could not recall the wisecracks that had enlivened our little group before the acidulous Countess joined us.

The Colonel's little dinners of eight or ten are a delight to the fortunate few who are bidden to them, but the banquets are an ordeal not easily survived and never to be forgotten. "Thank God," said the Colonel, "there is only one more and then I will have dined and wined all the delegates." Then he recovered his spirits. "Did you notice how, possessed as it were by an irresistible impulse, at the very first opportunity they all rushed away, even the stately Prince from Tabriz 'got a move on'? They did not stand on the order of their going. They went out pell-mell in the way, though in reverse, that Tom Jefferson sought to solve the plaguey question of precedence in the early days of the White House."

Three days after the banquet of unhappy memories a most gorgeously attired messenger from the Persian Legation appeared, and after running the gauntlet of our very suspicious sailors presented me with an invitation to dine at the residence of the Plenipotentiary of Iran on the following evening. Less picturesque duties for that evening, a séance with the drafting of the Covenant Commission, prevented me from accepting, but I called, as in duty bound, and in a few days there came another invitation. This was to a *déjeuner intime*. And intimate it was. The Prince from Ispahan, or was it Tabriz? and I sat down alone. I confess I came to this encounter with some trepidation. Persia was not on my beat, I had never been there. Some years ago the charming Professor Browne of Oxford or Cambridge, I cannot remember which, thinking that my wandering footsteps might lead me to Teheran, gave me a tip which he said would prove useful. "Once there," he said, "do not mention that you adore, as all foreigners do, that book of Morier's, *The Adventures of Hajji Baba of Ispahan*. It's a great book and a true picture of a Persian scamp that Morier drew from the life, but the Persians do not like it—small blame to them. It curdles their blood and on several occasions has embittered diplomatic relations. Leave the Hajji alone, but they will warm to you if you mention the kasidas of Jami, of Hafiz, and, last but not least, the verses of Hatif of Ispahan." And that is exactly what I did, and the Prince glowed with pride as he showed me a painting of the still-scented garden where the great Hatif had written his sonnets and his odes.

But after an excellent lunch it developed that this was not to be a poetry party. His ancient country had not received an invitation to participate in the drafting of the Treaty of Versailles, he told me, yet he had no reproaches to make to anyone on this score. He admitted that after all the injuries that the Russians had inflicted on his country it would have been unpopular in Persia to ride boot to boot with the unspeakable Cossacks at the outbreak of the war.

"Fortunately," continued the Prince, "our great and good friends in France understood and appreciated the difficulties of our position during the hostilities and were content that we should maintain an attitude of benevolent neutrality. Despite our justified hatred of the Russians, we fought like tigers to prevent the Turks from using our territory as a basis for their operations against them. And we were successful, but at what a cost! Our most fertile territories were devastated and our priests, at least many of them, were in open rebellion. How can we stand aside, much less aid the infidels, in a war which the most holy men of our religion have pronounced a holy war? However, we stood firm, and with the exception of Serbia and Belgium none of the participants in the war suffered as great losses as we did in maintaining our neutrality. And yet here at the Great Peace—well, we are regarded as interlopers." I told the Prince that as an actual declaration of war on the part of the Shah was lacking, however favorable to the Allies this inaction had proved, Persia could not participate in the Treaty, but I felt confident his historic land would be bidden to join the new comity of civilized nations and be asked to sign the Covenant. He gave me several documents which he thought might be helpful in securing this boon. One was a declaration by the Parliament and the Shah denouncing *les violations du droit des gens commises par l'Allemagne, spécialement dans la guerre sous-marine.*[5]

April—undated.

I should not, and do not, claim to have firsthand information as to the initial stages of the Irish problem as presented at the Conference —with it I lived on friendly but distant terms. I only came in at what might be called the comic-strip page of the proceedings. I do know, however, that in March three distinguished Irish-Americans arrived in Paris in the hope of placing the long-unsolved problem on the agenda and to secure the support of the President to having De Valera and Count Plunkett recognized as delegates to the Conference from the ever-verdant and ever-turbulent isle.

This would have been a difficult task at any time. There were many and most troublesome problems before the great World Assizes without this additional load. But it was particularly difficult at this moment, when, at the insistence of the President (with a goodly number of United States Senators in the visible background), the delegates were being asked in the Monroe Doctrine reservation to exclude all American questions from their field of operations. With what grace, then, could he barge in with Ireland? Further, the President had had quite a set-to with Judge Cohalan on the subject before leaving

[5]With this proof of eligibility Colonel House had no difficulty in having an invitation to Persia issued by the League. It was indeed the first or second that went out to a neutral nation. The Prince went back to Ispahan delighted. I trust he did not lose his head when the League failed to live up to its promises.

While undoubtedly the Prince from Tabriz was immensely pleased to have his long-established monarchy invited to join the league of parvenu nations that was forming, he did not rest content with this privilege and honor. A few days before he left Paris he filed with the Colonel and with the Secretary General of the Conference perhaps the most exacting demands of all the petitioners and suppliants. He demanded (1) that Consular Courts and jurisdiction be abolished. (2) That ample compensation be made to Persians for the devastation of their territory by the combatants in the course of the war. (3) That all concessions to foreigners, however ancient, be cancelled, and (4) the territorial demands which even the proved friends of Iran conceded were excessive. The distant Oxus was designated as the Central Asian boundary and "all Transcaspia. Merv, Khiva, Kurdistan, and Mosul were to be returned to their rightful owners and lords." So far as I know these demands were never taken up by the Conference.

New York. He had vetoed the Irish plan then and there was little reason to hope that he would reconsider his attitude now, when, as was apparent, the only hope of a successful issue to his labors was to pour barrels, even hogsheads, of conciliatory oil upon the troubled waters.

House, however, did succeed in having the President receive Frank Walsh. He proved to be a reasonable and a very intelligent man, and the interview went off without fireworks. But neither he nor his colleagues were what you would call shrinking violets, and soon it became known to the press that they were in Paris and also some details of the difficult mission upon which they had come—and its purpose. Unfortunately for him, as it proved, these notices were brought to the attention of Lloyd George by his press bureau, and still more unfortunately there was born in his mercurial breast the hope that an opportunity was near at hand to settle the century-old problem that had so often affected disastrously Anglo-American relations. House having turned his deaf diplomatic ear to several verbal suggestions from the British Prime Minister that he would like to meet the distinguished visitors, Lloyd George wrote a formal letter requesting House to bring about an interview. Nothing could have been easier. The Irish-Americans called; Lloyd George found that they were indeed "very high-class men." He was not only delighted with them but a few days later he ordered passports for them to visit Ireland (which had hitherto been refused) made out for them, and also a destroyer to be placed at their disposal to facilitate their journey.

And now I entered the scene; I had gone to a party, apparently like all the other members of the staff. Not finding it to my liking, I had returned about nine o'clock to the Crillon and found the Colonel pacing up and down the corridor in a condition which, for one so invariably calm and collected, could only be described as perturbed. His face brightened as he saw me. "I'm sorry for you—but I'm glad too. I must entrust you even at this hour with a mission which is important for me, for Lloyd George, indeed for all of us. The Irish delegates have been raising Cain in Dublin, as was indeed to be expected, and the result is a tremendous row in London. Lloyd George has forgotten that he brought it all on himself and announces that, although with great regret, he will have to make public what he calls 'my responsibility' in the matter. He has arranged to publish his version of the incident in the papers tomorrow. He writes cheerfully: 'DEAR HOUSE: It will soon blow over. It is just one of those things which we public men have to expect—and must grin and bear.' Take these letters, read them carefully, and read them also aloud to Lloyd George, and then hold on to them like grim death. You must see him tonight and save the man—from himself. But make it quite plain that if he publishes the statement he proposes to make tomorrow I will have to make the real facts plain, perfectly plain."

Before I left I read the letter from Lloyd George asking House to induce the Irish-Americans to call and the carbon from House telling Lloyd George he had passed on his request, also the letter of Lloyd George thanking House for his friendly good offices and his gratification at meeting such reasonable people. I sallied out into the night with the sheaf of letters stowed away in a most unsoldierly looking despatch case. I went to the Prime Minister's apartment in the Rue Nitot, then to the Majestic, and to many other places reputed to be his evening haunts. But all in vain; I had no luck. Apparently Lloyd George had vanished from the familiar scenes. After midnight I returned to the Rue Nitot. Philip Kerr was not there, a young Foreign Office clerk was on guard, and he raised his eyebrows when I told him that my instructions were to await the return of his chief. "But," he expostulated, "at this hour of the night—or rather of the morning— I'm sure the P.M. could not see you—unless it is a matter of life or death."

"It is," I answered firmly, "the life or death of a newspaper sensation."

Our vigil lasted until nearly two in the morning and then Lloyd George appeared. He had been in the country for a round of golf and had stayed on for a drive and a late dinner. He, too, raised his eyebrows as I placed the letters before him. He gave them a swift glance, muttered, "Good Lord," and then in a challenging, almost defiant, tone said, "Of course I wrote these letters! Who says I didn't?"

"No one, no one," I said softly, deprecatingly. "Only Colonel House concluded that in the press of more important matters the fact that you did write them might have escaped your memory."

"And it had," admitted Lloyd George. "But, good Lord! how natural it is that those Irish-Americans should feel this way. They talk just as I used to do in my early days in Carmarthenshire and South Carnarvon. Yes, I, too, made the welkin ring with my trumpet notes of Cymric patriotism. But of course we cannot permit it now. Just fancy! Those fellows as they were driving down Sackville Street, under the patronage of His Majesty's Government and with an honor

escort from the castle, broke out with Fenian speeches and denuncia-
tions of what they called the Sassenach. Tell House I'm glad we have
gotten them out of Ireland without further incidents and that he
should not give the matter further thought. Why should we engage
in a newspaper controversy when there are so many more important
matters to engage our attention?"

The Colonel chuckled when in the morning I gave him a restrained
account of the interview—and the end of the controversy. "Great
man, Lloyd George," he commented. "A wonderful fellow. What a
flexible memory he has, and that is why it's wise to keep his letters." . . .

Yesterday, and again today, I noticed in the hotel lobby a familiar
face. Truth to tell this was not unusual, but the fact that the man behind the familiar face avoided me was unusual and not to be tolerated.
So I cornered him and drew him into a window recess. He threw up
his hands and stuttered "*Kamerad.*"

"You are Judge —— of Illinois," I charged.

"I am indeed," he answered, "but oh, how I wish to remain incog-
nito." When I laughed, he relaxed and began, "I am that ashamed of
myself. If it was myself alone I wouldn't mind so much. I could say I
yielded to an hereditary or prenatal and uncontrollable influence and
let it go at that. But there's the Colonel! I'm afraid I have compromised
him. I would rather have cut off my right hand than done that."

"The Colonel is very wary," I suggested. "He is a most difficult
man to compromise. Many have tried it—but have failed."

His face brightened and, "But didn't he go bail for us?"

"No, he merely introduced you to the Prime Minister. He vouched
for you as Irish-Americans and introduced you as such."

"Thank God for that."

"But how did it happen?"

"How can I tell you when I don't know myself? But I'll tell you
what they said happened. I wasn't born in Ireland and even my
father was born in Chicago, but I suppose it's true, as my grandfather
used to say, there's not a drop of blood in our veins that's not Irish,
and proud of it we are. The Prime Minister shipped us on a torpedo
boat and the young fellows on board were just as nice as they could
be, but I can't honestly advise a landlubber to cross the Irish Sea in a
torpedo boat in February. So we were feeling pretty peaked when
we landed at Cork or Cobh, I'm not sure which, and as is, I suppose,
natural, with such a warm-hearted people, perfect strangers came up

to us and said, 'We welcome you back to the ould sod,' and then they offered us nips and indeed they forced them upon us. I won't say anything against Irish whisky, but it must be dangerous until you get used to it, and you see all of us had been brought up on 'Berban.' If we had gone slow with the new tipple perhaps nothing would have happened."

"But what did happen?" I inquired now with some impatience. I was a busy man, and there were problems awaiting me upstairs in which we were more nearly involved than in this Anglo-Irish fracas.

"Of course I don't know," came the answer, "but I'll tell you what they say happened. We were driving down Sackville Street in a jaunting car and all Dublin was cheering us. They say I took the driver's seat and announced that we Irish Yankees had come to proclaim Ireland a nation, and the police inspector who escorted us back to the dock—not Execution Dock, but a quay where another torpedo boat was tied up—said that I called upon all within the sound of my voice to join the boys from America and throw George the Fifth into the Shannon!

"We had another rough sea trip, but what I suffered from most was remorse. The idea of all the trouble I had gotten the kind little Colonel from Texas into."

"He can take care of himself," I assured the now-penitent agitator. "Perhaps you were rash in switching so suddenly from 'Berban' to——"

"Well, I guess that's it, but on nearer acquaintance I found their usquebaugh was no bad tipple and that if you don't rush matters it leaves a pleasant farewell. I know, because the police inspector who put us on board left a few bottles with us. He said it was a very small price to pay for the getting rid of us."

The judge had not, however, been entirely weaned away from "Berban." He now just naturally gravitated to the bar where it was dispensed in large quantities and of excellent quality, but I rushed upstairs where more acute and certainly less-amusing problems awaited my attention. The last words of the judge from Illinois that reached me were, "Was it whisky, that strange new whisky, or was it old Dame Heredity?"

April—undated.

Makino and Chinda, the two Dromios of the Japanese delegation, came to see House this morning and talked, which they so rarely do, in the most forthright manner. They assured the Colonel of their warm support of the Monroe Doctrine reservation in the Covenant which was so near to the President's heart. When they left I agreed that their support would be helpful, but I did point out that not only, according to the language of the reservation, was the Monroe Doctrine excluded from the sphere of the Covenant but also "other regional understandings." "It seems to me," I commented, "that this means a tacit recognition of the Okuma-Ishii doctrine which confers upon the Japanese much the same guardianship over East Asia as that we asserted over Latin America in the days of the Holy Alliance."

An hour later Wellington Koo appeared, greatly agitated. He took practically the same view of the reservation as the one I had suggested as at least a possible interpretation of it. He said he was cabling Peking and feared that he would not be authorized to sign the Covenant if this reservation were retained. The Colonel was distressed and again expressed his regret that the unofficial action of the Senate had forced the President to make the move which had landed him in the troubled waters of Far Eastern politics. Makino now seems to be walking on air and I have no doubt that he regards this concession—as he interprets it—even more important than the race-equality provision[6] and the settlement of the Shantung problem which the Big Four are still debating.

April 1st.

It is increasingly clear that the Conference is in the doldrums and that heavy weather awaits the ship upon which it is planned to embark the Covenant of the new-world order. Our delegates are whistling for wind from a favorable quarter, or merely to keep up their courage, which it is not quite clear. The Colonel is as busy as a bee in missionary work to secure the insertion of the Monroe Doctrine reservation in the Covenant which is now to be amended, and the President, poor man! has taken to his bed. It was high time. Five weeks ago he sailed away, the picture of confidence—some (those who like him not) thought the picture of arrogance. Today he is broken in health and in

[6]The Japanese amendment presented at the previous session read as follows:
"The equality of nations being a basic principle of the League of Nations, the High Contracting Parties agree to accord, as soon as possible, to all aliens nationals of States members of the League, equal and just treatment in every respect, making no distinction, either in law or in fact, on account of their race or nationality."
This is also the amendment that Baron Makino presented to the Plenary Session of the Conference later on, April 28th, although he admitted it was but a formal gesture and that he had no intention of reopening the discussion until later.

spirit. The realization that has come to him so belatedly of the power of those who oppose his policies while it was long in coming has at last crushed him to the earth. At least two of our delegates are advising him to summon the *George Washington* and go home, thanking God that three thousand miles of Atlantic Ocean roll between us and the European mess.

It does seem strange that until now the President did not realize that Clemenceau received a tremendous vote of confidence from the French Chamber in December in support of his peace policies, and that Lloyd George about the same time swept Great Britain in the Khaki election, while our voters have placed the control of the Senate in the hands of his enemies. When he first arrived here and the Colonel pointed out some of the obstacles in his path, the President smiled and said, "Men die, but ideas live." But except when the plague is raging men do not die very fast. Those who favor an open break with the powerful war premiers (and there are some here who do) whose mandates have just been renewed do not, it seems, envisage possible developments of the situation which at times seem quite probable. Bad as are the war premiers to deal with, or so it seems from our viewpoint, there are worse men in reserve. Let us suppose, for an instant, and it is by no means a far-fetched supposition, that Foch and Briand and Poincaré and Franklin-Bouillon and other open as well as secret enemies of the Tiger should overthrow him (and hardly a day passes but what some threat of this is heard in the Palais Bourbon), what would happen then and what would Mr. Wilson's position be? Certainly not an enviable one! And suppose that Northcliffe, now in open opposition to his former idol aided by the far-from-harmonious groups of Tory-Conservatives, should vote against Lloyd George's peace plans?

And suppose that Orlando should be replaced (and he admits he is in danger, and the admission is not due entirely for bargaining purposes) by some of the noisy Imperialists in Rome who are harassing him and stirring up mobs to hang him in effigy, what would be the situation then? No one knows, but it would certainly be worse than the present—bad as that is. It is forgotten, or so it seems to me, that all these war premiers have accepted the Fourteen Points and pledged themselves to their observance. True it is that Lloyd George has reserved the right to "reinterpret" the Freedom of the Seas clause and also that he agrees with Clemenceau that France and Britain are still bound by the secret treaties and that these treaties are as solemn and consequently as binding as any their respective countries ever entered upon—in the words that Clemenceau so frequently uses. If our President should go over the heads of these recognized rulers and appeal to the people, and he is undoubtedly toying with the idea, of course he might win, as some suggest that he would, but the best opinion is that he would fail and that he would then have to deal with people in comparison with whom the Tiger would be gratefully remembered as an amiable lamb. And not only that—these new people would claim for themselves and their governments perfect freedom of action. To them the acceptance of the Fourteen Points by their predecessors would be classed as mere diplomatic literature. These considerations are having weight with the President and undoubtedly they should. After all, he has to show a decent respect for the attitude of large groups of European legislators, who almost any day may develop into majorities, particularly so as he now stands before the Conference with a request to amend the Covenant at the behest of a fairly large group of American Congressmen.

Undoubtedly this demand from America (and that is clearly what it is) to insert the Monroe Doctrine reservation has opened wide the gates to other and very radical changes. With perfect frankness the President and Colonel House have explained to the delegates that without this reservation the Treaty and the Covenant will have hard sledding in the American Congress, might even fail of ratification, and quite naturally this has been the signal for the war premiers to confess their own difficulties—and undeniably they are considerable. Many important groups in the French Chamber are denouncing Clemenceau for his apparent failure to secure the Rhineland and other vital interests of France. Poor Orlando is booed in Rome and Milan, Lloyd George is being harassed by the delegates from the self-governing Dominions, so the hard-driven war premiers can say, and certainly they are saying, that the wishes of their people expressed in legislatures, or in public meetings, have to be considered quite as much as the will of the American people as voiced in that Congress over which, unfortunately, President Wilson has, apparently, lost control.

So while he won the war the President must realize today that he has lost the ideal peace he dreamed of. What should he do? Wash his hands of the whole matter and go home? In this case there would be no treaty, and a state of anarchy not only in Europe but throughout the world would follow. The predatory powers would pitch in and take what they want, and the democracies we thought to help, and most certainly promised to help, would be despoiled. Or should the President consent to a treaty that will reveal some compromises in principle but at least one that will contain the Covenant, a bright star of hope and guidance in the dark heavens by night and a rainbow of promise in the troubled skies by day?

"I think the President will reject the counsel of despair," said the Colonel today. "He will not run away. He has lost the first battle, but with the Covenant accepted and in force he will win the campaign although I admit years may pass before the war psychosis that enthralls the world is cleared away." I showed the Colonel then an excerpt from a great speech of Gladstone, spoken by him in a somewhat similar moment of distress long ago, which I came across and have kept on my desk for weeks. He admitted that the reading of it was timely and the sentiments applicable to the situation with which the Conference is confronted. "I shall show it to the 'Governor,'" he added. "Not many encouraging words are reaching him today." And he read it aloud several times:

"Men ought not to suffer from disenchantment; they ought to know that ideals in politics are never realized. W. E. Gladstone."

April—undated.

Both the French delegates are still bitterly opposing the Monroe Doctrine reservation openly in the Commission and anonymously in the press. Larnaude, at least, speaks beautiful French and has a sharp legalistic mind. M. Bourgeois, on the other hand, is dull and repetitious. On this subject alone he has now spoken for twenty hours! On this I am the best authority, as I have to translate his every word, the President with a bitter smile having refused a plea that I be allowed to "condense." In his opening Bourgeois said, "I oppose this change because I see clearly that if it is adopted there will be two separate and distinct groups of States under the Covenant; the United States on the one hand and the European states on the other," and in all the hours he talked he added nothing to this but simply poured out a Niagara of words.

House and many others ascribe the opposition of Bourgeois to the fact that its acceptance or rejection offers a broad field for trading. This may be so, but, on the other hand, I think his feelings have been hurt and he resents the way in which he has been ignored. As a matter of fact, he has been talking, at great length, which is his habit, about "a Society of Nations" in France for the last ten years, and now that the League is on the carpet he is not consulted or even listened to; that rankles and naturally.

Wellington Koo, evidently greatly worried over what seems to him implicit in the Monroe Doctrine amendment, wishes these clarifying words added—after regional understandings "which are not in conflict with the Covenant." But on the advice of Miller the President opposed the suggestion. "It would seem to intimate that there are provisions in the articles not in complete harmony with the spirit of our new-world charter—and that would never do," were the President's final words.

A feeling akin to remorse comes over me as I look at the picture I have drawn of M. Bourgeois. In extenuation of what I have written I can say, however, that my criticism is mild in comparison to that of the President as he listened, because he had to listen, to the interminable speeches of the former French Premier. Yet it was from M. Bourgeois that I received the only praise for my services as the interpreter of the proceedings that I can recall, rack my memory as I will. One evening after he had delivered a discourse even more discursive than was his habit, and I had put it into English as best I could, M. Bourgeois came over to me and said, *"Il faut avoir de l'esprit pour saisir la parole au vol et recueillir dans ce qu'on entend ce qu'il importe de conserver* [One must have intelligence to catch words in flight and to note in what one hears the words that should be remembered]." In recalling this nosegay I must, however, in fairness, admit that M. Bourgeois' knowledge of English is most fragmentary—that he could not really have known how I acquitted myself, that his praise came from the heart rather than from the head!

April 12th.

Last night M. Larnaude again drooled along for hours in criticism or rather in misrepresentation of the Monroe Doctrine reservation, and many of his hearers feared that a filibuster was under way, but such was not the case. Suddenly pulling out his watch with an expression of alarm that was comical to behold, the learned dean muttered: *"Ciel!* I have only twelve minutes to catch my train, but I warn you, M. le Président, that I shall resume the statement of my objections at the next Plenary Session." So it happened, as often before, that domestic arrangements impinged on international proceedings of great moment! The fact is that Larnaude always becomes nervous when the sessions are prolonged after midnight. He lives in a distant suburb of

Paris to which at midnight all transportation facilities are discontinued. The President intimated more than once that the discussions would be humanized and above all shortened if some permanent and reliable arrangement could be made to restore Larnaude to the bosom of his family every evening. "He would call the attention of our transportation pool to this opportunity for service."

On this occasion the President again made an eloquent speech in defense of the Monroe Doctrine, its purpose and its limitations, but unfortunately a stenographic report of it is not available.[7]

House was deeply impressed, indeed we all were, with the President's defense of the All-America Doctrine, and while the President had no notes he helped the Colonel to draw up for his records the substantial paragraphs of this address, which in the opinion of American listeners, at least, was the most eloquent speech delivered during the Conference. And we ought to be grateful for the vitriolic heckling of Larnaude which provoked these extemporaneous and historic remarks. The President was pleased but modestly admitted that his effort should not be regarded as extempore. "To me at least," he said with a chuckle, "it had a very familiar ring. I was, or professed to be, a teacher of American history for twenty years, and rarely a month passed that I did not preach what the Monroe Doctrine meant to me, and now we are offering it to the world."

Here follow the words of the President's appeal to Europe which House retrieved:

"A century ago, when the nations of Europe were crushed by absolutism, the United States declared that that system should not prevail in the Western Hemisphere. That declaration was the first international charter of human liberty, certainly the first in modern times, and the real forerunner of the League of Nations. In this last war against absolutism in Europe which has brought about its fall throughout the world, the United States entered the struggle in accordance with the principles and precepts of liberty which it had announced and adhered to for a century, indeed throughout its history.

"And now I ask you, is she to be denied recognition of the fact that she was the first in this glorious field? Is there to be denied her the small gift of a few words which, after all, only state the undoubted fact that her policy for the past hundred years has been devoted to principles of liberty and independence? Indeed are we not assembled

[7]In fact, from the beginning of the sessions, at the President's insistence, and with the purpose of shortening the records, shorthand writers have not been admitted.

here to consecrate and extend the horizon of this document as a perpetual charter for all the world?"

April—undated—probably April 14th.

Looking over my recent notes I find them skimpy and perhaps they do less than justice to the forensic battles that have here taken place, the results of which, soon or later, will reverberate throughout the world. The most desperate struggles took place in the session of March 24th and in that of April 11th, and they were waged over the very contentious questions of (1) an international force to put teeth into the League, (2) the Japanese demand for racial equality, (3) the prohibition of military preparations in days of tension and stress when, and at the time, the problem is before the Council for its decision or ruling, and (4), and above all the rest, the Monroe Doctrine reservation. The somewhat fuller accounts that follow I have expanded from the hurried notes made a few hours after the heated antagonists had expressed their, I should say, equally sincere points of view. For this reason they may not be *verbatim and literatim correct,* but I am inclined to think they are because in the prolonged discussions everything was said, and restated, and repeated, at least a dozen times with but little if any variation of language.

At the meeting on *March 24th* we got pretty far ahead, reading down to Articles XV and XVI. However, it was not all solid progress much as we wished to consider it so. Many changes were proposed and many reservations suggested, and those who made them could only be quieted by repeated assurances from the President that ample opportunity would be given later on to consider carefully all these amendments—if not sooner, at least upon the second reading.

This meeting, which ran along into a five-hour session, was marked as usual by long, almost interminable discussions between M. Bourgeois and Lord Robert Cecil. The former was for making everything very precise, and, above all, clear. M. Bourgeois frequently went into ecstatic rapture over the advantages that would accrue to the League and to the world if only his standards of *clarté*, of clearness and lucidity, were maintained. There should be an international force, he insisted, the respective quotas of the participating countries should be fixed right now, and an international chief of staff should be named immediately. Again and again the English representative, Lord Robert Cecil, stated that unless the impending danger was in plain view it would be impossible for a responsible Minister of the British Crown to place a portion of the British Army under the command of a general who was not a British subject. As for himself, he stated that he would not presume to place such a suggestion before the constitutional advisers of the King. The President stood with Lord Robert Cecil. He assured the Committee that in his judgment, before any portion of the armed forces of the United States could be placed permanently under foreign or even international control, an amendment of the Constitution would be required. Then he conjured M. Bourgeois not to be so precise, but unfortunately this was of no avail as *préciser* was the word that the senior French delegate was always using and the condition that he was continually insisting upon. Things were going very badly, and the outlook for progress was poor.

The President appreciated the situation and did what he could to improve it. He made a very charming little speech full of pleasant things that evidently mollified M. Bourgeois, at least momentarily. The President stated that when he was a lawyer he had learned that "definition was limitation" and looking back he considered this lesson the most valuable that he had derived from his short year as a practicing lawyer. "I beg you to believe, M. Bourgeois," he stated, "that our only objection to the precise provisions in the Covenant which you urge is that later on they would hamper and perhaps limit our action. We do not wish to define what we shall do when the emergency arises because it is our wish and also it is our firm belief that the measure of our assistance, when it becomes necessary, shall be without limit."

Nevertheless, M. Bourgeois came back and back again to his original proposition. There must be a permanent international army encamped on the Rhine. Agreement upon this point was an indispensable preliminary to further discussion of what in France are regarded as less important, less vital matters. This permanent army was regarded in France as the cornerstone of the whole peace edifice. It would be impossible, it would be sheer madness, to attempt to erect the edifice of security upon any other than this concrete military foundation.

With increasing agitation and considerable vehemence, Lord Robert explained that there were things, however desirable they might appear to be when viewed in certain aspects, that were absolutely impossible, and this international army was one of them. He expressed the opinion that it would be wise right now to eliminate from the discussion this and such kindred matters. If the French proposition could not be modified, it would be wiser for him and his colleague to withdraw, as neither of them approved of it and neither of them would assume the responsibility of even submitting such a plan to the Crown. He further argued that the plans which by mutual concessions could be brought into acceptable shape were so many and varied that all the available time, and it was none too much, had better be expended in discussion where there was at least a possibility of profitable results.

But M. Bourgeois came back once more. Lord Robert in his youth evidently had acquired some knowledge of French and out of pure good nature he would from time to time interject into the discussion a French phrase that was sometimes helpful and sometimes was not. Lord Robert now expressed the opinion (to help out the interpreter) that it was stupid to waste time, but as M. Bourgeois got it, he thought that his amendment and perhaps his whole point of view were regarded by the senior English representative as stupid. There was, of course, a tremendous uproar, and three quarters of an hour passed before the incident was closed by the English representative and the French representative mutually admitting that they had for each other the greatest personal admiration and that when they clashed it was from an overpowering sense of duty and not, as it were, from personal incompatibility or want of mutual appreciation.

Unfortunately, when at this juncture M. Bourgeois at last showed signs of being exhausted by his own oratory, M. Larnaude, the dean of the school of law and the second French delegate, sailed in and he was, it must be admitted, more exasperating and more positively insulting to the other delegates than his senior colleague had ever been. And again, probably in recognition of one of Lord Robert's bitter and cutting remarks and his impatience of stupidity, these tirades were directed at the English delegate, and each of the long, involved accusations of the Frenchman would conclude with a challenge something like this, "Now, do me the honor, Lord Robert, to answer me that," but Lord Robert would only nod his head affably. When about the tenth accusation had been sent, fulminating with crushing force through the armor of perfidious Albion, M. Larnaude at last paused, and this time he insisted upon a reply.

It was forthcoming. Lord Robert said: "M. Larnaude, there is no expression of appreciation of your legalistic mind that I could make that would not fall short of what is appropriate. But I cannot answer your question; how can I, when nothing has been said and nothing new has been advanced? I would only be repeating what I have said a hundred times and what has been said at least twice by our honorable President (Mr. Wilson) in his inimitable and charming way."

M. Larnaude was very angry; his eyes grew very small and his nose swelled; he shook his finger across the Peace table and shouted: "Unless you promise us an international force stationed on the Rhine, and unless steps are immediately taken to carry out your promise, there will be no League of Nations and perhaps no Peace." And M. Bourgeois pounded upon the table in complete approval of his colleague's ultimatum.

While they gave us no new information, or even a promising lead, I should say that whenever the French plan of putting force behind the League was projected into the discussions it was warmly, if but briefly, supported by Dmowski (Poland), Vesnitch (Serbia), Kramář (Czechoslovakia), and Hymans (Belgium). They, too, demanded, first, that the League should have at its disposal an international force, always ready to be sent to the point of danger; second, a posse composed of contingents drawn from the armies of the states, members of the League, proportioned to their population; and, third, as a last resort, an international general staff to keep close watch on the political scene and to have prepared plans to meet aggression wherever it showed its head—and, if possible, before it developed into a menace to world peace. When the meager sop[8] of consolation (Article IX) was handed out Dmowski said sadly:

"I had hoped that our distinguished and most welcome visitors from across the seas, broad as well as narrow, would carefully weigh the unanimous opinion of those unfortunate peoples who dwell so near the cave where the wolf pack lowers."[9]

Then, despite the lateness of the hour, Baron Makino (Japan) who, calm and imperturbable like Buddha on his lotus throne, has generally remained silent throughout the stormy sessions, arose and developed into a portentous troublemaker. As an amendment to Article XII he again proposed "that no military preparations of any kind should be permitted to contending nations while their respective claims were being investigated and while the question at issue awaited a decision" (by the Council of the League).

It was now thought to be a good time to adjourn and indeed it was.

[8]The "sop" in its greatly slenderized form finally was inserted as Article IX and reads: "A permanent Commission shall be constituted to advise the Council on the execution of the provisions of Articles I and VIII, and on military, naval, and air questions generally."

[9]It is sad to admit that these five countries were the first to suffer from the failure of the Conference to take the precautionary measures which they so repeatedly advocated.

Sleepy eyes were raised toward the clock, and it was found to be twenty minutes past one in the morning. The President was aghast, and he relieved the tense situation in which the delegates were separating by saying that his mind absolutely refused to function after midnight and that the something that took the place of his mind after this hour was wholly unreliable. M. Larnaude admitted somewhat ruefully that the last Metro train for Neuilly had left at eleven o'clock. Lord Robert Cecil gallantly offered the hospitality of the Hotel Majestic which was frigidly declined, and accompanied by M. Bourgeois he insisted upon wandering out in the drizzling rain to look for a taxi or a *sapin*, as he put it.

Fifteenth meeting, April 11, 1919.

I return once again to this crowded session. Lord Robert Cecil at this his first opportunity called the attention of the Commission to the difficulties which would arise if the Japanese amendment forbidding military preparations in a day of crisis, which had been presented as Article XIIa, should be adopted.

Such a provision would give an important advantage to such states as maintained their military establishment in a highly developed state. Should a crisis arise, the small and peaceful nations with a low military establishment would find themselves at a serious disadvantage if they could not make use of the period of three months (the delay imposed by the Covenant) in order to prepare a better defense against a nation with superior armaments and larger effectives.

Baron Makino observed that the whole spirit of the Covenant was opposed to the principle that nations might make military preparations in a crisis. If they should undertake warlike measures, a tense atmosphere would be created which would hardly conduce to a peaceful settlement. Moreover, if the nation whose military preparations were inadequate should augment them, the better armed nation would do the same and the discrepancy between the two military forces would remain the same.

The Committee (drafting the Covenant) had raised the objection that the Japanese amendment would result in forcing nations into a military program of serious dimensions. In answer, it might be said that the purpose of Article VIII was to lay down limits of armaments which might not be exceeded.

President Wilson said that he understood the provisions of Article VIII as they had been interpreted by Baron Makino. Nevertheless, without violating the obligations imposed by this Article, the states members of the League might increase their armaments up to the permitted maximum even during the period of time which would follow recourse to arbitration.

Lord Robert Cecil imagined the following hypothetical case. Suppose that an unscrupulous nation should be considering an attack against a neighboring state. She mobilizes all her troops, masses them on the frontier, and thereupon starts a dispute of a nature calculated to lead to a rupture. The dispute would then, in conformity to the Covenant, be submitted to arbitration, and while the case was being examined, the aggressor state would have all its forces ready for action. On the other hand, the state which was threatened would not be able to take any preparatory measures. As far as naval power was concerned, a state might quite easily, without violating Article VIII, mobilize its fleet with a view to aggression. The Japanese amendment would seem, therefore, to impose obligations too great for human nature and to put tremendous advantages into the hands of unscrupulous states.

M. Larnaude supported these observations of Lord Robert Cecil, which had previously been discussed by the Drafting Committee. He himself thought that the Japanese amendment would compel states to increase the number of their effectives. On the other hand, if they knew that they might take advantage of the period of three months, they would not maintain in time of peace forces equal to the maximum allowed them.

Viscount Chinda asked whether it was the idea of the Committee that military preparations might be made during the period of three months.

Lord Robert Cecil replied that if the forces of any state were less than the maximum fixed by the program of reduction they might be increased up to the maximum, but not beyond this point. Moreover, he recognized the force of the argument made by M. Larnaude, if the amendment were adopted, it would compel each state to maintain its forces at the maximum in order that it might be sure of defending itself against any aggressive act.

M. Bourgeois remarked that in this matter, as in many other matters, the whole difficulty lay in the fact that a *control of armaments such as he advocated* would not exist.

Mr. Orlando said that the Japanese amendment was unquestionably in harmony with the spirit of the Covenant. If the three months' period were to be considered as a period of military preparation, the first thing which every state would do in case of dispute would be to mobilize its armies on the frontier and increase its output of material. Could anyone imagine a state of things less favorable to a peaceful settlement? It would be a kind of invitation to war.

Mr. Vesnitch thought that the states about to become members of the League would become uneasy if they were not able to make military preparations in case they thought themselves threatened by a more or less open aggression. For this reason, he thought that it would be better not to adopt the Japanese amendment.

Mr. Koo said that he only wished to add a few words to what had already been said. The spirit of the proposed amendment pleased him inasmuch as it had unquestionably been conceived in the interests of peace. He thought, however, that it would not achieve the desired object inasmuch as it would encourage certain states, as M. Larnaude had so justly said, to maintain throughout a period of peace the maximum military force. Finally, such a situation would turn the world into a veritable armed camp just as it had been before the war. Military preparations were contagious. Should one nation maintain its forces at the maximum, another nation would do the same, and still another nation would follow the example set by the two. Moreover, the possibility of taking military steps during the moratorium would make it possible for nations to pay less attention to military preparations and would not compel such nations as were favorably disposed toward a program of disarmament to keep their establishment up to the maximum permitted. Therefore, Mr. Koo thought that the amendment should be rejected.

Lord Robert Cecil said that the League of Nations looks toward a program of complete disarmament and that the Japanese amendment would tend to force nations into maintaining the maximum of armaments in order to avoid finding themselves at a military disadvantage.

Mr. Reis (Portugal), as a representative of a small power, said he was opposed to the amendment. The Great Powers always could impose their will upon the small powers and the only salvation of the latter lay in their being able to arm themselves as well as possible in case of need in order to re-establish the balance as well as they might.

President Wilson explained why he had welcomed the adoption of the Japanese amendment at an earlier meeting. In a Treaty concluded by the United States with twenty-six other states, an unsuccessful attempt had been made to introduce a provision like the one before the

Commission. In other words, he had a sentimental interest in the Japanese amendment inasmuch as it had given him a momentary feeling that he was taking a friendly revenge upon those who had opposed the insertion of a similar clause in those other treaties (the Bryan Treaties). He admitted, however, that he had perhaps not given sufficient consideration to all the consequences which a provision of this sort might lead to. Every member of the Commission must be in sympathy with the generous impulse which had inspired the Japanese amendment, but he thought that a majority now saw the inconveniences which would arise if it were accepted.

Baron Makino did not insist upon the retention of his amendment, but expressed the desire that the Council would strictly supervise the performance of the program of armament reduction laid down for various states.

Thereupon the amendment was withdrawn.

Fifteenth meeting.

April 11th was indeed a day of battle! It broke when Baron Makino (Japan) made the following statement: a renewal of the plea first made on February 13th:

"I have already had occasion to bring up this subject before the Committee, but it was in another form and with a different meaning. The subject is a matter of such great moment and concern for a considerable part of mankind, and especially to the nation I represent, that I deem it my duty to present it again for your consideration. My reasons, having already been set forth, I shall now be as brief as possible.

"This League is intended to be a world instrument for enforcing righteousness and defeating force. It is to be the highest Court of Justice. It will, besides providing for social reforms, also look after the welfare and interests of the less-advanced peoples by entrusting their government to mandatory states. It is an attempt to regulate the conduct of nations and peoples toward one another, according to a higher moral standard than has obtained in the past, and to administer justice more fairly throughout the world. These ideas have touched the inmost human soul and have quickened the common feelings of different peoples scattered over the five continents. It has given birth to hopes and aspirations, and strengthened the sense of legitimate claims they consider as their due.

"The sentiment of nationality, one of the strongest human feelings, has been aroused by the present world-wide moral renaissance, and is at present receiving just recognition in adjusting international affairs. In close connection with the grievances of the oppressed nationalities there exist the wrongs of racial discrimination which were, and are, the subject of deep resentment on the part of a large portion of the human race. The feeling of being slighted has long been a standing grievance with certain peoples. And the announcement of the principle of justice for peoples and nationalities as the basis of the future international relationship has so heightened their legitimate aspirations, that they consider it their right and their duty to see that this wrong should be redressed.

"It must be admitted that it has been possible to bring our work to this advanced stage only because the prevailing world opinion has backed the different governments in working it out, and that the enduring success of this undertaking will depend much more on the adherence to (and espousal of) the noble ideals, set forth in the Preamble, by the various peoples concerned than on the support or acts of respective governments that may change from time to time. The peoples constituting the states members of the league must be the future trustees of this work, and their close harmony and mutual confidence are necessary for insuring such success.

"Believing these conditions to be indispensable, I think it only reasonable that the principle of the equality of nations and the just treatment of their nationals should be laid down as a fundamental basis of future relations in this world organization. If this reasonable and just claim is now denied, it will, in the eyes of those peoples who with reason are vitally interested, have the significance of a reflection on their racial quality and status. Their faith in the justice and righteousness of the Pact which is to be their guiding spirit may be shaken.

"Such a frame of mind may, it is to be feared, lead to their unwillingness and reluctance to carry out obligations, such as military contributions, which certain emergencies, foreseen in different Articles, may require. A most deplorable situation may thus be created, now that the world is to move on a higher plane of international political life. It will not be easy for people to reconcile themselves to the idea of submitting to a call for heavy and serious obligations, perchance in defense of those at whose hands they are refused just treatment. Such a contingency must be borne in mind, for pride is one of the most forceful and at times an uncontrollable cause of human action.

"I state in all seriousness that although at this particular juncture of political life the practical bearing of such a dangerous development of the question may not be fully realized, I, for one, entertain much anxiety about the possible future outcome of this question.

"My amendment to the Preamble is simply to lay down a general principle as regards the relations between at least the nationalities forming the League, just as it prescribes the rules of conduct to be observed between the governments of the member states.

"It is not intended that the amendment should encroach on the internal affairs of any nation. It simply sets forth a guiding principle for future international intercourse. The work of carrying out this principle comes within the indisputable competence of the proper authorities. This amendment does not fully meet our wishes, but it is an attempt to conciliate the viewpoints of different peoples, and it was arrived at after a most thorough and mature consideration of various aspects and the plain, unavoidable realities of present international relations."

Baron Makino concluded by formally asking that after the words "relations between Nations" in the Preamble, the following clause should be inserted: "By the endorsement of the principle of the equality of Nations and the just treatment of their nationals."

Lord Robert Cecil regretted that he was not in a position to vote for this amendment although he was personally entirely in accord with the idea advanced by the Japanese delegation. The British Government realized the importance of the racial question, but its solution could not be attempted by the Commission without encroaching upon the sovereignty of states members of the League. One of two things must be true: either the points which the Japanese delegation proposed to add to the Preamble were vague and ineffective, or else they were of practical significance. In the latter case, they opened the door to serious controversy and to interference in the domestic affairs of states members of the League. There were a great many things which the states themselves ought to do, but these were not included in the Preamble. For example, it had been found impossible to include in the text matters so unquestionably right as those of religious liberty, the claims of the International Council of Women, and a great many other principles of this sort because they would result in infringements of the sovereignty of states. Furthermore, Japan would be permanently represented on the Executive Council, and this fact would place her in a situation of complete equality with the other Great

Powers. This being so, it would always be possible for her to raise the question of equality of races and of nations before the Council itself.

Viscount Chinda, the second Japanese delegate, replied to the objections raised by Lord Robert Cecil. He pointed out that the Japanese delegate had not broached the question of race or of immigration. He asked for nothing more than a formal recognition of the principle of equality of nations and the just treatment of their nationals. These words might have a broad significance, but they certainly meant that all the members of the League should be treated with equality and justice. He thought it quite as important to introduce this principle into the Covenant as it was to introduce such other questions as the supervision of labor conditions, public health, traffic in arms, etc. Acceptance of the Japanese amendment would mean nothing except that the League of Nations was to be founded upon justice. Japanese public opinion was so strongly behind this amendment that he asked the Commission to put it to the vote. If the amendment were rejected, it would be an indication to Japan that the equality of members of the League was not recognized and, as a consequence, the new organization would be most unpopular. The formula which he proposed was of great importance, and the national aspirations of Japan were depending upon its adoption. Public opinion in Japan was very much concerned over this question, and certain people had even gone so far as to say that Japan should not become a member of the League of Nations unless she were satisfied on this point.

Mr. Orlando supported the Japanese amendment. He said: "Originally the Commission had been inclined to adopt an Article proclaiming the most important of all liberties, that of religion." He himself would have been glad if this Article had been retained in a Covenant which was intended to bind together nations of a democratic character. The equality of nations was a question which perhaps ought not to have been raised; but once having been raised, there was no other solution except that of adopting the amendment. Lord Robert Cecil had spoken of the practical reasons why its application would be difficult. Such an argument would carry weight if the Commission were considering the addition of an Article in the Covenant which put the members of the League under a definite obligation. All that was now asked, however, was the statement of a principle in the Preamble. If this principle were rejected, it would give rise to feelings which were hardly in harmony with the purpose of the new organization.

M. Bourgeois agreed with Mr. Orlando. He felt that it was impossible to vote for the rejection of an amendment which embodied an indisputable principle of justice.

M. Larnaude remarked that the Japanese amendment had now reappeared in an entirely different form and that it would be difficult not to adopt the principle of equality of nations as now proposed. Moreover, it was intended that this declaration should appear in the Preamble, and preambles ordinarily laid down broad declarations of principle which did not impose obligations so strict as those of subsequent articles. For these two reasons, he thought that the Commission could not avoid voting for the amendment.

Mr. Venizelos (Greece) reminded the Commission that he had been largely responsible for the disappearance of the religious-liberty clause from the Covenant. He had thought and hoped that if this clause were cut out the difficulty relative to the racial question would likewise be eliminated. Today, however, the question had appeared in a different light and Japan had taken her stand upon another ground; they were talking not of the equality of races, but of the equality of nations themselves and of just treatment of their nationals. It would be very difficult to reject such a proposal especially since Baron Makino had carefully pointed out that his proposal did not involve any state in the obligation to pass any measures whatever with respect to immigration. If the Japanese amendment were accepted and were written into the Preamble, a clause relative to religious liberty might also be introduced.

Mr. Kramář (Czechoslovakia) could not see how any danger could arise out of the Japanese amendment. He himself was pretty well acquainted with a state where a certain Article provided for the equality of nations and where these nations had been cruelly oppressed over a long period of time. He thought that the words of the Japanese amendment were entirely in harmony with the rest of the Preamble and particularly with the expression "open, just, and honorable relations."

M. Dmowski (Poland) expressed himself as in entire sympathy with the Japanese delegates, but he did not see how a general declaration could be included in the Preamble when it was not to be enforced by particular provisions in subsequent Articles.

Mr. Koo (China) read the following statement:

"I believe that the principle contained in the Japanese amendment involves a number of questions to which time alone can give a universally satisfactory solution. Nevertheless, I should be very glad indeed to see the principle itself given recognition in the Covenant, and I hope that the Commission will not find serious difficulties in the way of its acceptance. I should like to have my statement appear in the Minutes."

President Wilson felt that the greatest difficulty by which they were confronted lay in controversies which would be bound to take place outside the Commission over the Japanese proposal, and that in order to avoid these discussions, it would perhaps be wise not to insert such a provision in the Preamble. The equality of nations was a fundamental principle of the League of Nations. It was the spirit of the Covenant to make a faithful and loyal attempt to place all nations upon a footing of equality, in the hope that the greater nations might aid the lesser in advantageous ways. Not only did the Covenant recognize the equality of states, but it laid down provisions for defending this equality in case it should be threatened.

Baron Makino said that he did not wish to continue an unprofitable discussion, but in these matters he was representing the unqualified opinion of the Government of Japan. Therefore, he could not avoid the necessity of asking the Commission to make a definite decision in this matter, and he had the honor of asking his fellow members to vote upon the question of the insertion of his amendment in the Preamble.

A vote was taken, and eleven votes out of seventeen were recorded in favor of the amendment.

President Wilson declared that the amendment was not adopted inasmuch as it had not received the unanimous approval of the Commission.

M. Larnaude called attention to the fact that a majority had voted in its favor.

President Wilson admitted that a majority had so voted, but stated that decisions of the Commission were not valid unless unanimous, and the Japanese amendment had not received unanimous support. There was only one case where a decision of the majority had prevailed, and that was in the case of determining the seat of the League. In that case, it had been necessary to accept the opinion of the majority inasmuch as no other procedure was possible if the question was to be decided at all. In the present instance there was, certainly, a majority, but strong opposition had manifested itself against the amendment and under these circumstances the resolution could not be considered as adopted.

Mr. Vesnitch said that he had voted for the amendment because it laid down a principle of international law, that of the equality of nations. As for the question of "just treatment of their nationals" one could depend upon the honor of self-respecting nations to respect the citizens of other states. No one could deny these principles, and the vote taken by the Commission must have given satisfaction on this point to Baron Makino and to Japanese opinion at large.

Lord Robert Cecil thought it better that the Covenant should be silent on these questions of right. Silence would avoid much discussion.

President Wilson said that no one could dream of interpreting the vote which had just been taken as condemnation of the principle proposed by the Japanese delegation.

Baron Makino said that he was sorry to insist upon the point, but asked that the number of votes which had been cast in favor of the Japanese amendment should appear in the Minutes. He would take the question up again on the first appropriate occasion.

Fifteenth Meeting, April 11, 1919, at 8:30 P.M. (evening session).

M. Larnaude presented in a new form a compromise with regard to the Monroe Doctrine. When discussed at the last meeting it had been agreed that the provisions relating to this doctrine should be inserted under Article XX. He thought that the Commission was not wholly in agreement on this question; so, in order to obtain unanimity, he now proposed the following text:

"International understandings intended to assure the maintenance of peace, such as treaties of arbitration, are not considered as incompatible with the provisions of this Covenant. Likewise with regard to understandings or doctrines pertaining to certain regions, such as the Monroe Doctrine, in so far as they do not in any way prevent the signatory States from executing their obligations under this Covenant."

This wording indicated that the Monroe Doctrine must not create obstacles to the fulfillment of obligations arising out of the present Covenant, and stated in so many words what President Wilson had said at the previous meeting. "The President's statement, however, would only appear in the Minutes," argued Larnaude. "If they should be included in the Covenant, they would relieve the apprehension suggested by the present form." President Wilson had said the day before that the Monroe Doctrine was compatible with obligations arising out of the Covenant; it was the purpose of M. Larnaude's amendment to state this fact rather than leave it unstated. Furthermore, in mentioning the Monroe Doctrine a special and privileged place had been given to the United States.

President Wilson feared that the proposed text would create the impression that there was an incompatibility between the Monroe Doctrine and the obligations of the Covenant and that an unwarranted suspicion would thus be cast upon the Doctrine.

M. Larnaude protested against this interpretation. He said that the proposed text was intended to clarify the situation by correcting the ill-informed opinion that the Monroe Doctrine prevented Europe from taking a hand in American affairs and America from participating in the settlement of European questions. This misapprehension would be corrected if it were specifically stated that the Doctrine was not incompatible with the obligations arising out of the Covenant.

Lord Robert Cecil said that he did not desire either to support or to oppose the amendment. He merely wished to inquire whether this amendment would be likely to satisfy the criticisms and the fears which had arisen in the United States.

President Wilson remarked that there was no fear in America that the Monroe Doctrine was contrary to the obligations of the Covenant. There was, however, a fear that the Covenant might to some extent invalidate the Monroe Doctrine. If there were anything in the Doctrine inconsistent with the Covenant, the Covenant would take precedence over the Monroe Doctrine not only because it was subsequent to it, but because it constituted a body of definite international engagements. No one could doubt that if the United States subscribed to these engagements, they would carry them out.

M. Larnaude was of opinion that his amendment would satisfy French anxieties and would not cause any dissatisfaction in the United States. What objection could there be to stating explicitly something which was known the world over? If there were the least implication of suspicion in his amendment another formula might be found which would eliminate this suspicion and still preserve the principle of his amendment. He thought it was necessary to do this in order to secure the unanimous approval of the Commission.

M. Bourgeois remarked that the French amendment was based upon two different ideas: First, it was intended to state that there was no incompatibility between the Covenant and the Monroe Doctrine; second, it associated with this Doctrine a group of ideas and understandings which likewise were intended to secure peace and which, consequently, were to be considered as understandings compatible with the Covenant. In this way a general principle was laid down and the Monroe Doctrine was made a particular application of this principle.

Mr. Kramář asked whether in case of dispute between Paraguay and Uruguay the League of Nations would have the right to come to the aid of whichever of the two states was supported by the decision of the Executive Council.

President Wilson replied in the affirmative.

Lord Robert Cecil believed that the Monroe Doctrine would in no wise prevent the forces of a European state from going to America in order to defend the rights of the oppressed. The sole object of the Monroe Doctrine was to prevent any European power from acquiring any influence, territory, or political supremacy on the American continent. The idea that the Monroe Doctrine would prevent the Executive Council, in the execution of a unanimous decision, from acting in Europe, America, Africa, or Asia, was a perversion of the Monroe Doctrine, and citizens of the United States would be the first to disclaim it.

President Wilson agreed.

Mr. Koo said that he was reluctant to prolong discussion of this amendment inasmuch as the Commission had discussed it for a long time on the previous day. Nevertheless, he thought that if the amendment which he had proposed at the previous meeting were adopted, the objections of the French and Czechoslovak delegations, as well as his own, would be met. He had suggested adding after the word "Understandings" the following clause:

"Which are not incompatible with the terms of this Covenant and which are intended to assure the maintenance of peace, such as the Monroe Doctrine."

President Wilson made the same objections to this amendment which he had made to the French.

Mr. Koo proposed to add the words "or understandings" after the word "obligations" in the second line of the first paragraph of Article XX.

This amendment was adopted.

M. Larnaude proposed a new draft which was intended to correct the impression of suspicion in his first draft. The second sentence of his amendment was now to read as follows:

"Similarly with regard to all other arrangements, particularly those pertaining to certain regions, such as arise out of the Monroe Doctrine, in so far as they conduce to the maintenance of the peace which it is the object of this Covenant to assure."

President Wilson thought that this draft was not satisfactory. Moreover, a provision with regard to the Monroe Doctrine had been accepted the day before, and the Commission had decided to make a separate Article of it.

M. Larnaude declared that if this were the case the French delegation would be obliged to make a reservation.

President Wilson asked whether this reservation indicated that the French delegation would publicly oppose the American amendment. He thought that such a situation would create a most unfortunate impression on the other side of the water.

M. Bourgeois had no intention of creating such an impression in the United States, but he wanted to avoid discussions which might take place before the Plenary Conference and in the press. He thought that this result would be secured if the draft proposed by M. Larnaude were adopted.

President Wilson declared that the amendment was not adopted.

It is quite apparent that the French are determined to make a final stand and thresh the whole subject out once again in the Plenary Session of the Conference. To prevent this the Colonel is girding up his loins!

April 12th.

The fact that John Bull is out for a bargain, and, as it appears, a pretty sharp bargain at that, has been apparent ever since the President returned from Washington with his belated appreciation of the power of the Senate and with the peremptory demand of a group of Senators to secure the Monroe Doctrine reservation. At first this change of course was revealed but certainly not stressed by a remark here, and a suggestion there, which left no trace and most certainly could not be ascribed to an official source. Then, however, the extreme timeliness of the present moment for reaching a naval agreement between the two great sea powers was mentioned by important men in more or less formal conversations. Finally, on April 8th, after conferring with the President, House decided to put on record this unwelcome development, and on that day he wrote Lloyd George as follows:

"When I asked you yesterday if you had any objection to the affirmation of the Monroe Doctrine (in the Covenant), you told me, as you have told me before, that you could not consent without coming to an agreement with the United States regarding our naval building program."

House had decided to write this letter forcing the issue not only because of the somewhat vague talks with Lloyd George, but because of the way in which Cecil had described the situation in a letter to him written several days ago. This letter read:

"I have found in exalted quarters that some of the recent utterances of high officials connected with the United States Navy (he referred to a statement ascribed to Admiral Benson, naval adviser of our delegation) have produced a very unfortunate impression. Very possibly they have been misunderstood, but they have, in fact, conveyed the idea that the naval policy of America is one of expansion, that the American ambition is to have a navy at least as strong, or stronger, than that of the British Empire. It is urged, with some force, that such an attitude is wholly inconsistent with the conception of the League of Nations and that if it really represents the settled policy of the United States, it could only lead, sooner or later, to a competition in arms between us and them. . . . Would it be possible, for instance, for you to say that when the Treaty of Peace, containing the League, has been signed, you would abandon or modify your naval program? I am sure the British Government would be only too ready to give corresponding assurances. That would be what the French call a *beau geste* with which to inaugurate the League."

House replied the same day in these terms:

"I have been unable to see any connection between the two questions (the Monroe Doctrine reservation and the Naval Program proposal). If the kind of peace is made for which we are working, and which includes a League of Nations, it will be necessary for us to live up to its spirit. To do this, none of us can consistently continue to increase our armament either by land or by sea."

On the ninth this letter was submitted to him by House, and having been approved by the President, was sent on to its destination. Late in the afternoon Cecil informed House that the letter was not satisfactory to Lloyd George and quite a discussion followed. House told Cecil with more than his usual bluntness that the United States was not open to a bargain on the Monroe Doctrine reservation but was going to take the position it believes to be right. He did not want his letter as to the Naval Program sent back (Cecil had offered to do so) because it represented the settled policy of the United States and it would not be reconsidered.

"We are presenting the Monroe Doctrine amendment to the Commission this evening. We would like your support, but of course you can oppose it if you see fit."

Cecil was evidently greatly worried and admitted that he could not promise British support. He was given a copy of the amendment as finally drawn up. It now read:

"Nothing in this Covenant shall be deemed to affect the validity of international engagements such as treaties of arbitration or regional understandings, like the Monroe Doctrine, for securing the maintenance of peace."

A few hours later (at the fourteenth meeting) the President formally presented his amendment and it was adopted. By his silence, Cecil gave his consent, and the President was pleased. He recognized that an outstanding obstacle to ratification by the Senate had been successfully negotiated, and House also breathed more freely. Cecil did suggest that the amendment be not added to Article X, but should form a separate Article, and this was agreed to.

When Cecil accepted the Monroe reservation, which evidently he had always wished to do, he again opposed a definition of it, frequently asked for and even demanded by Larnaude and Reis, and this was most pleasing to the President.

"If we attempted that," he said in his supporting plea, "we might well run the risk of limiting or extending its application and none of us wish to do that." But the French delegates were far from being appeased. Bourgeois was boisterous in his dissent and Larnaude said he would fight it out in the Plenary where all Europe would hear.

"That sounds quite menacing," I said to House. "Are you not afraid of a row in the Plenary?"

"Not at all," answered the Colonel suavely. "I spoke to Clemenceau this morning and he assured me he would not recognize either one of his delegates on the great day, and then the Tiger added, 'Larnaude is getting on my nerves and Bourgeois is sapping my vitality.' No," concluded the Colonel, "have no fear, the Monroe Doctrine reservation is in the bag."

April 20th.

While it is still feared by some that there will be a shindy later on in the Plenary Session, the selection of the minor powers to be represented on the Council of the League has been more easily arrived at than was to be expected. First off, a subcommittee of the delegates was named, composed of Vesnitch, Venizelos, and Bourgeois; House was to preside, but owing to pressure of work he asked Miller to sit for him. But, while he had great confidence in Miller's tact, the Colonel could not keep from shaping one of the important features of his great project. Balfour and Cecil dropped in, and they had a long and, apparently, an exceedingly amicable talk. When these exchanges were concluded, House said:

"I have an idea; I hope you will approve of it. At least it would save time, and that is so valuable; let each of us take a card and write upon it the names of the member states we nominate for the Council."

All agreed, and then a strange thing happened. On each card the states named were the same, and while one was written by Balfour and another by Cecil, it was apparent to me that the Colonel's fine Italian hand directed both pens.

Of course this is not the whole story. There were preliminary and far-reaching exploratory talks; China, to the great disappointment of Mr. Koo, was left out because it was held that at the time it did not enjoy a responsible government. Also, it was agreed that the new nations which had so recently put in appearance at the baptismal font should be ignored because they were involved in so many contentious matters that would come before the League in its first sittings. Greece was given a chair out of compliment to Venizelos; as to the Greeks themselves, there was apparent a great lack of enthusiasm. Lord Robert agreed that a Latin-American state should sit in the Council, and House nominated Brazil, as the greatest of them all in resources and in population, and in recognition of her early and frank assistance to the Allies during the war, plus her traditional friendship for the United States. Pessoa is the ranking Brazilian delegate and he has also just been elected president of that great South American republic. I was sent to advise him that he had been chosen. He was immensely pleased at the honor bestowed. He is a very able man, and his choice should give prestige to the League in the new world south of Panama.

April 22d.

The British want to make some changes even at this late hour in the Covenant when everyone has agreed to sign it with his John Hancock in its present form. They want to have the words "Members of the League" inserted instead of "States, Members," etc.

Lord Robert Cecil writes that the change would merely correct a failure on the part of the drafting committee to express what was obviously the sense and purpose of the Commission.

"If all members (of the Committee) agree, it would not be necessary to hold another meeting of the Commission," he suggests.

But Miller maintains it is not quite so simple as that. Of course the purpose of the proposal is to make the representatives of the British Dominions eligible to membership on the Council. Miller holds that this change is not merely a matter of drafting and that consequently it must be submitted to the whole Commission. The President shares Miller's view, but he does not want to oppose the British, who have been so helpful to him throughout the more recent proceedings. The matter has hung fire for several days and now it is brought to head by a written inquiry from Sir Robert Borden (Canada). After mulling over the incident for several days, on May 6 Wilson, Lloyd George, and Clemenceau signed a memorandum which reads:

"Representatives of the self-governing Dominions may be named as members of the Council."

Probably the President did not foresee the developments that would follow upon this incident. The rearrangement gave the British Empire six votes in contrast to our one. Perhaps the President was under the impression that in future controversies the Dominions might vote with America rather than with the Mother Country. It was doubtless fresh in his memory that a few days before, in a formal meeting of the Council of Ten, Hughes (Australia) had stated (although it was omitted from the record) that the next time Britain went to war "Australia would go in or stay out—as she thought best."

Of course the six votes meant nothing, even if they could be controlled by Downing Street (by no means a certainty); for, with but unimportant exceptions, unanimity on all decisions was required in the Assembly and in the Council also. However, in the Covenant as presented to and approved by the Conference April 28th, the change desired by Cecil was inserted.[10]

April—undated.

Much appears in the press, and there is even more talk in the corridors of the Crillon and the other meeting places of the delegates, in regard to what is termed the President's stubborn determination to "intertwine or interweave" the Covenant with the Treaty. If there has been a struggle on this point, as many claim, I did not know anything about it—and this seems strange. The "intertwining" was

[10]It is a regrettable fact that during the debates in the Senate in 1919 and in the presidential election that followed, this change helped to kill the Covenant and perhaps, as thought by many, prevented America from entering the League.

definitely decided upon in the conferences which took place between
House and Lord Robert Cecil[11] about January 22d (probably because
of the manifest of the opposing Senators under the leadership of Lodge
published a few hours before, the delegates got down to work) and
the President was very insistent that his point of view should prevail.
But he really does not have to be insistent as, in so far as I can see, there
is little or no opposition to his plan—at least not to binding the two
documents together. His argument is, and I have heard him develop it
in conversation with House three or four times and always in practically identical language, "While I hope for the best, the Treaty, like
all human documents, may prove imperfect. It may not live up to our
ideal, but with the Covenant an integral and inseparable part of the
Treaty, the mechanism to perfect our work, to adjust it to the needs
of situations which may arise, will be close at hand." And in this
attitude the President was supported warmly by Cecil.[12]

Lloyd George and Clemenceau, whatever their real feelings may
have been, remained neutral in the fray if there can be said to have
been one. On at least one occasion Clemenceau said to House in my
presence that he regarded the Covenant of doubtful present utility but
he hoped that the President was not mistaken in basing high hopes
upon its ultimate value. It is, however, quite true that at the beginning
of the negotiations, early in January, both Lloyd George and Clemenceau were as slow moving as the President was eager and indeed
impatient to go ahead with both the Treaty and the Covenant. In
explanation of his desire for speed the President said on several occasions that he could not remain for long in Paris—that in a very few
weeks he would have to return to Washington. Many think that the

[11]The Colonel was an old acquaintance and a very strong supporter of the League.
He, with the President, represented the United States on the Commission or Committee to which the question was referred. He was a high-minded and clear-sighted
American, devoted to the President and profoundly convinced that a good understanding between the British Empire and America was vital for the peace and prosperity of the world. If men may be divided into those whose ambition is to do something and those who want to be something, he emphatically belonged to the first class.
He cared nothing for position. But he cared immensely for what he believed to be
in his country's interest. He was consequently a delightful person to work with. In
discussion he always put forward his real opinion supported by his real reasons. There
was never any danger that agreement reached on that basis would be upset for personal and private considerations. It was a bad day for the League when, some months
later, the collaboration between Wilson and House ceased. But for that, the League
might have been successfully steered through the American Senate and the course of
world history might have been very different." (Comments on the situation at this
time by Viscount Cecil, in his book, *The Great Experiment*, pp. 63-64, London, 1941.)

[12]Younger son of Lord Salisbury, many times Prime Minister of England, and later
raised to the peerage under the title of Viscount Cecil of Chelwood.

outstanding delegates who heard these words did hope that the President would return to the White House and that once there his presidential duties would make his return to Paris difficult, if not impossible. This sounds plausible, and it may be the true explanation of their attitude. On one occasion at least I heard Clemenceau say to House: "Your President is a *mauvais coucheur!*"—an "ugly" not an accommodating fellow—and from his point of view this was an apt description of the President's attitude at the time.

April 16th.

Two of the most bitterly contested battles over the final shape of the Covenant were not fought out in the closed sessions of the Commission but in the Colonel's study and conference *salle* which, with a touch of characteristic humor, he called his "cloakroom," for as usual it was the silent man from Texas who bore the brunt of the struggle, and was only concerned to escape public notice much less acclaim; the praise of his chief and of his conscience for him was reward enough.

These less-spectacular but vital struggles, in which great bitterness was displayed, centered around two reservations (although of course, officially, this too-revealing word was avoided) which are insisted upon by men of both political parties in Washington who have studied the outlook for ratification of the work of the Conference. Indeed here all are in agreement. These changes are pronounced indispensable.

The first is "no Power need accept a Mandate against its will," or, as it was later phrased, only to be vested in those "who are willing to accept it" (Article XXII, second paragraph). Many of the delegates made bitter charges on this proposal, and personally the President was in agreement with them. They argued and the President was at least in tacit agreement, "Should not all the enlightened and democratic peoples share the responsibility for those who because of oppression throughout the generations, or for other reasons, are clearly unequal to the task of self-government? Verbal blueprints are not enough, all the more fortunate and better equipped nations must accept their fair share of the duties of trusteeship and above all of guidance." It was only after a long struggle and much recrimination, which left scars, that this exceptional clause went into the Covenant.

If possible there was an even more bitter if also quite clandestine battle over the decision which now at last is inserted as paragraph 8 of Article XV, which reads:

"The Council is to make no recommendation in cases affecting a member's domestic jurisdiction." And this leaves the United States, as well as other powers of course, in complete control of its immigration laws and its school regulations. The Japanese are bitterly disappointed. The Colonel likes Makino and admires the dignity with which he has received several rebuffs and also the brickbats which are hurled at him from the Younger rather than the Elder Statesmen in Tokyo. I think—wisely—the Colonel avoids detailed discussion of these prickly problems. He simply says, "My dear Baron, without these explanatory clauses, rather than reservations, the Congress of the United States will not, I fear, accept the New Order, they may not enter the League. They may not be bound by the Covenant. It is as simple as that. There is no room for discussion. We can take it or leave it." Makino, without even making a wry face, took it. But of course it is not a total defeat for him. The reservation as to the Monroe Doctrine and "similar regional understandings" (Article XXI) has a soothing influence on his wounds.

In regard to avoidance of a mandate, for the moment at least, House argued at greater length and in more detail. "We have no desire to shirk our share of responsibility in re-establishing the world upon an even keel. No, not that; but we, at least many of us, doubt that our form of government is suitable for a people of different mentality and alien traditions. Some of our leaders, and very important and influential they are, think that our stewardship in the Philippines, although unselfish and certainly most costly to us, has not been an unqualified success. These are but small groups, it is true, but there is a strong and very powerful group who wish to confine our political activities to the American hemisphere. They argue that for one reason or another mandates degenerate into imperial appendages—and they would have none of them. I may, of course, be mistaken—I hope I am —but I confess that unless these prejudices are humored, the Senate and even the American people will not subscribe to Article X on which our hope of world peace and national security depends."

I admit that only the four walls of the "cloakroom" know all that was said in these interminable conferences, but I think that these few words reveal the arguments that were advanced and oh, so often repeated!

April 27th.

The President secured, in the Committee at least, the Monroe Doctrine reservation and also the amendment to the Covenant which permits the powers to withdraw from the League and escape its responsibilities on two years' notice. It is a victory which Senators in Washington, both supporters and opponents of the Treaty, say will smooth the path to ratification, but it cannot be denied that both these changes have weakened the President's position here. It is true, of course, that none of the powers represented on the Commission, with the exceptions of Japan and of China, attach much real importance to the Doctrine. They, the Europeans, argue that as it did not keep America out of the World War in 1917 America will come in again if it is in her interest to do so and that President Monroe has been dead a long, long time. And it is quite clear that much of the opposition to the reservation was inspired by a belief that here was a situation that would facilitate trading, and undoubtedly "trades" have been made. Orlando argues openly, and Clemenceau more discreetly, that as the President has been helped by them in his struggle with the recalcitrant Senators in Washington they have every reason to expect his assistance in their parliamentary battles, which to them, at least, are also of vital importance.

But in insisting upon the right to withdraw from the League and to cast off the responsibilities assumed under the Covenant upon notice the President has suffered a tremendous loss in moral prestige. Many of those who deplore this step were until the last few days the most unwavering supporters of the President. Today they are not, and they are quoting many expressions in the Wilson speeches at the Conference which certainly do not tally with his later action. "We were told," they are saying, "that the word Covenant connoted something sacramental, and by it the peace of God could and would be secured. How the President denounced man-made pacts, and protocols and agreement which men and nations only had to keep as long as it was to their advantage, but the Covenant, he thundered, 'had the sanction of God.' It, the Covenant, was a sacrament, and those who partook of it drank the blood of the Prince of Peace, but now it appears it is only binding for twenty-four months. You can stay in or get out, as your national interests dictate. In other words, it is merely another scrap of paper—like all the old-style treaties." These are reported to me as the sentiments of M. Larnaude—but he has not gone so far in the public debates.

Orlando, however, supported the President in a long speech, and it is evident that he expects a substantial return. Under his honeyed words the President suffered visibly, and indeed nothing could have been more destructive of the League ideal than those that the eloquent Sicilian used. No wonder the original Covenanter writhed. Orlando's words were: "However precious the privilege of membership in the League may seem today, it is a comfort to know you can divest yourself of membership and its responsibilities in case you want to, in case the new society does not work out in the way we all hope it will."

It is to be hoped that these sacrifices will smooth the path of the Treaty, and of the President, in Washington, but it cannot be denied that here, at least, they have entailed a loss of prestige and of faith in the Wilsonian ideals in quarters which have hitherto been the most steadfast.

April 28th.

Today, to our immense relief, the Conference in Plenary Session approved the amended Covenant with the Monroe Doctrine reservation. The great *salle* was chockablock with dynamite, but thanks to the masterly handling of the situation by Clemenceau none of it was touched off. Hughes, the weird little Prime Minister of Australia, was simply bursting with an anti-League, anti-Japanese speech, and M. Bourgeois was all primed to advance once again his demand, so frequently rejected in the Commission, for an international army, or at least an international sheriff's posse, to enforce the decisions of the League. And there was the Portuguese delegate primed with a speech, said to have been a mile long, setting forth the fact that his was a deeply religious country and that not since the days of Pedro the Cruel had his people ever consented to a treaty which was not placed, in the preamble at least, under the benign protection of the Holy Trinity. The Tiger certainly knew how to manipulate the "steam roller" in a manner worthy of the best traditions of our party conventions. He frequently admits that he had given this matter, so important in politics, some attention during his residence in America, and his memory has evidently been refreshed by several dress rehearsals under the "seeing" eye of the Colonel.

An amendment to Article V which appeared in the Covenant as approved today, it must be admitted, was far from familiar to many of the delegates. It had been introduced by President Wilson without fanfare and quietly put through. It justifies and sanctions the ruling of the President that the Japanese equality proposal, or amendment, was defeated, although a majority voted for it. And it also means that it cannot be reintroduced with any hope of approval as long as a representative of Australia is present. This change in procedure, as some call it, is authorized by the first paragraph of Article V which now reads:

"Except where otherwise expressly provided in this Covenant or by terms of the present Treaty, decisions at any meeting of the Assembly or of the Council shall require the agreement of all the Members of the League represented at the meeting." . . .

This memorable meeting, the last, was held in the afternoon, and the shadows of an early evening after a dark, dull day were lengthening in the great *salle* when the word was given to the President. I must admit that the tired man who was now called upon to promulgate his new Gospel was not at his best. Certainly the trumpet notes with which on former occasions he had electrified the delegates from all over the world were missed, and what he said was lacking in the beauty of language with which he had presented the first draft to the same assembly on February 14th. In the main this was not the fault of the President. He was not and could not be as confident of his panacea for the world's ills as he had been ten weeks ago, before he had been exposed to the guerrilla wars of the Conference and the equally discouraging sniping tactics on the home front. Further, what he had to say, and what he had to explain and make clear, did not lend itself to the graceful diction in which he is past master. He had to go into somewhat matter-of-fact details, to describe how the Articles had been transposed, the changes in nomenclature that had been found advisable, and certainly, wisely I thought, he did not dwell on the provisions which had been inserted at the behest of men the President does not regard, and quite correctly, as 100 per cent Covenanters. However, when he closed with the words "I now move the adoption of the Covenant," there was a ripple of applause in which Clemenceau joined with the muffled sound of his gray-gloved hands.

When M. le Président now closed his eyes, after announcing "Monsieur Bourgeois has the floor," Colonel House's face was a study. Was this to be another illustration of the fact that the best-laid plans of even the most astute of men "gang agley"? Perhaps the Tiger had forgotten about the arrangement he had entered upon so gleefully, or more probably he had decided not to be schoolmastered by the man from Texas—that he had decided to achieve the desired result in his own way. Be this as it may, it was a dark moment. The President slumped wearily in his chair, Mr. Balfour gazed intently at the ceiling, Clemenceau closed his eyes, and the delegates prepared to listen once again to the thoughts and the fears that the father of the French League of Nations Society expresses in such halting phrases. But I must try to be fair, and as I was on this occasion not involved in the mechanism of interpreting (Montoux was on the griddle; as always during the Plenary Sessions) I could see how arresting if not convincing his plea was. "I do not conceal from you the fact that if we are to have a League, and thereby security for all, sacrifices will have to be made. Some of our historic traditions and our long-accustomed rights will have to be abandoned, but how insignificant is this loss of independent action when you contrast it with the menace that will hang over us all—if the League is not established *with force behind it*."

M. Bourgeois had talked along this line for about ten minutes when, unwisely, he stopped for breath and dived into the pyramid of manuscript notes before him. Suddenly Clemenceau opened his eyes wide and rapping sharply with his gavel on the table before him, in a loud, clear voice announced: "As I hear no objections, I declare that the Conference has considered and adopted the revised Covenant as presented by the Commission of the League appointed for that purpose." A ripple of applause ran through the brilliant *salle* in which all joined except poor Bourgeois. Amazed and stunned, and bitterly disappointed, he sank back in his seat, the very picture of woe. Some of his friends surrounded him and offered what consolation there was in the assurance that his undelivered speech, although for the most part a twice-told tale, would be included in the official record of the historic session. Tardieu whispered to House, "You see we have introduced into France the practice of printing unspoken speeches as in Washington through the medium of the *Congressional Record*." House said nothing but evidently was very happy. The Tiger had achieved their joint purpose—but in his own way.

As the delegates prepared to leave, Lloyd George turned to Clemenceau with—"Tell me! How did M. Bourgeois ever get to be Prime Minister?"

"What a natural question. Many, very many, people ask it. Perhaps I can explain. It was long, long ago when, perhaps as you know, very unfairly I think, I was called the *tombeur* or the *démolisseur des Ministères*—the destroyer of Ministries—but they fail to explain that those I smashed were formed out of pseudo-republicans, really camouflaged Bonapartists, Orleanists, and what have you. I did my duty, playing no favorites, and when about twenty presidents of the Council, the possible and the impossible alike, had been placed on the shelf, or were licking their wounds in some political hospital, the supply gave out—only Bourgeois was left and they had to take him. Strange, isn't it?"

Then Balfour joined the group, but what a changed Balfour he was! Gone was the self-control which had baffled the Irish in the House of Commons thirty years ago and left me, an observer in the press gallery, speechless with admiration.[13] Now he placed a trembling hand on Clemenceau's shoulder (a tactical mistake, as the Tiger dislikes physical familiarity). His usually placid features were distorted with anger. Glaring through his glasses at the equally myopic Bourgeois, he said in his best Oxford French in a voice so loud it must have been heard by many, "*Oh vous ne savez pas comme je déteste cette homme, c'est un imbécile!*"

But that was too strong for Clemenceau. After all Bourgeois was a Frenchman and his appointee. So he answered dryly, "*Pas ça, mon ami. Pas ça. C'est un homme de second plan comme il y'en a beaucoup par ici.*"

A petty incident at the Plenary amused me unduly, but my amusement was shared by many, and it certainly relieved the solemnity of the proceedings. The French delegates, including M. Pichon, the Minister of Foreign Affairs, have been peeved by the introduction into the League of what they call "satellite states" but which we regard, and properly, as the overseas dominions of the British Commonwealth of Nations and our sister republics of the Caribbean world. And so from time to time Pichon has suggested that the principality of Monaco should be admitted as a trainbearer to France. In private conversation with House, Pichon brings the matter up and with great vehemence, especially when the admission of Newfoundland is proposed by Cecil. As to the admission of Monaco, House always turns his deaf ear, but when Newfoundland is mentioned, he inquires jovially if that is not where the big, handsome dogs come from, and should not every dog have his day before the League, as well as elsewhere?

But for reasons that are variously interpreted, Monaco, where gambling flourishes, bulks large on Pichon's horizon and today in the Plenary he asked that an invitation to join be sent.

"Of course—I only make the proposal—if nobody objects."

To which Clemenceau snapped:

[13]Described in my *Heyday in a Vanished World*, New York—London, 1937.

"You know everybody objects; that's where we have all lost our money."

The word-artist who drew up the official *procès-verbal* of this session described this spat as: *"Un échange de vues entre M. Pichon et M. le Président du Conseil."* And it was a very characteristic one.

As we walked away from the triumphant session General Smuts joined the Colonel, who knew only too well that the Afrikander was torn with doubts as to the justice and even the efficacy of the Treaty in its present incomplete form. For several weeks now hardly a day had passed without a suggestion of changes coming from him. He seemed very tired. Certainly he was not sharing the exultant mood that shone on the faces of at least a majority of the delegates. He shrugged his shoulders in answer to an unspoken inquiry from the Colonel and then, "The Peace Treaty may fade into oblivion—and that would be, I sometimes think, a merciful dispensation of a kind Providence—but the Covenant will stand—as sure as fate. It must and shall succeed because there is no other way to salvage the future of civilization."

At the last, indeed the latest minute, when Bourgeois and Larnaude, licking their wounds and sulking in their tents, had abandoned the long struggle, the very intelligent and more practical Tardieu took a hand in the game and wheedled from the Big Four another consolation prize which under circumstances other than those that followed on the World War might have been adequate and certainly would have proved helpful. Tardieu asked not for an armed force, not for a posse, not even for a commission of surveillance manned by staff officers. No, he simply asked for an international commission in liaison with the League, *chargé des constatations nécessaires*, and this modest request prospered. It became a few days later Article 213 of the Treaty, which reads: "So long as the present treaty remains in force Germany undertakes to give every facility for any investigation the League of Nations, acting, if need be, by a majority vote, may consider necessary."[14]

[14]This might have sufficed had there been any unity of purpose in the Council of the League; unfortunately there was not. The military and naval observers soon learned that while their zeal in exposing infringements of the Treaty clauses was appreciated, their efforts went into the "dead" files of their respective governments. In 1924 one, and not the least, of these intelligent and industrious observers showed me the official acknowledgment of his painstaking report. The substantial sentence read: "The highest members of the Government hold that it is not advisable to raise questions as to how the manifold infringements of the clauses of the Treaty should be met. Certainly not at this moment." This intelligent officer made no further reports. Shortly afterwards he was promoted and sent to another field of activity. A word to the wise man had sufficed!

April 29th.

Some of the French writers, and this is natural enough, and some of the American correspondents, and this I think is not as it should be, are making labored jokes over the quick work of the Covenant Commission. They admit that the world, according to Genesis, was created in six days, but they contend in those days supernatural assistance was available. "Things are different now, but all the same Wilson and House have been fast workers. In ten committee meetings they have reshaped the world."

In view of this intended slur, and more are to be expected from those who are devoted to power politics, and have battened on them in the past, I think I should put down in black and white the calendar of the Committee meetings. The first was held on February 3d at the Crillon, Wilson presiding, with fifteen to nineteen delegates present. After ten meetings, which totaled forty-nine hours, the First Draft of the Covenant was submitted to the Conference on February 14th. In all there were fifteen official sessions of the Commission and the revised Covenant was practically finished on April 5th.

But this is by no means the whole story. Of course, as described elsewhere in my diary, many months of study and discussion had been expended on the new-world Charter long before the Conference assembled. From the moment House arrived the Leaguers and the Covenanters surrounded him. Innumerable committees, official and otherwise, met from time to time at the Crillon and elsewhere. It would be guesswork, a stretching of the imagination, to say how many hours these subconferences ran to; but frequent, long, and somewhat tedious they were.

April 30th.

House had a long talk with Clemenceau today and they made me sit in with them. House told the Tiger that while Wilson thought it was quite unnecessary, the matter of possible invasion being fully covered by the terms of the Covenant, he would fight for the Rhine Agreement. In a general way he told the Tiger that the President was heartsick over some of the compromises he had been compelled to make, but that now he would not yield another inch either at home or abroad. The Tiger then went on to admit that we Europeans "are a tough bunch" and again he insisted, as often before, that the *preparation des Âmes* for the Wilson creed had not been very thorough and certainly far from complete. "You most certainly have not in-doctrinated little Hymans with your beautiful ideas," he said. "He wants to annex Limburg, where the strong cheeses come from, and both banks of the Scheldt, and he scowls when I say, 'But, *mon Ami*, do they not belong to the Dutch?' How he scowls when I say that." After a pause the Tiger continued, "Hymans is a small man physically, and in many other ways, but his imagination is simply prodigious. He is confident that Belgium put ten million men in the field and saved the Great Powers from enslavement by the Huns, but if we don't give him Limburg he may not intervene another time. Yes! take it from me, dear friend, some of the little pups are just as bad as the great black bears, and if the Lodge group in the Senate succeeds in abandoning Mr. Wilson's beautiful creation on our doorstep we shall hear from them." House laughed and pooh-poohed the possibility and the Tiger said, "I hope you are right."

I have never been as confident of the outcome of the Crusade as House certainly was, and may be yet. I recall with misgiving what the President said in that great speech to Congress in joint session, on December 4th, I think, in 1917. He said:

"Statesmen must by this time have learned that the opinion of the world is everywhere wide-awake and fully comprehends the issues involved. No representative of any self-governed nation will dare dis-regard it by attempting any such covenants of selfishness and com-promise as were entered into at the Congress of Vienna. . . . The Congress that concludes this war will feel the full strength of the tides that run now in the hearts and consciences of free men everywhere. Its conclusions will run with those tides."

Certainly he cannot believe that now. Certainly little Hymans does not feel that tide, or if he does he minimizes its strength, and certainly the subtle and slippery Scialoja, the back-stage brains of the Italian delegation, does not; and these Founding Fathers (!) will assuredly be on hand when the League meets next November and will seek to reshape it and to nullify many of its provisions that were nearest to the heart of the man who inspired it and gave it the breath of life. Suppose the prophets who say that the pendulum is swinging away from Europe, and that America is about to withdraw into her shell, are justified by the course of events, what will become of the Covenant? True it is that Bourgeois, although the most obstinate opponent of some of its provisions, told House today that while he regarded it as pitifully insufficient he would fight for its ratification in the Senate, of which he is an influential member, "as a step, although a short step, in the right direction." And of course Cecil and Smuts, the able lieutenants to whom the President owes so much, will put up a good fight for what he fought for and for what they believe, but will they be there? Their duties may call them to distant fields in their far-flung Empire. But Hymans and Scialoja will be there and judging by their past activities with no helpful purpose.[15]

One question is on every lip: have we made the world safe for Democracy? Time alone will bring the answer. Fresh from my contacts with the peacemakers, I am not optimistic. I recall the eloquent words with which the President announced to Congress in February 1918 the purpose and the plan of his world crusade. He said: "We fight for a new International Order; without that new Order at the end of the war the world would be without peace." Well, it can only be asserted while the battle is not won the struggle continues.

True, as the President said in the clarion note with which he later opened the battle for peace. There is abroad "a great compulsion of the Common Conscience," and he has spoken as he promised to do with the "Great Voice of Humanity." Unless these words are heeded at home, and abroad, generations yet unborn will rue the day they came into a war-ridden world.

[15]As a matter of fact, these fears were realized: from time to time Cecil and Smuts took part in the League debates, but Hymans and Scialoja were there from the first session until they passed on to a better world. In this way the enemies of the League achieved and claimed the rights of seniority so important in all parliamentary assemblies.

Berlin – after the Whirlwind

(Late in May Colonel Bonsal was sent from Paris to Washington to secure certain information as to the situation there. Early in July he rejoined Colonel House in London and with his chief worked with the commissioners of the powers there assembled to shape, classify, and allocate the mandates over countries that as yet could not stand alone, as had been agreed in general terms, by the Peace Conference.

As the possibility of America failing to accept any of the mandates, in view of the increasing opposition to the step, developing in Congress and elsewhere, Colonel House became reluctant to take part in drafting the terms of the trusteeships, the burden of which America seemed little inclined to share. Consequently, he returned to Paris early in September (1919), and ten days later he sent Colonel Bonsal to report on German conditions, after the whirlwind of war had passed, and to enter into relations with the new German leaders, who, it was hoped, unlike Count Brockdorff-Rantzau, would be disposed to fulfill the conditions of the Treaty that had been accepted in Paris on June 28th.

Excerpts from Colonel Bonsal's diary, after his arrival in Berlin, follow.)

Berlin, September 20 (1919).

Another swift change and a new destination. Once again I am in Berlin and at the Adlon. Both are quite shabby, and how natural that is. I cannot say I was surprised when my orders came. For several weeks I had "sensed" (to borrow the language of the successful novelists) that the Colonel (House) was brooding over the unsatisfactory German situation. It was clear to me that he was shooting up antennae or aerials, whatever they may be called, to secure better contact and communication with German people and with the prevailing thought and opinion beyond the Rhine. It was certainly no secret to me that the Colonel had expected the negotiations with the late enemy to follow quite a different course. Sequestered at Versailles, as they were, behind a stockade (not intended as a humiliation but as a greatly needed protection), the exchange of long notes was not the kind of co-operation between the recent antagonists which my Colonel thought at all likely to bring peace to the world. He did not, as many do, hold the chauvinistic French solely responsible for this unhappy state of affairs. He admitted that the new German Republic and its inexperienced leaders were proving most disappointing. Judging by the information that had reached him through many channels, an unhappy spirit was in control of the Imperial Reich so suddenly and by such artificial means converted into a republic, or, as some preferred to call it, a democratic realm. He could not see that a single one of the terms so gladly accepted at the Armistice was being fulfilled. He regarded Brockdorff-Rantzau as the evil genius of a people, the merest tyros in self-government, now suddenly called upon to reach decisions of vital importance to themselves and indeed to the world. My new, by-no-means-an-enviable job, is to make a survey of Germany in convulsions and if possible to find a man who will help the Colonel and the few others who are not still suffering from the war psychosis to save the situation—in a word, to find the "balm in Gilead," if there be any left.

September 20th.

The first man I ran into today as I surveyed the wreckage of Berlin "after the whirlwind of war" was poor old XYZ. He would have a fit if he thought I put his name in my diary. Ten years ago I knew him as a daring rider at Baden-Baden, once at least the winner of the famous steeplechase. He was a gallant regimental officer three years ago; today he drags one leg and there is a curious tic to his left cheek, which suggests something quite serious that is to come. He was cold and standoffish when I ran into him in the café, but half an hour later he had tracked me to my room, and how he talks! There is nothing for him here, he says. He wants to go to China with Colonel Bauer, but there is the physical examination and he fears he cannot pass that, and I am sure his fears are well founded.

He talks and talks but, unlike so many, he really is worth listening to. How the war came and who provoked it I thought was threadbare, but certainly he looks at it from quite a different angle. He admits that the Serbian mess and the resulting murder of the Archduke complicated the situation, and that the new railway plans of the Russians to build strategic lines leading to the German frontier, as outlined by the ukase of the Tsar in March 1914, contributed to make a continuance of peace, of even a merely armed peace, impossible, but—and now I will quote his very words:

"The war came because of the inferiority complex which oppressed the *hohe Herren* of our Foreign Office and had caused even the All Highest many sleepless nights. We lost out at Algeciras. We truckled at Agadir. The Entente was too much for us. They had all the winning cards and our diplomatic prestige was in shreds. Then came the blow to our military prestige; the German-trained Turks were walloped by the French-trained Slavs and Greeks in the Balkan war—immeasurable disaster! Then came Gray's plan for a conference, but for once all of our people were united against that. Since Bismarck was gone we always lost out at conferences. There was only one thing to be done and that was to re-establish the prestige of Prussian militarism by striking swiftly and hard! Unfortunately the army was in the hands of a man who had the great name of the victor of 1870 but who lacked most of the qualities that went with that name. The younger von Moltke had charming personal traits, but when the Emperor said his name was worth ten divisions to the army, he was romancing. In war it's battalions and brigades, not names or personal qualities, that tip the scales. It is only fair to say that the younger von Moltke was not eager for his job and he admitted it. He said he was too slow for the swift-moving wars of the day, and he demonstrated this self-diagnosis at the Battle of the Marne, when he failed to assume the risks which the situation demanded and so condemned us to a war of attrition.

"He had another failing which so often besets slow-thinking, slow-moving men. Every now and then he revolted against his naturally sluggish bent and reached a lightning decision. That is illustrated by his letters to Conrad von Hötzendorf, the chief of the Austrian Army in 1909, which the *Arbeiter Zeitung* secured and maliciously published. In that year he tried to make the Austrians attack the Serbs, although they were even less prepared than they were in 1914. Conrad held back, but those taunts had much to do with the headlong onslaught five years later. They rankled—those taunts—and so they contributed to the outbreak of the war at the time it came. It might have been postponed, and to our advantage, but sooner or later inevitable it was."

"And now?" I inquired.

"*Vae Victis*," he answered. "That, of course, will be the decision of the triumphant democracies—as it was of the victorious kings."

"Your Austrian Allies?"

"*Niederträchtiges Volk*," he mumbled. "It took an Occupation Army of two hundred thousand men to hold them in line."

He stumbled to his feet, coughed a gas cough, and hobbled away, a sad picture of humbled arrogance. I shall pray tonight that we may never be defeated in war!

Berlin, September 25, 1919.

Count Bernstorff, former German Ambassador in Washington, called upon me on Monday afternoon. He was looking well. He said he had enjoyed his nearly three months' vacation in the country. He had left Berlin on the last day of June, after his party, the so-called National Democrats, had split upon the question of signing the Peace Treaty. He said to me that he, himself, had been in favor of signing, but as the majority of his party voted against it, he felt he could not accept the post of Permanent Undersecretary of the Foreign Office which had been offered to him at the time. Bernstorff said that he was present at the recent caucus of the Democrats in the Parliament building, several days before our interview, and that he had success-fully urged his party to accept the offer of the Ebert administration, that is, they were to support the present government (the Majority Socialist) and in return the Democratic party was to have three men in the Cabinet, that is, the Minister of Justice, the Minister of Trans-portation, and one Minister without portfolio. While this deal was in progress, Bernstorff told me that he had been offered once again the position of Permanent Undersecretary of the Foreign Office, but the condition with which it was saddled had proved unacceptable. He was willing to serve in the Foreign Office, but he wished also to be per-mitted to run for the National Assembly at the approaching elections upon the Democratic ticket. He had not heard definitely, but was in-clined to think that President Ebert did not see his way to allow-ing him to serve both in the Assembly, as a party leader, and in the Foreign Office as a government official. It was quite evident from much that he said and much that he left unsaid that Count Bernstorff regards himself as a political possibility of the greatest importance in Germany. I was also struck with the fact that the Germans of all political colorings with whom I have spoken since my arrival here were inclined to think that if his advice from Washington had been followed, the Empire would not have gone down in the great dis-aster by which the Reich is now involved.

He said, "Of course I do not have to tell you that our situation politically as well as economically is very critical. What should be most emphasized, particularly to an American inquirer, is the question of raw materials. If we get the raw materials and the present administration secures a little moral support or even merely countenance from America, as against our reactionary and radical opponents, we may pull through. I say 'pull through,' but only and always if the winter is a mild one and we can manage to get along with the coal that is in sight or available to us now after the various annexations have been put through. But if we have a severe winter, I am afraid nothing can save the government of the day, which will be made responsible for the weather as well as for so many other untoward events which, however, as you know, are quite beyond our control."

The Bernstorff who stood before me was far from being the "glass of fashion and the mold of form" he had undoubtedly been during the long years of his mission in Washington. His shoes were cracked, his cuffs were frayed, and his trousers—how they needed pressing! Those who were in Washington during the last tense months of his mission (I was in foreign parts) are in agreement that the vast propaganda sums that were placed at Bernstorff's disposal were not all wasted in printing pamphlets or even in blowing up munition plants. Much was spent in furnishing his table with delicacies, and it was conceded that his wines and his cigars were superb. With this reputation in mind I had some natural hesitancy in offering the Ambassador one of my army cigars, a crime of the Service of Supplies, and indeed I only did it in answer to his silent but hungry appeal. (When, later, I turned over to him a box more than half full of these stogies, Bernstorff, though long trained to conceal his feelings, went to pieces, and the thanks he proffered bordered on the hysterical. "You cannot appreciate the pleasure you are giving me," he stuttered. "And I hope you never will, for that would mean that you had lived as I have for months without the soothing influence of the Divine Weed. Yes, for the last six months I have been reduced to smoking brown paper, brown flypaper, I think, puah!")

"The German revolution," explained Bernstorff, "was after all but a disease of demobilization, and we cannot be sure that maladies of this nature have run their course or that our people can be said to be immune to a recurrence in the near future. The very stiff notes, I use a mild word, though of course you must know that the great majority of our people regarded them as insulting—those very stiff notes that came from the Peace Conference, or the Supreme War

Council, certainly have had a very unfortunate effect on the country. I estimate, conservatively, I think, that each one of them costs our present government at least fifty thousand votes in the elections which are impending, which will be put off as long as possible, but which, after all, will have to be held at a relatively early date.

"It is true our people want to go back to work now, though it is also true that many of the men who were long in the trenches are unfit for hard labor and also not a few are not anxious for it. Whether they work or whether they just wait for something to turn up, we keep on paying them just the same pittance and, as long as that continues and as long as our depreciating currency buys something that will at least keep body and soul together, the Government can hobble along, but (as every new printing of currency reduces the value of the paper already in circulation) it is only too evident that the time is fast approaching when printing-press promises to pay will only be worth the paper they are printed on—if indeed that.

"Please tell Colonel House that I recall my official and personal intercourse with him and the negotiations upon which we were engaged as by far the most interesting incidents of my career. I only regret, as I am sure he does, the circumstances beyond our control, which rendered our negotiations fruitless and made it impossible to achieve the results for which we worked with, I am sure, equal sincerity, and which, I think (and I believe the Colonel will agree with me), came so near at one time of being crowned with success."

At this point I called the former Ambassador's attention to the German forces under General von der Goltz, active in Finland and in several of the other Baltic States, a problem that was causing the Supreme War Council in Paris considerable anxiety. I asked would these men obey orders from Berlin? Was Berlin disposed to bring them home?

"This question," said Bernstorff, when I broached it (as instructed), "is complicated enough, but not nearly so complicated as it would appear to observers in western Europe. The Supreme Council in Paris seems to forget that shortly after the Armistice von der Goltz had begun to disband his forces and he was withdrawing from the territory which we had conquered, when, at the request of the still-weak governments of the new Baltic States, he was urged to remain, and later in fact he was ordered to remain by the Supreme War Council as a bulwark, and perhaps for the moment the only available bulwark, against the advance of the Bolshevik forces. The members of the

Supreme War Council in Paris have also probably forgotten that these German troops were in large numbers transported back to where they now are, in English ships, placed at their disposal by the British Government.

"So much for that phase of the question. Now, of course, other aspects of the situation are attracting the attention of these men and should be considered. These soldiers of the Baltic armies, and the young adventurers from home who have joined them since, know at least one thing, and that is, that they are better off where they are than their fellows in Germany. They are living without strenuous manual labor and without very great physical effort. They are living off the country which they control and occupy. Courland, and the surrounding districts, is a rather vacant land today, and each of these men thinks it may be possible for him to carve a farm out of the unoccupied or deserted districts. I should say that General von der Goltz is an opportunist. He may change his plans, but at present he undoubtedly hopes to link his forces up with Kolchak and Denikin for the purpose of fighting Lenin. With this end in view, he probably hopes to secure money and material support from the Allies of the west and perhaps from Berlin. Most of the people who are with him and their reactionary friends at home in Germany are inclined to think that when the Russian Reds are beaten, von der Goltz and his men will come home laurel-crowned and begin to drive out of office and government those whom they regard as the Reds in Germany. This is what they think, and it may be correct, but it is taking a long view of the situation and looking much farther ahead than I would care to do at this moment when our national life is a daily and an unremitting struggle for existence.

"As to my own activity, I try to talk sense and to turn my countrymen away from the dreams and from the fantastic mirages with which their eyes and their thoughts have been put out of focus for so many years. I tell them that Japan and America have money but that the rest of us are *caput*—'down and out.' Some people think that I am a little too pessimistic and ought to speak words of cheer, but as I am convinced that the winter that is approaching is going to be the worst of our war experiences, I think I am right in trying to prepare our morale for the last great test to which it must be subjected. Tell Colonel House if we could get a little raw material, a little moral support, a little of what would be regarded here as common civility to the unfortunate men who are at the head of the German state today,

we will get out of the woods, I think, BUT—that is quite a considerable 'but.' Please tell the Colonel I believe in a League of Nations,
but of course only one in which all are represented, the vanquished as
well as the victors. I also hope the Colonel will use his influence to
see that our armed forces are not reduced immediately to 100,000
men. We agreed to this when we were ordered to do it, but it would
mean anarchy if we comply today. We have about 300,000 men
under arms, and we shall need them until next spring. Today, if the
Government only had 100,000 men at its disposal, von der Goltz
with his 70,000 men in the Baltic States would be in control of the
situation. As it is, he is merely a factor of considerable importance."

On the following day (September 26th) I called upon Walther von
Rathenau in his office in what was once the palatial quarters of the
famous Allgemeine-Elektrizitäts-Gesellschaft. It is now in need of
paint and run down at the heels and everywhere else. I should say
he is not immediately accessible to all callers, but a copy of his most
recent letter to the Colonel, which I had been authorized to use,[1] soon
swept away all defensive barriers. He is nervous and greatly depressed,
unlike the hopeful Bernstorff, and he opened our talk by saying:

"What has been done in Paris is a crime against humanity and
civilization, none the less great because some of the gentlemen who
did it were perhaps not aware of what they were doing. They have
Balkanized and Mexicanized the Continent of Europe—east of the
Rhine. Today there remains only one relatively strong power on the
Continent of Europe, and that is France."

In answer to my remark that the few people I had met in Germany
seemed fresh and hopeful, especially the country people, he said: "Of
course they do, and they are hopeful and planning energetically for
the future. They have not the remotest suspicion of what has happened to them. They have all been war-crazy for five years and as yet
they do not appreciate the straits into which defeat has thrown them.
Let us hope that the realization of the true situation will not come to
them suddenly—or yet completely; that would indeed be a fatal
awakening.

"Yes, as you say, they are cheerful and not disinclined to work.
They are beginning to put their shoulders to the wheel but if they had,
as I have, and perhaps a score of other economists in Germany have,
a realizing sense that however industriously and ardently they may put

[1]It bore the notation in the Colonel's handwriting: "Colonel Bonsal is my alter ego.
Speak to him as frankly as you would to me."

their shoulders to the wheel they will never get the cart out of the mire—not under present conditions—that would be the end of Germany and of the Germans as a nation. They would scatter to the four winds, as you see they are doing today—that is, the few who can secure transportation. Fifteen millions of Germans must emigrate or starve, so the posters say. Well, that statement is not exaggerated. The crisis is so terrible that it cannot be met, however, by emigration to the Argentine, and to Paraguay, and Brazil; some may escape in that way, indeed some have, but the great bulk of us have to face the situation here, and what we shall have to face will depend in a large measure upon America."

Here again Herr Rathenau came back to the remark which I had made to the effect that I found Germans almost everywhere going about their business and seriously taking up the struggle for life with good courage, although to my mind by no means unaware of the great catastrophe in which they and their fortunes were involved.

"Yes, of course," he said, "they are bearing themselves bravely, as you have noticed. They are in the plight, I take it, of fever patients. People come in, look them over, and they are surprised to find how well the patient looks; they say, never did he have a better color; never were his eyes so bright. But the doctor knows what the flushed cheeks and the flashing eyes portend and knows also that the course of the fever may well in a few hours leave the patient a corpse or a skeleton. In this latter case, it is still uphill work, and careful nutrition is necessary to bring the patient back to life and usefulness again. Now, the fever of misunderstanding, the great madness under which we Germans and some others of the peoples of Europe have been suffering in a hardly less degree, mind you, has not run its course; it may be fatal still, or we may escape a fatal issue, but look, what is there left us to build up upon? How can we reconstruct the waste of tissue? No one can contradict me when I say there is absolutely nothing left us beyond a possible bare subsistence. Our potash is gone with Alsace-Lorraine, and our export coal with the Saar Basin. Of coal and iron, we have not enough of them left in sight for our own needs, and for years to come there will be nothing to export. For the last sixty years before the war the Germans had ceased to be a self-sufficient people, and we could not survive except by and through our export trade. That, you see, was our money crop. What is to take its place? Remember, we have no ships now. We have simply idle factories and a peasant population that is working hard to fill its belly, and an industrial population that is drawing non-employment pay. Even if you let us do it, how can we purchase raw materials with our mark quoted at about three American cents? Mind you I am not discussing these questions politically, but merely from the standpoint of the economist. It seems to me some leading people in western Europe are expecting us to pay for all the damages caused by the war and at the same time are inflicting a fatal knockout blow not only upon our prosperity and our capacity to pay, to repay as they say, but upon our very existence. Today, economically, Germany is dying, and the gangrened corpse that will result, I tell you again, speaking as an economist and not as a politician, I tell you that gangrened corpse will infect the whole world.

"I must try to make you see that outside of France you have not left standing a single strong state east of the Rhine. I must tell you again, the Paris Peace Conference has Balkanized and Mexicanized Europe. Of course I know that the American representatives in Paris did not propose to do anything of the kind, and I am inclined to think that many representatives of other powers are equally guiltless of planning this thing in cold blood, but you have done it all the same. What are these states of Poland, Czechoslovakia, and Yugoslavia which you have created? Let me tell you: nothing that will last except the shame of them; nothing that will advance humanity; nothing that will redound to the credit of civilization. Should you, Colonel Bonsal, come back here in ten years you will shudder with horror at the sight of the human suffering and the human destruction for which your country will be in a large measure to blame. This is a terrible outlook, and the consequences, the inevitable tragic consequences of it, I believe, unless the peace conditions are radically changed, will not be borne by us Germans alone. The whole world will be involved and permeated by the lawlessness of the new situation, and the era in our history which began with a laudable attempt (I have no doubt of this) to civilize the Balkans and to bestow civilized government and respect for the law where it was lacking, will end, indeed it has ended, as I have already told you several times, by the Balkanization of that Europe from whence came life-giving blood and the heart impulse of the whole civilized world.

"What a waste of time it is to talk about the responsibility for the war," continued Rathenau. He was here referring to the flood of pamphlets and controversial books about the peace negotiations with which the newsstands and bookstores of Berlin are flooded. "The only vital, the only important thing to do today is to get together and see whether we can save ourselves and our children from the terrible consequences of the disaster in which, whatever may be our separate responsibility and individual guilt, we are all involved. Even our Emperor (what folly to think otherwise!) he did not plan or plot out the war. He and those who were with him stumbled into the war like a lot of drunken sailors who did not know how to take care of themselves, much less to take care of the people whom it was their bounden duty to protect. The Kaiser," he continued, "what an idiot! What a coward he was! In the end, why did he not place himself at the head of a chosen band and throw himself upon the enemy? There are many who would have rallied around him, had he shown a spark of manliness, who would have been happy to have accepted their probable fate. But, after all, this repining is foolish too. The only thing to do, that is worth while, is to plan and build, to put up the barriers and the dykes, to save what yet remains, from the threatening floods of devastation and demoralization which the war has left without control."

At this point Herr Rathenau went into, with great wealth of detail, what he considers was his momentous, indeed his all-important interview with Field Marshal von Ludendorff at the headquarters of the army in June 1917. "It was then that the worst that could happen had happened, and America had entered the war against us," he said. "Everything was lost, and everybody knew it, apparently, except the blind *bande* in control. Colonel House will, I am sure, remember what I told him in our talks in 1915 and in 1916 when he was in Germany, before you entered the war. I recall with pleasure that he thanked me for the frankness with which I spoke and that in 1916 he congratulated me upon the correctness of my predictions in our 1915 talks. I was as frank as I dared to be, and there were, as Colonel House intimated at the time, very few who cared or dared to talk frankly. Well, I told him then that the war could only end in two ways: By the energetic intervention of the United States to enforce peace, or by her intervention on the side of the Entente Allies. And again, and as a last resort, on my return from a short trip to America, I tried, for the last time, these arguments upon Ludendorff, upon whom I literally forced myself. In the interview, we talked in terms of chess, a game in which we are both adepts, and I said to him I was trying all the time to save my country and the thousands of lives that were being thrown away every minute. I am not so sure that I then fully appreciated that I was also trying to save the life of the world. Ludendorff, of course, stressed his 'invincible army,'—as became the *miles gloriosus*.

" 'Yes, these, your successes,' I said. 'I admit them, but where are they leading us? What is your end play, your victory stroke, to be? What is the result that will justify all this wastage of blood and treasure? Can you inform me?' I found out (he admitted it when I forced him into a corner) that our great general had no end play planned. He was just hoping that the other fellows would grow weary of the butchery before we did. Well, I talked with him until noon, and when our interview was interrupted by official business, I found the general still interested, and he asked me to come back in the afternoon and we would talk some more. When I came back in the afternoon, I drew my illustrations as to the hopelessness of the situation from the war of 1870. Then I said, 'General, we had Paris surrounded, was that an end?' 'No,' he admitted. 'Then we had Paris under bombardment; was that an end?' 'No.' 'Then came the revolution. Now was that an end play? So,' I continued, 'you have got today to besiege London, Paris, and New York. You have got to bombard them, one and all, and then revolutions have to follow. Can you do that, are you sure of your ability to do that?'

"He was silent for a long time and then he said: 'You have convinced me of many things. I recognize how serious is the situation, but I still have a feeling that we are going to win, that our victory stroke will come by means of the ruthless submarine warfare.' Well, we talked on that subject until nightfall. I think I conclusively proved that you Americans would be building more ships in six months than we could sink in nine. As it now turns out, I overestimated your effort of the first six months and I underestimated what you did in the second six months. I still think you could have lived up to my figures or even exceeded them in the first six months, only you were not fully aroused to your danger. I think Ludendorff was forced to see that I had him in logical argument or else a man of his admirable mental gifts would not have taken the course which the field marshal now did. Suddenly he swept all our figures and all our memoranda from the table. 'All you say may be so,' he admitted, 'but you do not convince me. I have a feeling that the U-boat warfare is what will prove our salvation,' and he repeated it over and over again. *'Ich habe das Gefühl*—I have the feeling—that through it we shall win.' Well, there was nothing more to be done or to be said. Our leader had taken refuge in the guidance, not of his brains, but of his feelings. All indeed was lost!

"I will give you a direct answer to the inquiry you bring from Colonel House, but I should warn you not to attach any great importance to it. Neither I nor those who think as I do are in the Government now and we may not even be listened to in the council chamber. But we have agreed to urge a policy of fulfillment. The fact that the Treaty cannot be carried out does not release us from the duty of trying. We lose no opportunity of insisting upon this attitude. Of course the terms of the Treaty are impossible, but we think that the only way to demonstrate this is to attempt a policy of strict fulfillment. In this we are not guilty of bad faith to you or to our own people, but we do think that in this way, and in this way alone, can we hasten a return to sanity which it seems to me is as greatly needed in Paris as it is with us here."

Often in the course of our long interview, which continued for several hours, Rathenau would turn his thought from the turmoil in Europe and from the many groups of armies which still faced one another in hostile array, and in some quarters, particularly in eastern Europe, were still fighting. "If the world is to survive, and I am not too sure of that, although I admit that this is a tough old world," he repeated, "a new society must be formed, and in my judgment the basic principle of that new society will be the insistent demand that every man and every woman shall perform every day some useful physical labor. The dignity of labor must be re-established. In the new society there must be no place for hereditary landlords controlling large areas of idle lands or for coupon-clipping parasites." And he added somewhat sadly, "I may not witness this transformation, but you will, I hope. It is absolutely necessary if civilization is to survive."[2]

Some months later Rathenau became Minister of Foreign Affairs in the Weimar government and in June 1922 he was assassinated[3] because,

---

[2] It is noteworthy that this thoughtful and farsighted man should have developed in this way, and to me at this time, the idea of compulsory labor battalions which is the only innovation in the new Germany that is approved by the democratic countries and by some is even imitated. Today it is a fact that in Germany no man, however learned, can receive a degree or take up professional duties unless he has worked with pick and shovel in a labor camp for at least six months. (1936)

[3] Little did his murderers, who, at least two of them, committed suicide when about to be arrested by the police, appreciate that in some twenty German cities within the next few years monuments were to be erected in their honor or that they were to be unveiled with great pomp and ceremony by the leading men of the Hitler regime.

within what he considered were the limits of the possible,[4] he attempted to carry out the Versailles Treaty. Rathenau was the leading spirit in the second Wirth ministry, and the fate that befell him did not encourage any of his successors to continue the policy of "fulfillment." Indeed, a very few weeks after their conviction his assassins were liberated—and feted!

Rathenau continued to talk at length, and, I must admit, with great eloquence, of the socialized society of which he dreamed. It was only with difficulty that at last I brought him back to the living, struggling world with which we are confronted—with which my mission in Berlin is immediately concerned.

Berlin, September 25, 1919.

In war there are always mysteries, and the Great War is no exception to the rule. The all-engrossing mystery here, in military circles at least, is why the High Command detached two army corps from the Western Front just before the Battle of the Marne, where they might well have exercised a decisive influence. Even more mysterious is the fact that they were sent to the Eastern Front, where, evidently, they were not needed and certainly not asked for. By this step, the right wing, the famous right wing of the German invasion in France, was greatly weakened and the "pincer" operation failed. When I was on the Eastern Front in the spring of 1915, a Colonel Bauer, who was in the Bureau of Operations, and the most active member of it, told me that while the battle of Tannenberg was under way, and apparently there was no doubt as to its successful outcome, Ludendorff was called to the field telephone by General Headquarters. Appreciating that the message would be of importance, Colonel Bauer was asked by his chief to listen in at a second phone. He told me that he heard Colonel Trappen from Headquarters announce that three army corps

[4]While the regular Commissions of Control appointed by the Supreme War Council to regulate disarmament, and above all to keep watch over secret rearming, only reached Germany several weeks later, Berlin at this time (September 1919) was certainly cluttered up with military observers who were making voluminous reports to their respective governments as to how the new authorities were, or were not, fulfilling the disarmament agreements. It soon became clear that these special agents were handed a difficult job. It was apparent to me, and it must be to them, that the returning troops are being fed into a number of camouflaged organizations, such as the Sicherheits Polizei, the Einwohner Wache, and even into sport clubs whose activities are purely military, and in this way it is clear that the potential military strength of the German people is being maintained. But in view of the Spartacist danger, with munitions and subsidies coming to them from Moscow, was this not only permissible but even advisable? It was a difficult problem, and, as the sequel demonstrated, it never was solved.

and a division of cavalry were to be sent to re-enforce the Eighth Army on the Eastern Front, and he asked to what points they should be directed. Ludendorff gave the necessary information, but added that he did not need re-enforcements. Trappen countered with the statement that these troops were superfluous on the Western Front. On the following morning Trappen called again and said that only two corps would be sent and a cavalry division, but that the Fifth Corps would be held in the west.

These unwanted troops that were detached in this mysterious manner were, with the exception of a reserve division of the Guards, all first-line troops. What became of them, I do not know. But I do know that in March 1915, at least six months later, I heard Hindenburg complaining that Headquarters would not let him have any first-line troops, and then he added whimsically, "All my men are grandfathers." Certainly during my stay with his army I saw no first-line troops, with the exception of a very smart regiment of Baden cavalry, whose activities I have described elsewhere in my account of the retaking of Memel.[5]

September 26, 1919.

I could not have imagined that the war records of the Great General Staff would have been opened to me at this early day, or indeed at any time, but as a matter of fact this surprising thing has happened. I understand, of course, the political reasons which have induced prominent members of the Weimar government who must be nameless to take this step; in any event, I am glad to profit by it. Ever since the Armistice old Prussian officers without number have been insisting that at the front the army could have continued to face a world in arms, but that it was the disloyal strokes, the *Dolchstösse* in the back, inflicted by the Social Democrats, that brought about the military debacle (it was only months later that a large measure of responsibility was assigned to the Jews).

These legends will, in the course of time, be generally accepted, I have no doubt, the Germans, like other peoples, being inclined to believe what they want to believe, and the records which prove the contrary will be doctored or entirely suppressed. But the fact is that, as the archives now opened to me disclose, Ludendorff lost hope of a military victory after August 8th, which he describes in his official report as "a day of mourning for the German Army." Weeks later, as

[5]*Collier's Weekly,* March 1917.

archives further reveal, lamenting the disaster to the Bulgar and the Austrian contingents on the Salonika front (September 25, 1918), he wrote:

"This seals the destiny of the Quadruple Alliance."[6] A few days later in an official report he describes how six or seven German divisions with hitherto fine records have allowed themselves to be cut to pieces. There is also in the dossier an unsigned memorandum describing in detail the War Council of September 29th (1918), at which, among others, were present Hindenburg, Ludendorff, and von Hintze, the new Secretary for Foreign Affairs, whom I knew so well in China. The Emperor presided and the soldiers and the diplomats, for once in agreement, said:

"Sire, the army demands and requires an immediate armistice."

The Emperor protested against this decision, advancing "face-saving" arguments, but finally was forced to the following admission: "We have come to the end of our tether. I, too, recognize we must end the war as best we can."

Let us examine further the tale of disaster and humiliation which the record discloses. On October 1st Ludendorff sent Lersner, his liaison officer, to the Chancellor with an urgent demand for peace, and in these words explained the necessity of it. He wrote:

"The troops hold today, but no one can foresee what will happen tomorrow. The break-through may occur at any moment, and upon a vital point a division may fail to do its duty."

In another dispatch, under the same date, Ludendorff admits that in round numbers some forty thousand of his men, mostly infantry, have deserted and crossed the frontier into Holland. In the same dispatch the field marshal officially conceded the increasing demoralization of his army and for the first time speaks of propaganda. He says: "The minds of many are poisoned by the tracts that are dropped upon them at the front." (This "poison" would seem to have been distilled or at least purveyed by open Allied fliers and not from the "traitors who skulked at the rear," of whom we are hearing so much now.)

On the third of October the height of the crisis was reached and Hindenburg sent this blistering message to Prince Max of Baden, the new Chancellor:

"As a consequence of the disaster on the Macedonian front, and owing to the disappearance of our reserves, making it impossible to secure replacements for our heavy losses, there is not the least hope

[6]Germany, Austria-Hungary, Bulgaria, and Turkey.

left of imposing peace upon our enemies. We insist upon our demand for an armistice."

A letter from the Crown Prince, or rather the certified copy of it that was sent on to the Reichstag Committee by the War Ministry, was also placed before me. It is dated September 18th (1918), and reads:

"After the Battle of the Marne I never believed that a complete victory was possible. After the check of the 1918 offensive, the situation became truly critical. It is necessary to make peace as quickly as possible."

Letters from the Archduke Ruprecht in command of the Bavarian Army are equally enlightening, and they seem to have had great influence on his cousin, Prince Max, the new Chancellor. They came from the man who commanded the Bavarians, generally regarded by the Allies as more sturdy and obstinate fighters than even the Prussians.

"I do not think we can hold on throughout the coming winter," he wrote (on October 4, 1918). "It is even possible that disaster will overtake us before then. The Americans are increasing very rapidly, much more rapidly than was foreseen; they have already thirty-one divisions in France. Our reserves do not suffice to replace our daily losses, and owing to the lack of officers, and to sickness, and to the wretched food, they are inferior to our adversaries."

On October 18th Ruprecht wrote again and more insistently to Prince Max:

"Our troops are vanishing in an alarming manner. The number of fighting men in our infantry divisions rarely equals three thousand. We have lost many machine guns and we lack good marksmen; the resistance of our troops diminishes hourly. If we do not receive more petrol from Roumania, our air force will have to be grounded. I do not think we can hold out beyond December, and a disaster may occur at any moment. Ludendorff does not appreciate the gravity of the situation; it is absolutely necessary to secure peace before our adversaries have forced their way into Germany."

So much for the ever-victorious, the unconquered army!

If I had the time I should copy these records[7] more fully than I am

[7] I should say here that these letters that were shown me were not the originals that came to the General Staff from officers in the field, but certified copies that were sent on by the War Ministry to the Reichstag Committee on the Conduct of the War for their information and understanding of the situation. In subsequent visits to Berlin I was frequently told that one of the purposes in burning the Reichstag building was to destroy the evidence so damaging to the prestige of the Prussian military caste. When General von Seeckt and his brother officers of the old army were placed in control of the Reichswehr, permitted under the Versailles Treaty, they undoubtedly destroyed

doing. I have an idea that they will not always be available. There are people out of the picture now who may come back and who have a vital interest in their destruction. But time is lacking, and, after all, the purpose of my mission here is to ascertain and weigh future probabilities and not to hold a post-mortem over the corpse of what was so recently a "mighty empire."

In this account, however fragmentary and sketchy, that I am taking from the official reports, I must not overlook the part, indeed the very leading part, that the navy played in the debacle.[8] These reports show that as far back as six months before the end a sharp lowering of morale was noted and deplored by the ranking officers in both Kiel and Wilhelmshaven. The climax came when (October 9th) Admiral Scheer ordered the sailors to take the ships, so long harbor-bound, to sea, to break the strangle hold of the British High Sea Fleet, to fight a liberating battle, or to go down with flying colors. Whereupon the men not only refused to sail but murdered quite a few of their officers who pointed out to them the path of duty. In some of these reports it is noted that Prince Henry of Prussia, who was given the command of the devoted fleet by his imperial brother, failed to rise to the heroic occasion, that in fact he stayed on shore in the arsenal. It is also worthy of notice that the first outbreak of disobedience took place in the navy, where there were no Jews, while in the army there were many whose gallant conduct was rewarded with Iron Crosses. Admittedly, the naval forces afloat and in the yards and arsenals were purely "Aryan" bodies; however, once they were convinced that the army was defeated, the sailors were unwilling to sacrifice their lives for a cause that was already lost. It was these practical men, certainly not heroes, who started the uprising in Kiel on November 1st, and a few hours later in both the naval bases the Social Democrats joined with them—and the much-vaunted German marine came to an inglorious end.

Twice-told tale though it was, I copied these revealing dispatches in part because my new-found Social Democratic friends were in-

the originals of this illuminating correspondence. Hans von Seeckt who won his spurs as chief of staff to Field Marshal von Mackensen in the Roumanian campaign was chosen, and well chosen, to rebuild the clandestine German Army that was suddenly unmasked in 1938.

[8]It seems to me the last word on this subject was spoken by the War Committee of the Reichstag, which, after painstaking investigation, finally, in March 1928, reported that: "The defeat was due to the military and economic superiority of the enemy." One might imagine that this verdict would end the *Dolchstösse* legend, but such is not the case. The Germans are a remarkable people!

sistent that I do so. And the fact that I had sat at Halle with Bebel and the elder Liebknecht in the first *Sozialisten-tag* that was held after the repressive Bismarck laws had been repealed, made them regard me as one of "theirs." They wanted the widest publicity given to these confessions of failure and defeat. They knew how persuasive was the "dagger-in-the-back" slogan, as an explanation of the military collapse to a people who have always had an exaggeratedly high opinion of their military prowess and wished to hold fast to it.

But I made one condition, although I did not emphasize it. One good turn deserved another was the line I took; and I did want to know, as far as the documents revealed, under what circumstances and through what pressure the unrestricted U-boat warfare was decided upon, the step that brought us into the war, the Emperor to flight, and the German people to ruin. Readily they agreed to my proposal—for such it was—and as a matter of fact it soon became clear to me that the members of the National Assembly, at least those with whom I came in contact, were as ignorant of the circumstances leading up to this tragic decision as we were on our side of the Atlantic. Perhaps indeed even more so; but they set about getting the incriminating documents with considerable enthusiasm. As they said, proudly and truthfully, "no member of the present National Assembly was involved in those fateful decisions."

The official records show that while the debates had raged for a year, it was only during the session of the Reichstag Committee on January 31st (1917) that final approval of unrestricted U-boat warfare was secured, the German Empire signed its death warrant, and Admiral von Capelle achieved an immortality which will prove irksome with the passing years. This admiral is not now highly regarded, and apparently never was, in naval or political circles, but as he was accepted at this critical moment as the mouthpiece of von Tirpitz, his words carried weight. And according to the record these were his words:

"We do not have to worry about the United States; not one ship or its complement of men will reach this side of the ocean; that is why we have U-boats and that is just the kind of prey we wish to hunt down and destroy."

Admiral Koch followed. He was less theatrical but equally positive. "U-boat warfare will force England to sue for peace," he insisted.

The chairman of the Committee then drew up the following resolution:

"As conditions are now, it is clear we shall by means of a rigidly enforced submarine campaign be able to compel England to accept peace at our hands within five months."

The resolution, the order for full steam ahead, the removal of all restrictions on the steel sharks, which many of the naval men had wanted for so long, was then sent on by special messenger to both the Admiralty and to von Hindenburg at Army Headquarters. On the following day von Capelle returned to the Committee room bearing with him what he said was the grateful thanks of the navy, and he added: "I can also give you the assurance that, viewed from the military standpoint, the assistance which will result from the entrance of America into the war on the side of our enemies will amount to exactly nothing." That also is in the record.

In the face of these demands, for an "all-out U-boat campaign" now in January 1917, insisted upon both by the army and the navy and enthusiastically endorsed by the press, the position of Chancellor Bethmann-Hollweg clearly became exceedingly precarious. He was now even deprived of the slender prop he had availed himself of six months before in his conflict with von Tirpitz. He could no longer claim that there were not available enough U-boats to accomplish their diabolical purpose; at least one hundred and twenty new and more formidable submarines had been launched during the intervening months and as many more were in the yards, nearing completion.

A Herr Schultze-Brombert, who, though a member of the new National Assembly, is fighting, almost single-handed, to preserve the fair name of the old imperial crowd, has brought me another long letter from the former Chancellor, not addressed to me, but to a friend who was urged to use it in any way he sees fit, which, he says, sets forth the essentials of the defense which Bethmann-Hollweg proposes to make before the Committee now in session, if given an opportunity to do so.

In this communication Bethmann-Hollweg argues: "It is not fair to say that our alternative was U-boat warfare to be pushed in the most unrestricted manner, or a continuance of the military stalemate on the Western Front and increasing starvation at home.

"There was the chance of a negotiated peace through the mediation of President Wilson. While our Washington plans had not prospered fully, I am sure Count Bernstorff will bear me out that hope in that direction had not been abandoned when the new navy policy ended abruptly and absolutely all negotiations.

"It is true we had been disappointed; the something forthright and tangible we had long expected from Washington had not come, but I could see the difficulties of President Wilson's position and at this time, at least, I did not question his good faith. Clearly Wilson could not afford to make a proposition to us which the Allies would decline. What would they accept in the way of terms to end the war so disastrous to us all? Wilson did not know, nor did he know what terms we would accept, and, frankly, I did not know myself what terms would be accepted by the Emperor and the Reichstag. Bernstorff could not pin Wilson or House down to a concrete proposal, and most certainly I could not present one that had any but the most remote chance of success. We should all bear in mind that only fifteen months later would the army even consider the restoration of occupied Belgium and that step was for the Allies, of course, a *sine qua non*. So we kept swirling around in a vicious and what seemed a hopeless circle.

"We were in this dilemma when in January 1917 the formal demand for the U-boat campaign was made by the army, the navy, and the press, and, in this instance, there can be no doubt, the press was interpreting the well-nigh unanimous will of the people. The demand was now formally reduced to writing, and it read, 'unrestricted U-boat warfare must be undertaken immediately and be prosecuted with the utmost resolution.' It also asserted that there was complete agreement in the fighting forces that the war situation demanded the employment of this weapon to the fullest extent of its possibilities, and the admirals, on their high authority, gave the assurance that 'so used this weapon would prove invincible.'

"Now what did this mean?" said Bethmann-Hollweg. "Surely it was an admission that the land war had ended in a stalemate and that in view of the increasing severity of the blockade the day was not far distant when in all probability we would not be able to maintain even our present far-from-brilliant positions. 'Without the use of this weapon we cannot guarantee a successful conclusion of the war—with it we can,' asserted the High Command.

"If anything definite in the way of possible mediation and acceptable negotiation had come from Washington I might have continued to oppose this step as I had done successfully in 1916, but nothing definite came. In view of the attitude of the Entente powers I had no reason to expect anything would come, and so I could not advise the Emperor to reject the plan which his military advisers considered as offering a chance of success, even though I thought, as I most certainly did, that the chance was not a very good one."

Berlin, September 26th.

I am not getting about as much as I would like, the line-up of my visitors is long, and the unfortunate people who wait and wait to see me seem to find comfort in the "sight," though why they should, the Lord only knows. I can do nothing for them. I did, however, get out to Potsdam on Sunday and attended service, a penitential service, in the Garrison Church. It was thronged with the widows and the mothers of the Junkers whose broken bodies are rotting all over Europe from the Baltic to the Black Sea, from the Channel to the Volga. Well, there they were, as far as I could see through the long crepe veils not as fleshy as they had been when their arrogant spouses rode away to war. But I did not gloat over them. I imagine I'm a poor hater, as Mme. Georgitch said when I refused to enthuse or dance a hornpipe on hearing the news, the good news, that Stambolov, who had used me despitefully, had been set upon and cut to pieces with the ugly yataghans which the Macedonians use so skillfully and, above all, so silently.

But I did see that the streets, once so stately, were grass-grown and the atmosphere rank and even putrid with uncollected garbage. At times it seemed to me that the air was fresher even in the hotel lobby than Unter den Linden. And a saunter along the Friedrichstrasse in the afternoon was certainly not uplifting. (I was warned to avoid it at night.) There it was that, in prewar days, the life of Berlin, of Gross-Berlin, surged. Well, it did not surge now. The great artery was cluttered up with war cripples, who hobbled along as best they could or made imploring gestures for help from vestibules and the entrances to houses. Some of these unfortunates were bold and not a few indulged in menacing gestures. Others, and these were the more numerous, crouched against the cold, damp walls as though ashamed for the stranger to see their distorted leg and arm stumps, their dead eyes, or their faces scarred almost beyond recognition as human beings by the flame throwers which one of their great men invented—not thinking it could and would be turned against their ever-victorious army. All these unfortunates were alike in one respect. They were all talking, or rather mumbling, to themselves, their tales of woe, rather than to those callous folk who hurried by as fast as they could. Russian refugees, often barefooted, always in rags, milled around in groups too. They had escaped the revolution and apparently had no fear of the starvation with which they seem to be confronted. But how unlike they are to the Junker ladies now beaten down upon their long-unbending knees. They are not and never have been *hoffähig,* nor can they boast of heraldic quarterings, but they hold high their heads, and if die they must, they will die as free men and masters of their souls—an ideal which seems to be beyond the grasp of the average German.

On one of my few walks I saw a sight which made me wonder if the world, the Berlin world at least, which I had known so well in other days had not come to an end. On the Friedrichstrasse Kempinski's restaurant and café which Pemberton Grund and I had inaugurated (well in the last century) was not only closed, but all the doors and windows were boarded up. This extra precaution is due to the fact that Kempinski, the *Feinschmecker* from Warsaw, was a Pole and doubtless during the welter of war had dabbled in politics. Certainly I had come to this shrine of excellent food and drink with no thought of talking about the Curzon line. This was the peach month, and I wanted to quench my thirst with a deep draught of peach *Bowle* which Grund had invented and which bore his name for so many years in thirsty circles. I had wanted to know why this warm-weather drink was now known as Maryland Club punch and is no longer associated with the name of my old companion, who carried the Herald tabard to so many battle fronts in Europe, Asia, and Africa. Grund sleeps in a little English churchyard near Brighton and the peach *Bowle* of his mixing bears an alias. Well, Kempinski has vanished and Grund, their benefactor, is no longer remembered by the fruit drinkers of Berlin. And I could also find no trace of Karl von Kleist, who had gotten into trouble by knocking down an impertinent waiter at Kempinski's, and unfortunately in court the waiter revealed that he had a wooden leg and the *Rechtsanwalt* maintained that poor Kleist was known in all the cafés as "Boxer Karl." As a witness I disputed this and demonstrated that Kleist was a dub with his fists. However, the judge held that Kleist was a redoubtable fighter *für die hiesige Verhältnisse*[9] and gave Kleist a stiff sentence. Certainly in these days fist fighters were not approved of in Berlin.

The Social Democrats who, while far from united, are in control, seem more inclined to ventilate and emphasize the mistakes of the im-

[9] In view of local conditions.

perial regime than they are to prepare to face the actual situation or the hard winter that is so near. Now and again, it is true, I hear of a shadowy plan, *Winterhilfe*—winter help—they call it, but nothing practical is being done in the way of feeding and clothing the thousands in dire want. More, much more zeal and energy are displayed in giving the widest possible publicity to the mistakes of imperial diplomacy which are held to share responsibility for the national defeat, with the confessed collapse of the forces in the field. (Confessed at least in Social Democratic circles!)

I try to avoid, or at least limit, these time-consuming discussions; clearly my job is to peer into the future, not to hold an inquest over the past, but I fear I am far from successful. This campaign to "place responsibilities" now under way, and in which against my will I am becoming involved, I should state was initiated by a resolution of the National Assembly (that has succeeded to the Reichstag) which three weeks ago provided for the appointment of a committee to ascertain (1) upon whose shoulders rests responsibility for the war, and (2) who they were who insisted upon the proclamation of unrestricted U-boat warfare in January 1917, which forced an evidently reluctant America into the war and sealed the fate of the Central Empires.

The private hearings of this Committee, whose members are nearly all Majority Socialists, are now under way, and it is announced that the investigation will be kept upon a high, consequently upon a nonpartisan, plane. The chairman has been authorized to hold secret sessions when it may seem advisable in the public interest, but judging from the communications with which I am deluged, sooner or later much soiled linen will be hung on the lines—publicly.

The controversy which resulted in the fateful decision goes back farther than was generally known before the records were opened. They reveal that in January 1916 von Tirpitz, then at the head of the navy, demanded the proclamation of unrestricted ("ruthless," as we may well call it) submarine warfare. With the support of the Foreign Office, Bethmann-Hollweg stoutly opposed the plan, not because it was barbarous or politically unwise, but for the reason that at the time the German Navy did not have available a sufficient number of submarines to clear the seas of hostile and neutral shipping. Many here— and they are very vocal—assert that this statement on the part of the unfortunate Chancellor was a subterfuge, that he greatly feared the political consequences of the new policy on the still-neutral nations, and that he merely advanced the argument he did because he recognized it was the only one that would be listened to in Berlin. With his darling project defeated, von Tirpitz resigned, and for some months nothing further was heard of his plan—born of desperation.

As to what followed is a matter of hot debate; no one is as well informed as Bernstorff but, trained career-diplomat that he is, he shows no eagerness to enter into the controversy. He will await his day in court and that is coming in a week; in the meantime he says he is fully occupied in reviving the long-dormant Democratic party, which he insists is the hope of Germany.

"If we are to gain control of the National Assembly," the former Ambassador said to me yesterday, "we shall need recruits from all the prewar parties. Only with their co-operation can we hope to bring our tempest-tossed Vaterland back on an even keel."

Naturally in these circumstances he does not wish to alienate any of the political groups which later on might prove invaluable. But Bernstorff is very human. While he will not flaunt in the faces of his former critics the dispatches from Washington that would justify him in saying, "Well, I told you so. I warned you what would happen," he is not displeased to know that the Washington correspondence will be placed before the Inquiry. One of the members of the Commission has already given me an undoubtedly authentic copy of the dispatch which the Chancellor sent to the Ambassador in Washington on January 16th (1917) and his reply which clears the skirts of the much-maligned diplomat and places the responsibility where it belongs. It reads:

I know full well that by taking this step (unrestricted U-boat warfare) we run the danger of bringing about a break, and possibly war, with the United States. We have determined to take the risk. But I request your Excellency to advise me as to any possible means likely to afford an opportunity for taking steps to diminish the danger of a break.

(Signed) BETHMANN-HOLLWEG.

The Ambassador's answer, although couched in diplomatic language, was to the effect that the only way to avoid a head-on collision with America was to rescind the order.

. . . With evident reluctance Bethmann-Hollweg, at the second meeting of the Committee, placed into the record some details of his long fight against the new submarine campaign and in doing so he showed conclusively that he had delayed it for at least twelve months. He testified: "On October 1, 1916, I was informed by Admiral von

Holtzendorff, in strict confidence, that the Naval High Command, the Army General Staff concurring, had decided to inaugurate unrestricted submarine warfare on October 18th. I immediately sent the following telegram to Baron Grunau, the representative of the Foreign Office at Imperial Headquarters:

" 'I cannot conceive of a final decision being taken on this momentous question, and of my being merely informed thereof, confidentially, by the chief of the Admiralty Staff, without an agreement, sanctioned by His Majesty, having been reached on this point with me, and I desire to make the following comment. It is well known that we are now pledged to the United States to carry on U-boat warfare solely under the rules of prize. We can recede from this position only after making an impressive statement of our reasons for so doing and after allowing a certain period of time to elapse in which, in theory at least, the American Government would be enabled to prevent the sailing of American ships with passengers to England. It should be borne in mind that, at the personal command of His Majesty the Emperor, Count Bernstorff in Washington has been instructed to approach President Wilson on the subject of issuing an appeal for peace. In case President Wilson is prevailed upon to do this, the probable rejection of the appeal by England and her Allies, taken in connection with our acceptance of it, will constitute good grounds for us to withdraw our promise to the United States and permit us to do so in a manner which would justify us in the sight of the world at large, and particularly in the eyes of the European neutral powers. It is evident that this course could not fail to have important influence upon the attitude they will probably assume later. Until the situation here described is cleared up, at least in respect to our relations with the United States, the proclamation of U-boat warfare, to be followed by steps for putting it into execution according to the present orders of His Majesty, is absolutely impossible.' "

For the time being the Chancellor was successful. But the evil day had only been postponed for a few months.

While defeated and retired from the scene, as the records now brought to light clearly reveal, it is apparent that von Tirpitz still clung to his darling project and that he remained all-powerful at the Admiralty. In November, undoubtedly at his instigation, a memorial to the Emperor was drawn up. It is signed by five senior admirals and his name does not appear, but the original draft of the letter now before the Committee is in his handwriting. It reads:

"If the Imperial Navy is permitted to carry on unrestricted U-boat warfare, Britain will be forced to sue for peace within five months."

In the secret hearings of the War Committee of the Reichstag, according to the accounts now brought to light, there was advanced only one thought in a less confident spirit. It was voiced by Herr Helfferich, then Minister of Economy and Finance, later Vice-Chancellor, who said: "This (unrestricted U-boat warfare) is a card we must play. If it is not trumps, Germany is lost for the ages."

While Bernstorff himself will not speak on the subject of his treatment on his return from Washington, his paper, the organ of the new Democratic party, is not so discreet. The fact that the Emperor for three months refused to accord the Ambassador back from his post the usual audience, is referred to frequently and in terms of deep indignation. Also the insulting words of Ludendorff, who apparently accosted the waiting envoy outside the imperial audience chamber, are given much publicity. The Generalissimo, then supreme in political as well as military matters, is reported to have said, indeed to have shouted: "With our U-boats running free we shall end the war in three months. On that day you will regret your opposition, which delayed its adoption for some months. A heavy, a very heavy responsibility, Herr Botschafter."

"I do not think so," answered Bernstorff, and the paper adds: "He was dismissed like a lackey because he told the truth."

The only remark Bernstorff made to me on the delicate subject is as follows:

"I do not know why I was not received. When I was admitted to the imperial presence four months later, the die was cast: we were at war with America. His Majesty asked me no questions and I offered no information. I had said all I was entitled to say; our conversation should be described as conventional; certainly it had no political significance."

As the prospect of a decisive military victory on the Western Front grew more doubtful, many civilians rallied to the position taken by the Army and Navy Command. The testimony before the Reichstag Committee, to clarify the situation and advise as to a course of action, became more voluminous and, so at least it seemed to me, distinctly more one-sided. Particularly striking was the statement of Admiral von Capelle, the successor of von Tirpitz in January 1917. It carried great weight and is thought by many to have shaped the final decision.

"I am aware," he said, "if our plan is approved and carried out America may enter the war, but I am confident that the military assistance she may give our enemies will amount to nothing. On the other hand, we of the navy are unanimously of the opinion that U-boat warfare, if pushed to its logical conclusion, will relieve the food situation in six weeks and give us complete victory over our enemies in four months—at latest." In response to an inquiry from a member of the Committee, von Capelle said: "We should not worry about American reinforcements to the Allied armies. We can assure you that not a single ship with troops will reach this side of the Atlantic. To stop them we have the U-boats; that, indeed, is why we have the U-boats."

Berlin—undated.

. . . In the War Office records which the Majority Socialists open to me apparently without reserves of any kind, everything that is damaging to the "Imperial clique and the stupid High Command," to use the language of the men of Weimar, is emphasized and spotlighted. In nearly all of them Ludendorff, who with prudence and wisdom fled to Sweden,[10] is made the scapegoat. But with due allowance for the animus behind these revelations, the conclusion is inescapable: the imperial armies on the Western Front yielded because they were stopped and then defeated in battle, and that the "dagger strokes in the back" wielded by the starving civilian population of which we hear so much today were the inevitable consequence rather than the cause of the military collapse.

One of these records of defeat and failure appeals to me as having vital, lasting value, and on this account I shall give it at length.

It should be recalled how early in 1918 the Germans were cheered by an announcement of the High Command that the Ukraine, the "granary of Europe," had been overrun, was in complete control of the invaders, and that the good people of the Vaterland, long on short rations, would soon be able "to eat their fill." It was even suggested by a few sentimentalists in Bonn that once the iniquitous British blockade had been broken there would be quite a little food available for the starving people of Belgium and northern France. . . .

But suddenly a rude awakening. The "Bread Peace" proved to be

[10]Many of the Weimar people say Ludendorff took to his heels because he feared that Foch and Haig and Pershing reserved for him the fate that Old Blücher promised Napoleon after Waterloo. "If I get my hands on him I will hang him—in the service of humanity," said the Prussian field marshal.

another illusion—an invention of the hard-pressed propaganda agencies. The countless army trains returning from Kiev (August 1918) were laden, not with breadstuffs, but with wounded and invalided soldiers, and those who had eyes could see that the plan of "economic collaboration" with the Ukrainians, preached so cynically at Brest-Litovsk, was a complete failure. At this moment of crisis Karl Helfferich the Vice-Chancellor was dispatched to Kiev (August 1918) posthaste to ascertain why the promised "Bread Peace" had proved to be such a tantalizing mirage and also why the German agents who were bringing the blessings of Kultur to the benighted inhabitants of the fertile steppes were being assassinated. And indeed Field Marshal Eichhorn, the army chief, and Count Mirbach, the diplomatic agent, had both been shot down in the midst of their guards by men the Germans called "terrorists," although the simple peasants of the devastated land hailed them, and worshiped them, as patriots who would not stand idly by while the bread was taken from the mouths of their starving children.

Herr Helfferich did not stay long in the Ukraine, probably not more than two weeks. He returned almost immediately to Berlin because, for once in perfect agreement, the High Command and the Rada government, imposed and maintained by German bayonets, told him that his life was in danger and that they could not guarantee his safety. They both admitted that the peasants were united in opposing the "economic collaboration," as they saw it in practice. Here are a few excerpts from the doleful report which Helfferich made to the Reichstag Committee on the Conduct of the War immediately on his return to the safety and gloom of Berlin.

"Our armies of nearly half a million men," he said, "have not liquidated the war on the Eastern Front as was hoped, and indeed announced, and the actual situation gives no promise of liquidating it in either a military or an economic sense in the months to come. We meet, it is true, with no important mass resistance either from the peasants or from the Bolsheviki, but our losses in the Kleinkrieg (guerrilla warfare) are very heavy and the audacity of these peasant marauders and other irregulars increases with every day. The Skoropadski government which we sustain with our bayonets would collapse immediately if we withdraw, but even while we sustain it with our bayonets, with great losses in men and matériel, none of the expected 'economic potentialities' of this land, so often reported as fabulously rich, are realized. The government which we sustain has not fulfilled any of its promises and clearly the hoped-for 'Bread Peace' is an illusion. Our army is not living off the country, which was the very least we were given to expect, but is daily drawing on the meager resources of the Fatherland for its rations. True, the Ukrainian authorities we have installed are ineffective and supine, but when the army detachments have taken over the collection of grain we have had no better results. The peasants refuse to sow the rich black earth plains for the next year, and what is left over from the last harvest they hide underground and keep for their own consumption. The hetman we selected to lead his people in the paths of peace and production is profuse in his protestations of good will but he produces no food. Unfortunately, too, the oil harvest is equally negligible. By the aid of British and American technicians, the wells in the Caucasus were put out of business before we arrived, and it will be months before we can hope to see them flowing again. There is, it is true, a little oil stored and still available but the Turks, our Allies, who are living on our subsidies, have the shameless audacity to challenge our right to this supply."

In conclusion the Vice-Chancellor urged the immediate and complete withdrawal of the armies from the Ukraine. He insisted that they be sent to the Western Front, where Ludendorff, at last realizing his critical situation, was clamoring for reserves and replacements. They were sent, but arrived too late, and they came, as the High Command reports, "with a greatly deteriorated morale—as a result of their Russian experiences."

As one good turn deserves another, I gave the Weimar people some excerpts from President Wilson's speech in April 1918, which reveals the contempt felt throughout the civilized world for the *Herrenvolk* of Berlin now controlled by submarine pirates and land robbers, as demonstrated in the Ukraine. It reads:

"I am ready to discuss a just and honest peace at any time that it is sincerely purposed. But the answer, when I proposed such a peace, came from the German commanders in Russia, and I cannot mistake the meaning of the answer. I accept the challenge; Germany has once more said that force and force alone shall decide whether Justice and Peace shall reign in the affairs of men. There is, therefore, but one response possible from us: Force, force to the utmost, force without stint or limit, the righteous and triumphant force which shall make Right the law of the world and cast every selfish dominion down in the dust. . . ."

After reading and rereading this announcement, of which, apparently, so close had been the censorship in war days, they had never heard, the Weimar people agreed with me that far from becoming its granary, the Ukraine had proved to be the graveyard of the German Empire.

"That foray into Russia was our undoing," was the conclusion that most of the members of the National Assembly now arrived at.[11]

A short and saddening meeting this afternoon in the back room of Hiller's restaurant with Mathias Erzberger, the plenipotentiary who received the Armistice terms from Foch at Rethondes ten months ago, and after tumultuous debates forced the acceptance of the Versailles Treaty upon the bewildered members of the National Assembly in Weimar last June.

He has played a notable part in German politics under the Empire, and he most certainly is a striking contrast to old Windthorst whom he succeeded as the leader of the Center or Catholic party in the Reichstag. Windthorst, whom I met several times at the Bierabenden held in the olden days in the Chancellor's residence, was a small, placid little man, apparently fashioned out of cotton wool and much given to prolonged and eloquent silences, while Erzberger's speech rushes along like an Alpine torrent, sweeping everything away with it, including reason and comprehension.

The poor man has a hunted look, and well he might, as in the last three months he has but narrowly escaped three attempts to assassinate him. Among his friends, as well as with his more numerous enemies, it seems to be agreed that his days are numbered.[12] In the press he is generally spoken of as *Der Verderber des Reiches* ("The Destroyer of the Realm"), and quite respectable people, or those who pass for such, expectorate when his name is mentioned. In my judgment, this treatment is most unjust, as in accepting the Armistice he saved what was left of the disintegrating German Army and gave the present shaky government the chance, not a very brilliant one, I admit, it has to survive. He had little to say, but he did suggest that while America had won the war it had not shaped the peace in strict accordance with the Fourteen Points. I countered with pointing to the fact that at least three great powers had contributed to the victory and

[11]Strange perversity of the German character. Hitler made the same mistake in 1940 when he, too, invaded the Ukraine. This false step will prove a decisive factor in the complete collapse of his armies, now in plain view.

[12]A few months later, retired from the government, Erzberger was murdered. His assassins received but a nominal sentence and shortly afterwards they were liberated.

that it was natural they thought they should be consulted in drawing up the peace. He agreed, and then concluded our talk with the words which have become a slogan here: "The future of the German people hangs upon Wilson and the decision that must soon be made in Washington."

September 27th.

Browsing in the Zimmerstrasse bookshop this afternoon, a familiar haunt in other days, I came across a sheaf of propaganda broadsides that were put out by Finance Minister Helfferich early in 1918 to push the Seventh War Loan, which apparently was not going like hot cakes and needed pushing. The many advantages of these bonds were set forth in glowing language, but there was one feature as to the collateral behind these scraps of yellow wilted paper which amused me. It read: "OUR ENEMIES WILL PAY." Now that the uncomfortable boot is on the other foot, the loser in the conflict is indignant that payment should even be mentioned.

As I was about to barter for this and other sheafs of wartime literature, Theodor Wolff, long famous as the editor of the *Berliner Tageblatt*, came in. He recognized me as an American correspondent he had known before the war, but he was evidently unaware of my present mission and I did not enlighten him. The Weimar people or the local Soviet have confiscated the evening edition of his paper and the status of the morning *Ausgabe* is somewhat uncertain, so the great editor proposes to take a vacation. His thoughts had turned to Italy, and he wanted a copy of young Goethe's *Reise-Bilder* of that fair land.

"In these days it is not in great demand," explained the clerk, but he scurried around in the hope of securing a copy of the rather outmoded classic.

"If they will let me—and of course I am not at all sure that they will—I plan to descend the Brenner, see once again that *gelobtes* land, breathe in the fragrance of the orange and the lemon blossoms, if they still bloom, and above all I hope to get rid of this war cough, which is wearing me down," said the once greatly feared and still-influential editor.

As to the future of the Vaterland, Herr Wolff was oppressed by gloomy forebodings. "The new men who have to face the problems of today are without political experience, and the task that awaits them would tax the most expert. Yes! the Social Democrats will miss

Bebel and Auer and Singer, who are gone. I did not approve of their politics but they at least knew what they wanted."

Turning then abruptly from the domestic scene, Wolff gave me a message which he evidently hoped would in some way reach Paris, or even America. "At the Conference the victors could have chopped Germany into fragments and remnants. That would have been a solution, although a bad one. Or the Allies, under the guidance of America, could have bound the Germans to them by a treaty of friendship, which might have resulted in peace and security for all. Unfortunately the Conference pursued neither of these courses."

Herr Wolff likes Count Brockdorff-Rantzau, although he is ready to admit that his selection for the post of plenipotentiary at Versailles was a mistake. "Bernstorff wanted the job, but Erzberger greatly admired Brockdorff and so he was chosen. What, in addition to this personal liking, that counted greatly in his favor, was the fact that during the war, when so many of our diplomats fell down, Brockdorff did a good job in Denmark where he was Minister. More than any other of our men he was successful in circumventing the British blockade. More than any other man, I think, he helped to keep our war machine going—and greased."

When I mentioned that the Count's attitude on the historic day at Versailles had been subjected to severe criticism, he nodded. "I have no knowledge of the facts," he admitted, "and perhaps I should say nothing. But for the little it is worth, this is what I think. For years he has been in delicate health, and particularly under the strain of his mission in Copenhagen he, always addicted to the bottle, has been drinking enormous quantities of cognac. He admitted to me once that without these deep potions he simply could not keep going. But this, I think, is the real explanation of his tantrum that led to the fiasco of his mission, and fiasco it was, I admit. You see, Brockdorff is an imaginative, high-strung fellow, and he had persuaded himself that at the Conference he would have the opportunity to play, in reverse, the role of Talleyrand at the Vienna Congress. He 'conceded' that he was abler than any of the men with whom he would have to cross swords, that he knew more than any other delegate the deep cross-currents that would clash. It was an opportunity to save Germany from the wolves and also to place Brockdorff on the pinnacle to which he had long aspired. Then when he arrived they placed him behind a stockade! I readily admit that this precaution probably saved his life, but it also prevented him, at least so he thinks, from playing the Talleyrand role, from acting the great part of which he had dreamed so often that to him, at least, it had become a reality. When this dream dissolved—well, I admit he acted very foolishly. But if you knew Brockdorff you would see how natural it was. Having failed in the west, his eyes are now turning to the east. In Russia he hopes to find our salvation. In a few weeks, unless I'm greatly mistaken, he will be sent to Russia."[13]

Herr Wolff did not think much of the men that the Colonel has in mind for German leadership (though of course I did not reveal his hopes). He said Rathenau was an "hysteric, a weathercock." When defeat and collapse in the west were undeniable he had, doubtless with his tongue in his cheek, suggested a *"levée en masse* of the civilian population"—and then he went to Holland.

"Stresemann," he thought, "was a much abler man, but he doubted the Allies would be inclined to trust him. In the early years of the war he had been an ardent disciple of von Tirpitz and an Annexationist—on a large scale. When poor Bethmann-Hollweg suggested in 1917 that we had better let Alsace and Belgium go, because we could not hold them, Stresemann made a savage attack on the Chancellor in an executive session of the Conduct of the War Committee of the Reichstag. No, the new men are our best bet. They at least bring fresh minds to the problems, but even so we are gambling with fate."

A pathetic incident awaited me on my return to the hotel. Two stalwart Russian girls were helping into the elevator a tottering old lady swathed in black. Wearing dark glasses, she hardly saw at all and evidently was bewildered and in great distress. One of the girls said to her: "But, Countess, the Artz says if you but submit to the operation he will rid you of those horrid cataracts and you will see again just as in the old days."

"But I don't want to see again," protested the old lady. "The world is so ugly, so ugly."

After depositing them and carrying me higher to my floor, Karl, the elevator attendant, explained: "That is the Countess Kleinmichel, once a great lady at the court of the Tsars. She but barely escaped the Bolsheviki and she arrived here without money and without her jewels. A syndicate of Russian dressmakers who also escaped have taken charge of her and are keeping her afloat. They secured for her, in remembrance of the days when she was the best-dressed woman in all the Russias, a little cottage down at Baden-Baden, and every now and

[13]He was; and remained as Ambassador in Moscow until his death years later.

then they bring her up to Berlin to see if her sight cannot be restored."

Countess Kleinmichel! That indeed was a name to conjure with at the Tsarist court before the ten days dawned "that shook the world." I had never met her, but often in those distant days I had seen her driving down to the island or along the Neva behind her famous Orloff trotters. Hers had been the role of Princess Pauline in Vienna; to be seen in her salon was a title of nobility; to sit at her dinner table, well, that simply opened all doors. As a matter of fact, at least so I have been told by those who were in St. Petersburg at the time, the smashing of her banqueting hall was the first overt act of the Revolution. The Countess had ignored the rumblings, paid no attention to the "common" people, until this historic night when they invaded her palace, stole the silver and the jewels, tore from the court ladies their Parisian gowns. Lucky were those who, like the amazed hostess, were able to make their escape to the refuge of a friendly legation. Poor lady! I can well understand she has no desire to see the world that is so different from that in which she was the queen.

B.[14] came in this morning with a bulky manuscript written, not typed, by Herr von Jagow, who presided over the Imperial Foreign Office for the first two years of the war—until he was eased out by the military men. It is a defense of his stewardship, and even the hasty glance I was able to give it reveals its value as source document. It is written in Latin letters and not the "Gothic" characters which Bismarck loved and urged his countrymen to retain.

I told B. once again I was not in Berlin for a post-mortem, as many seemed to think, but to assess the possibilities of the future. I could only suggest that I be authorized to send it on to the Congressional Library, where it would be available to future historians, but this was not agreed to, so I kept the manuscript for twenty-four hours and then returned it to the ex-diplomat, who, now entirely out of the running, is vegetating in a little cottage near Potsdam.

Even during the hasty reading, at least of most of it, I found the document of absorbing interest, although not by any means convincing. Jagow insists that in permitting the existence, and indeed in encouraging the activities, of the Narodna Obrana in its anti-Austrian propaganda, the Belgrade Government incurred moral responsibility for the murder of the Archduke. Then he asserts, "It is not true that we drifted into the tense situation lightheartedly. We knew full well

[14]Count Bernstorff.

that the position we took up brought us near, very near, to war, but for obvious reasons we had no choice but to stand by our Ally. For some years now the South Slavs, spurred on by Russia, had threatened the integrity of the Danubian Monarchy and also the position and security of the German people in Mittel-Europa. We could not advise the Austrians, our partners in an endangered Deutschtum, to pursue an unworthy course even if it promised a postponement of hostilities—and that is all anyone, even the most optimistic, hoped, as the ultimate conflict was clearly inevitable.

"We had to assist Vienna to secure satisfaction for the dastardly murders, but after all the men at the Ballplatz were the representatives of a great power—we could not treat them as children in leading strings. Had the Austrian demands for satisfaction, which the Entente called an ultimatum, been shown to us we would most certainly have asked that it be 'toned down.' Indeed our archives will reveal that as soon as we were permitted to have an inkling of what the note contained, I was instructed by the Chancellor to ask that it be softened, but the reply came that it was too late, that the fatal message had gone forward to Belgrade and had in all probability been delivered. In any event, it was beyond recall. But admitting the stiffness of the note and deploring it, as the Imperial German Government did at the time, is far from conceding that we agreed with Sazonov in saying it aimed at reducing the Serbs to a state of vassalage. So, unhappily, it was on these irreconcilable interpretations of the Austrian demand that the issue was joined. Then Russia mobilized and war was inevitable.

"We, and I personally, with especial vehemence, are reproached for not having given more wholehearted support to Grey's plea for a conference. I agree that his sincerity cannot be questioned and that he wanted to avoid war, or at least to localize it, to keep Britain out; but he did not appreciate our position. We were bound to the Danubian Monarchy not only by a solemn treaty but by the ties of the common danger with which we were confronted. To protect Austria from the disruptive schemes of the South Slavs, to maintain her as a strong and independent power, was a *Lebensfrage* for us; it was truly a matter of life and death for the German Empire and the German people as well. Looking back, I think we went to great lengths in our endeavor to escape war. Had we gone any farther we would have lost our self-respect and endangered the future of the German race. I say again, Grey was sincere with his conference idea, but I assert he went about it the wrong way. As always, I fear he demonstrated his complete ignorance of Continental conditions. Practically he proposed that Austria should submit her case to a jury, the members of which through their organs of public opinion, the press, and the pulpits, had already voted disapproval of her course. It would have looked as though Austria, the culprit, was brought before a jury of her peers merely to receive condign punishment. To that humiliation we could not expose our Ally; the form of her demand we disapproved of, but its purpose was a just one and we could do no other than stand by it and by her."

More briefly Jagow speaks of the march through Belgium. "In the Entente countries, and in America, this move is regarded as a blunder, one of those that are more disastrous than crimes, but no one there views the question from our standpoint or realizes the difficult choice with which we were confronted. With our General Staff for twenty years it had been axiomatic that when the inevitable renewal of war between France and Germany came, our armies would have to advance through Belgium. Many voices were raised in civilian circles against this plan because of the nearly century-old neutrality treaty to which we were a party, protecting Belgium from invasion by any and all of her neighbors. Now from 1904 on our General Staff was quite satisfied that military conventions had been arranged by Belgium with England and France authorizing England to send an expeditionary force to the Low Countries upon the outbreak of the expected war. In this case—and the fears of our soldiers, as it now appears, rested on solid foundations—a direct frontal attack, say by the way of the Vosges or by Verdun, would have left us with an exposed flank, a most precarious position to be placed in, so the view of the soldiers prevailed.

"That was the situation—our predicament, if you like—that the Chancellor hinted at when on August 4, 1914, he defended the march through Belgium with the words 'Not kennt kein Gebot,' or 'Necessity knows no law.' It is also a fact that the Imperial Government gave to King Albert every assurance that if his government and people did not resist the passage of our troops any possible damage done or supplies requisitioned would be paid for, and compensation given even for the interruption of commerce and civilian activities, and that when the military emergency was over, the civilian authorities would be reinstated and the independence of Belgium would be maintained against all comers by Germany. Unfortunately for them, and I admit for us, the Belgians would not accept these terms. They preferred to join up with France and England, and so the duel between the two powers who had so much to fight about became a world war."

Still more briefly Jagow dismisses the story of the War Council in Potsdam on July 5th, at which the Kaiser presided and, as frequently reported, yielded to the arguments advanced by Hindenburg to the general effect that the crisis was a heaven-sent opportunity to settle for all time political and military supremacy in western Europe.

"No such council was held on that date or any approximate date. All those stories are *Geschichten nicht Geschichte* (gossip—not history). Hindenburg, who is charged by his fiery eloquence with having turned the scale in favor of war, was not even in Berlin at the time. He was living the placid life of a retired officer in his cottage in Hanover and was not called back to active service until several weeks later, when he was sent to East Prussia where the Russian invaders were meeting with better success than the Army Command had anticipated."

Berlin, October 1st.

I have not written a line or raised a finger, and yet it has been arranged that I am to see Herr Ebert, the former harness maker, now the chief magistrate of the new German Republic-Reich on Tuesday next. What a change in procedure and protocol since the imperial days of William der Siegreicher and Frederick the Peace-loving, and of Bismarck, the Man of Blood and Iron! It will be difficult to display no surprise at the way all doors fly open, in the Berlin I once knew so well, when they were all close shut, especially to newsmen. How well I remember my first approach to the great men here, the treasured letter from the Ambassador in Washington to a Vortragender Rath at the Foreign Office, and the surly greeting of the sentry as I sought to present it. "Zehn Schritte vom Lieb [Ten steps from my body]" were the words with which he greeted me. Warm—yes—but certainly not cordial. I had come up the wrong stairway, the one reserved for mighty men in uniform.

What a contrast this confrontation will be with the hours I spent in Friedricsruh with the Old Pilot, who had so recently been tossed off the bridge into the stormy waters by the young Sailor-Emperor, who maintained that the future of his Germany was on this uneasy element which Britannia had ruled for so many years. How Bismarck growled and grouched over the decay of the Hohenzollern brood which he ascribed to the unfortunate marriage with "Vicky," the English princess.

B. urges me, if I must wear a collar when I call on Herr Ebert, to leave it unbuttoned, the fashion which the new chief magistrate follows, but he insists that Ebert is an honorable man, and all seem to agree that a better choice for this unenviable post could not have been made.

Unfortunately I left Berlin before the day of this meeting, which would have proved interesting, I am sure.

. . . In the second of the October (1919) meetings of the Committee investigating the conduct of the war, an effort was made by several of the members to induce the former Chancellor, while on the stand, to admit that his peace moves were hampered and in the end nullified by the inflammatory propaganda and false statements that were issued by the press bureaus of the army and the navy, and they placed in evidence a statement for which they made a certain Herr David responsible. He had been a Minister of State in the Bethmann-Hollweg administration and he was reported as saying:

"While the political branch of the government was urging upon Wilson the advisability of making a peace move, which might well have proved the salvation of our country, a poisonous hatred of Wilson and the people of America was being instilled into the hearts of our folk by the publicity machinery of the High Army Command."

The former Chancellor did not wish to go into this question. He protested that he had been far too busy with more important matters at the time. The chairman then produced a telegram which he said the then Chancellor, and the present witness, had sent to von Falkenhayn, who had now succeeded von Moltke in the command of the German armies. After but a moment's hesitation, Bethmann-Hollweg admitted: "Yes, I sent that telegram under date of February 5th (1916). I complained to the army commander that the censorship, largely under his control, was giving complete license to such papers as the Cologne *Volkszeitung* and the *Kreuzzeitung* to continue their campaign in favor of a renewal of U-boat warfare in its most rigorous form despite the engagements we had given to the American Government. As you see, I told the general that these publications were hampering my government and interfering with a satisfactory settlement of the *Lusitania* controversy which we sought. I did all I could to stop this press campaign, with some temporary success, but after a very few weeks it was resumed. Yes, I cannot deny the statement of Herr David, but I will say it was difficult to place responsibilities. There was much confusion in the situation and at times sharp conflict between the civilian, the naval, and the military authorities in matters of press control and censorship."

At this point in his examination—his second appearance on the stand—Bethmann-Hollweg was shown a memorandum dated January 2, 1917, drawn up and signed by the steering committee of the Catholic Center party, the most numerous and powerful group in the Reichstag at the time. He was asked if he remembered having received it. He said he did.

"What did you think of it?" inquired the chairman.

"I thought it very important," was the answer.

This document, perhaps the most revealing of the series, reads: "As to the question whether the new U-boat warfare is necessary, the decision should rest with Field Marshal von Hindenburg. It is our desire that the Imperial Chancellor conform his course to the wishes of the field marshal. If he does he will have the unanimous support of our party."

The comment on this made by the national assemblyman who guided my researches was: "That ended Bethmann's weak and ineffective resistance to the war lords. Without the support of the Center he could not have survived for a day. Of course he could have resigned from the government, but probably because he saw he could not change its course by an inch he decided to swim with the flowing tide."[15]

Out of these interminable hearings, many of which I attended and at all of which I was represented, I have drawn one excellent suggestion; at least I think so. On the eve of my departure from Berlin, I put to Count Bernstorff the following question:

"What, in your judgment, would have happened in January 1917 if, instead of declaring for the indiscriminate use of the submarine weapon, Berlin had said to Washington: 'We would welcome the mediation of America. We believe that if negotiations are initiated a reasonable peace would result'? What, in your judgment, would have happened?"

"I believed then, while still in Washington," said Bernstorff, "that

[15]As a later entry in my diary makes plain, I had left Berlin some days before the last two meetings of the Commission "to place war responsibilities" were held. The information here disclosed reached me through one who was present. It would not be fair to disclose his identity.

there was a fifty-fifty chance of success, but with the more complete knowledge of the military, political, and economic situation which I acquired within a few days of my arrival in Berlin, I was and still am confident that the negotiations would have been successful."[16]

So, two years more of devastating war might have been avoided if there had been in existence practical machinery for bringing the enemy states into a conference. Well, while as yet untested, certainly the League of Nations provides that very agency.

[16]It should be stressed more emphatically than appears to be the case in these excerpts from my diary that the testimony which I here reproduce was given before two committees duly authorized to take it. These committees functioned at different times and their members were drawn from very different classes and political groups, which is natural enough in view of the fact that during the interval (1917–19) between the sessions the war had been lost, the German revolution had taken place, and the Empire had been transformed into the Republic-Reich. But it is clear that the members of these committees represented the sentiments of the German people at the time they were called upon to function. Their very different attitudes and purpose illustrate once again how rapidly the views of people change in times of stress and how quickly these changes find expression through the ballot, even in the hands of amateurs, as was most certainly the case in Germany at the time.

The first committee "to advise on the conduct of the war" was composed of members of the Imperial Reichstag and the sessions were held in the old Reichstag building during the last days of December (1916) and the first days of January (1917). Out of these deliberations came the approval of the plan, so long urged by the navy, and by nearly all the army leaders, for unrestricted U-boat warfare, which brought us into the struggle and ended in the fall of the imperial regime. The second committee, recruited from members of the National Assembly, that sought to implement the policies of the new Weimar government, was appointed to place the responsibility for the defeat and collapse of Germany where it belonged. It got down to work late in September (1919), also in the Reichstag building. Its purpose was to establish the responsibilities for the war and, more pointedly, for the defeats and the disasters that resulted from it. I think its members tried to be fair to the old regime—but in this I do not think they were always successful. More often than not these selectmen of the National Assembly welcomed with great favor any evidence that was damaging to the regime they had displaced.

All the data as to the hearings in January 1917 that were communicated to me were in printed form, but the pages were marked confidential and were evidently furnished exclusively for the information of members of the Reichstag. So far as I know, they were never made public, and I do not believe that this information is now available in Germany. It is more than likely that the original stenographic reports were destroyed in the fire that wrecked the Reichstag building in 1933 and doubtless that was one of the purposes of the highly placed Hitler incendiary. I have reason to believe that full reports of what I describe as the post-mortem hearings of October and November 1919 are still in existence but they are closely held. In frequent visits to Germany of recent years I have not been successful in securing a copy.

PART VII

Blackout in Washington

Paris, Hotel Crillon, October 4th.

Well, here I am again, but not without having been subjected to quite a few trials and tribulations on the journey. And the Colonel has flown! Well, not exactly flown; he was able to make the journey to Brest on his own feet although suffering from another acute attack of the gallstones. He was in much pain himself, and of course greatly distressed at the news of the President's illness; there was ample room for him and his large party on the *Northern Pacific* and for the following week few sailings were scheduled so, making a quick decision, he embarked. He urged me to join him as soon as possible in New York, if I failed to reach Paris in time to sail with him, and with characteristic thoughtfulness he had arranged before leaving that when I arrived at the port of embarkation I should have priority over other "casuals" who might, and indeed most certainly would, be waiting on the dock.

I should now explain in greater detail how this swift change of plan and of base came about. In Berlin on the afternoon of September 27th I read in the *Tageblatt* a laconic cable to the effect that, broken in health and yielding to the insistent demand of his doctors, the President had interrupted his Western tour and was returning to Washington. I confess that the news did not surprise me. All through May I had been convinced that Mr. Wilson was in for a serious illness. Indeed, on the day I left Paris for Germany, the Colonel had shown me a letter from his constant correspondent, Mr. Kohlsaat, the Chicago editor, to the effect that the President was looking wretched, that he evidently needed a long, soaking rest, and that, unfortunately, was precisely what he seemed unable to secure.

An hour after reading the announcement in the paper there came to me a wire from the Colonel, telling me he was sailing shortly and asking me to join him as soon as possible.

While rushing about the hotel lobby in an attempt to get what information I could in regard to the infrequent international trains, I ran across Warwick Greene, who had at one time headed the Public Works Bureau of the Insular Government in Manila. Our last contact had been when, three years ago in the Philippines, we had together climbed the mountains to Haight's Place, several thousand feet higher than Baguio, where the perspiring dweller in the tropics could at times wear a sweater and revel in the sight of hoarfrost glistening on the mountain pines.

Like everyone else, Greene was in the army now and on his way back from Riga, where he had been *en mission* for the Food Administration. He was leaving for Paris on the following day with an empty army car at his disposal. He invited me to join him, and added confidently: "We shall beat the International train by a day—at least." I accepted on the spot, and bright and early the next morning we sallied out of the now grass-grown and garbage-littered streets of Berlin. By the time we reached Weimar it was plain, even to me, that our car was not a racer. In what was once the Athens of Germany we stopped for an hour, and while Greene "looked under the hood" I wandered about and visited the shrine where for so many years my old professor Erich Schmidt had presided over the Goethe *Nachlass*, or archives, and I also had a look at the modest rooms where the Committee of the National Assembly was at work on the new Constitution which was to bring happiness to the German people, some participation in their government at least, and peace to the world outside—it was hoped.

Even before we pulled into Erfurt at the end of our first day's run, it was evident that Greene's belief that we would reach Paris before the twice-a-week Berlin express arrived was an iridescent dream. Somewhere and somehow our car had been tampered with: our gasoline had been watered, our inner tubes had been extracted and replaced with others of very inferior *ersatz* quality, and our spark plugs had been swiped. However, Greene was a resourceful mechanic as well as an expert chauffeur, and somehow we kept plugging along. . . .

While exasperating, our leisurely progress gave me an opportunity to see things that would have escaped me on the railway. In the agricultural districts we passed through there was much plowing in progress, and with grim determination the peasants, at least, seemed to be resuming their former tasks. At the entrance to each of the villages we passed through there were arches of pine branches now bedraggled and battered by the autumn storms and upon each and every one of them was inscribed the legend, *"Willkommen zu unseren siegreichen Soldaten* [Welcome to our victorious soldiers]" and often the message, *"Mit Stolz und Liebe erinnern wir uns an unsere Verblichene* [We hold in affectionate remembrance those who died]"—who are not coming back.

But in the manufacturing towns the aspect of affairs was less reassuring. Men, women, and children, all thinly clad, were standing around or wandering aimlessly about, pale and hungry. Few if any of them seemed to be sustained by the thought that now the war was over the future promised better things; all they knew was that they were cold and hungry—and winter was coming on. . . .

As we generally reached our destination after midnight and left at crack of dawn, I cannot say that we spent our nights anywhere, but we were bedded for a few hours at Frankfort and again at Mayence. I suggested to Greene that the spectacle of our limping car would not enhance the fame of the American automobile industry and that in justice to the makers of the car, which had obviously been tampered with, we should haul down the flag which we had flown ever since we started out so hopefully from Berlin—to put the iron horse to shame. Greene thought well of the suggestion, but decided he could not comply with it. It seems that our transit visa from the German *Kommandantur* demanded that we fly the flag, and so we continued to do so. It is only fair to say that the showing of these colors which had brought imperial Germany to her knees provoked less hostility than it was natural to expect. It is true not seldom dark and dirty looks followed us as we made our way through the slums of manufacturing towns, but generally, when noticed at all, the appearance of our car and the flag that flew over it attracted nothing more than apathetic amazement. You could not startle people who had lived through the last four years. They appreciated that in these days anything might happen.

There did occur one near-altercation, but I could well understand the motive behind it. We were at a halt, tinkering with the motor, as so often before, in a street on the outskirts of Mayence when an old man, staggering from starvation weakness, or from drink, came toward us. "I gave the Kaiser my two sons!" he shouted. "Hans died at Verdun and Franzl was blown to bits at Ossowice on the East Front, and now I see I gave them for nothing, *vergebens, vergebens*. Why did you *Kerls* not stay where you belonged?"

"Tough luck, old man," I answered, "but quite a lot of fine American boys died too. And you began it."

He looked about him for a brick, but fortunately none was near at hand, and a minute later we were back in our coughing car and crawling out of this danger zone. . . .

I have pleasant memories of the night we spent in Vasa, a little village in the Thuringian forest. The air was cool and bracing and the near-by mountain streams were alive with speckled trout, several of which, with robust appetites, we devoured for supper. Soon half a dozen of the village elders gathered around us and we enjoyed much friendly talk. "Thank God the war was over," and we all agreed on the familiar formula—"What a pity it happened." (*Schade dass es so gekommen ist.*) Soon, however, some debate developed as to the Emperor's flight into Holland. Most of the villagers now gathered at the Stammtisch in the inn were of the opinion he should have died at the head of his troops, but one old man insisted, "No, it was his duty to survive, to live on. He personified the monarchial principle. It was his duty to live to fight another day when the *Käfers* (cockroaches) now in power in Berlin and Weimar would get their deserts."

Naturally Greene and I kept out of this.

The following morning, bright and early, greatly refreshed, we pulled out of the village along a beautiful forest road. However, the night had not been as refreshing to the car as it had been to us, and soon it was again coughing—horribly. Then a flat tire developed and when that was replaced in silence, because all we had to say on that subject had been said before, we peered under the hood. Baffled as usual, for the survey gave no explanation of the weakening of the engine, I turned away and saw a weather-beaten and ragged German soldier coming along the road toward us. He was leaning heavily upon a stick or rather a staff about eight feet high, and certainly he was making but little progress. He reminded me of the many veteran grenadiers Grimm describes in his tales, plodding their weary way on the road back from Moscow in the Napoleonic days. As he drew nearer, I saw that the poor fellow was feeling his way with his staff rather than leaning on it and that his uncertain step was rather that of a blind man than a weary walker, although as it developed he was both. Just as he came up with us and I saw that the poor fellow's face was a raw mass of red flesh, the result of a flame-thrower's blast, and that his eyes were bandaged, Greene suddenly burst out into explanations of what really was the matter with the engine and how it could not possibly be remedied until we arrived at Mayence, where American mechanics and replacements would perhaps be available. The effect of these words in a strange tongue on the lonely traveler was startling. He staggered to the side of the road and fell with convulsive sobs to the ground. This was an unexpected sip of gall and wormwood in his bitter cup. *"Die Englander sind schon in Thuringen* [The English have already reached Thuringia]," he gasped. "I did not think they would have come so far, so soon," he moaned. *"Wie weit sind die Kerls vorgeschritten."*

We gave him a stiff drink, which he swallowed mechanically, and also several packages of cigarettes, which he pocketed without a word. Then, as it began to rain, we bundled him into our car and drove him back to Vasa, where we turned him over to the kind Wirth of the inn, by whom we had been so well received. It was a good deed and a daring one, to put an added burden of four miles upon our weakening motor—but we did it. As usual at sight of a personal disaster or continued suffering, my war "front" crumbled. To me the shambles of an impersonal battlefield was as nothing to the catastrophe that had overtaken this poor devil, and so I went to pieces. How far I went, I only realized many hours later when I discovered that in loading the blind soldier into the car I had left on the roadside bank both my camera and my much more valuable raincoat. But there was no turning back now. Even the ever-optimistic Greene was doubtful that we could reach the Rhine under our own steam. . . .

The mechanic in Mayence did not prove to be the magician we had hoped to find there, but with the engine panting and coughing we pushed on and, about midnight, the broken, improvised bridges and the crater-marked roads revealed the fact that we were drawing near the immortal citadel of Verdun. The streets were still blocked with rubble and many barricades had not been removed. We wandered around within the town for another hour before we found an inn that was in operation, and certainly it was not operating on all cylinders. But even in the darkness I spied a mail rack and a telegram addressed to "General Bonsal, American Army." Without doubt Frazier, whom I had advised as to our probable route, had promoted me in the hope of securing quicker service. When I opened it, I found that the message was dated the very day I started from Berlin. It told me that our colonel was far from well, would sail at the first opportunity, and urged me to hurry, hurry, hurry!

At crack of dawn we pulled out of the ruined city and for an hour or two made good progress. Our hopes had revived when suddenly the old noises were heard, more intense if possible than ever before, and then with a wail of finality the engine stopped, and this time even Greene admitted that he was at the end of his remedies and panaceas. I thanked him warmly for the lift he had given me and, burdened with my bag and the Bosch magneto I was bringing for Frazier, I staggered along the railway track. I had walked on for an hour when I came to a station and looking up I read the word which under any circumstances would have been electrifying—"VALMY." In my wanderings I had stumbled upon the field where on that never-to-be-forgotten day, September 20, 1792, modern warfare had been revolutionized.

I confess that for some minutes I forgot my weariness—even the weight of the magneto. In me, as with all others doubtless who have approached it, the name of Valmy awakened memories and invited reflection. It was, perhaps, on that very hilltop that the tourist, Goethe, stood, and watching the raw recruits of the French Revolutionary Army rushing into successful battle, made this memorable entry in his diary:

"From this place and on this day a new era in World History begins, and you who are here can say you were present at its birth."[1]

---

[1]Goethe's prophetic words have been entered upon the imperishable tablets of history, and that may be the reason why his description of his own baptism of fire on this occasion has been ignored. Culling it from his account of the campaign in France, 1792, I hereby rescue his words from oblivion and present the Sage of Weimar in the role of war correspondent:

"I rode along to the left," he writes, "and then I could plainly survey the favorable position of the French. I fell in with good company, officers of my acquaintance belonging to the General Staff, greatly surprised to find me here. I had now arrived in the region where the balls were playing across me; the sound of them is, curiously enough, as if it were composed of the humming of tops, the gurgling of water, and the whistling of birds. They were less dangerous by reason of the wetness of the ground; wherever one fell, it stuck fast, and thus my foolish experimental ride was secured against the danger of the balls rebounding. I was soon able to remark that something unusual was taking place within me. It appeared as if you were in some extremely hot place and, at the same time, quite penetrated by the heat of it, so that you feel yourself, as it were, quite one with the element in which you are. It is remarkable, however, that the horrible, uneasy feeling arising from it is produced in us solely through the ears; for the cannon thunder, the howling and the crashing of the balls through the air, is the real cause of these sensations. After I had ridden back and was in perfect security, I remarked with surprise that the glow was completely extinguished and not the slightest feverish agitation was left behind. On the whole, this condition is one of the least desirable; as indeed among my dear and noble comrades I found scarcely one who expressed a really passionate desire to try it."

The station was alive with historic memories, but apparently quite dead as to opportunities of transportation. For the time being there was not even a stationmaster, but I did not complain, for my motor mishap had landed me at the scene of the battle where modern warfare began, at least according to Goethe, who chanced to be there and who described what he saw as a poet rather than as a military expert. But his words have prevailed, as the words of poets generally do, and so it would be unwise to dissent from his view that here on this hallowed spot the "Nation in arms," the young conscripts of the French Revolution, prevailed over the long-trained, the veteran Brunswickers. The truth is, of course, that in the army of valiant and enthusiastic citizens a number, quite a large number, of veterans trained under the monarchy had been enrolled and that it was very fortunate for the French Revolution that they were on hand. The whole truth is, however, that here as well as at Yorktown and later still at New Orleans the *élan* of the volunteer, who was also a sharpshooter, prevailed and a great change took place in what had been for centuries formal battle tactics.

Little Gneisenau, the father of the Prussian Army, an ensign in the Anspach regiment that had been hired out to the English and probably surrendered with Cornwallis at Yorktown, drew a profitable lesson from his humiliation. He appreciated the Virginia militia with their sure aim and supple movements at their true value, and when he returned to Prussia he put into practice the lessons he had learned. He limbered up the movements of Frederick's Grenadiers, with the result that they won the War of Liberation and brought down to earth the Napoleonic eagles.

Having apparently no trains to announce, the *chef de gare*, when he appeared at last, was most desirous of showing the soldier from America over the battlefield; particularly he wanted to show me the historic ridge where years later Kellerman, the hero of many greater battles in foreign lands, who had been honored with a Napoleonic dukedom and a marshal's baton, in his last testament ordered that his ashes be scattered to the winds that had been kind to his epochal victory here. But I was not to be decoyed away from the rusty steel rails over which so many hundred thousand gallant Frenchmen had rolled to their last rendezvous with destiny at Douaumont. An unannounced train might come sneaking by, I feared, and so I stuck to the battered platform and listened to the *chef de gare*, who, I concluded, was stronger on history than on timetables. And he certainly knew his Lamartine and loved to quote the poet-historian.

"As today," he said, "on September 20, 1792, an autumn mist hung over the ridge." Then he described how the battle was lost and how it was won. "It was the very day on which our first republic was born in faraway Paris," he explained, "and, Monsieur, believe me, right in the cradle it was within a hairbreadth of destruction." The *chef* was so eloquent that I soon fell in with his mood and I, too, could see the raw Carmagnoles rushing ahead, shouting *"Vive la Nation,"* and singing the songs of freedom.

"The King of Prussia himself reproached his men for yielding before the onrush of our *sans-culottes*—but in vain." Then, departing from the lyrical and speaking in the professional tones of a soldier who had been an *auxiliaire* in the Great War, he added: "But what a small expenditure of personnel there was! When they fled, the Germans only left six hundred dead on the field." Somewhat arrogantly he added: "In our war such a petty casualty list would not have been recorded in the communiqués."

Yes, as I was soon to realize more fully than ever before, ours had been a bloody war, and the battered bodies and the crippled lives had not all been buried underground, out of sight forever.

. . . My hours in Valmy, and those that immediately followed, will mark a period in my own war memories. The train I ultimately caught was crowded, jammed, with the wreckage of war; it had been chartered, apparently, to carry the crippled and the crushed survivors of battle to Verdun, where they were to celebrate the anniversary of some great feat of arms which was, I think, the recapture of Douaumont, and now it was carrying them back to darkened homes. This train, crowded with those who survived, was a more horrible sight than any of the many ghastly battlefields I have witnessed in so many lands. It was clear to me that those who had died in a moment of exaltation and of inspiration were the lucky ones; to many of these death had been merciful, often it had come instantaneously, but the overcrowded train in which I now stood up for hours was filled with men and women who were dying slowly, the long-drawn-out death of conscious agony. All about me were groups of *grand blessés,* many with grotesquely distorted faces which even their loved ones could not look upon save with a feeling of repulsion that must have been difficult to conceal. Very much alone were the groups of war widows left to struggle for existence in a pitiless world, with perhaps a child, wearing as its only heritage the Médaille Militaire as substitute for the guiding hand of a father. As I traveled with this cavalcade of misery and of suffering, I realized more fully than ever before the terrible price our generation has paid for its victory. Is it not possible that we have learned our lesson? Can we not see to it that such a crime shall never happen again? Is not the panorama of calamity and distress by which we are surrounded a sufficiently crushing indictment of the military epoch out of which no one has emerged victorious? Gone are the gay little wars and the picturesque and cheerful campaigns of but a few short years ago. They gave impetuous youth a field for service and opened avenues to high distinction. Casualties, of course, there were, but relatively few, and more often than not they were concealed by the smoking clouds of black powder. And the poets sang the songs of personal heroism. But the smokeless-powder campaigns, with the engines of greater destruction that are brought into action today, lead to mass slaughter, and the shambles of undistinguished mass graves are revealed in all their stark grimness. Yes, as the old ballad had it years ago, although the world would not listen: "*Malbrouck est mort, et enterré* [Malbrouck is dead and buried]." "*Il ne reviendra pas* [He will not return]." And with him has gone what there was of chivalry on the battlefield.

How I wish all who will be called upon to shape world policies in the next decade could have been exposed to this heart-rending spectacle. Out of such an experience might come something more substantial than our halting Covenant for peace and non-aggression, with reservations, signed by men well beyond the fighting age; perhaps might be reached even a universal decision not merely to disarm but to beat our swords into plowshares and to join in the forgotten prayer, "Peace! peace unto Jerusalem. They shall prosper who love Thee."

. . . From the moment I had abandoned the crippled car the Bosch magneto had proved a heavy burden. As the hours lengthened, it seemed to weigh a ton and I thought seriously of abandoning it, but I could not let down my loyal comrade of the Conference, and then was it not a harbinger of the peace and prosperity that might now come to the war-racked, devastated world? In sending me the commission Frazier had written: "There is no magneto in the world like that of Bosch and, the war being over, now again I must have one for my car." Perhaps it was inventions such as this that would put the

Germans on their feet again, and so I staggered on under my burden. . . .

The train hobbled into Paris about midnight. After standing in the crowded corridor with my heavy pack for eight hours, I found I could hardly walk. I leaned against an iron pillar and watched and watched and waited. Slowly the silent mob of the lame, the halt and the blind, the crape-draped widows, and the pale-faced, sad-eyed orphans of some of the four hundred thousand gallant soldiers who died defending the great fortress against the onrush of the invading Germans, dissolved. For me the pomp and pageantry of war had vanished for a long time, perhaps forever, and what remained was misery and tears, loneliness and squalor. It was hours before the last of the war widows, carrying children who would never see their fathers, disappeared into the darkness of the city where victory perched. But I shall see them always—always.[2]

Paris, October 5th.

Authority to ratify the Treaty of Versailles was given the President of the Republic by the Chamber yesterday, by a vote of 372 to 53. It was not the *victoire éclatante* which Clemenceau hoped for but hardly expected. The fact that 73 deputies abstained from voting was a significant feature of the balloting. I hope we shall do as well in Washington.

Barrès made quite a few "critical observations" (as he called them) on behalf of his group. He said the Treaty was accepted as a "continuing creation—that the Chamber must be allowed to work hand in hand with the government in the practical execution of the Peace arrangements. Frequent reports to the Chamber must be made by the various commissions on reparations and control, and with this understanding we accept the Treaty."

Many deputies like Jacques Piou voted "yes" "*mais avec quelques réserves.*" Delahaye spoke against, and M. Maginot, the former Minister of War, said, speaking for himself and his colleagues of the liberated regions, he voted to reject the Treaty because it did not give *les certitudes* to which the French people were entitled. "It is not

[2] I gave my friend, Edouard Conte, an account of this cavalcade of misery with which I had traveled from the glorious battlefield of Verdun, and several days later he supplied me with the official figures, the catastrophic cost of defense and victory. They reveal that there were one million and fifty thousand war widows in France and they were charged with the support of twelve hundred thousand war orphans. "The lists of the crippled, the *grands blessés,* have not been completed, but," he added, "they are countless—like the sands on the seashore."

acceptable to the people of the frontier provinces," he shouted, "because by it their security is not fully safeguarded." The Socialists split; some approved "because it wipes out 1870." Another group rejected it in the words of Ernest Lafont, "because it does not bring peace."

Barthou, certainly no friend of Clemenceau, at considerable length expressed his regret that the annexation of the Rhine provinces had not been secured, but he added: "Can anyone deny the imposing force of the guarantees which we receive? Things are not as they were in 1914. Great Britain and the United States have recognized that the security of France is indispensable to the peace of the world; in fact, they now concede that a threat from Germany is not merely a danger to France but a menace to the Allies, to Europe, to the world."

Franklin-Bouillon denounced the League of Nations as deplorably weak, "and, if the United States does not come in, it would prove to be merely another scrap of paper." He added, "Of course the Rhine Agreement promising aid from Britain and from the United States in case of another German invasion is in some measure reassuring, but will the United States ratify the pledge of the President? And if ratification is secured, the guarantee seems to me very limited. To illustrate my doubts: suppose Germany invades Poland and France goes to her aid, as she is pledged to do, what would the Allies do? In my judgment, the guarantee would not be operative and they would be at liberty to stand aside, to consult their own exclusive interests, *quoi?*"

This debate really began on August 26th and its course at first was rather languid. Tardieu glossed over what he admits are the shortcomings of the document, but dwelt with satisfaction on what he calls "the inestimable advantages of the Treaty and the pledge of immediate assistance from Great Britain and America in case of aggression."

Certainly it cannot be said that the news of the ratification in the Chamber (it is understood there will be no opposition in the Senate) has been received with rapture. There is little comment, and when interrogated, people generally say: *"C'est une paix de vigilance—mais c'est la Paix"* or "It is a peace pact that will require watching—but after all it is peace." After four long years of war that is something; in fact a great deal.

In the *Figaro* of October 4th, Alfred Capus of the French Academy hails the parliamentary victory of Clemenceau with these words: "This vote, particularly significant because of the way the Socialists fell apart, will certainly contribute to calm the nerves of our people, and above all to exorcise the phantoms by which so many have been obsessed for months. Now the petty discussions are finished. The most *éclatante victoire de notre pays* has received popular approval. It will bring safety and prosperity if from this day we turn over a new leaf and cease to tear ourselves to pieces."

Everybody is asking me about the Treaty outlook in Washington, but as I know nothing, I say nothing. What information reaches me would indicate that the Treaty is in for hard sledding on the other side of the water, but that I keep to myself, in the hope that when in a few days I reach home the outlook will be brighter.

A few hours later the Treaty of Guarantee, as it is called here, by which Great Britain and the United States are pledged to come to the assistance of France to repel an unprovoked attack by Germany was submitted to the Chamber and approved unanimously. The guarantee is joint, not single. Britain will only be bound in case America ratifies. Well, in any case, Foch and Briand are defeated but I fear not routed.[3]

Washington, October 30th.

Three days after my return from Germany, at Brest, I was squeezed on board the *Siboney*, a narrow, slim-waisted vessel, on which I had often sailed the summer seas of the Caribbean. She was now masquerading as a troop ship; as a talking point to the tourist trade the *Siboney* boasted windows instead of narrow portholes. She was certainly not the craft I would have chosen on which to buck the autumnal gales of the Western Ocean. She rolled and she pitched and she wallowed in a gray world of fog and mist and drizzling rain and for twenty-four hours we lay hove to, but I gave little thought to my damp surroundings; after all, I was better off than the doughboys crowded on board and most certainly less deserving; indeed, with the prospect that with every turn of the screw I was nearing the glorious pageant of the red oaks and the scarlet maples at my home in northern Westchester, rather than put up with further delay, I would most willingly have pushed off from the shores of France on a raft. . . .

The joy of my homecoming was marred by bad news of the physical condition of my chief. On the 12th (October) he had been carried from the transport on a stretcher; again the persistent gallstones were harassing him. Now the repentant Colonel was ready for the

[3] I radioed the news to the Colonel, and in his reply was a message of congratulations to the Tiger and an expression of hope that the Treaty would be even more successful in our Senate. The Colonel is convinced that this is the moment for Clemenceau to resign, and has told him so, frequently.

operation, but the doctors would not undertake it. His general condition would not permit him to stand the shock, and their decision was that he must wait—and suffer. When he was stronger they would do what he should have permitted them to do six months before.

"The medicine men always have the last word," admitted the Colonel ruefully.

From another quarter the Colonel was also being harassed. The fight on the Treaty had reached an acute stage. From the White House there came no word of guidance; in fact, no word at all. Some said the President was dead; others, and at least one of these was a Senator, said the President had lost his mind! A few of the correspondents, even those who were generally regarded as conservative, were wiring from Washington sensational conjectures, and their wild yarns were being printed under scareheads. They seemed to be in agreement that Lodge, Johnson, and Brandegee, the most truculent of the opposition Senators, were sharpening their knives. "They mean to learn from the Colonel what *really* happened in Paris—or else."

A week before my arrival, the naval medico in charge, as in duty bound, had called on the chairman of the Foreign Relations Committee and explained the condition of the witness they yearned to examine. He had been civil, the medico reported, and agreed to wait—but not for long!

"While you have come a little late," said the Colonel, "I regard you as a messenger from Heaven. You know these men, and they will believe you. They are probably suspicious of doctors' certificates. Of course I do not want to escape the cross-examination which they plan, but I do not want to be grilled until I can sit up and defend myself. And naturally I want to confer with the President first as to the strategy, and, above all, as to the tactics of his campaign, of which at present I am wholly ignorant. Kohlsaat telephoned me yesterday that the President is absolutely *incommunicado*. No one is admitted except Mrs. Wilson and now and again a tight-lipped doctor. You know Lodge, and while you like him personally, politically you abhor him and all his deviltry, as I do. But dissemble, tackle him with asbestos gloves, and secure for me a respite, 'a cooling-off' period."

With but twenty-four hours' delay, which I spent enjoying the autumnal glories of Whitefields, I went to Washington to do what I could. Through my old schoolmate, "Gus" Gardner, his son-in-law, now dead, in an army training camp, I had been on pleasant social terms with Lodge. Outside the field of politics, to me he was the most interesting man in the Senate. It would be a joy to me if I could avail myself of these terms of intimacy, though not of friendship, to help the Colonel in his hour of need.

Conceding to them the very best of intentions, a charitable attitude not shared by many, House thought it most unwise of those in charge of the situation to shroud in deepest mystery the President's illness. One notable result was that many alarming rumors were current, and some believed (and these were not exclusively the President's political enemies) that Mr. Wilson had suffered a mental as well as a physical collapse.

"At a moment when energetic action is imperative, I am bedridden," moaned the Colonel, "and all we fought for is in grave danger."

Though physically run down, admittedly not up to his fighting weight, the Colonel was not a prey to imaginative fears. Lodge and his colleagues had made no secret of their determination to subject House to the most severe cross-examination, and they were very active in extracting "information" from a number of people (the Colonel called them "coyotes") who had been on the fringe of the Paris Conference and were most eager for the flashlight of publicity.

"As soon as you can," pleaded the Colonel, "go to Washington and see the Senator. You know him well, and I trust from you he will accept a frank statement. Assure him that the moment I am able to travel I shall be most eager to appear before his committee. We have nothing to conceal, indeed quite the contrary."

I went to Washington on the 28th (of October) and saw Lodge the same day, and he authorized me to send House a reassuring letter. "We shall be glad to see the Colonel when he can travel with safety, but assure him there is no particular hurry. We flatter ourselves we know what happened in Paris, all the wild talk of the rumor mongers notwithstanding. We are fully informed as to the past, but we do think that House's presence will be most useful later on, when Congress has to face the situation created in Paris."

Lodge was extremely courteous, even, it seemed to me, considerate, and in the course of the conversation that followed what might be termed our business talk, I got the impression that he was not as confident, as some of his ardent adherents claimed to be, that he could defeat the Treaty and so alter the Covenant as to "hamstring" it, the expression used by both Wilsonians and anti-Wilsonians with, of course, very different purpose and meaning. Indeed, I came to the conclusion that the chairman of the Foreign Relations Committee was in the mood to compromise, but with whom? I telephoned my impression to House and he urged me to stay with Lodge and to secure from him, if possible, a statement of his minimum demands.

We had two talks, and I sent on the result to House, and he was delighted. "The situation is brighter, much brighter," was his comment. I trust he is right—he generally is—but after all the President is still silent and darkness enshrouds the White House. The vote on ratification in the Senate cannot be much longer delayed, everything favorable as well as everything unfavorable to the Treaty has been said scores of times, and the world needs, and indeed demands, action.

Washington, November 5th.

Frazier, who had rejoined House, wrote me yesterday:

"The Colonel was most complimentary about the work you have done for him in Washington, and he is especially appreciative of your interviews with Senator Lodge. The Colonel expects to go to Washington himself next week."

(As no answer came from the silent White House to his letters, this expectation was not realized.)

November 12th.

For several reasons I did not retain a copy of the memorandum which I sent on to House within an hour of my last interview with Senator Lodge. The first was, as a result of my telephone talk with him, I had expected House to come to Washington in a very few days and that this was his plan is indicated by the letter to me from Frazier, who was with the Colonel at this time. But there was another and a more powerful reason for my apparent negligence. The copy of the Covenant which the Senator and I had before us during our talks was in printed form from the document room and on it the Senator had penciled with his own hand (and under his signature) a number of unimportant verbal changes which I do not clearly recall except that they were few and unimportant. But in about thirty words he made additions to Article X and Article XVI which, in his opinion, restored to the Senate, and also to the House, as the "money power," the authority which, as he claimed, was their constitutional right and which he asserted the President had ignored. These changes and additions, having been made by the Senator with his own hand, authenticated the document, and it was in these notations that the value of the memorandum lay. A copy by me would have been of little or no value—so I thought at the time.

November 16th (1919).

I am now making a record of my talks with Lodge, although the high hopes with which they inspired House and myself, rather less so, two weeks ago are gone. Not a word has come to House from the White House, not even an acknowledgment that the important communication has been received.

The Senator and I went over the Covenant, Article by Article. Here are some of the details. In our final session there was an official copy of the Treaty on the library table, also one of the so-called Lodge Reservations before the Senate but, so far as I can remember, we did not once refer to them. It was on the printed copy of the Covenant that I brought with me that the Senator made the changes and inserted the interlineations which if accepted, he thought, would smooth the way to ratification. The changes ran to about forty words, the "inserts" to about fifty. It seemed to me they were more concerned with verbiage than with the object and the intent of the instrument. In my judgment, they were complementary to, rather than limiting, any substantial purpose of the Covenant. In this they differed sharply from the Reservations Lodge had introduced into the Senate and which are now blocking the path to ratification.

The Senator, frankly and repeatedly, stated that his interest or, as he put it several times, his anxiety, centered around Article X, which the President often refers to as the "heart of the Covenant," and his suggestion, indeed his demand, was to the effect that none of the obligations or commitments incurred under this provision should be undertaken without the approval of the Senate and the concurrence of the House. When Lodge had finished what he had to say, I expressed my pleasure at the helpful collaboration of the chairman of the Committee, and with reason, I think. What he asked for now was decidedly milder than the reservations before the Senate, but there was, I ventured to point out, one drawback to any change, even if merely of verbiage, because, in this case, the document would have to be referred back to all the co-signers of the Covenant and this might open the gates to other changes and would certainly result in delay. I also ventured to say that the clarification of Article X which he urged was implicit in the Article itself. I argued "it goes without saying," for a variety of obvious reasons, that the sanction of the Senate and the approval of the House, which alone can furnish the money, would have to be forthcoming before aggressive or even defensive action against an aggressor nation could be undertaken.

"If it goes without saying," commented the Senator somewhat tartly, "there is no harm in saying it—and much advantage."

Good-naturedly the Senator now chaffed me about the expression I had used, "it goes without saying," which he thought was a "barbarism." He then went on to express his opinion of the language in which the world charter was drawn, and it was a poor one.

"As an English production it does not rank high." Then more in chaff than in earnest, he said: "It might get by at Princeton but certainly not at Harvard."

I agreed, but absolved the President of personal responsibility. The Covenant was, I explained, "the product of many minds and not a few pens. Every sentence had to be translated into several languages and then retranslated back a dozen times, and each time every word was subjected to the suspicious scrutiny of eyes which were looking for something other than grammatical mistakes or awkward phrases."

As an illustration of how the document grew, I repeated the words of General Smuts on presenting to the Commission his Article dealing with mandates. "I can see many places where there is room for improvement and clarification," he admitted. "But this agreement has been reached through long and weary nights of discussion within the Committee and I warn you that if even a word is changed or perhaps even a comma, the whole edifice will collapse. We would have to begin all over again."

This interested and rather softened the hitherto austere outlook of the Senator, and he said: "Of course I admit that the Covenant has a noble objective in view. But will it stand up? And if it crashes, will we not be involved?"

I admitted that both the League and the Covenant, like all instruments that sprang from the brain of man, could bear watching, but I added: "We can get out on two years' notice. If I am not mistaken, that method of escape from possible disaster was suggested by you or your committee. To put it over, and the adoption of the Monroe Doctrine reservation, insisted upon by many Senators, cost the President his most bitter struggles."

As to this Lodge made no admission or even comment.

The business of our meeting having been concluded, the Senator began to talk, as he had so often before, about George Borrow, that strange, vagrant genius for whom he had a rare cult. Here at last was a subject upon which we were in perfect agreement, and when I furnished him with one or two items of interest in regard to the less-known chapters in the wanderer's life, that Arthur Evans, also a great Borrow fan, had passed on to me in Paris, the Senator was profuse in his thanks.

Once out of the house, I hastened to the post office at Union Station and registered the copy of the Covenant on which Lodge had made his notations. And when this was out of the way I by telephone called up the Colonel, who was in bed, and told him in veiled language of the important document that would be in his hands in the morning. I was rewarded by a whoop of joy. So much for the record.[4]

November 18th.

I had another talk with Senator Hitchcock today in regard to the battle for ratification of the Treaty and the Covenant which under his leadership is about to be resumed. I admire Hitchcock greatly and I regret that I am not permitted to be as frank with him as he is with me. House still holds that in view of the fact we have no way of

[4]*January 10, 1926.* What really happened to this paper eventually I do not know. Probably, with the exception of Mrs. Wilson and Admiral Grayson, no one knows, and as they never showed the slightest appreciation of its importance, whatever they may have known, they have probably forgotten. In the course of the following winter and spring the President and Colonel House exchanged letters on four or five occasions. The letters of the President, dictated (as all his letters were now) from his sickroom, while cordial, were certainly not gushing, and yet, of his many letters which I have read I can only recall two or three that could be so classified. In the following June, on leaving for Europe, House advised the President of his plans, and I was struck by the friendly tone of the answering letter. But in the meantime those who had sought to bring these two men, so mutually helpful, together, had reached the conclusion that Mrs. Wilson stood in the way and that as long as the sickroom regime lasted, and it lasted until the President's death, it would be impossible to re-establish the old accord.

I cannot shed any further light on the question so often asked as to whether from the beginning of the struggle Lodge was determined to defeat the Treaty and that throughout the negotiations he was merely sparring for time by introducing delaying amendments or crippling reservations. Most certainly, he told me, he would vote for the Covenant in the revised form obtained by me and sent on by House to the President, and he told me that, in his judgment, not many votes would be cast against it in this shape. I do not mean to suggest, however, that Lodge approved wholeheartedly of everything, or indeed of anything, that was done in Paris—assuming that the Senator ever did anything wholeheartedly. In the last evening in his library he even said: "You good people who were over there in Paris seem to have been entranced by the President's eloquence. You thought that his was the voice that breathed over Eden, proclaiming a new era, that the old Adam was dead. . . ."

"Not at all," I replied. "We knew he was not dead, but we did believe he had a wicked clutch on the throat of civilization, and that unless it was broken the world which men of good will loved was doomed to end."

knowing that the President received his letter, based on my interview with Lodge and urging the acceptance of his slightly diluted reservations, it would not be fair to make him (the President) publicly responsible for what House considers one of the main difficulties in the situation. Having frequent contacts with Lodge, and also with Kellogg, Hitchcock is in the best possible position to know what they are driving at, and he urged me to communicate these, his impressions, to House, which I did.

"I and most of the members of our party in the Senate," he said, "are personally in favor of getting the Treaty ratified in almost any form. In any form, if even in one of the least desirable forms, it would, we think, end the present disastrous anarchy that prevails in world relations. I have to act under instructions, but those in control at the White House prevent me from receiving instructions direct. I am merely told 'the President will not budge an inch.' His honor is at stake. He feels he would be dishonored if he failed to live up to the pledges made to his fellow delegates in Paris."

As to his relations with Lodge, Hitchcock could shed but little light. "I confess," he said, "the Massachusetts Senator is an enigma to me. At first I had the impression that he merely wished to weave into the Covenant some of his great thoughts, so that this world charter would not, in the future, be regarded as a party document. His hatred of Wilson is very deep and his talking point is that, as the President did not permit any real Republicans to participate in the drafting of the Treaty, they have a perfectly free hand in the matter of ratification, also a greater responsibility than would have been theirs had they been consulted during the drafting process.

"I admit that in some of my unofficial cloakroom talks with Lodge he expresses views which even to me seem reasonable, but when I ask him to get down to cases and state what changes he would suggest, his attitude stiffens and his face hardens. I think he would like to induce me to offer changes and concessions. Of course, by my instructions, although, owing to the President's illness, they are somewhat out of date, I am precluded from doing so. So my conviction deepens that whatever may have been his purpose two months ago, today Lodge has decided to defeat the Treaty and the Covenant—if he can. Please tell Colonel House that this is my firm impression and further assure him that unless we agree to compromise on what so many of us think are minor points, the Treaty will fail of ratification."

November 20th.

I sent this bad news on to House immediately. In his reply he expressed regret but no surprise over the situation that is developing here. Once back in America, he had picked up again his innumerable lines of "grapevine" information. He in New York understood the situation better than I did in Washington.

Perhaps I should mention that in our talk I called Senator Hitchcock's attention to the fact that Republican criticism, as voiced by the Lodge resolution of last year, and by the letters of Root and Taft to House, while in Paris, did help shape the Covenant and, further, that in carrying out some of these suggestions, the President had run into noisy, loud, and at times very serious opposition. Hitchcock laughed. "I made the same remark to Lodge—not once but at least twice. His only answer was a blank stare. Evidently all that has been wiped off the Republican slate."

It is amazing, and also not a little humiliating, to hear the wisecracks in circulation here and the nonsense that is talked by some men, Democrats as well as Republicans, many of whom are high in congressional circles, as to what our national policy should be with respect to our international relations. Lodge is reported as saying, "All will be well as long as we do not loosen our present hold on the lunch basket and keep the paws of the bandits with whom we have lately been associated out of it." And the blatant, preposterous Borah is reported as saying: "League of Nations? A crazy quilt of crazy notions, I call it, hatched out by a man who never sat in a deliberative assembly and shows his want of legislative training every time he opens his mouth."

Today (November 26th), a week after the vote in the Senate[5] by which the Treaty and the Covenant failed of ratification, Colonel House made to me the following comments on the resulting situation:

"We do not know that the President ever saw the Lodge reservations in the modified form in which he offered them to you on November 2d. We do not know if the President received the numerous letters

[5]The ratification enactment was defeated in the Senate on November 19th by a vote of 55 to 39. Acting under instructions from the stricken President, entirely out of touch with the situation by which they were confronted, the Democratic members of the Senate voted with the "bitter-enders" and defeated the new world charter in the form it had been modified in Paris at the instance of so many Republican Senators and other party leaders. Had these instructions not been given, or had they been ignored, the Treaty and the Covenant would probably have been brought into the haven of ratification by a vote of 81 to 13.

and petitions, from scores of men who had been his lieutenants and supporters in all the League battles, urging him to accept the Treaty even with important modifications—and so avoid world anarchy. We do not know the date of the President's letter urging the Democratic Senators to vote against the Treaty in any form but the one in which it was first sent to the Senate—an instruction which they obeyed and so in combination with the Lodge men and the 'bitter-enders' encompassed its defeat.

"We do not know if this instruction was drawn up by the President in September, when the President and many others thought that the Treaty could be ratified in its original form, or whether it was issued later in October or November, when most of its most loyal supporters, men who had stood with the President through thick and thin, recognized that the outcome was doubtful.

"Even more important than answers to these queries is the question that cannot and should not be avoided: who was the President of the United States during these crucial weeks when decisions vital to the security of our country, and to the peace of the world, had to be, and certainly were, made? Who acted in his name in the days and weeks when the President was not in touch with his constitutional advisers? Here is a situation that may occur again under, if possible, even more tragic circumstances. It is to be hoped that congressional action on the matter will not be long delayed."

Washington, November 27th.

I must try to be fair to Lodge, although it is difficult in view of the developments of the last two weeks (reference, no doubt, to the vote in the Senate on November 19th). At the time of my talks with him, first in his little room in the Capitol itself, not in the office building, and the final talk in the library of his house on Massachusettes Avenue the following evening, I did not receive the impression that the Senator was out to defeat the Treaty and scrap the Covenant, although he did express the opinion that it had been unwise to "intertwine" these great documents. Indeed, I concluded—and his words justified my conclusion—that once the changes he advocated were accepted and all commitments under the Treaty subjected to review by what he referred to several times as the "constitutional authority," the Senate, the ratifying power, and the House, which would hold the purse strings, his opposition would cease. He also believed this would be the attitude of his friends who were at the time opposed to the Treaty in the form it was before Congress.

The Colonel is of the opinion that the stiffening attitude of Lodge and the others who now are called the "irreconcilables" is due to the growing opposition throughout the country. That it is growing cannot be denied. Now that Wilson is perforce silent there is certainly no one competent to take his place and "sell" the Treaty to the people. But I have another impression which I shall keep to myself—and my diary. I think Lodge was hurt in his vanity, which is enormous, by the fact that the President did not accept with enthusiasm the olive branch, if you can call it that, which he extended through House, of which I was the humble intermediary and bearer. This is a situation about which we can do nothing. Doubtless with the best intentions, the President is kept a prisoner in his sickroom by Mrs. Wilson and Grayson. Even the secretary, Tumulty, is not admitted, and all the efforts of House and his friends to establish relations with our stricken leader have failed. Lodge may well think that with his "accustomed arrogance" the President has snubbed him; on the other hand, the olive branch may never have reached him—altogether an unfortunate mess.

Washington, December 20th.

No one at this time appreciated more fully the danger of the situation and the probability of impending tragedy in world affairs than did President Lowell of Harvard, an ardent advocate of harmonizing the views now in open conflict. He had several conferences with Colonel House at this time and also with key men here in Washington. His final report is revealed in these words to House and other supporters of the League:

"It has seemed to me that the differences between the League as adopted in Paris and as changed by the reservations reported and apparently approved by the Senate Committee on Foreign Relations are not very important, and that with good will they might be reconciled. But I must admit that even with the utmost effort I have found it impossible to mediate or even to bring the President and the Republican Senators who are in favor of slight amendments together for a conference."

Washington, December 23d.

My last days in the Army were troubled—not to say hectic. It is not so easy to get out of the Army as it is to join up, especially if your services have been unimportant. My troubles were emphasized by a personal complication. Dennis Nolan—who in the last months had commanded a brigade at the front, who for his services had been at least brevetted with a star, who would have been made a major general but for the fact that with the Armistice all promotions were suspended —had been, by some mechanical process known only to the War Department, "demoted" and in the guise of a mere major was slinking about Washington. Hearing, incorrectly I think, that I was "strutting around the Capital as a lieutenant colonel," in an outburst of rage he announced in the club that he would shoot me on sight! By strategy I avoided a meeting until I, too, had received my discharge and had returned to my former insignificant status as the senior camp follower of the Army. Then all was forgiven, and we enjoyed a merry dinner of reconciliation and of farewell at which several survivors of the San Pablo "push" in the Santiago campaign were present.

When in the spring of 1922, for at least the twentieth time, the question as to whether the President should have presented himself personally at the Great Assizes in Paris became a matter of newspaper discussion, I interrogated the Colonel on the subject and also placed before him some of the contradictory entries in my diary.

"The first entry, November 1918, discloses that you opposed the coming of the President and that you left nothing undone, that you thought proper, to stop him. My second entry registers approval, indeed enthusiastic approval, of the President's activities. This was in January 1919. Two months later your enthusiasm has cooled. You intimate that the President's return to Paris in March was a blunder, one of those blunders that the French cynic characterized 'as worse than crimes.' "

The Colonel laughed. "I must confess your diary in this respect mirrors the truth. And that is quite a feather in your cap. Some of the entries in my own diary—well, today I find them baffling—to use a mild word. It is quite true that in November 1918, when it was first suggested, I regarded the coming of the President to Paris as a tragic mistake. And I worked against it in all ways that I considered proper. The public record shows that as well as your diary. I opposed his coming by a frontal attack and then by flank movements—all to no purpose. He came and, as you know perhaps better than anyone else, I did all that was possible to avoid the consequences of what was undoubtedly a mistake in strategy and in tactics. By the middle of January I began to think that I, not the President, had been wrong, and by the end of the month I was sure of it. Soon I was convinced that but for the presence of the President the Peace Conference never would have convened at all; certainly never have gotten down to work. The powers would have split up into groups, peace treaties would have resulted, quite a number of them in fact. They would have been contradictory and none of them would have been worth the paper they were printed on. Without his presence our peace ship never would have been launched. The pressure which he exercised upon his motley coworkers never could have been exerted by cable. The President's first sojourn in Paris had been an astonishing success, the future course of the world had been charted in broad lines, the recalcitrants had been brought to heel. Of course there were details to be filled in. We, the minor delegates, could attend to that, at least to most of them, and the rest could, with advantage, have gone over to the first sessions of the League. This at least was my thought.

"In other directions, too, the prospect was brighter, much brighter. The defeat of the President in the 1918 elections had been either forgotten or explained away—or so it seemed. Anti-League sentiment may have been a contributing factor to this election setback, but there were certainly others, such as local issues and the hostile feelings certain to accumulate after six years of drastic legislation. How clear was the support that the people were giving to the plan for world peace by February 1919! Thirty-four out of thirty-six state legislatures had endorsed the League without reservations and thirty-three governors had come out for it.

"In these circumstances it would have been wiser for Mr. Wilson to have stayed at home and to have been a little more conciliatory with those who still believed, in their blindness, that we could with advantage keep aloof from the living, struggling world, but he returned to Paris and became a party to the guerrilla wars of the Conference, which, viewed from America, seemed so alarming. Soon many began to think that, as we interfered in every one of their problems and above all in the quarrels which they had long regarded as private, those devilish war-mongering Europeans would intervene on our side of the Atlantic. That unfortunate idea spread like a prairie fire, and soon the Senators, or at least some of them, who at first had only meant to heckle Mr. Wilson, or who merely wanted to put some of their own verbiage into the Covenant, saw a chance for political advantage, perhaps for a party victory. They won it, but I do not envy them their responsibility for the present world situation." . . .

. . . A few days before Christmas, in 1922, I saw the ex-President for the last time. Though broken in body, it seemed to me that his mental powers were not impaired. I had escorted M. Clemenceau in his tour of the country and when we arrived in Washington, word had reached the former French Premier that Mr. Wilson was not only able, but most anxious to see him.

"I would like to talk with you about our battles of not so long ago. You were a stanch friend as well as at times an open foe," the message ran.

At the conclusion of this interview, which greatly affected M. Clemenceau, hearing that I was downstairs, the ex-President sent for me and talked in an appreciative way of my services as interpreter throughout the meetings at which the Covenant was drafted. "You disproved the old saying to the effect that the translator is always a traitor." He then spoke favorably of several contributions I had made to the magazines and the newspapers on the League of Nations controversy, then a word of criticism: "But why have you not said that you were there, an eye and ear witness to all that took place while the Covenant was being drafted?"

"I was determined to be discreet, Mr. President. I thought I should cast off my newspaper skin when I was called to serve you in an official and most confidential capacity."

At this Mr. Wilson laughed heartily, but went on to say: "You can't be too indiscreet to please me now. I give you full absolution in advance. We at least have nothing to conceal. I glory in the ideas that we defended in France and they will triumph. Perhaps the world charter which we fashioned in Paris will be redrawn in a happier form, but as to its ultimate acceptance I have not the shadow of a doubt. The world will not commit suicide." The President sighed, and I think in thought he was not as confident as his words indicated. There he sat, wounded and paralyzed, a victim of the shortsighted greed and ignorance of his own countrymen.

Clemenceau was deeply affected by this close view of the tragic fate that had overtaken the man who had been his honorable antagonist in so many of the Treaty battles in Paris. He asked Henry White, whose guest he was, to excuse him from appearing at dinner that evening and he dined alone with me in his room.

January, 1929.

In the nearly seven years that have elapsed since my last entry in this diary, hardly a month passed that I did not, at home or abroad, have the privilege of discussing the world situation with Colonel House, my old chief. But generally we talked of the exciting present, or of the disturbing future, rarely of the past, although it was far from dead. But when his *Intimate Papers*, edited in such a scholarly manner by Professor Seymour, were published a few weeks ago, and the Colonel sent me a copy with a flattering inscription and a far-too-generous acknowledgment of the small part I had played in his mission, I ventured to question him as to several incidents upon which I needed enlightenment. Again I called his attention to the entries in my diary, and asked him to help me, if possible, to harmonize the contradictions, the rather flat contradictions that resulted from them.

"I must compliment you on your diary; both statements as to my feelings and my attitude are correct. I did not want the President to come to Paris and I told him so; I wanted him to stay 'behind the curtain' in Washington. True, at that moment my position was an awkward one, because there were some who whispered that my course was inspired by the thought that in the absence of the President I would become the No. 1 American delegate. There was, of course, absolutely nothing but malicious gossip in this. I had all the responsibility I wanted or cared to shoulder in the secondary place that had been allotted me. But in December and in January, as I came in contact with the discordant delegates as they assembled, I reached the conclusion that without Wilson's prestige the negotiations would never have been started. In March, however, the President should never have returned from Washington; but it is only fair to say that he did not come this time on his own volition, or as a free agent. Here the responsibility that rests on the Senate is very great. Senators, friendly as well as unfriendly, had advised him that without the Monroe Doctrine reservation and the provision permitting withdrawal from the League upon two years' notice, which they demanded, there was little chance that the Treaty could be ratified. It was extremely difficult to put through these amendments with all the driving force which Wilson's presence in Paris exerted. If he had not been there, I do not know what would have happened, so I shall not indulge in pure guessing."

I then went on: "In the *Intimate Papers* you include my letter to you (November 1, 1919) in regard to your expected appearance before the Foreign Relations Committee of the Senate, and also my memorandum as to my talks with Lodge on this subject, but you omit all reference to the two interviews which I had with the Senator in the days that followed. You may recall that when I advised you that in my opinion Lodge was in a mood to accept the Covenant with reservations considerably less drastic than those which under his name were before the Senate, you immediately telephoned me to follow up this lead without delay."

"That, I recall it, is putting it mildly; it came like a rainbow in a lowering sky."

"Following your instructions, three days later I sent you a letter describing the interviews and a memorandum detailing the concessions which Lodge was prepared to make and which he thought, although he admitted he could not guarantee it, would bring the Treaty into the haven of ratification."

"I sent your letter and the memorandum on to the President, giving it my warmest support. That letter was never acknowledged. And now I will tell you why I make no reference to it, and why I omitted the incident entirely when I published my *Intimate Papers*. I didn't know at the time, and I do not know now, that the President ever saw the letter or that the memorandum enclosed, so tragically important in my judgment, ever came to his notice, or, if it did, that he was in a condition physically and mentally to appreciate it. Now if I had included that memorandum which, you might say, apparently indicated that Lodge, at least privately, was making concessions from his public stand, the criticism of the President's unbending attitude, already strong, even from his close adherents, would have increased in violence. I could not bring myself to be responsible for that. And I had another thought: was this really the President's affair? It seemed to me that he was in the position of a soldier who falls desperately wounded in leading an attack. Should he alone be the arbiter of how the forces that had failed should execute an orderly retreat, reform, and fight another day under more favorable circumstances? It seemed to me that this duty should have devolved upon other shoulders. And so the question presents itself, in whose hands was the executive power of the United States Government in November and December 1919? I do not know—nobody knows. That is a mystery which Congress never solved, so far as I know, never tried to.

"And there was another consideration: If I had published the concessions that, apparently, Lodge was willing to make, it would have meant that I accepted what might be called his proposal, and that I believed in his good faith. Frankly, I could not do that. In my judgment, from the very beginning the good faith of Lodge was questionable. What was the motive that induced him to take this, apparently, conciliatory step? I did not know then and I cannot say that I know now. Did Lodge, and those who went along with him, wish to defeat the Covenant which Wilson had drafted, and signed, absolutely and irretrievably, or did they wish only to weaken some of the obligations that were incurred under it? Did Lodge merely want to assert the Senate's right to advice and consultation, which, as he publicly claimed, Wilson had sought to ignore? Again, was he seeking a partisan victory, or did he merely desire to make of the Covenant a bi-partisan document?

"Perhaps by voicing these surmises I am doing less than justice to Senator Lodge. I should dislike to do that, but not half as much as I would hate to do an injustice to the stricken President; to make him responsible for ignoring an opportunity which perhaps was never presented to him. No, I would not add by a feather's weight to the burden which the President would have to bear, if he had knowingly ignored the offer, which, if made in good faith, might have led to a nearly complete victory.

"Had the President called me into consultation, and, as you see by my diary, that is what I expected, the moment your memorandum had been studied, I do not know what I would have advised, but I am sure I would have given this new phase of the controversy very careful consideration. It seemed to me a 'lead' that should have been followed up very carefully but of course with great caution. Our handicap in the whole matter was, of course, our want of faith in Lodge—it all goes back to that. This I can best describe in the words of one of my Texan friends, who said: 'To have followed the trail of Lodge in that Treaty battle would have broken the back of the most supple rattlesnake.' "

House was deeply moved as he recalled the incidents of those tragic days. After a short pause I made this comment:

"I see one danger in the course you pursued. At some future time someone rummaging in the Senator's papers may come across a record of the concessions which, ostensibly at least, Lodge was willing to make. What then?"

"I have thought of that," said House, "but no, I have no fear of such a development. When on November 3d Lodge, as you reported, was apparently willing to make concessions, even if they were merely of a face-saving character, he was not confident that he could defeat the Treaty, but in a very few days he grew more confident and bolder. On November 19th, by a vote of 55 to 39, he defeated ratification of the Treaty in the form that Wilson had presented it and which he insisted upon. And, unfortunately, every day the slogan of 'Away from Europe' was making converts throughout the country. Encouraged by these developments, the Senator from Massachusetts now determined to defeat the Treaty in any form, to smash Wilson, and damn the consequences! So I think we can rely on Lodge's discretion; after November 19th he would have destroyed any record of a move he would have regarded as having been made in a moment of weakness two weeks before. You should not forget that at this juncture Lodge was under the impression he would be the standard-bearer of his party in 1920. To him and to some others he seemed more worthy of this honor than the unfortunate Harding later chosen. Lodge was drawing up a platform for his presidential campaign. We can rely on him, I think, to eliminate from his record any signs of wavering in the Treaty battle in which he scored such a tragic victory.

"You will remember," continued House, "that the President stated publicly on several occasions that he regarded Article X as the 'heart of the Covenant'; also, you will recall that Lodge stated to you that he and those who stood with him would not accept responsibility for any action under this provision (Article X) unless the Senate had previously given its approval. This was, as you know, the rock upon which the project of ratification was wrecked; the President maintained that he would be dishonored in the eyes of those who had worked with him in drafting the Covenant if he compromised on this point. He stood firm, and our plan, our dream, if you will, came to nothing.

"I did not regard the addition which Lodge insisted upon as disastrous to our plan. I think you were right when you pointed out to the Senator that nothing could be done under the Covenant without congressional approval. Where would the funds have come from, if not from Congress, to meet the obligations which acceptance of Article X carried with it? You were quite right in maintaining that all this went without saying, but when Lodge insisted upon putting it down in black and white, I saw no great harm and sent on his proposal to the President with my endorsement.

"Now let us see what has happened to Article X; by the common consent of all who signed it, it has become a dead letter, with the result that we remained outside the League, although it has adopted the limited responsibilities urged by our isolationists, the very concession we were willing to acquiesce in. Perhaps at Paris we made a mistake in asking too much from war-distracted people. I sometimes think that you and those who thought with you, that the wisest course would have been to arrange for quarterly or even more frequent meetings of delegates from those we regarded as the 'righteous Nations' to review the state of the world and to pass such judgment as might be necessary upon the conduct of States, members of the League, and the others, were on the right track. These automatic meetings at stated intervals, unrelated to the passions of the moment, would have offered many advantages. You recall how Grey failed when in July 1914 he sent out a call for a conference of the powers. His call was regarded as an unfriendly intervention in a political crisis by some, and it went unheeded.

"With the wisdom of hindsight, I now think we saddled the Covenant with too many rules that are not flexible enough to meet developments that are, and always must be, unpredictable. Perhaps we should have preserved our freedom of action unhampered by rules and obligations which might have been more applicable to a different situation and another problem. Meeting automatically and at intervals fixed in advance of the emergency, we would have been swayed not by rules and regulations but by the public opinion of the world in an international congress assembled; it would then have been for public opinion to decide whether the natural processes of growth and decay in nations are to be decided by orderly processes or by wars which have never settled anything, since the day when Cain slew Abel.

"This, I think, is what the future has in store for us; true, it is not a reassuring prospect; the forces of public opinion are undoubtedly slow in crystallizing and at times they do go astray, but if they fail us, at least we can say that the world is being shaped as the majority of peoples wish it to be; that is democratic doctrine, and of that I shall never despair. I wish we could have blazed a straighter trail and reached a stronger and more reassuring position. But, after a careful consideration of all the criticisms that have been made, I do not see how we could have done better at the time. We were not dealing with angels, but with men who had come not unscathed through the most terrible period of world history and who were concerned in doing everything they could to avoid a repetition of it.

"There is one other charge which I think I should comment upon. It is said that 'by conferring with Lodge, his archenemy, I broke the President's heart.'[6] How unfair this is you know. You cannot fail to recall that through Henry White, acting as his intermediary, the President was himself, indirectly at least, conferring with Lodge throughout the Paris negotiations, and that upon his first return to Washington he invited him to the White House for an exchange of views. It happens, however, that I never saw Lodge while the Treaty was before the Senate, or indeed later, and that I never wrote him about the milder reservations, which he placed in your hands. I felt I was not at liberty to do so until I heard from the President. I was packed up and awaiting the summons to go to Washington, but, as you know, the summons never came.

"But if I had conferred with Lodge, I do not see the harm; I would have been merely following in the President's footsteps. And about the contacts which the President maintained with the Senator from Massachusetts, who was also, unfortunately, the most influential member of the Foreign Relations Committee, you are better informed perhaps than anyone else because you discussed with me certain memoranda and then, at my request, carried them to Henry White to be sent on to the Senator. You may recall that morning early in February 1919, on which White, honorable gentleman that he was, came into my office greatly disturbed. He said he had passed a sleepless night and had come to make a personal explanation. He went on to say:

" 'Last evening, it occurred to me that I had been doing something that I should not have done now that Lodge has come out openly against the proposed Treaty, as he understands it. This is how it happened, and I hope these circumstances may be accepted as extenuating my indiscretion. From the very beginning of my diplomatic career, I have kept in touch with Lodge, the friend of my youth. When in Washington, I saw him nearly every day, and when I was abroad, we exchanged frequent letters. When I was sent to Italy as Ambassador and later to France and, above all, when I represented the United States at the Algeciras Conference, as he was a member of the Foreign Relations Committee, I kept him informed and often asked for and received his advice. Following this practice, ever since the Armistice, I

[6]This charge was made by the second Mrs. Wilson in her *My Memoir*. For the details see Appendix B.

have been writing him almost weekly, describing the situation as I see it and expressing to him my hopes—and my fears. I hope you will make a clean breast of what I have confessed to the President and tell him I am sorry and that from now on this correspondence shall be discontinued.'

"I told White that his scruples did him honor, but I asked him to do nothing in the matter until I had consulted the President, and this I did that very afternoon. At first, as always when Lodge's name was mentioned, the President bristled and was evidently not a little displeased with White, but he listened as I explained to him how I thought this correspondence might prove valuable, and finally he agreed with me. The result was, as you know, I drew up from time to time memoranda, many of which the President read, and all of which he approved, which you carried to White to be sent on, in his own language, to Lodge, and in his own name, if he agreed. And this he did—invariably, I think.

"These are the only contacts, direct or indirect, that I had with Lodge during the negotiations in Paris or in Washington. They were carried on, it is true, at my suggestion, but with the President's express approval. In these circumstances I do not see how I can be charged with having broken the President's heart in so doing; although apparently the charge is made on high authority, that of the second Mrs. Wilson.

"I have no patience," the Colonel went on after a long pause, "with those who speak of the President's venture in altruism, although many say it with kindness in their hearts, as 'a magnificent failure.' Much was accomplished, and though, as we all know now, Wilson left the world far from safe for Democracy, he liberated in Europe many millions of people and gave hope and courage to many millions more who, as yet, are not 'redeemed.' Wilson died a martyr to the noble cause that will ever be associated with his name. It may be a trite saying, but it is a true one, 'The blood of the martyrs refreshes the tree of liberty as it also invigorates the Church.'

"If you look the scene over, not through the glasses of the short-sighted isolationists, however, you cannot fail to realize that our failure was far from complete. As I look at the wild world with which we are confronted today, I still find comfort and encouragement in some words of Carlyle which you may recall. I recall them every day: 'Nothing that was worthy in the past departs; no truth or goodness realized by man ever dies, or can die; but is all still here, and, recognized or not, lives and works through endless changes.'

"The President, the American people, and forward-looking men and women everywhere, lost the great battle, but it was not a total defeat. Those who in the future shall lead civilization to ultimate victory, and on that score I have no misgivings, may advance along a somewhat different route, but they will find extremely helpful the signposts and the steppingstones which Wilson placed on his way. Perhaps if we had been as familiar with Bunyan's masterpiece as our fathers were, we would have been better prepared for the dangers of the wilderness we had to cross. We might have visualized more clearly the castles of the robber barons and have avoided the quagmires and the pitfalls into which so many well-meaning but unwary delegates at the Conference fell. The path of the pilgrims leads through many dark glens, along many a precipice, and up many steep hills; but someday they will reach the Shining Gate and enter into the City of Peace."[7]

With this glance in retrospect I end my chronicle of words spoken and of things seen during the tragic year of 1919—and after. Should what I have written ever pass out of my personal files into the public domain, it may serve as a footnote to history and prove of some slight assistance to those who will share responsibility when the next Assizes are called to save the world from the plight in which it flounders today. As a last word I would recall the saying of General Smuts that should never be forgotten:

"Not Wilson, but humanity failed at Paris."

That places responsibility where it belongs.

[7]Colonel Edward M. House died in March 1938. World War II came September 1939. America's boasted isolation ended December 7, 1941, with the catastrophe at Pearl Harbor.

COVENANT OF THE LEAGUE OF NATIONS

WITH AMENDMENTS IN FORCE, OCTOBER, 1936[1]

THE HIGH CONTRACTING PARTIES,

In order to promote international cooperation and to achieve international peace and security

by the acceptance of obligations not to resort to war,

by the prescription of open, just and honorable relations between nations,

by the firm establishment of the understandings of international law as the actual rule of conduct among Governments, and

by the maintenance of justice and a scrupulous respect for all treaty obligations in the dealings of organized peoples with one another,

Agree to this Covenant of the League of Nations.

ARTICLE 1

Membership and Withdrawal

1. The original Members of the League of Nations shall be those of the Signatories which are named in the Annex to this Covenant and also such of those other States named in the Annex as shall accede without reservation to this Covenant. Such accessions shall be effected by a Declaration deposited with the Secretariat within two months of the coming into force of the Covenant. Notice thereof shall be sent to all other Members of the League.

2. Any fully self-governing State, Dominion or Colony not named in the Annex may become a Member of the League if its admission is agreed to by two-thirds of the Assembly, provided that it shall give effective guaranties of its sincere intention to observe its international obligations, and shall accept such regulations as may be prescribed by the League in regard to its military, naval and air forces and armaments.

3. Any Member of the League may, after two years' notice of its intention so to do, withdraw from the League, provided that all its interna-

[1]Amendments to Covenant which have come into force in accordance with Article 26 are printed in italics. Amendments approved by Assembly but not yet ratified by Member States are not included in this text.

tional obligations and all its obligations under this Covenant shall have been fulfilled at the time of its withdrawal.

ARTICLE 2

Executive Organs

The action of the League under this Covenant shall be effected through the instrumentality of an Assembly and of a Council, with a permanent Secretariat.

ARTICLE 3

Assembly

1. The Assembly shall consist of Representatives of the Members of the League.

2. The Assembly shall meet at stated intervals and from time to time as occasion may require at the Seat of the League, or at such other place as may be decided upon.

3. The Assembly may deal at its meetings with any matter within the sphere of action of the League or affecting the peace of the world.

4. At meetings of the Assembly each Member of the League shall have one vote and may have not more than three Representatives.

ARTICLE 4

Council

1. The Council shall consist of Representatives of the Principal Allied and Associated Powers [United States of America, the British Empire, France, Italy and Japan], together with Representatives of four other Members of the League. These four Members of the League shall be selected by the Assembly from time to time in its discretion. Until the appointment of the Representatives of the four Members of the League first selected by the Assembly, Representatives of Belgium, Brazil, Spain and Greece shall be Members of the Council.

2. With the approval of the majority of the Assembly, the Council may name additional Members of the League, whose Representatives shall always be Members of the Council; the Council with like approval may increase the number of Members of the League to be selected by the Assembly for representation on the Council.

2. *bis. The Assembly shall fix by a two-thirds majority the rules dealing with the election of the non-permanent Members of the Council, and particularly such regulations as relate to their term of office and the conditions of re-eligibility.*

3. The Council shall meet from time to time as occasion may require, and at least once a year, at the Seat of the League, or at such other place as may be decided upon.

4. The Council may deal at its meetings with any matter within the sphere of action of the League or affecting the peace of the world.

5. Any Member of the League not represented on the Council shall be invited to send a Representative to sit as a member at any meeting of the Council during the consideration of matters specially affecting the interests of that Member of the League.

6. At meetings of the Council, each Member of the League represented on the Council shall have one vote, and may have not more than one Representative.

ARTICLE 5

Voting and Procedure

1. Except where otherwise expressly provided in this Covenant or by the terms of the present Treaty, decisions at any meeting of the Assembly or of the Council shall require the agreement of all the Members of the League represented at the meeting.

2. All matters of procedure at meetings of the Assembly or of the Council including the appointment of Committees to investigate particular matters, shall be regulated by the Assembly or by the Council and may be decided by a majority of the Members of the League represented at the meeting.

3. The first meeting of the Assembly and the first meeting of the Council shall be summoned by the President of the United States of America.

ARTICLE 6

Secretariat and Expenses

1. The permanent Secretariat shall be established at the Seat of the League. The Secretariat shall comprise a Secretary-General and such secretaries and staff as may be required.

2. The first Secretary-General shall be the person named in the Annex; thereafter the Secretary-General shall be appointed by the Council with the approval of the majority of the Assembly.

3. The secretaries and the staff of the Secretariat shall be appointed by the Secretary-General with the approval of the Council.

4. The Secretary-General shall act in that capacity at all meetings of the Assembly and of the Council.

5. *The expenses of the League shall be borne by the Members of the League in the proportion decided by the Assembly.*

ARTICLE 7

Seat, Qualifications of Officials, Immunities

1. The Seat of the League is established at Geneva.

2. The Council may at any time decide that the Seat of the League shall be established elsewhere.

3. All positions under or in connection with the League, including the Secretariat, shall be open equally to men and women.

4. Representatives of the Members of the League and officials of the League when engaged on the business of the League shall enjoy diplomatic privileges and immunities.

5. The buildings and other property occupied by the League or its officials or by Representatives attending its meetings shall be inviolable.

ARTICLE 8

Reduction of Armaments

1. The Members of the League recognise that the maintenance of peace requires the reduction of national armaments to the lowest point consistent with national safety and the enforcement by common action of international obligations.

2. The Council, taking account of the geographical situation and circumstances of each State, shall formulate plans for such reduction for the consideration and action of the several Governments.

3. Such plans shall be subject to reconsideration and revision at least every 10 years.

4. After these plans shall have been adopted by the several Governments, the limits of armaments therein fixed shall not be exceeded without the concurrence of the Council.

5. The Members of the League agree that the manufacture by private enterprise of munitions and implements of war is open to grave objections. The Council shall advise how the evil effects attendant upon such manufacture can be prevented, due regard being had to the necessities of those Members of the League which are not able to manufacture the munitions and implements of war necessary for their safety.

6. The Members of the League undertake to interchange full and frank information as to the scale of their armaments, their military, naval and air programs, and the condition of such of their industries as are adaptable to warlike purposes.

ARTICLE 9

Permanent Military, Naval and Air Commission

A permanent Commission shall be constituted to advise the Council on the execution of the provisions of Articles 1 and 8 and on military, naval and air questions generally.

ARTICLE 10

Guaranties Against Aggression

The Members of the League undertake to respect and preserve as against external aggression the territorial integrity and existing political independence of all Members of the League. In case of any such aggression or in case of any threat or danger of such aggression the Council shall advise upon the means by which this obligation shall be fulfilled.

ARTICLE 11

Action in Case of War or Threat of War

1. Any war or threat of war, whether immediately affecting any of the Members of the League or not, is hereby declared a matter of concern to the whole League, and the League shall take any action that may be deemed wise and effectual to safeguard the peace of nations. In case any such emergency should arise the Secretary-General shall on the request of any Member of the League forthwith summon a meeting of the Council.

2. It is also declared to be the friendly right of each Member of the League to bring to the attention of the Assembly or of the Council any circumstance whatever affecting international relations which threatens to disturb international peace or the good understanding between nations upon which peace depends.

ARTICLE 12

Disputes to Be Submitted for Settlement

1. The Members of the League agree that, if there should arise between them any dispute likely to lead to a rupture, they will submit the matter either to arbitration *or judicial settlement* or to inquiry by the Council, and they agree in no case to resort to war until three months after the award by the arbitrators *or the judicial decision* or the report by the Council.

2. In any case under this Article the award of the arbitrators *or the judicial decision* shall be made within a reasonable time, and the report of the Council shall be made within six months after the submission of the dispute.

ARTICLE 13

Arbitration or Judicial Settlement

1. The Members of the League agree that, whenever any dispute shall arise between them which they recognize to be suitable for submission to arbitration *or judicial settlement*, and which can not be satisfactorily settled by diplomacy, they will submit the whole subject matter to arbitration *or judicial settlement*.

2. Disputes as to the interpretation of a treaty, as to any question of international law, as to the existence of any fact which if established would constitute a breach of any international obligation, or as to the extent and nature of the reparation to be made for any such breach, are declared to be among those which are generally suitable for submission to arbitration *or judicial settlement*.

3. *For the consideration of any such dispute, the court to which the case is referred shall be the Permanent Court of International Justice, estab-*

lished in accordance with Article 14, or any tribunal agreed on by the parties to the dispute or stipulated in any convention existing between them.

4. The Members of the League agree that they will carry out in full good faith any award *or decision* that may be rendered, and that they will not resort to war against a Member of the League which complies therewith. In the event of any failure to carry out such an award *or decision*, the Council shall propose what steps should be taken to give effect thereto.

ARTICLE 14

Permanent Court of International Justice

The Council shall formulate and submit to the Members of the League for adoption plans for the establishment of a Permanent Court of International Justice. The Court shall be competent to hear and determine any dispute of an international character which the parties thereto submit to it. The Court may also give an advisory opinion upon any dispute or question referred to it by the Council or by the Assembly.

ARTICLE 15

Disputes Not Submitted to Arbitration or Judicial Settlement

1. If there should arise between Members of the League any dispute likely to lead to a rupture, which is not submitted to arbitration *or judicial settlement* in accordance with Article 13, the Members of the League agree that they will submit the matter to the Council. Any party to the dispute may effect such submission by giving notice of the existence of the dispute to the Secretary-General, who will make all necessary arrangements for a full investigation and consideration thereof.

2. For this purpose the parties to the dispute will communicate to the Secretary-General, as promptly as possible, statements of their case with all the relevant facts and papers, and the Council may forthwith direct the publication thereof.

3. The Council shall endeavor to effect a settlement of the dispute, and, if such efforts are successful, a statement shall be made public giving such facts and explanations regarding the dispute and the terms of settlement thereof as the Council may deem appropriate.

4. If the dispute is not thus settled, the Council either unanimously or by a majority vote shall make and publish a report containing a statement of the facts of the dispute and the recommendations which are deemed just and proper in regard thereto.

5. Any Member of the League represented on the Council may make public a statement of the facts of the dispute and of its conclusions regarding the same.

6. If a report by the Council is unanimously agreed to by the Members thereof other than the Representatives of one or more of the parties to the dispute, the Members of the League agree that they will not go to war

with any party to the dispute which complies with the recommendations of the report.

7. If the Council fails to reach a report which is unanimously agreed to by the members thereof, other than the Representatives of one or more of the parties to the dispute, the Members of the League reserve to themselves the right to take such action as they shall consider necessary for the maintenance of right and justice.

8. If the dispute between the parties is claimed by one of them, and is found by the Council, to arise out of a matter which by international law is solely within the domestic jurisdiction of that party, the Council shall so report, and shall make no recommendation as to its settlement.

9. The Council may in any case under this Article refer the dispute to the Assembly. The dispute shall be so referred at the request of either party to the dispute provided that such request be made within 14 days after the submission of the dispute to the Council.

10. In any case referred to the Assembly, all the provisions of this Article and of Article 12 relating to the action and powers of the Council shall apply to the action and powers of the Assembly, provided that a report made by the Assembly, if concurred in by the Representatives of those Members of the League represented on the Council and of a majority of the other Members of the League, exclusive in each case of the Representatives of the parties to the dispute, shall have the same force as a report by the Council concurred in by all the members thereof other than the Representatives of one or more of the parties to the dispute.

ARTICLE 16

Sanctions of Pacific Settlement

1. Should any Member of the League resort to war in disregard of its covenants under Articles 12, 13 or 15, it shall *ipso facto* be deemed to have committed an act of war against all other Members of the League, which hereby undertake immediately to subject it to the severance of all trade or financial relations, the prohibition of all intercourse between their nationals and the nationals of the covenant-breaking State, and the prevention of all financial, commercial or personal intercourse between the nationals of the covenant-breaking State and the nationals of any other State, whether a Member of the League or not.

2. It shall be the duty of the Council in such case to recommend to the several Governments concerned what effective military, naval or air force the Members of the League shall severally contribute to the armed forces to be used to protect the covenants of the League.

3. The Members of the League agree, further, that they will mutually support one another in the financial and economic measures which are taken under this Article, in order to minimize the loss and inconvenience resulting from the above measures, and that they will mutually support one another in resisting any special measures aimed at one of their number by the covenant-breaking State, and that they will take the necessary steps to

afford passage through their territory to the forces of any of the Members of the League which are cooperating to protect the covenants of the League.

4. Any Member of the League which has violated any covenant of the League may be declared to be no longer a Member of the League by a vote of the Council concurred in by the Representatives of all the other Members of the League represented thereon.

ARTICLE 17

Disputes Involving Non-Members

1. In the event of a dispute between a Member of the League and a State which is not a Member of the League, or between States not Members of the League, the State or States not Members of the League shall be invited to accept the obligations of membership in the League for the purposes of such dispute, upon such conditions as the Council may deem just. If such invitation is accepted, the provisions of Articles 12 to 16 inclusive shall be applied with such modifications as may be deemed necessary by the Council.

2. Upon such invitation being given the Council shall immediately institute an inquiry into the circumstances of the dispute and recommend such action as may seem best and most effectual in the circumstances.

3. If a State so invited shall refuse to accept the obligations of membership in the League for the purposes of such dispute, and shall resort to war against a Member of the League, the provisions of Article 16 shall be applicable as against the State taking such action.

4. If both parties to the dispute when so invited refuse to accept the obligations of membership in the League for the purposes of such dispute, the Council may take such measures and make such recommendations as will prevent hostilities and will result in the settlement of the dispute.

ARTICLE 18

Registration and Publication of Treaties

Every treaty or international engagement entered into hereafter by any Member of the League shall be forthwith registered with the Secretariat and shall as soon as possible be published by it. No such treaty or international engagement shall be binding until so registered.

ARTICLE 19

Review of Treaties

The Assembly may from time to time advise the reconsideration by Members of the League of treaties which have become inapplicable and the consideration of international conditions whose continuance might endanger the peace of the world.

ARTICLE 20

Abrogation of Inconsistent Obligations

1. The Members of the League severally agree that this Covenant is accepted as abrogating all obligations or understandings *inter se* which are inconsistent with the terms thereof, and solemnly undertake that they will not hereafter enter into any engagements inconsistent with the terms thereof.

2. In case any Member of the League shall, before becoming a Member of the League, have undertaken any obligations inconsistent with the terms of this Covenant, it shall be the duty of such Member to take immediate steps to procure its release from such obligations.

ARTICLE 21

Engagements that Remain Valid

Nothing in this Covenant shall be deemed to affect the validity of international engagements, such as treaties of arbitration or regional understandings like the Monroe doctrine, for securing the maintenance of peace.

ARTICLE 22

Mandatory System

1. To those colonies and territories which as a consequence of the late war have ceased to be under the sovereignty of the States which formerly governed them and which are inhabited by peoples not yet able to stand by themselves under the strenuous conditions of the modern world, there should be applied the principle that the well-being and development of such peoples form a sacred trust of civilization and that securities for the performance of this trust should be embodied in this Covenant.

2. The best method of giving practical effect to this principle is that the tutelage of such peoples should be entrusted to advanced nations who by reason of their resources, their experience or their geographical position can best undertake this responsibility, and who are willing to accept it, and that this tutelage should be exercised by them as Mandatories on behalf of the League.

3. The character of the mandate must differ according to the stage of the development of the people, the geographical situation of the territory, its economic conditions and other similar circumstances.

4. Certain communities formerly belonging to the Turkish Empire have reached a stage of development where their existence as independent nations can be provisionally recognized subject to the rendering of administrative advice and assistance by a Mandatory until such time as they are able to stand alone. The wishes of these communities must be a principal consideration in the selection of the Mandatory.

5. Other peoples, especially those of Central Africa, are at such a stage

that the Mandatory must be responsible for the administration of the territory under conditions which will guarantee freedom of conscience and religion, subject only to the maintenance of public order and morals, the prohibition of abuses such as the slave trade, the arms traffic and the liquor traffic, and the prevention of the establishment of fortifications or military and naval bases and of military training of the natives for other than police purposes and the defense of territory, and will also secure equal opportunities for the trade and commerce of other Members of the League.

6. There are territories, such as Southwest Africa and certain of the South Pacific islands, which, owing to the sparseness of their population, or their small size, or their remoteness from the centers of civilization, or their geographical contiguity to the territory of the Mandatory, and other circumstances, can be best administered under the laws of the Mandatory as integral portions of its territory, subject to the safeguards above mentioned in the interests of the indigenous population.

7. In every case of mandate, the Mandatory shall render to the Council an annual report in reference to the territory committed to its charge.

8. The degree of authority, control, or administration to be exercised by the Mandatory shall, if not previously agreed upon by the Members of the League, be explicitly defined in each case by the Council.

9. A permanent Commission shall be constituted to receive and examine the annual reports of the Mandatories and to advise the Council on all matters relating to the observance of the mandates.

ARTICLE 23
Social and Other Activities

Subject to and in accordance with the provisions of international conventions existing or hereafter to be agreed upon, the Members of the League:

(a) will endeavor to secure and maintain fair and humane conditions of labor for men, women, and children, both in their own countries and in all countries to which their commercial and industrial relations extend, and for that purpose will establish and maintain the necessary international organizations;

(b) undertake to secure just treatment of the native inhabitants of territories under their control;

(c) will intrust the League with the general supervision over the execution of agreements with regard to the traffic in women and children and the traffic in opium and other dangerous drugs;

(d) will intrust the League with the general supervision of the trade in arms and ammunition with the countries in which the control of this traffic is necessary in the common interest;

(e) will make provision to secure and maintain freedom of communications and of transit and equitable treatment for the commerce of all Members of the League. In this connection, the special necessities of the regions devastated during the war of 1914–1918 shall be borne in mind;

(f) will endeavor to take steps in matters of international concern for the prevention and control of disease.

ARTICLE 24
International Bureaus

1. There shall be placed under the direction of the League all international bureaus already established by general treaties if the parties to such treaties consent. All such international bureaus and all commissions for the regulation of matters of international interest hereafter constituted shall be placed under the direction of the League.

2. In all matters of international interest which are regulated by general conventions but which are not placed under the control of international bureaus or commissions, the Secretariat of the League shall, subject to the consent of the Council and if desired by the parties, collect and distribute all relevant information and shall render any other assistance which may be necessary or desirable.

3. The Council may include as part of the expenses of the Secretariat the expenses of any bureau or commission which is placed under the direction of the League.

ARTICLE 25
Promotion of Red Cross and Health

The Members of the League agree to encourage and promote the establishment and cooperation of duly authorized voluntary national Red Cross organizations having as purposes the improvement of health, the prevention of disease and the mitigation of suffering throughout the world.

ARTICLE 26
Amendments

1. Amendments to this Covenant will take effect when ratified by the Members of the League whose Representatives compose the Council and by a majority of the Members of the League whose Representatives compose the Assembly.

2. No such amendment shall bind any Member of the League which signifies its dissent therefrom, but in that case it shall cease to be a Member of the League.

APPENDIX B

WOODROW WILSON AND COLONEL HOUSE

To the Editor of the *Post*—Sir: When in the days to come Macaulay's New Zealander surveys the ruins of Westminster and tries to make sense out of the records of the Parliament of Man (Paris-Versailles, 1919) what a difficult task awaits him. In the current issue of a popular weekly Mrs. Woodrow Wilson describes the meeting at Brest between the President on his return from his disastrous February visit to Washington, his unhappy encounter with the Foreign Relations Committee of the Senate, and Colonel House, who had during his absence represented him at the conference.

When House left, Mrs. Wilson states that the President seemed to have aged ten years and that his jaw was set in the way it had when he was making superhuman efforts to control himself. He smiled bitterly as he said that House had given away everything he had won before he left Paris, that he had compromised on every side, and that he, the President, would have to start all over again, and this time it would be harder because House had given the impression that his delegates were not in sympathy with him. But, as he threw back his head, the light of battle was in his eyes and he thanked God that he could still fight.

In the light of this statement it is right and proper to examine the records and ascertain how the President began all over again and whom he sent into the battle. A week later, when the President was undeniably ill, he asked Colonel House (the man Mrs. Wilson thinks had betrayed him) to take his place in the Council of Four and he warmly endorsed, as the records show, all that Colonel House was able to accomplish there in a difficult situation.

The records also reveal that all through the month of April the President entrusted House with the difficult negotiations with the French and English, and in writing he requested House to explain to Clemenceau the American position on the issues in dispute. He asked House to make known his views to Tardieu and he sent to him innumerable and vital papers with such notations as "March 18—Won't you be kind enough to give me your opinion? Affectionately yours, W. W." "March 20—Let me have your comments. Affectionately, W. W." "April 19—I would like a suggestion from you. Affectionately"; or as on May 13, "What do you suggest?"

When the hard battle was over and the Treaty was signed the President accepted the review of what had been accomplished, drawn up by Colonel House, and authorized its publication in the world press under the signature, Woodrow Wilson. On leaving for America the President chose Colonel House to represent him in the discussions that were impending with Lord Robert Cecil and other delegates as to the best way to set up the League of Nations, and when this was achieved, and gratefully acknowledged, the President sent House to London to work out the system of colonial mandates.

All these records are available in the Library of Yale University to those who care to examine them. Of course the charge of "betrayal" has been made before, but hitherto upon authority so irresponsible that it did not require notice, much less contradiction. However, it did justify me, I think, in speaking to President Charles Seymour, of Yale; to Hunter Miller, of the Department of State, and to Arthur Hugh Frazier, members of the delegation who were closest to Colonel House, and I found them in complete agreement that the "betrayal" story was entirely inaccurate. Today, however, it has seemed to me, and to others, that these corrections are due quite as much to the memory of our great war President as to the unsullied fame of his loyal lieutenant, Edward M. House.

STEPHEN BONSAL.

Washington, January 28, 1938.

APPENDIX C

To facilitate my final discharge from the Army on December 11, 1919, Colonel House wrote:

"Colonel Bonsal's linguistic accomplishments, his wide acquaintance, and his knowledge of world conditions have made him invaluable to me. It is with great reluctance that I sever connection with him; for besides being an adviser upon whom I have learned to lean, I have come to have a sincere affection for him.

"I wish to express to you my sincere appreciation for having made it possible for me to secure his services."

This was to General Marlborough Churchill, chief of Military Intelligence, General Staff. The citation the general gave me on granting my discharge follows:

WAR DEPARTMENT
OFFICE OF THE CHIEF OF STAFF
Washington, D. C.

December 17, 1919

MY DEAR COLONEL BONSAL:

Upon your final discharge from active service, I desire to take this opportunity of expressing my appreciation of the excellent service which you have rendered to the Military Intelligence Division, and to the American Commission to Negotiate Peace.

Your linguistic accomplishments, your wide acquaintance and knowledge of world conditions have made you invaluable not only to the War Department but to the American Peace Commission.

I trust that your return to civil life will not sever our cordial official and personal relations. If there is ever any way in which I can be of assistance to you, please let me know.

Very sincerely yours,
M. CHURCHILL

Lieutenant Colonel Stephen Bonsal,
The Parkwood,
Washington, D. C.

GLOSSARY OF NAMES

ASQUITH, LADY, afterwards Countess of Oxford, wife of H. H. Asquith, leader of Liberal party, long Prime Minister. Became famous as Margot Tennant, one of the founders of the famous Society of Souls, before she became wife of the man who was Prime Minister on outbreak of World War I.

BALFOUR, ARTHUR, later Lord Balfour. Founder of the Society of Souls, Chief Secretary for Ireland during the days of Parnellism and crime. Nephew of Lord Salisbury and himself Prime Minister several times.

BERNSDORFF, COUNT JOHANN, Imperial German Ambassador to United States until our entrance into the war. Frequently warned his government of the danger of the submarine threat.

BLISS, TASKER H., chosen by the President to represent the United States on Supreme War Council and later a delegate to the Peace Conference. He was military adviser to the President. An excellent soldier who had had much experience in legal and financial matters with our Army of Occupation in Cuba.

BRATIANU, JAN, Prime Minister and tireless worker for the Greater Roumania; often by methods which those who liked him not—their name was legion—qualified as Byzantinian.

BROCKDORFF-RANTZAU, COUNT ULRICH, scion of an ancient Holstein family. The unfortunate choice of Weimar government to receive Versailles Treaty. Resigned rather than sign and labored as long as he lived to prevent its fulfillment. Later, as Ambassador to Russia, sought to align the Soviets against the Western world.

CHOTEK, COUNTESS SOPHIE, daughter of the ancient but impoverished Bohemian family of that name, married morganatically to Archduke Francis Ferdinand and shared his fate at Sarajevo.

COBB, FRANK, long chief editorial writer of the New York World, a famous newspaperman, one of the few whom Wilson suffered gladly.

CLEMENCEAU, GEORGES, Premier and saviour of France at seventy-nine, at times a little sensitive as to his age, and yet not a little proud that as a first-line fighter he had contributed so powerfully to the salvation of France. The only survivor of the French Deputies who signed at Bordeaux the eloquent protest against the peace imposed by German bayonets in 1871. His four years of far-from-luxurious exile in America, to escape Napoleon the Little, had taught him much, including a command of nervous American-English. He had an engaging habit of standing between Wilson and House, saying, "Now we Americans must stand together," and then violently attacking their policy.

DIAMANDY, CONSTANTIN, second Roumanian delegate to the Conference, with many interesting experiences of his stay in Russia during the revolutionary period, 1917–18.

FRANKLIN-BOUILLON, HENRY, stormy petrel of French politics, often called "The Gadfly" of the Clemenceau ministry. Persistent in his attacks on Clemenceau in the Chamber, where, unfortunately, he was ranking member of the Foreign Affairs Committee. He prophesied that the American Congress would never ratify the Rhine Agreement to march to the aid of France if invaded.

FRAZIER, ARTHUR HUGH, veteran of the Foreign Service, long Secretary of our Legation in Vienna, Rome, and later at the Embassy at Paris. Sat in the place of House on the Supreme War Council while the Colonel was in Washington in 1918. Later U.S. Commissioner in Vienna and Athens during the unsettled period following the war, handling American affairs in the absence of normal diplomatic representation.

GARBAI, ALEXANDER, head of the Interim Government in Hungary between the Károlyi and the Bela Kun regimes.

GRAYSON, CARY, an extraordinarily ingratiating personality, a navy doctor who became an admiral and was successively the intimate friend of three Presidents as widely different as Theodore Roosevelt, William H. Taft, and Woodrow Wilson.

GREENE, WARWICK (son of Francis Vinton Greene, who commanded a brigade in the pacification of the Philippines, 1899), Secretary to W. Cameron Forbes, Governor General of the Islands; later Chief of the Bureau of Public Works.

HITCHCOCK, GILBERT, editor from Omaha, long Senator from Nebraska, ranking Democrat on Foreign Relations Committee in charge of the struggle to secure ratification of the Versailles Treaty.

HOUSE, EDWARD M., Texas-born world traveler, maker of governors in the Lone Star State for two decades. In 1911, seeking a wider field of activity, he contributed largely to the nomination and election of Wilson in 1912. Entrusted with many diplomatic missions, both at home and abroad, by the first Democratic President since the days of Grover Cleveland. The President's chief lieutenant at the Peace Conference.

HYMANS, PAUL, long Foreign Minister of Belgium, inclined to interpret the Fourteen Points in an imperialistic sense. After the war an unfortunate influence in all the meetings of the League of Nations. Most suspicious of the Great Powers.

JAGOW, GOTTLIEB VON, Minister for Foreign Affairs of German Empire during a critical period of the war. Eased out by the growing power of military leaders Hindenburg and Ludendorff.

KLOTZ, LOUIS LUCIEN, Finance Minister in the Clemenceau cabinet, an ardent advocate of extracting the last penny from Germany.

Kramář, Karel, Chief Minister of the Czechoslovak Republic under Masaryk, represented his newly born country on commission to draft the Covenant. In 1917, while still a member of the Austrian Reichsrath, he was charged with treason and condemned to be hanged. The only delegate to the Conference who enjoyed this high distinction. The sentence of the court, however, was not carried out.

Kun, Bela, the mysterious adventurer who proclaimed a Soviet republic in Hungary and defied the powers for five months.

Lansing, Robert, Secretary of State, legal adviser and counselor of the Department, succeeded Mr. Bryan when the Great Commoner disagreed with the President over the correspondence dealing with the sinking of the *Lusitania*. His usefulness at the Conference was limited by the fact that the President disliked lawyers, particularly international lawyers. "They have made such a mess of world affairs"—a remark that was often on his lips.

Lippmann, Walter, famous journalist and writer, secretary in Paris for a few weeks during the Armistice negotiations of the "Enquiry," a study group set up under Colonel House to prepare material and information for the guidance of the American delegation. Worked with Frank Cobb on the glossary, so-called—an amplification of the Fourteen Points.

Lloyd George, little "Davy" of Wales. Most hated man in Britain in 1900, the sword and buckler of the Empire in World War I. Succeeded Mr. Asquith as Prime Minister in the darkest hour of the war. Overthrown in 1922. The oldest member of Parliament today and an influential one, although without a party.

Lodge, Henry Cabot, long Senator from Massachusetts. Early in the war he advocated an association for the maintenance of world peace, but as Wilson developed his plan for the League and the Covenant Lodge bitterly opposed them; more than any other man he brought about the defeat of the Wilsonian policies.

McCormick, Vance, Pennsylvanian, chairman of the National Democratic Committee; filled many positions in the Wilson administration during the World War.

Miller, Hunter, legal adviser of the American delegation, member of drafting committee, later in charge of historical publications of Department of State.

Nubar, Pasha (Boghos), son of the famous statesman, member of the wealthy Armenian family, long seated in Egypt. Able and ardent advocate of the Armenian cause.

Pessoa, Epitacio, representative of Brazil at the Conference. While there elected President of Brazil; loyal supporter of Wilsonian policies.

Renner, Karl, first Chancellor of the Austrian Republic, most able and sensible man, long editor of *Arbeiter Zeitung*, organ of the Austrian Social Democratic party.

Scialoja, Giuseppe, Senator, later Minister for Foreign Affairs, a subtle opponent of the new order and everything that President Wilson stood for; a hard-working member of the Italian delegation under Premier Orlando.

Smith, Hoke, member of President Cleveland's cabinet, long Senator from Georgia, not overfriendly to the Wilson policies.

VENIZELOS, ELEUTHERIOS, Prime Minister of Greece, began as a guerrilla fighter in the mountains of Crete. Was one of the most polished of the delegates at Versailles. He suffered from the fact he was so charming that everybody was afraid of him.

VESNITCH, MILENKO, second Serbian delegate, lieutenant to Prime Minister Pasitch; had been Minister to Washington and Paris, and had an American wife.

WHITE, HENRY, Maryland-born, a resident of Rhode Island when at home—which was rarely the case. Secretary of the United States Legation in Vienna and London, Ambassador to Italy and to France, American representative at the Conference of Algeciras. He knew Europe well, but Mr. Wilson did not avail himself of this knowledge to any great extent.

WISEMAN, SIR WILLIAM, former British soldier, later in Intelligence work in United States; enjoyed the confidence of Lloyd George and Balfour, employed by them on many confidential missions.

INDEX